Yamada-kun and the Seven Witches

3

Miki Yoshikawa

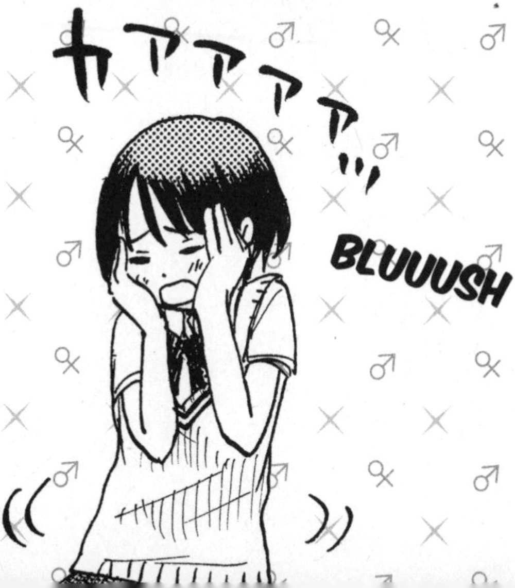
BLUUUSH

Ryu Yamada

A second-year at Suzaku High School and part of the Supernatural Studies Club. He's a former (and maybe current) delinquent and is loathed by his schoolmates for some reason. He possesses the ability to switch bodies with whomever he kisses.

Urara Shiraishi

A second-year at Suzaku High School and president of the Supernatural Studies Club. She's a cool-headed girl who is devoted to her studies. She's a problem child like Yamada, but for completely different reasons. Lately (thanks to Yamada?) she's started to make some friends.

Miyabi Itou

A second-year at Suzaku High School and part of the Supernatural Studies Club. She's the only member of the club who's into the occult. She's a bona fide idiot who rushes headlong into things.

Toranosuke Miyamura

A second-year at Suzaku High School. He's the vice-president of the Supernatural Studies Club and Student Council. The polar opposite of Yamada, he's the most popular kid in school. He's very curious and sharp, but his perverted streak is a problem.

Ushio Igarashi

A second-year at Suzaku High School. He is the loyal minion of the cunning Odagiri. He seems to have a history with Yamada.

Nene Odagiri

A second-year at Suzaku High School. She shares the position of Student Council vice-president with Miyamura. She sees Miyamura as a rival and ends up getting involved in the Supernatural Studies Club. Could she somehow possess powers of her own?

CONTENTS

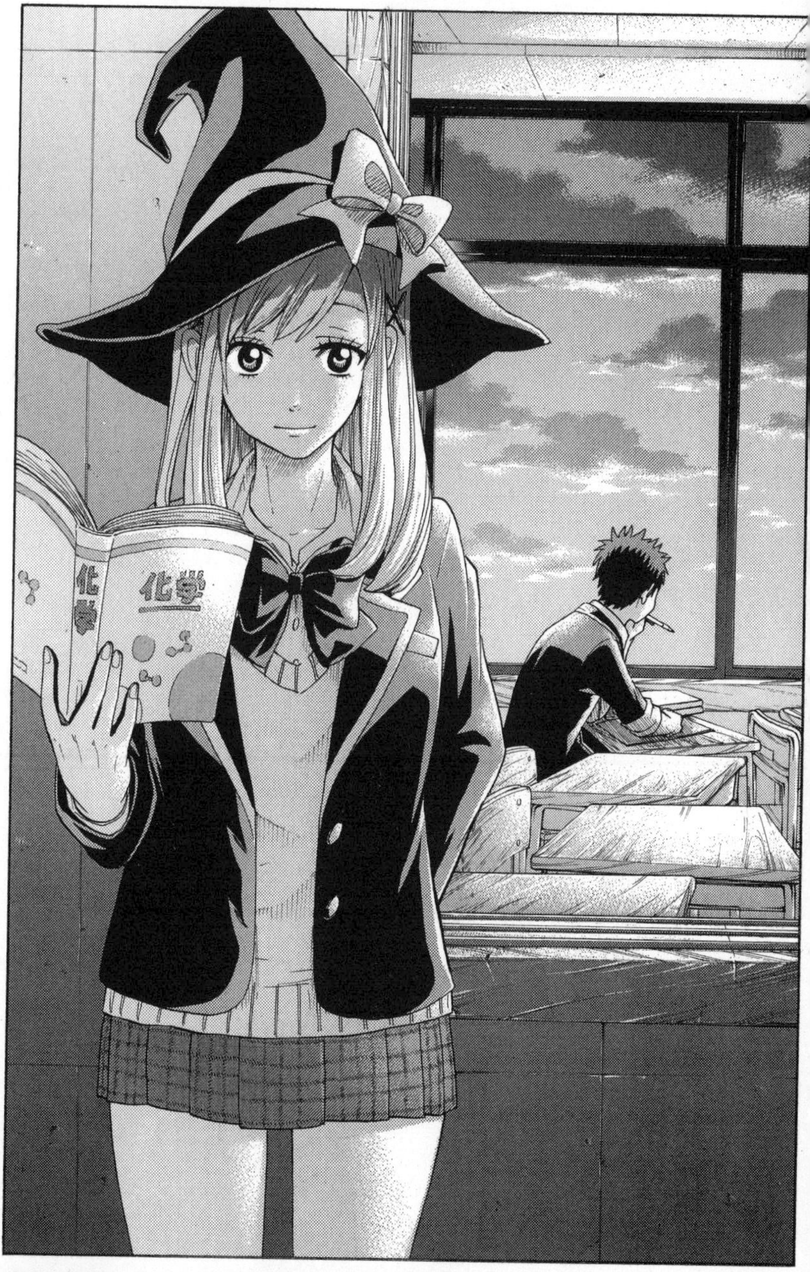
化学
化学

CHAPTER 17: I will give you a kiss.

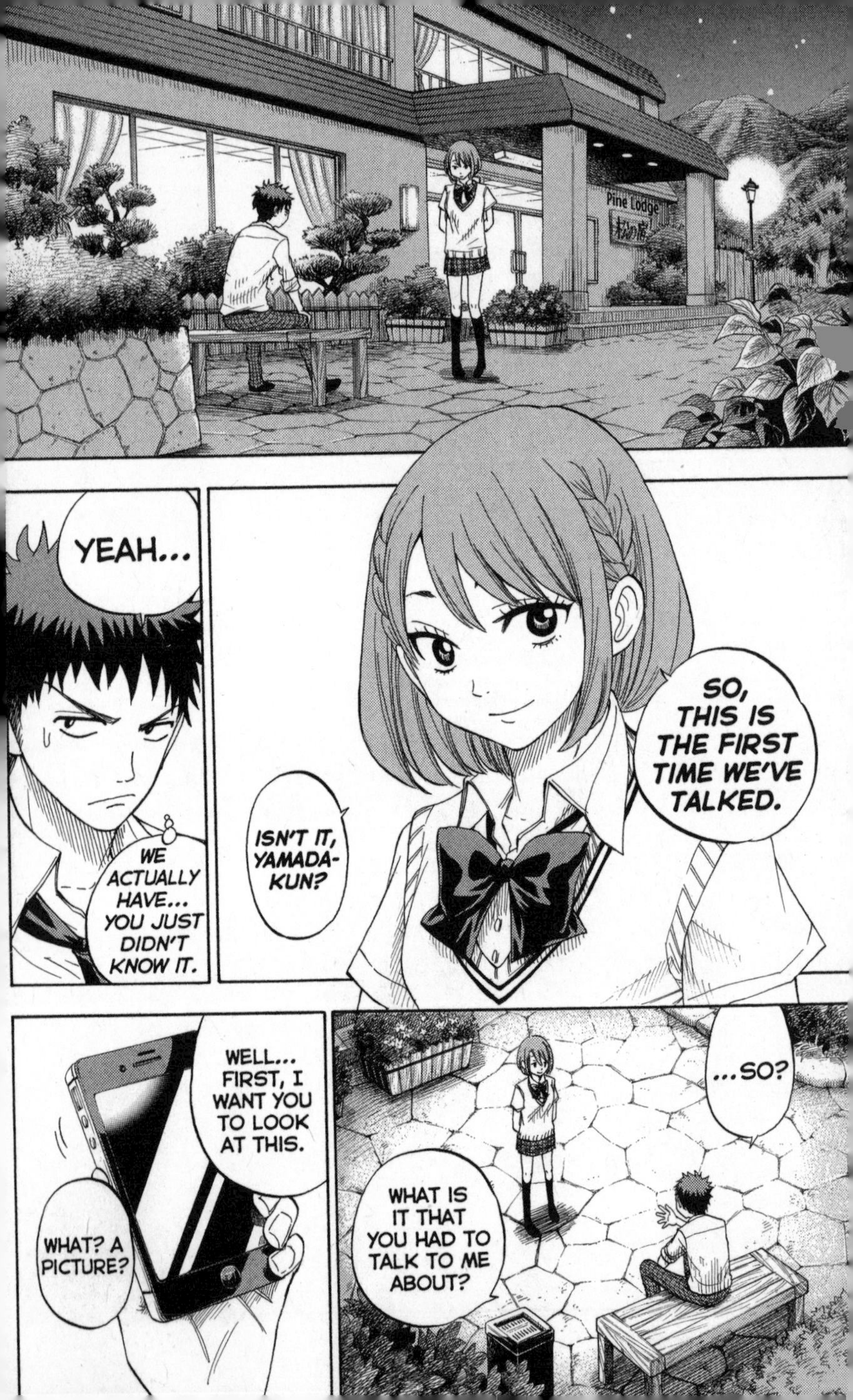
Pine Lodge
SO, THIS IS THE FIRST TIME WE'VE TALKED.
ISN'T IT, YAMADA-KUN?
YEAH...
WE ACTUALLY HAVE... YOU JUST DIDN'T KNOW IT.
...SO?
WHAT IS IT THAT YOU HAD TO TALK TO ME ABOUT?
WELL... FIRST, I WANT YOU TO LOOK AT THIS.
WHAT? A PICTURE?

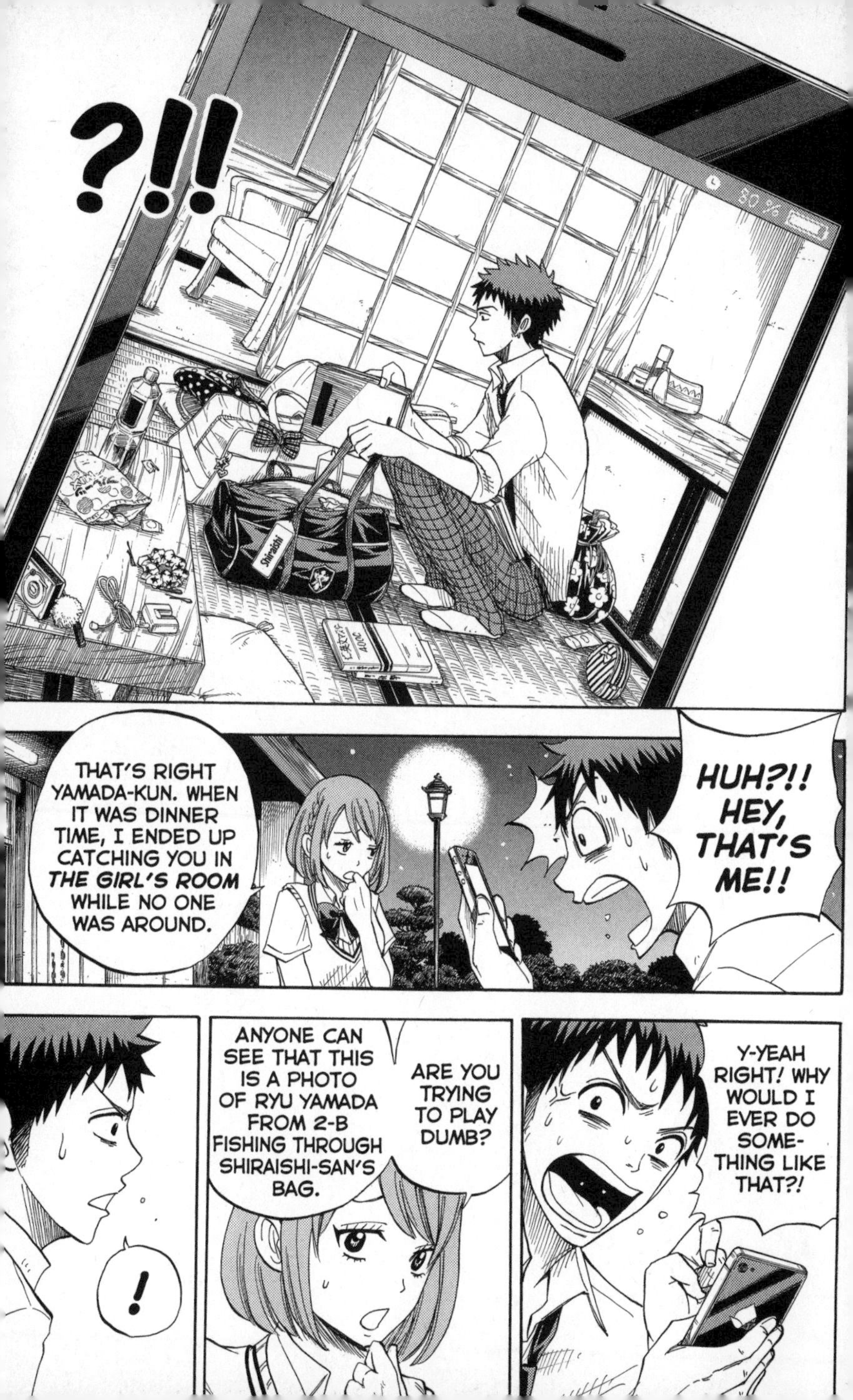
?!!
80 %
Shiraishi
HUH?!! HEY, THAT'S ME!!
THAT'S RIGHT YAMADA-KUN. WHEN IT WAS DINNER TIME, I ENDED UP CATCHING YOU IN *THE GIRL'S ROOM* WHILE NO ONE WAS AROUND.
Y-YEAH RIGHT! WHY WOULD I EVER DO SOME-THING LIKE THAT?!
ARE YOU TRYING TO PLAY DUMB?
ANYONE CAN SEE THAT THIS IS A PHOTO OF RYU YAMADA FROM 2-B FISHING THROUGH SHIRAISHI-SAN'S BAG.
!

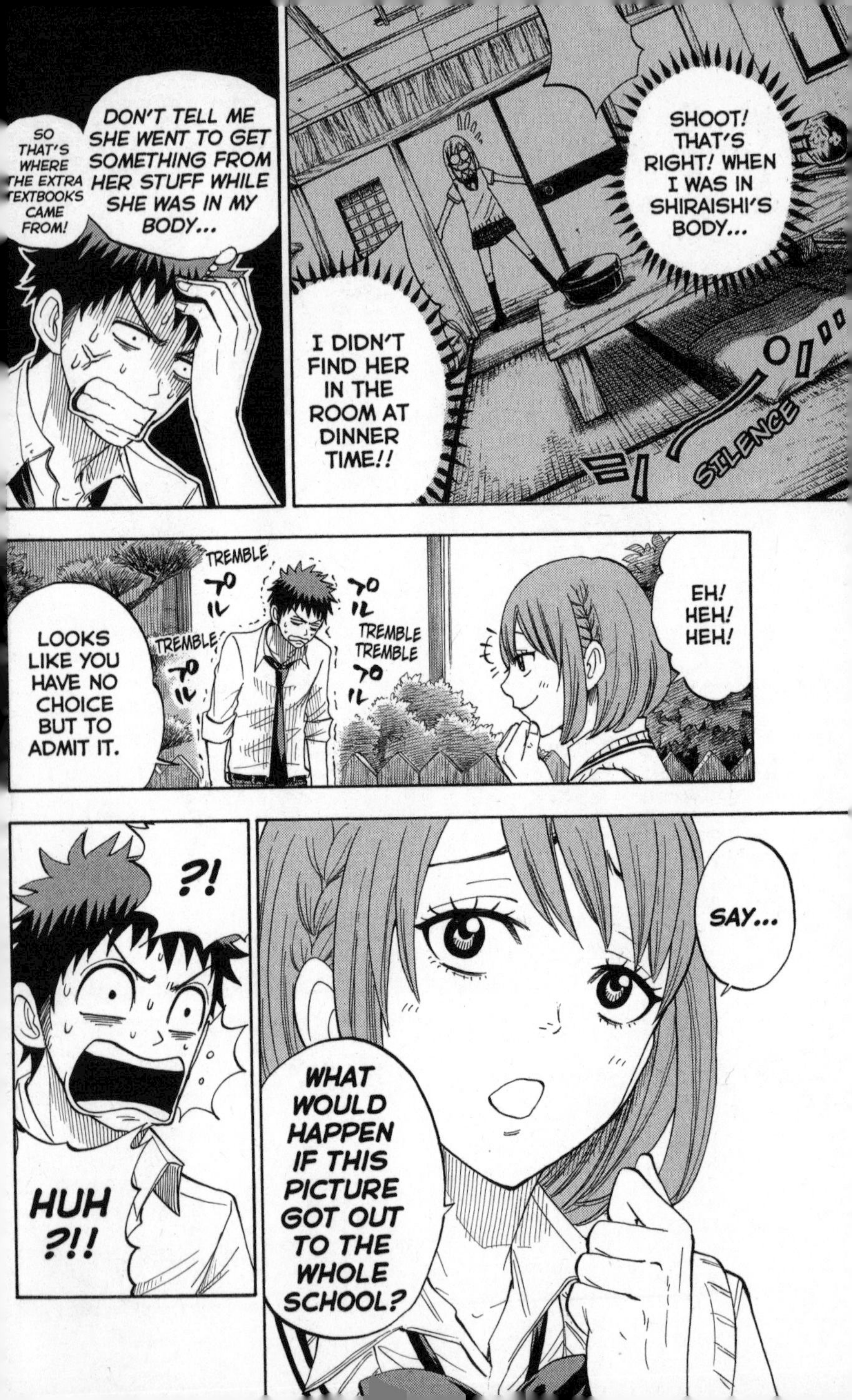
SHOOT! THAT'S RIGHT! WHEN I WAS IN SHIRAISHI'S BODY...
I DIDN'T FIND HER IN THE ROOM AT DINNER TIME!!
SILENCE
DON'T TELL ME SHE WENT TO GET SOMETHING FROM HER STUFF WHILE SHE WAS IN MY BODY...
SO THAT'S WHERE THE EXTRA TEXTBOOKS CAME FROM!
EH! HEH! HEH!
プル
TREMBLE TREMBLE
プル
プル
TREMBLE
プル
TREMBLE
LOOKS LIKE YOU HAVE NO CHOICE BUT TO ADMIT IT.
SAY...
WHAT WOULD HAPPEN IF THIS PICTURE GOT OUT TO THE WHOLE SCHOOL?
?!
HUH ?!!

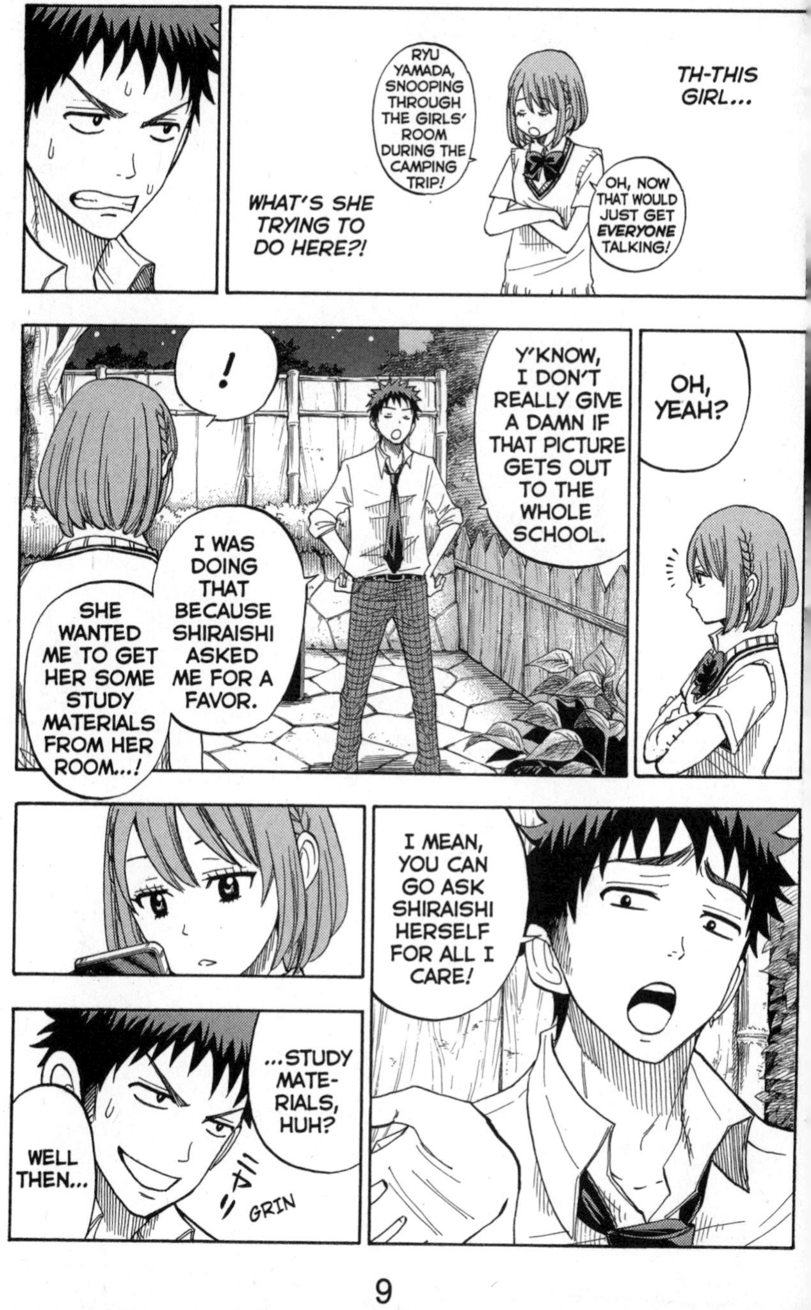
TH-THIS GIRL...
RYU YAMADA, SNOOPING THROUGH THE GIRLS' ROOM DURING THE CAMPING TRIP!
OH, NOW THAT WOULD JUST GET EVERYONE TALKING!
WHAT'S SHE TRYING TO DO HERE?!
OH, YEAH?
Y'KNOW, I DON'T REALLY GIVE A DAMN IF THAT PICTURE GETS OUT TO THE WHOLE SCHOOL.
!
I WAS DOING THAT BECAUSE SHIRAISHI ASKED ME FOR A FAVOR.
SHE WANTED ME TO GET HER SOME STUDY MATERIALS FROM HER ROOM...!
I MEAN, YOU CAN GO ASK SHIRAISHI HERSELF FOR ALL I CARE!
...STUDY MATE-RIALS, HUH?
GRIN
WELL THEN...

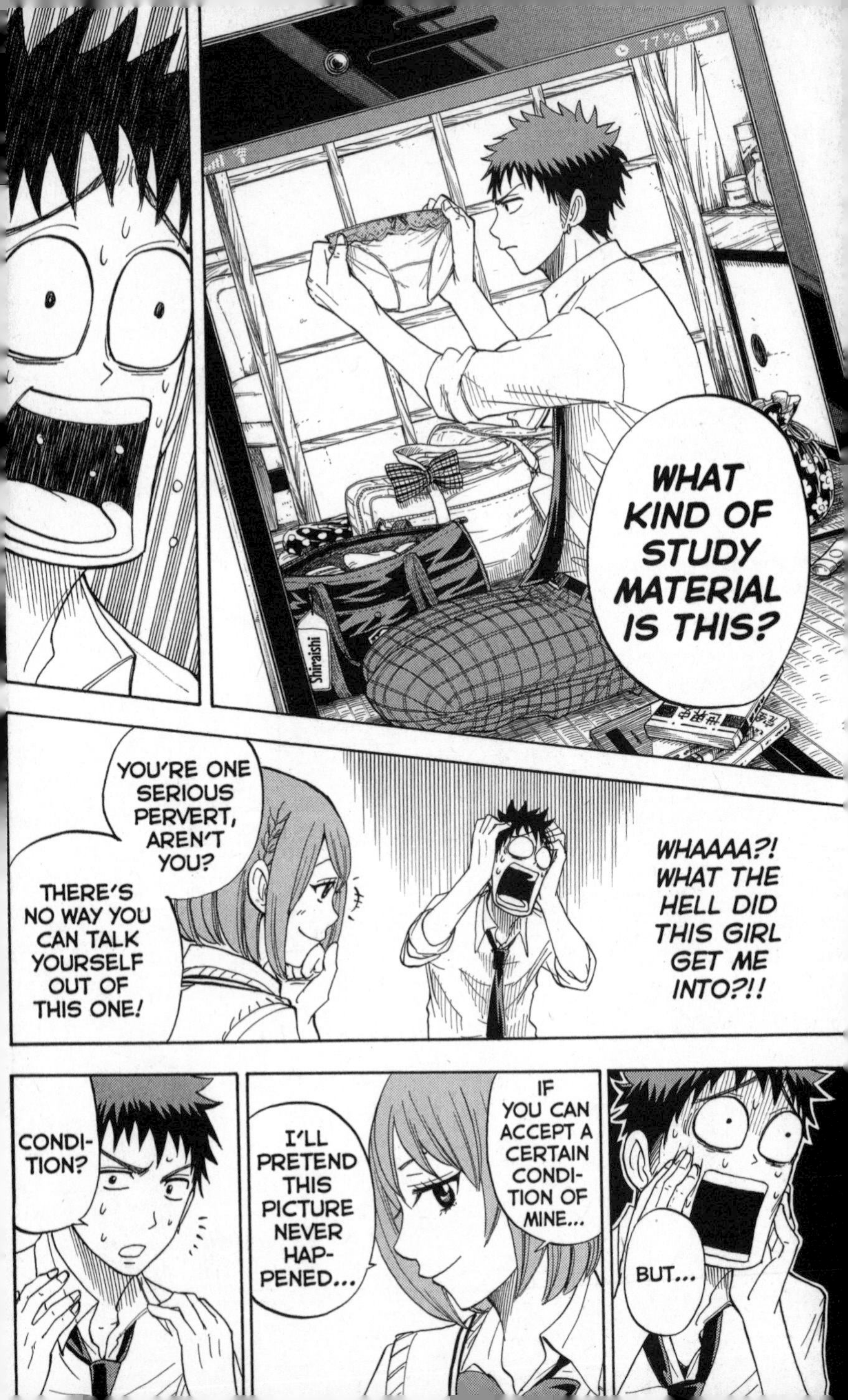
77%
Shiraishi
WHAT KIND OF STUDY MATERIAL IS THIS?
WHAAAA?! WHAT THE HELL DID THIS GIRL GET ME INTO?!!
YOU'RE ONE SERIOUS PERVERT, AREN'T YOU?
THERE'S NO WAY YOU CAN TALK YOURSELF OUT OF THIS ONE!
BUT...
IF YOU CAN ACCEPT A CERTAIN CONDITION OF MINE...
I'LL PRETEND THIS PICTURE NEVER HAPPENED...
CONDITION?

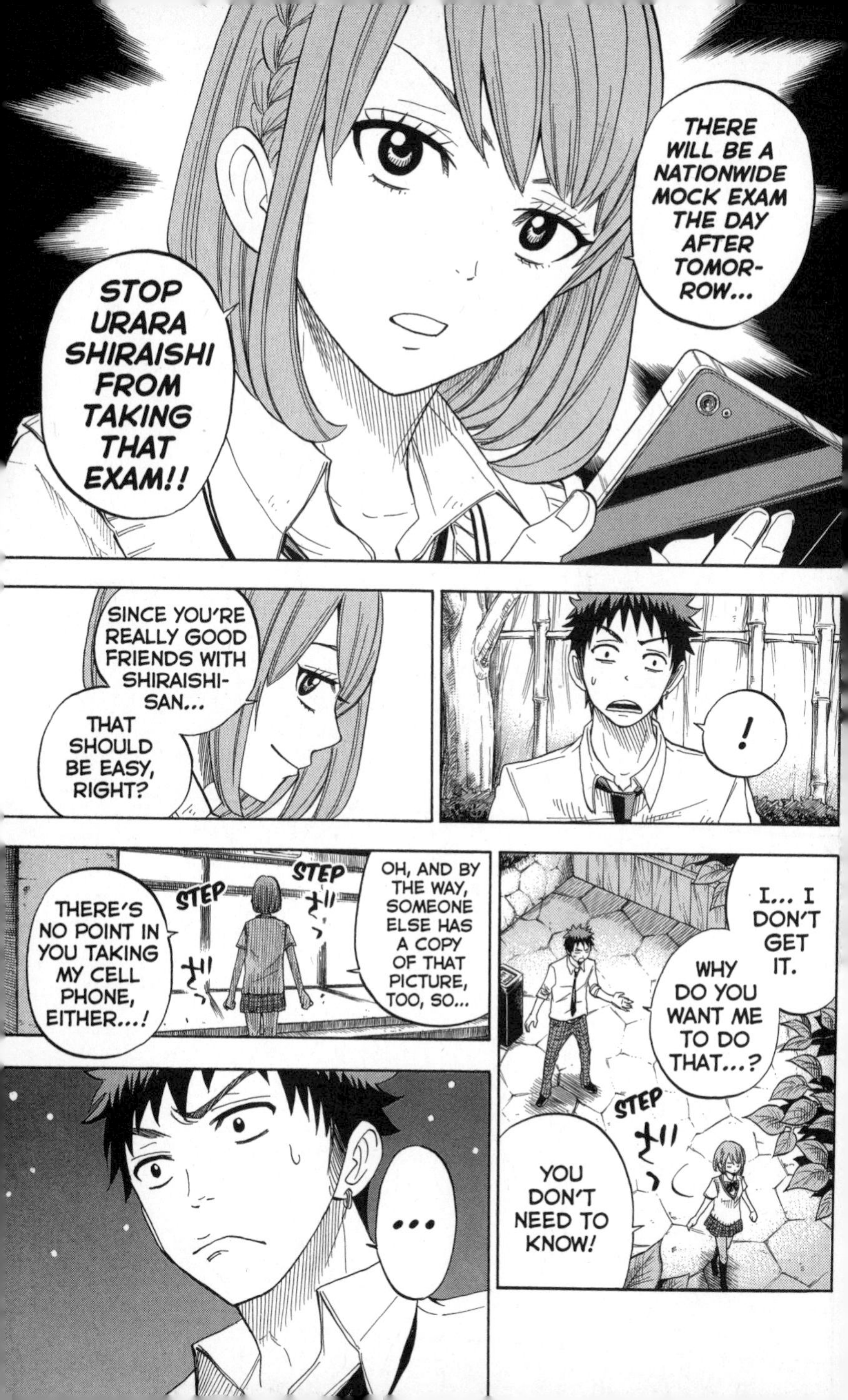
THERE WILL BE A NATIONWIDE MOCK EXAM THE DAY AFTER TOMORROW...
STOP URARA SHIRAISHI FROM TAKING THAT EXAM!!
!
SINCE YOU'RE REALLY GOOD FRIENDS WITH SHIRAISHI-SAN...
THAT SHOULD BE EASY, RIGHT?
I... I DON'T GET IT.
WHY DO YOU WANT ME TO DO THAT...?
STEP
YOU DON'T NEED TO KNOW!
OH, AND BY THE WAY, SOMEONE ELSE HAS A COPY OF THAT PICTURE, TOO, SO...
STEP
STEP
THERE'S NO POINT IN YOU TAKING MY CELL PHONE, EITHER...!
...

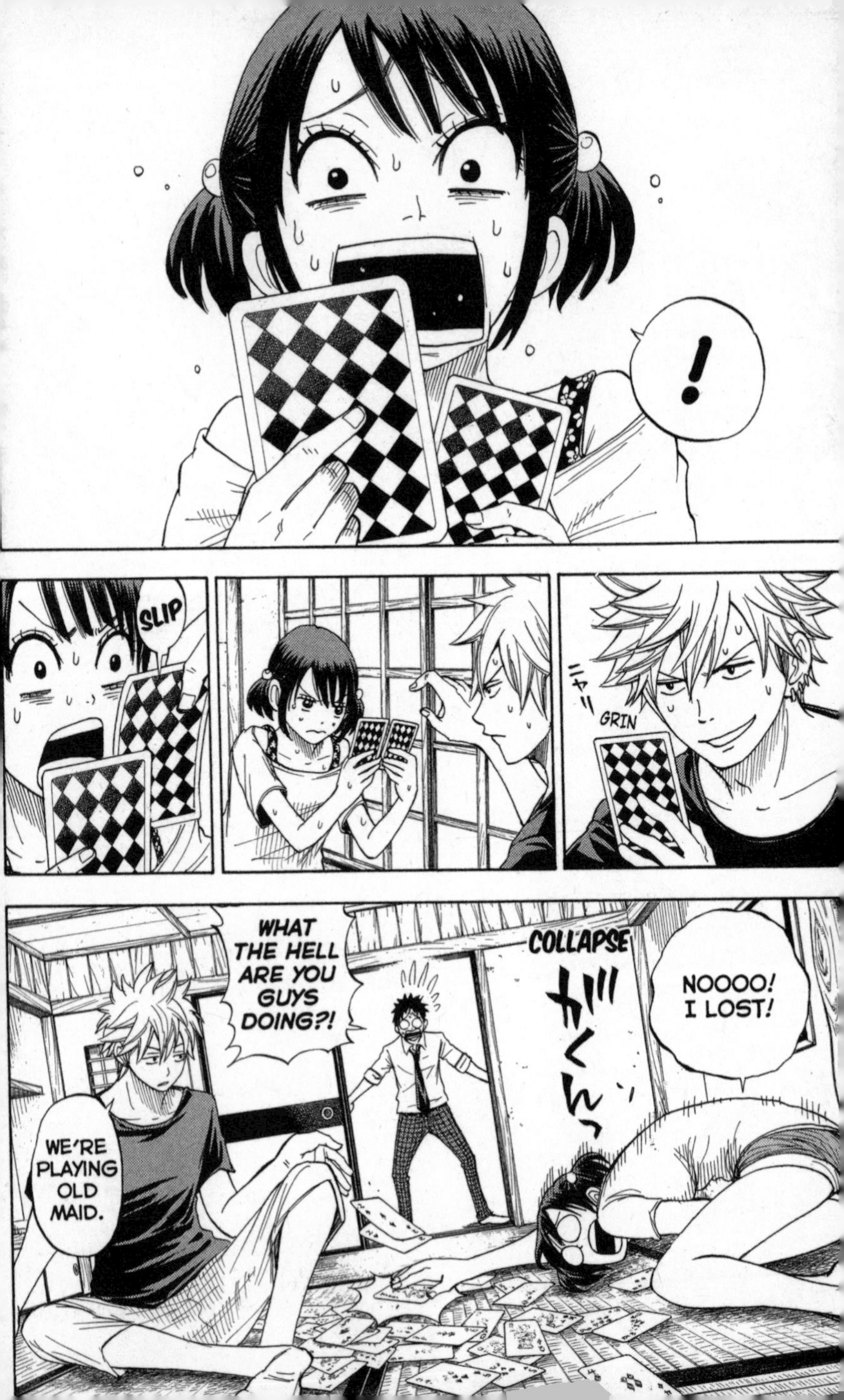
!
ニヤリ
GRIN
SLIP
NOOOO! I LOST!
COLLAPSE
がくんっ
WHAT THE HELL ARE YOU GUYS DOING?!
WE'RE PLAYING OLD MAID.

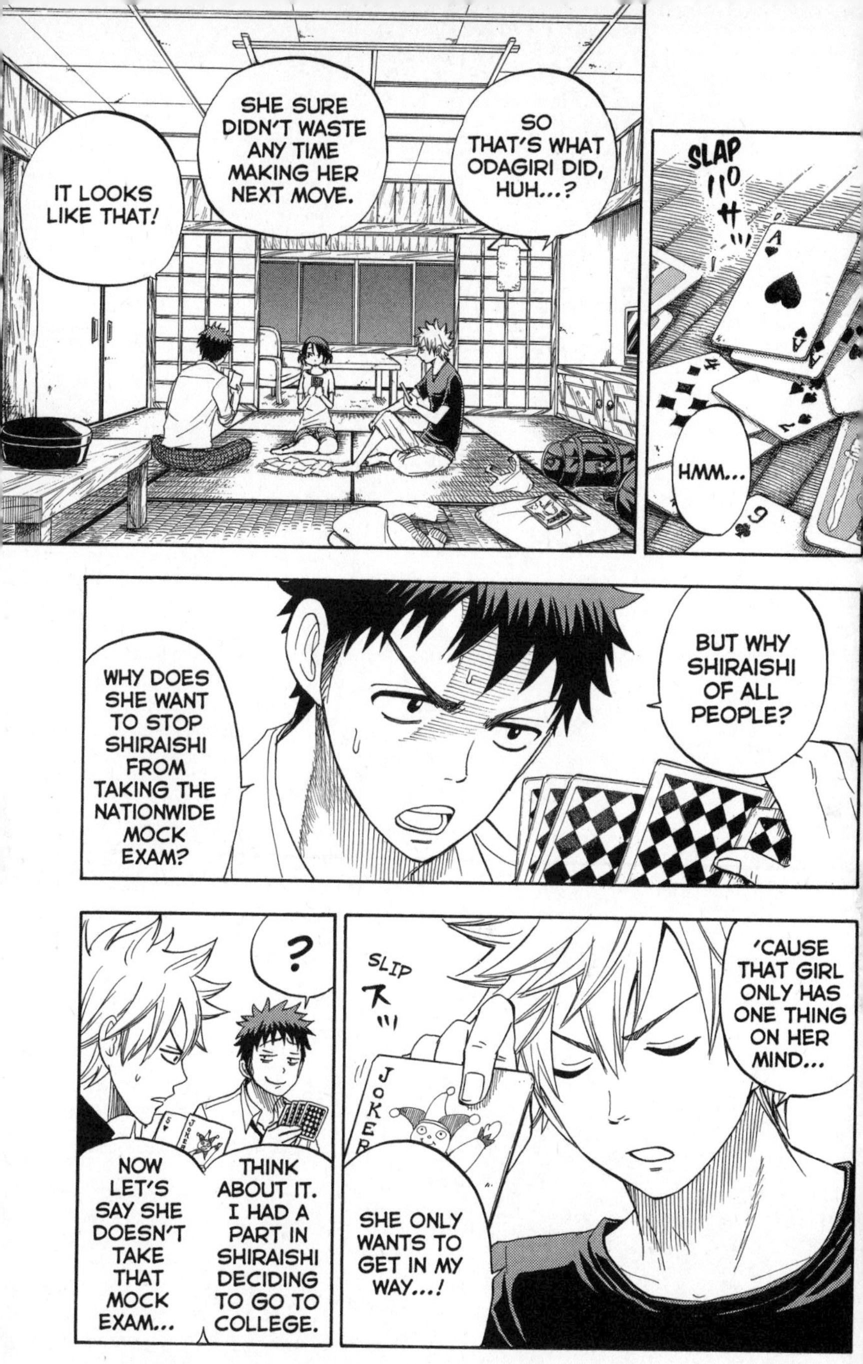
SLAP
HMM...
SO THAT'S WHAT ODAGIRI DID, HUH...?
SHE SURE DIDN'T WASTE ANY TIME MAKING HER NEXT MOVE.
IT LOOKS LIKE THAT!
BUT WHY SHIRAISHI OF ALL PEOPLE?
WHY DOES SHE WANT TO STOP SHIRAISHI FROM TAKING THE NATIONWIDE MOCK EXAM?
SLIP
'CAUSE THAT GIRL ONLY HAS ONE THING ON HER MIND...
SHE ONLY WANTS TO GET IN MY WAY...!
?
THINK ABOUT IT. I HAD A PART IN SHIRAISHI DECIDING TO GO TO COLLEGE.
NOW LET'S SAY SHE DOESN'T TAKE THAT MOCK EXAM...

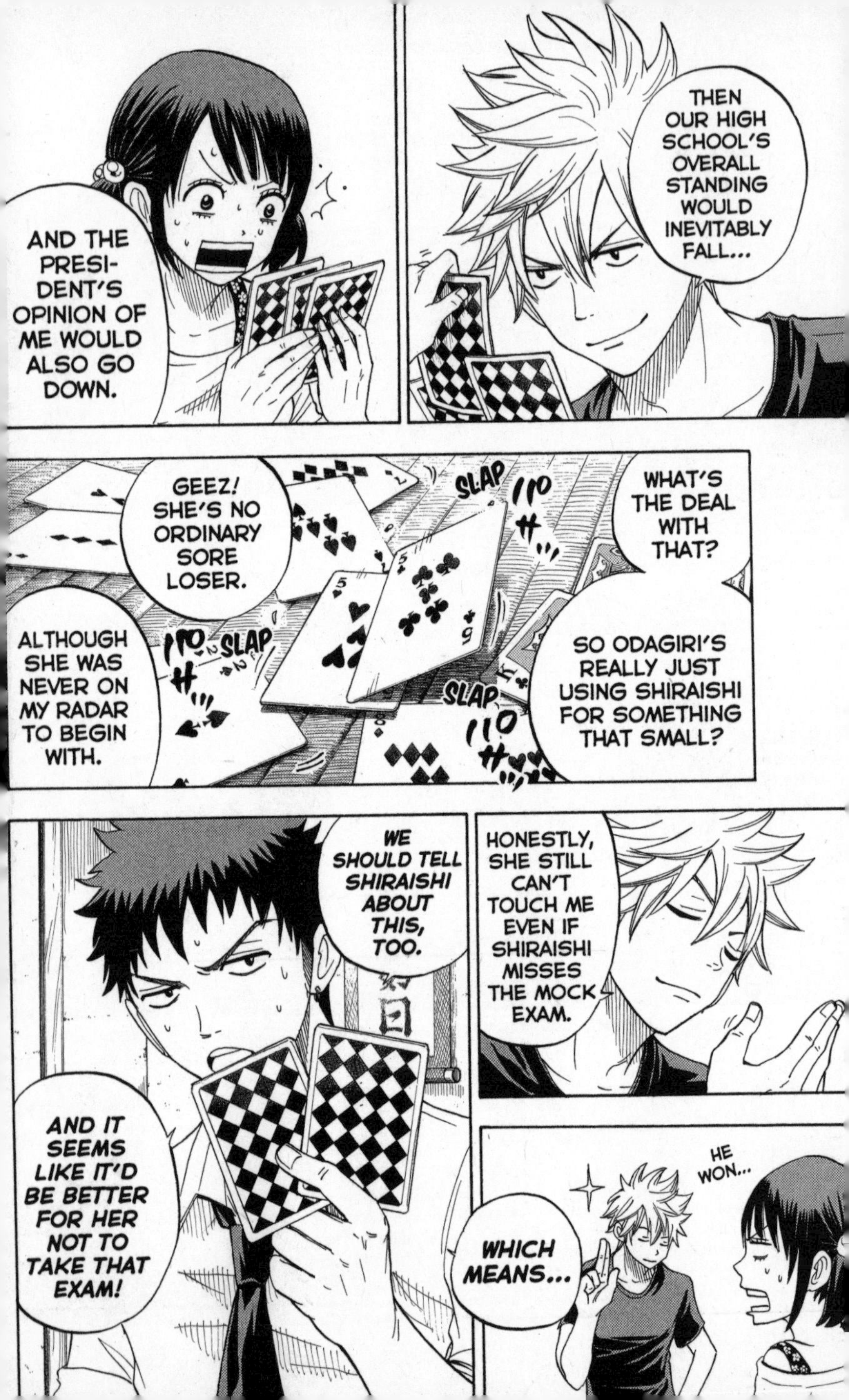
THEN OUR HIGH SCHOOL'S OVERALL STANDING WOULD INEVITABLY FALL...
AND THE PRESIDENT'S OPINION OF ME WOULD ALSO GO DOWN.
WHAT'S THE DEAL WITH THAT?
SO ODAGIRI'S REALLY JUST USING SHIRAISHI FOR SOMETHING THAT SMALL?
SLAP
GEEZ! SHE'S NO ORDINARY SORE LOSER.
SLAP
ALTHOUGH SHE WAS NEVER ON MY RADAR TO BEGIN WITH.
SLAP
HONESTLY, SHE STILL CAN'T TOUCH ME EVEN IF SHIRAISHI MISSES THE MOCK EXAM.
HE WON...
WHICH MEANS...
WE SHOULD TELL SHIRAISHI ABOUT THIS, TOO.
AND IT SEEMS LIKE IT'D BE BETTER FOR HER NOT TO TAKE THAT EXAM!

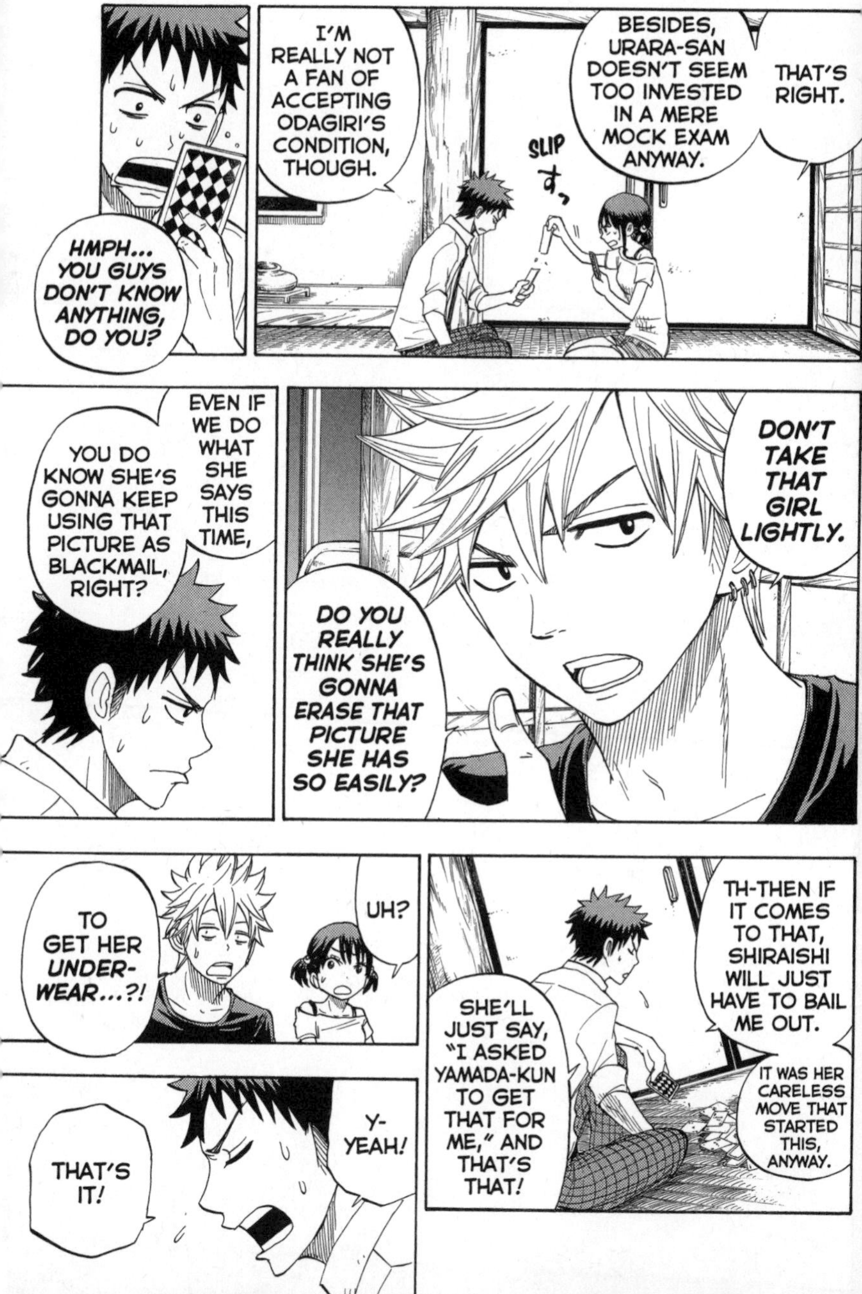
THAT'S RIGHT.
BESIDES, URARA-SAN DOESN'T SEEM TOO INVESTED IN A MERE MOCK EXAM ANYWAY.
SLIP
I'M REALLY NOT A FAN OF ACCEPTING ODAGIRI'S CONDITION, THOUGH.
HMPH... YOU GUYS DON'T KNOW ANYTHING, DO YOU?
DON'T TAKE THAT GIRL LIGHTLY.
DO YOU REALLY THINK SHE'S GONNA ERASE THAT PICTURE SHE HAS SO EASILY?
EVEN IF WE DO WHAT SHE SAYS THIS TIME,
YOU DO KNOW SHE'S GONNA KEEP USING THAT PICTURE AS BLACKMAIL, RIGHT?
TH-THEN IF IT COMES TO THAT, SHIRAISHI WILL JUST HAVE TO BAIL ME OUT.
IT WAS HER CARELESS MOVE THAT STARTED THIS, ANYWAY.
SHE'LL JUST SAY, "I ASKED YAMADA-KUN TO GET THAT FOR ME," AND THAT'S THAT!
UH?
TO GET HER UNDERWEAR...?!
Y-YEAH!
THAT'S IT!

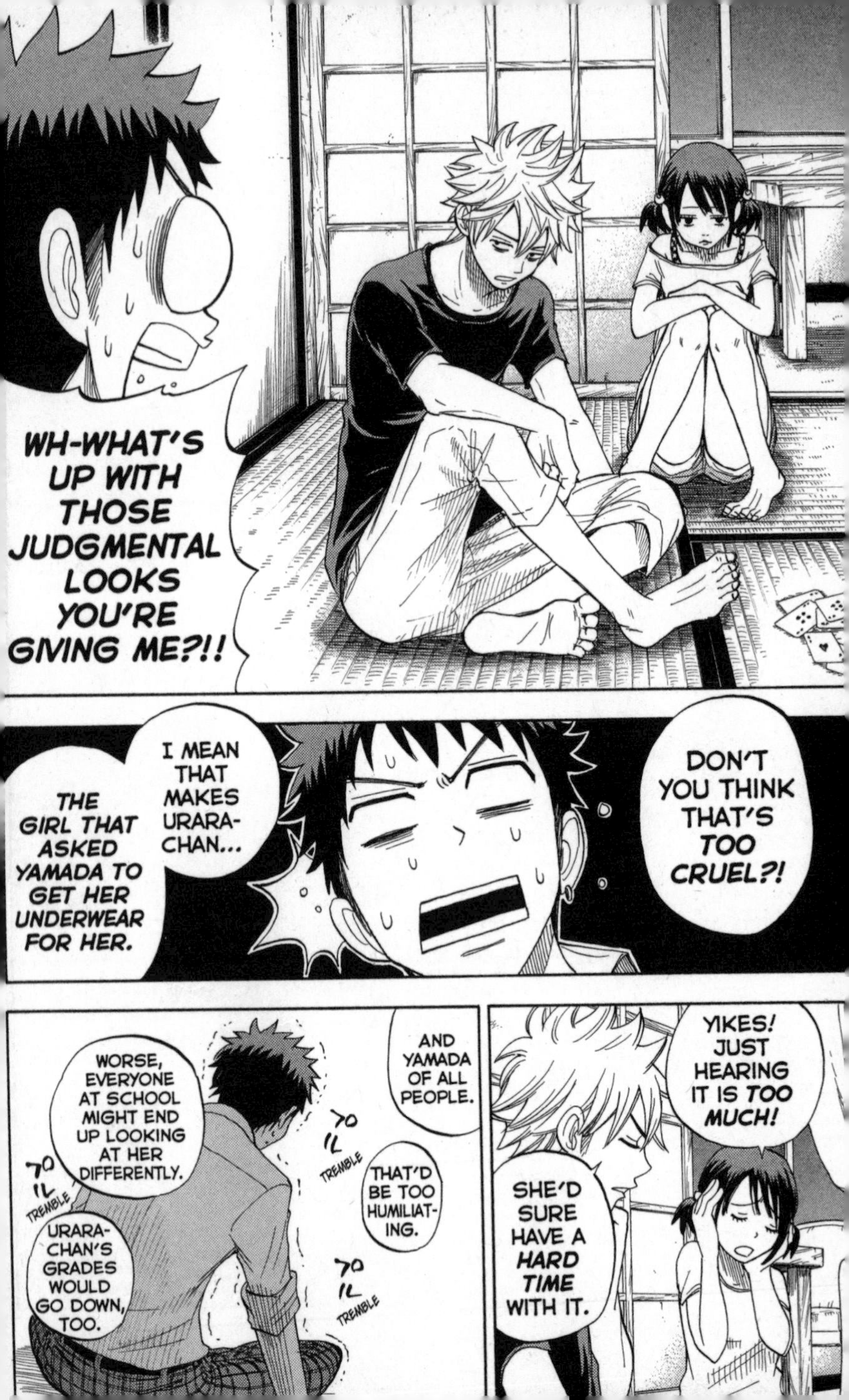
WH-WHAT'S UP WITH THOSE JUDGMENTAL LOOKS YOU'RE GIVING ME?!!
DON'T YOU THINK THAT'S TOO CRUEL?!
I MEAN THAT MAKES URARA-CHAN...
THE GIRL THAT ASKED YAMADA TO GET HER UNDERWEAR FOR HER.
YIKES! JUST HEARING IT IS TOO MUCH!
SHE'D SURE HAVE A HARD TIME WITH IT.
AND YAMADA OF ALL PEOPLE.
WORSE, EVERYONE AT SCHOOL MIGHT END UP LOOKING AT HER DIFFERENTLY.
TREMBLE
THAT'D BE TOO HUMILIATING.
TREMBLE
URARA-CHAN'S GRADES WOULD GO DOWN, TOO.
TREMBLE

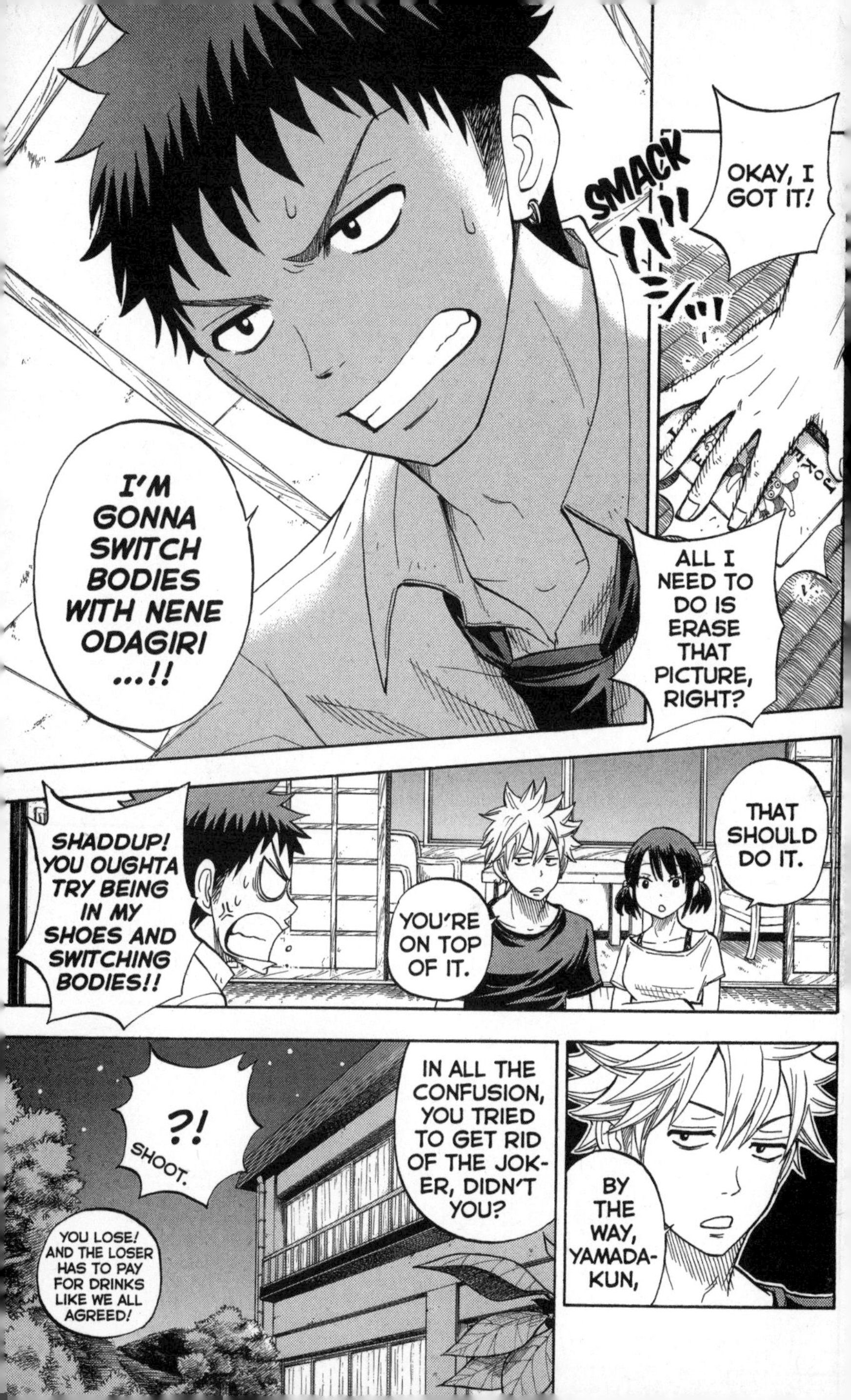

OKAY, I GOT IT!
SMACK
ALL I NEED TO DO IS ERASE THAT PICTURE, RIGHT?
I'M GONNA SWITCH BODIES WITH NENE ODAGIRI ...!!
THAT SHOULD DO IT.
YOU'RE ON TOP OF IT.
SHADDUP! YOU OUGHTA TRY BEING IN MY SHOES AND SWITCHING BODIES!!
BY THE WAY, YAMADA-KUN,
IN ALL THE CONFUSION, YOU TRIED TO GET RID OF THE JOK-ER, DIDN'T YOU?
?!
SHOOT.
YOU LOSE! AND THE LOSER HAS TO PAY FOR DRINKS LIKE WE ALL AGREED!

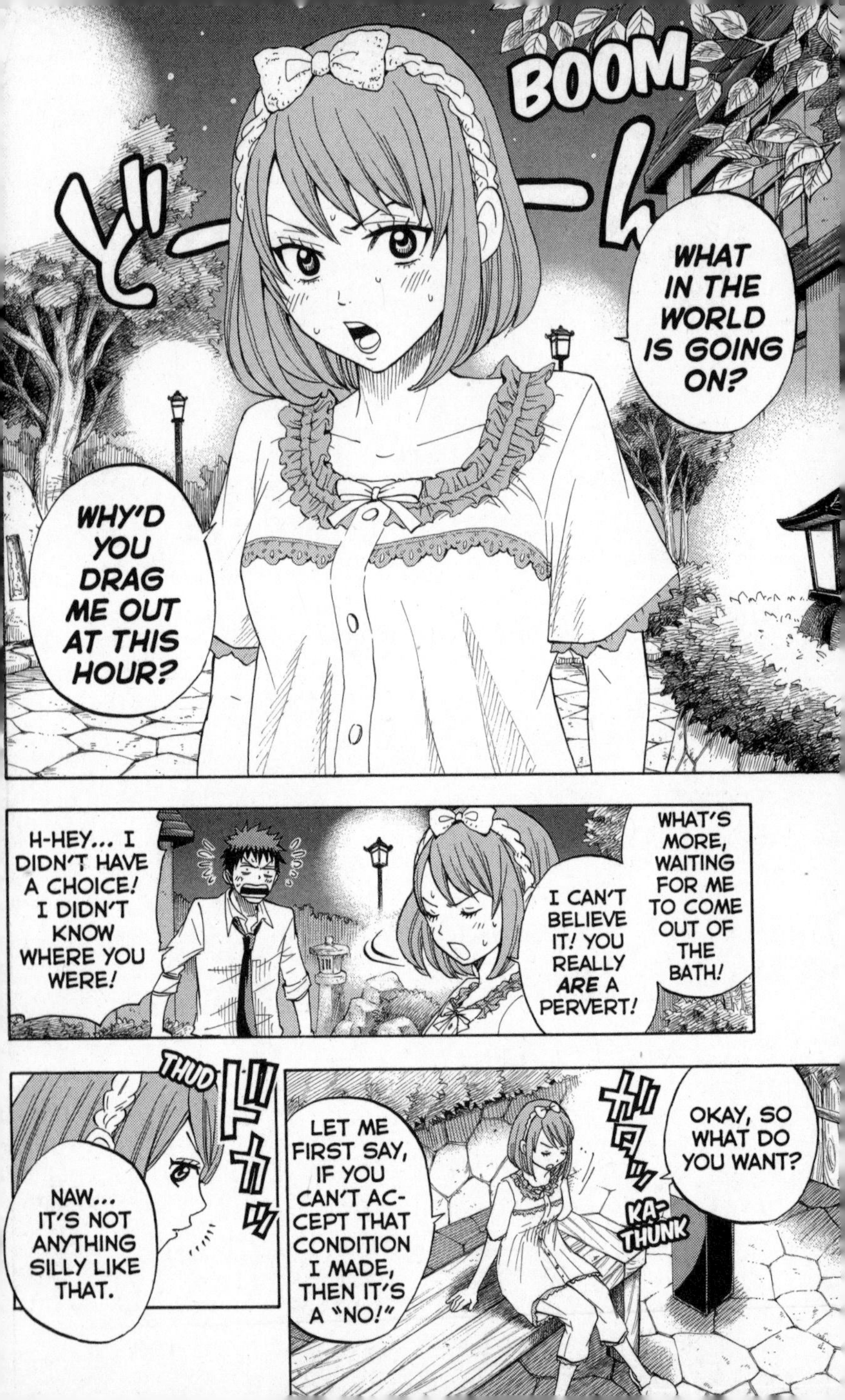
BOOM
WHAT IN THE WORLD IS GOING ON?
WHY'D YOU DRAG ME OUT AT THIS HOUR?
WHAT'S MORE, WAITING FOR ME TO COME OUT OF THE BATH!
I CAN'T BELIEVE IT! YOU REALLY ARE A PERVERT!
H-HEY... I DIDN'T HAVE A CHOICE! I DIDN'T KNOW WHERE YOU WERE!
OKAY, SO WHAT DO YOU WANT?
KA-THUNK
LET ME FIRST SAY, IF YOU CAN'T AC-CEPT THAT CONDITION I MADE, THEN IT'S A "NO!"
THUD
NAW... IT'S NOT ANYTHING SILLY LIKE THAT.

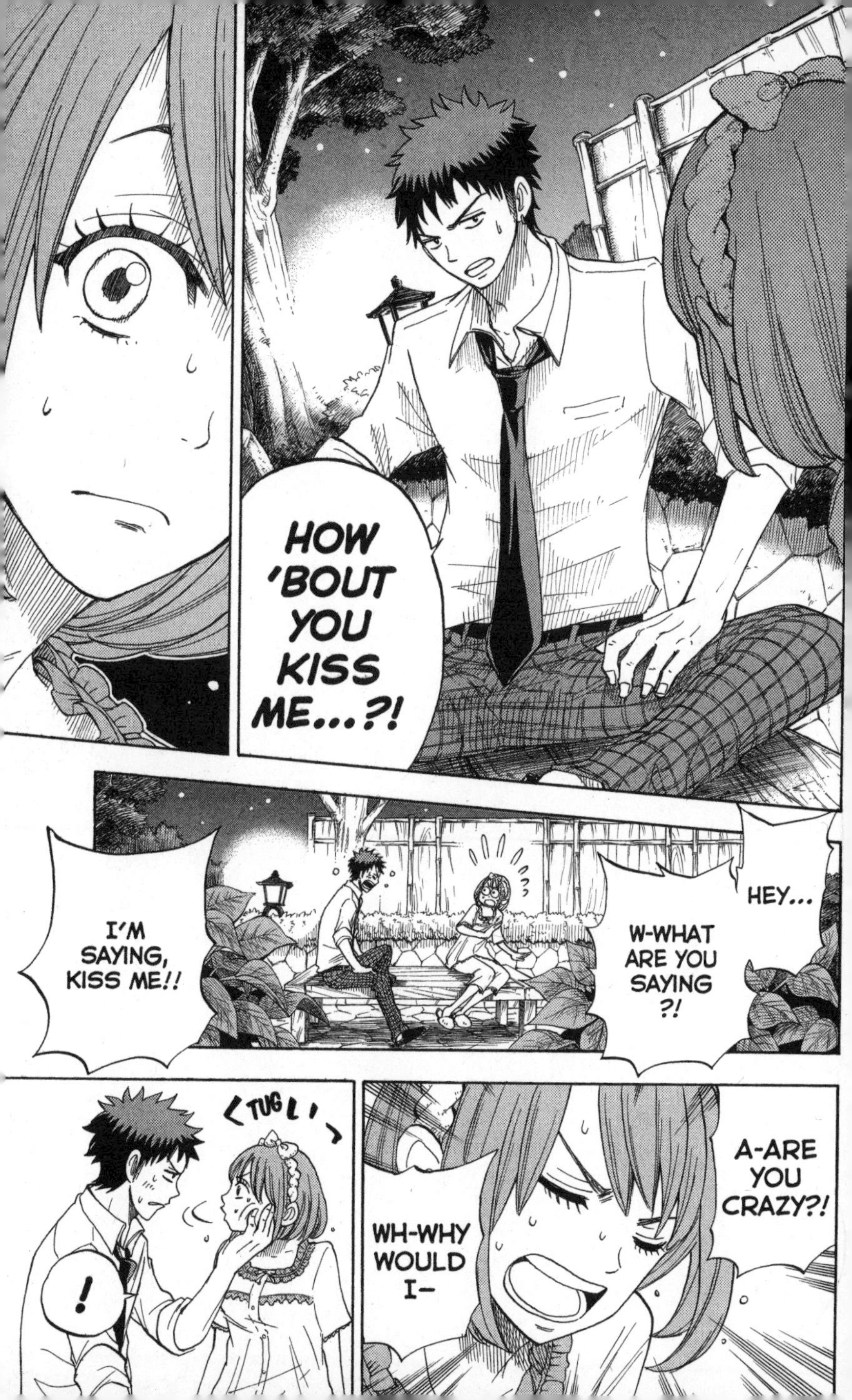
HOW 'BOUT YOU KISS ME...?!
HEY...
W-WHAT ARE YOU SAYING?!
I'M SAYING, KISS ME!!
A-ARE YOU CRAZY?!
WH-WHY WOULD I–
TUG
!

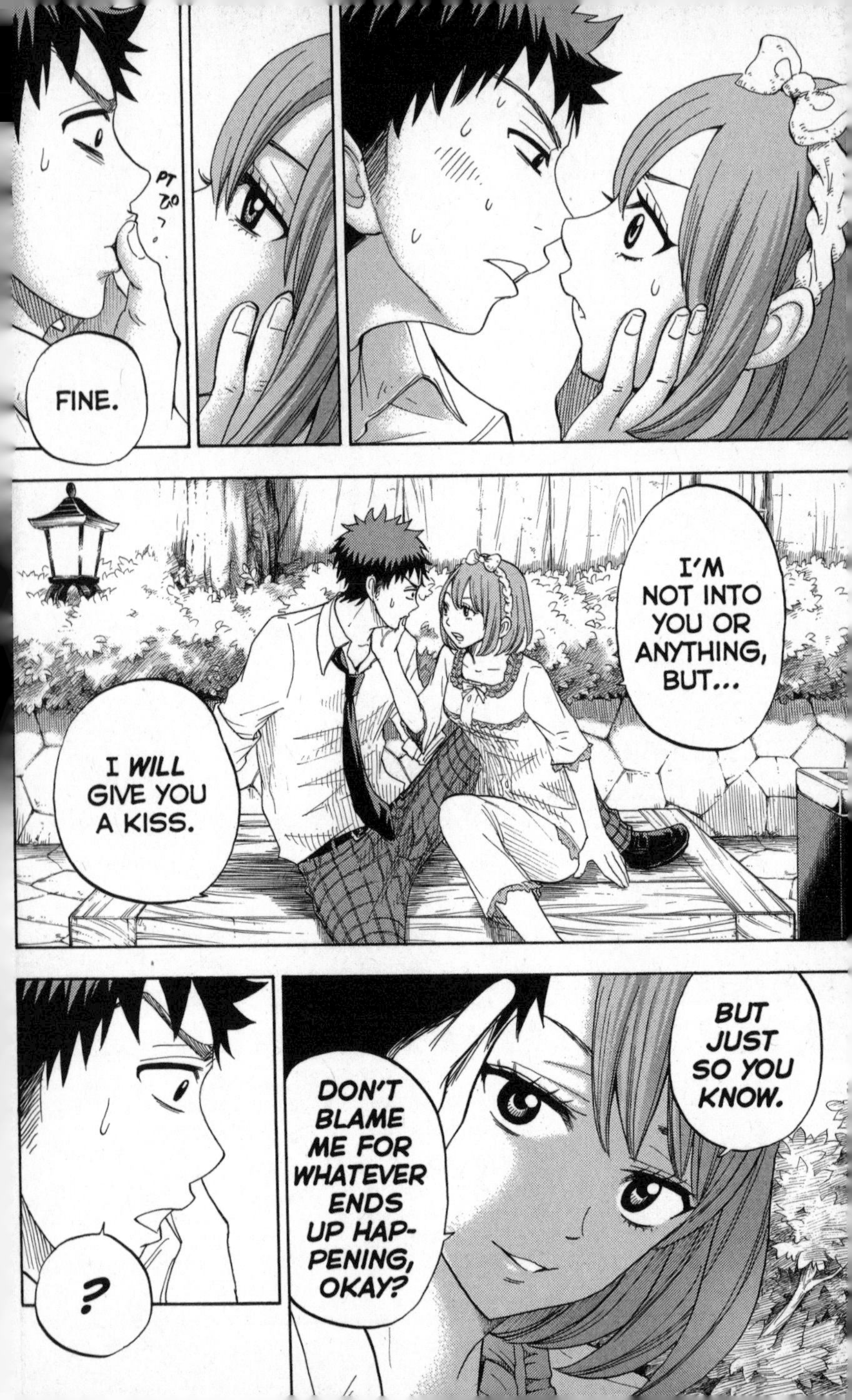
PT
FINE.
I'M NOT INTO YOU OR ANYTHING, BUT...
I WILL GIVE YOU A KISS.
BUT JUST SO YOU KNOW.
DON'T BLAME ME FOR WHATEVER ENDS UP HAP-PENING, OKAY?
?

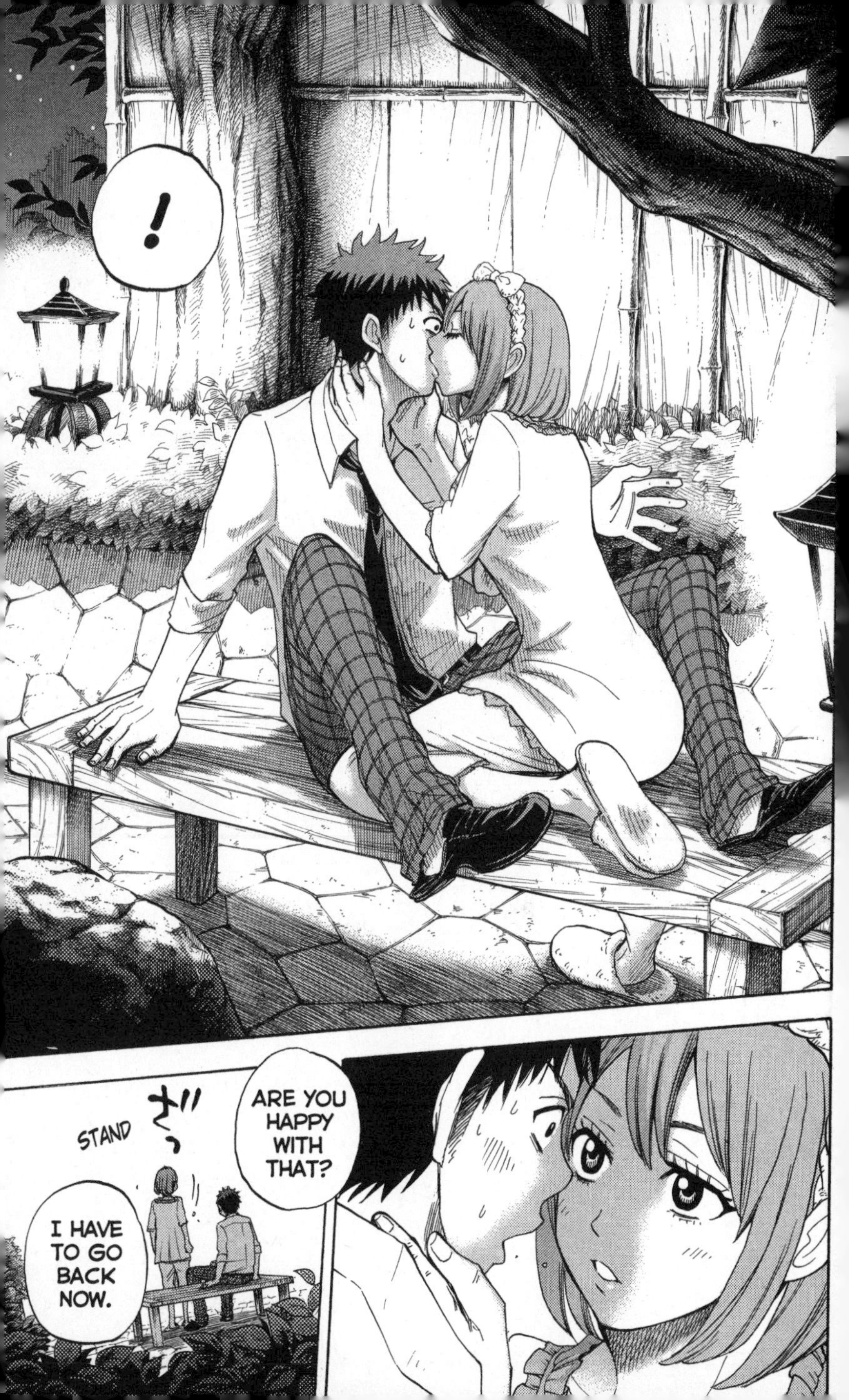
!
ARE YOU HAPPY WITH THAT?
ざっ
STAND
I HAVE TO GO BACK NOW.

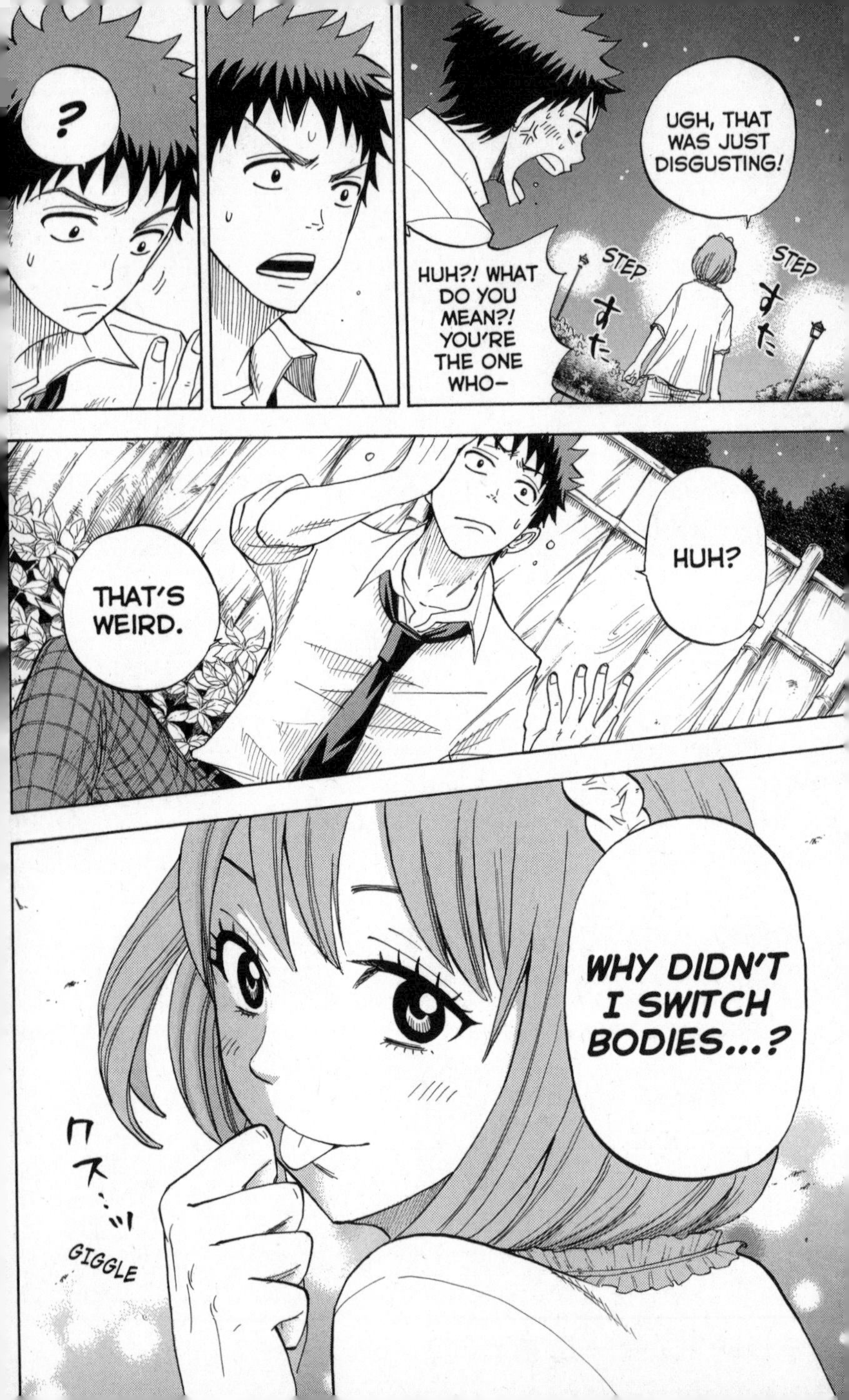

UGH, THAT WAS JUST DISGUSTING!
STEP
すた
STEP
すた
HUH?! WHAT DO YOU MEAN?! YOU'RE THE ONE WHO–
?
HUH?
THAT'S WEIRD.
WHY DIDN'T I SWITCH BODIES...?
GIGGLE

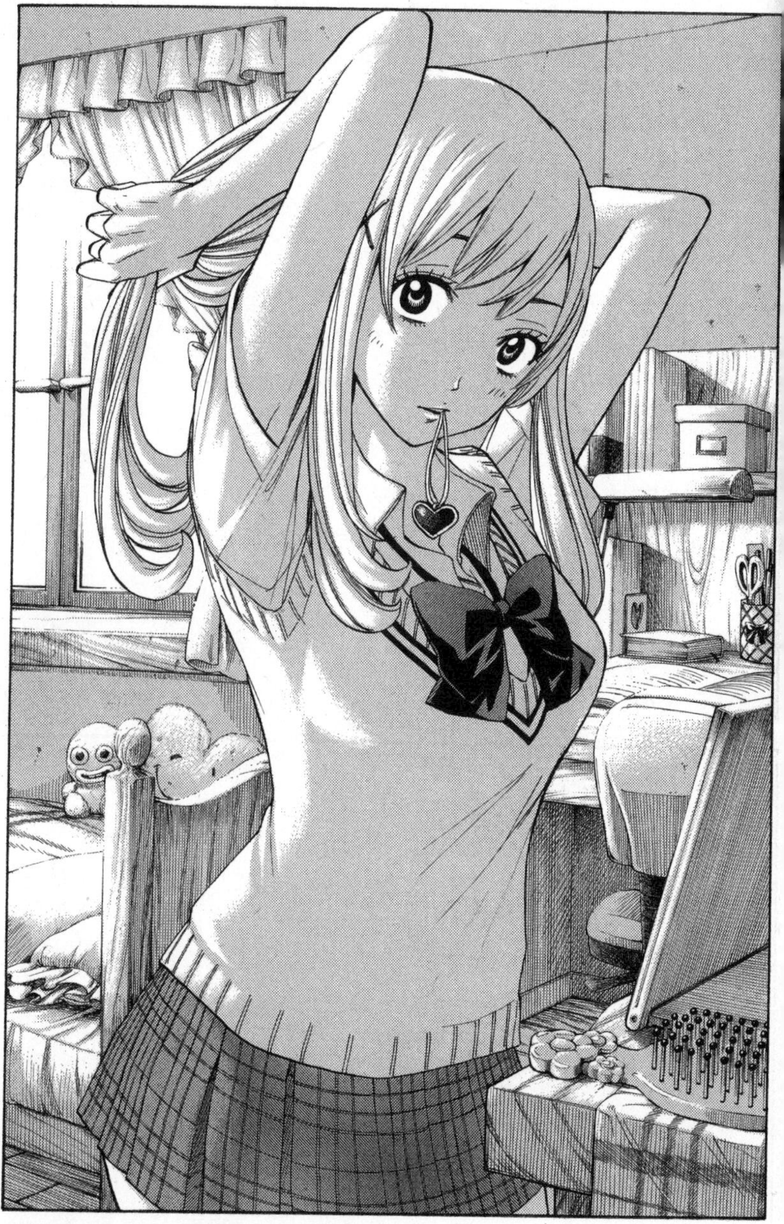

CHAPTER 18: Fidget Fidget.

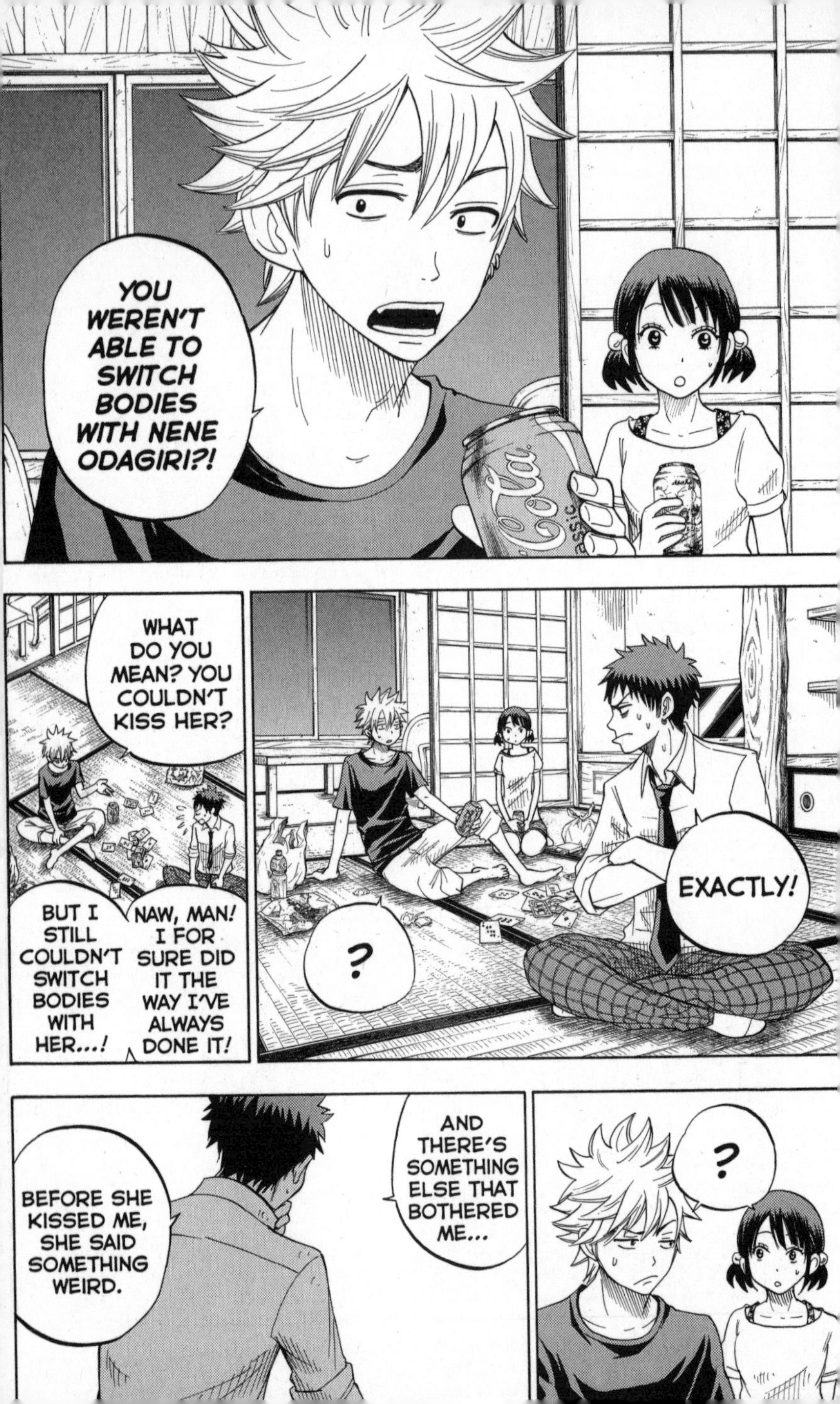
YOU WEREN'T ABLE TO SWITCH BODIES WITH NENE ODAGIRI?!
EXACTLY!
?
WHAT DO YOU MEAN? YOU COULDN'T KISS HER?
NAW, MAN! I FOR SURE DID IT THE WAY I'VE ALWAYS DONE IT!
BUT I STILL COULDN'T SWITCH BODIES WITH HER...!
?
AND THERE'S SOMETHING ELSE THAT BOTHERED ME...
BEFORE SHE KISSED ME, SHE SAID SOMETHING WEIRD.

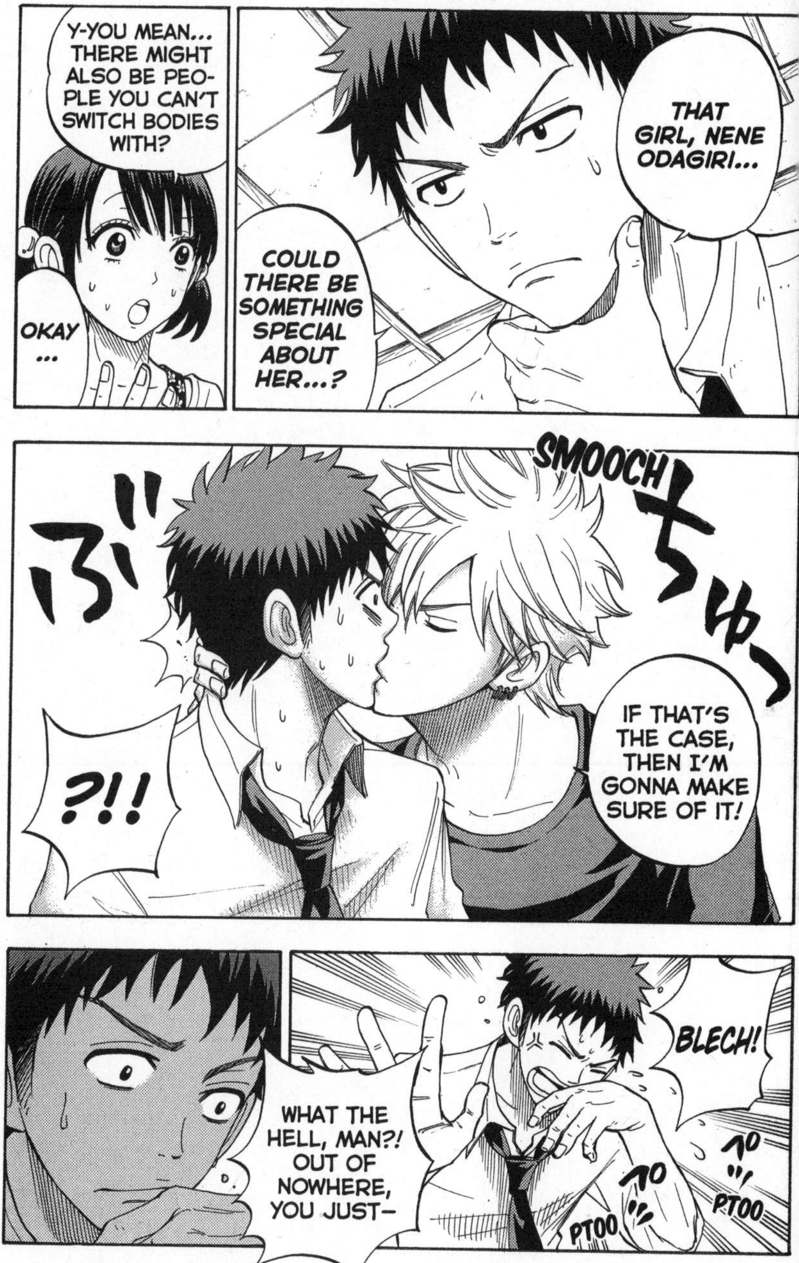
THAT GIRL, NENE ODAGIRI...
COULD THERE BE SOMETHING SPECIAL ABOUT HER...?
Y-YOU MEAN... THERE MIGHT ALSO BE PEO-PLE YOU CAN'T SWITCH BODIES WITH?
OKAY ...
SMOOCH
ちゅっ
IF THAT'S THE CASE, THEN I'M GONNA MAKE SURE OF IT!
ぶ
?!!
BLECH!
PTOO
PTOO
PTOO
WHAT THE HELL, MAN?! OUT OF NOWHERE, YOU JUST—

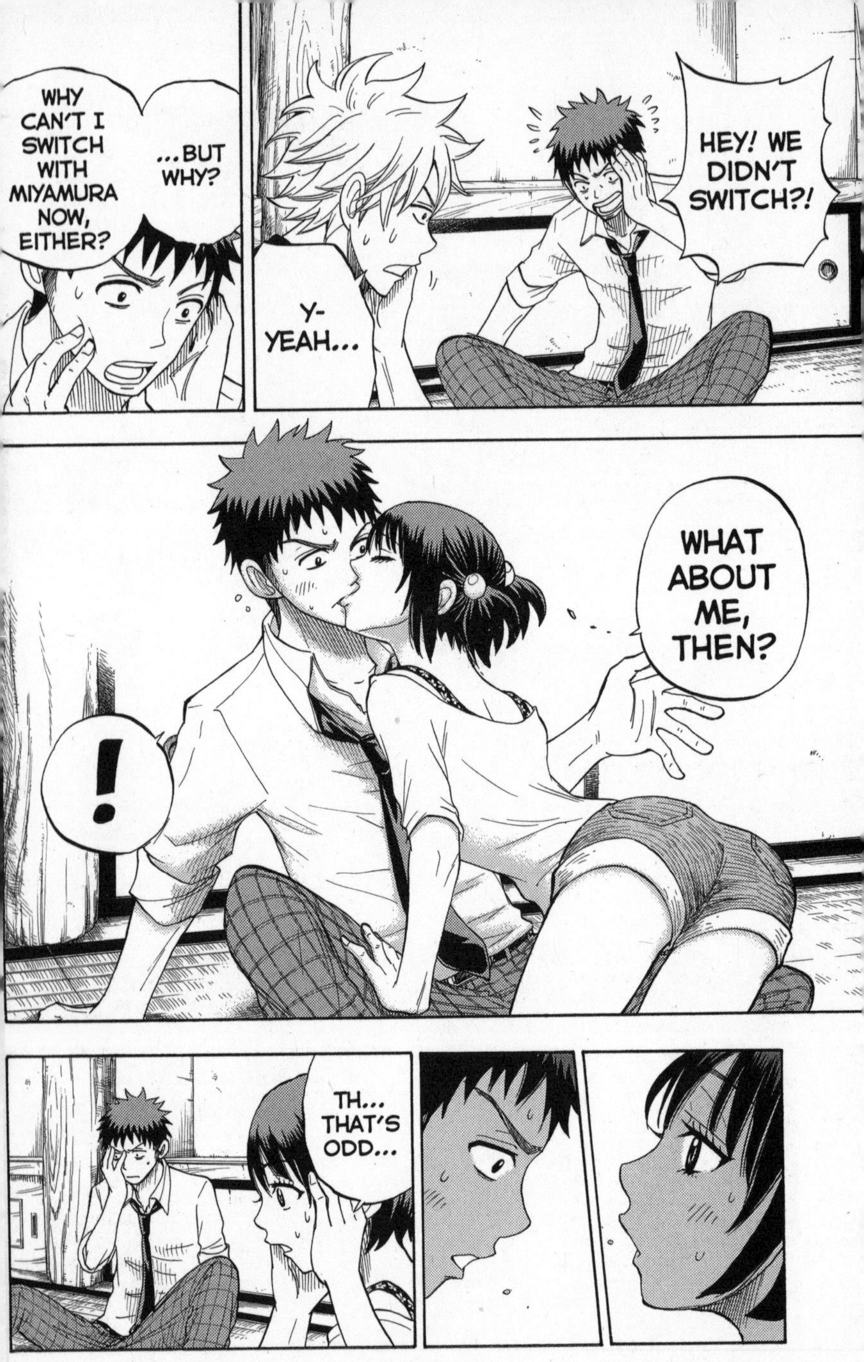
HEY! WE DIDN'T SWITCH?!
Y-YEAH...
...BUT WHY?
WHY CAN'T I SWITCH WITH MIYAMURA NOW, EITHER?
WHAT ABOUT ME, THEN?
!
TH... THAT'S ODD...

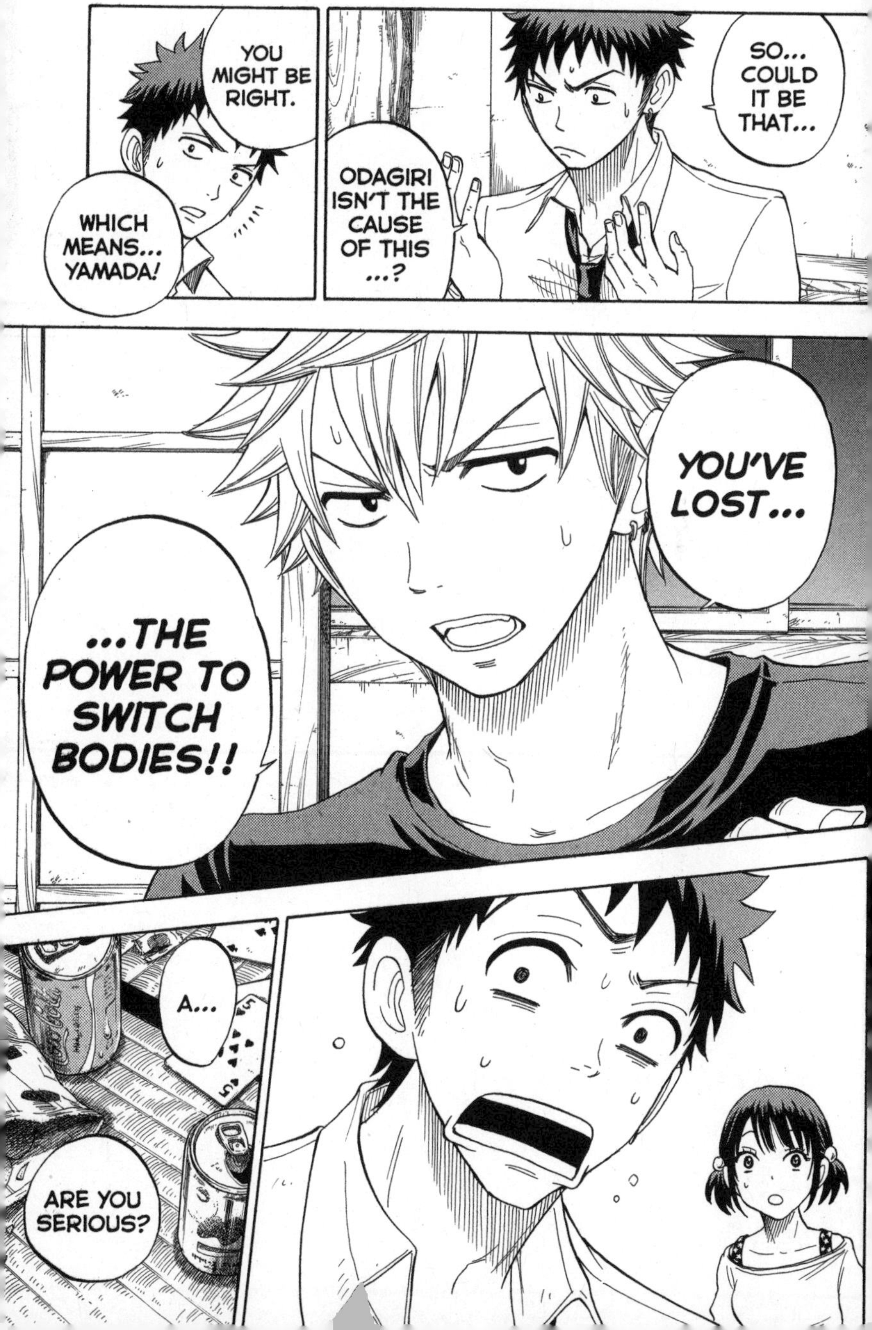
SO... COULD IT BE THAT...
ODAGIRI ISN'T THE CAUSE OF THIS ...?
YOU MIGHT BE RIGHT.
WHICH MEANS... YAMADA!
YOU'VE LOST...
...THE POWER TO SWITCH BODIES!!
A...
ARE YOU SERIOUS?

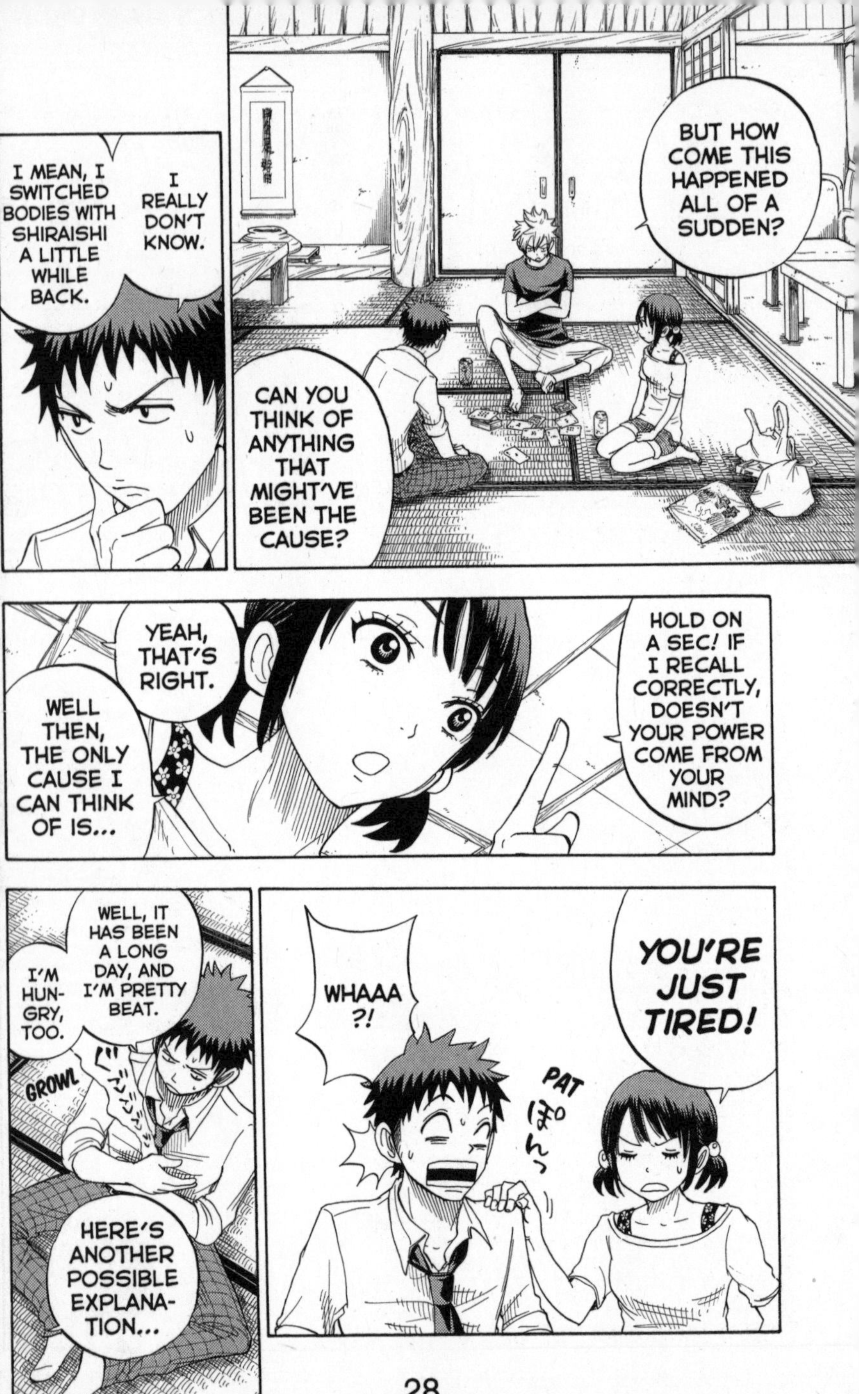

BUT HOW COME THIS HAPPENED ALL OF A SUDDEN?
CAN YOU THINK OF ANYTHING THAT MIGHT'VE BEEN THE CAUSE?
I REALLY DON'T KNOW.
I MEAN, I SWITCHED BODIES WITH SHIRAISHI A LITTLE WHILE BACK.
HOLD ON A SEC! IF I RECALL CORRECTLY, DOESN'T YOUR POWER COME FROM YOUR MIND?
YEAH, THAT'S RIGHT.
WELL THEN, THE ONLY CAUSE I CAN THINK OF IS...
YOU'RE JUST TIRED!
PAT
ぽんっ
WHAAA?!
WELL, IT HAS BEEN A LONG DAY, AND I'M PRETTY BEAT.
I'M HUNGRY, TOO.
GROWL
HERE'S ANOTHER POSSIBLE EXPLANATION...

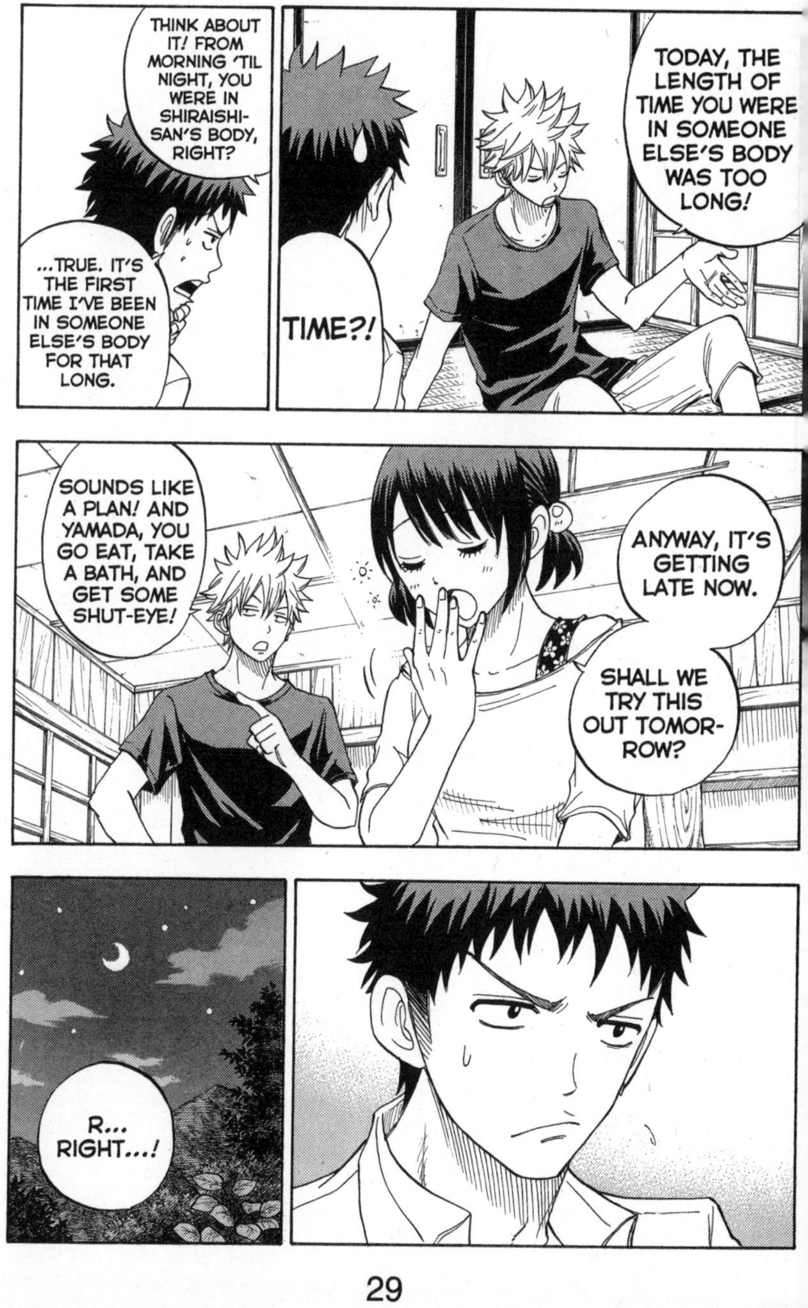
TODAY, THE LENGTH OF TIME YOU WERE IN SOMEONE ELSE'S BODY WAS TOO LONG!
TIME?!
THINK ABOUT IT! FROM MORNING 'TIL NIGHT, YOU WERE IN SHIRAISHI-SAN'S BODY, RIGHT?
...TRUE. IT'S THE FIRST TIME I'VE BEEN IN SOMEONE ELSE'S BODY FOR THAT LONG.
ANYWAY, IT'S GETTING LATE NOW.
SHALL WE TRY THIS OUT TOMOR-ROW?
SOUNDS LIKE A PLAN! AND YAMADA, YOU GO EAT, TAKE A BATH, AND GET SOME SHUT-EYE!
R... RIGHT...!

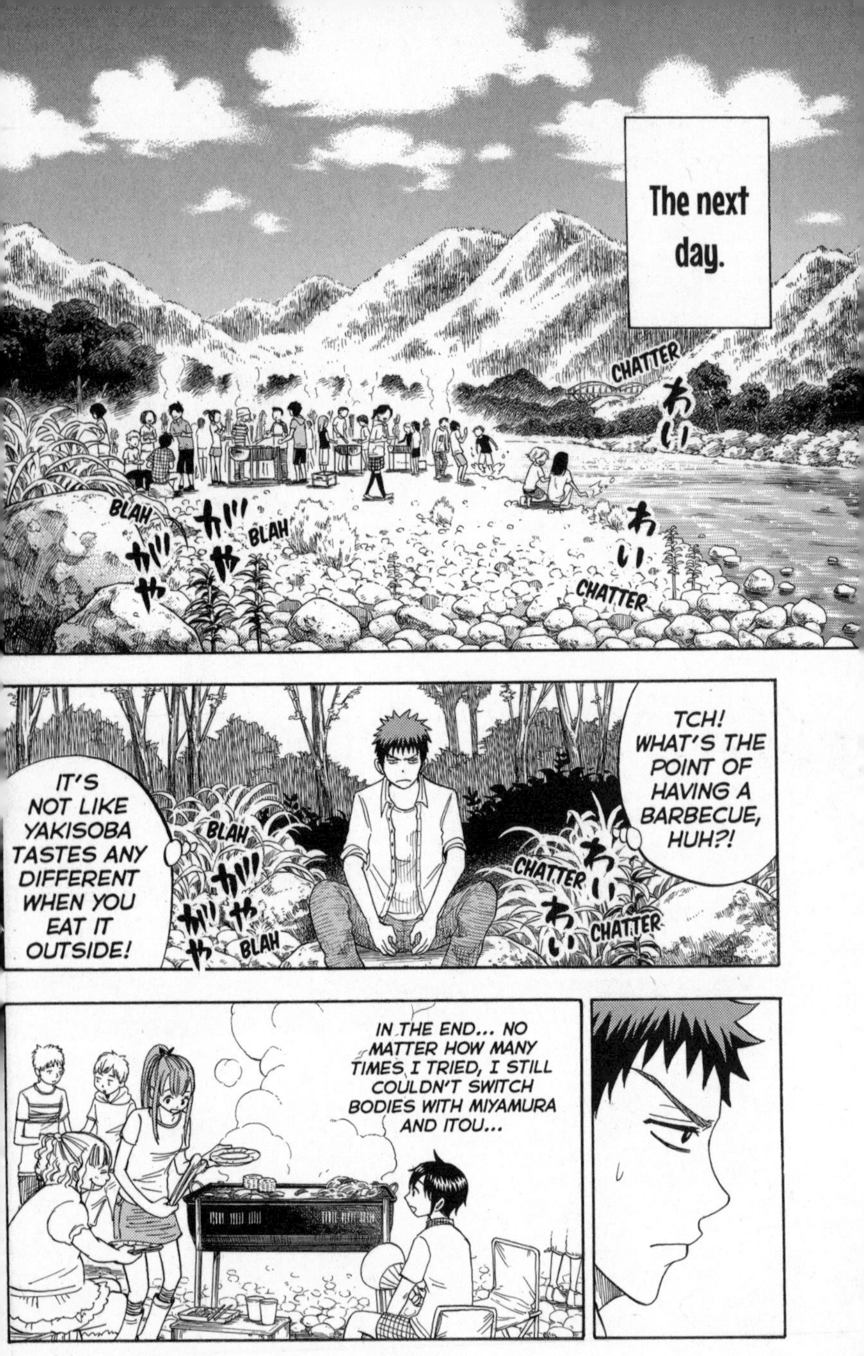
The next day.
CHATTER わい
CHATTER わい
BLAH ガヤガヤ
BLAH ガヤガヤ
TCH! WHAT'S THE POINT OF HAVING A BARBECUE, HUH?!
CHATTER わい
CHATTER わい
BLAH ガヤ
BLAH ガヤ
IT'S NOT LIKE YAKISOBA TASTES ANY DIFFERENT WHEN YOU EAT IT OUTSIDE!
IN THE END... NO MATTER HOW MANY TIMES I TRIED, I STILL COULDN'T SWITCH BODIES WITH MIYAMURA AND ITOU...

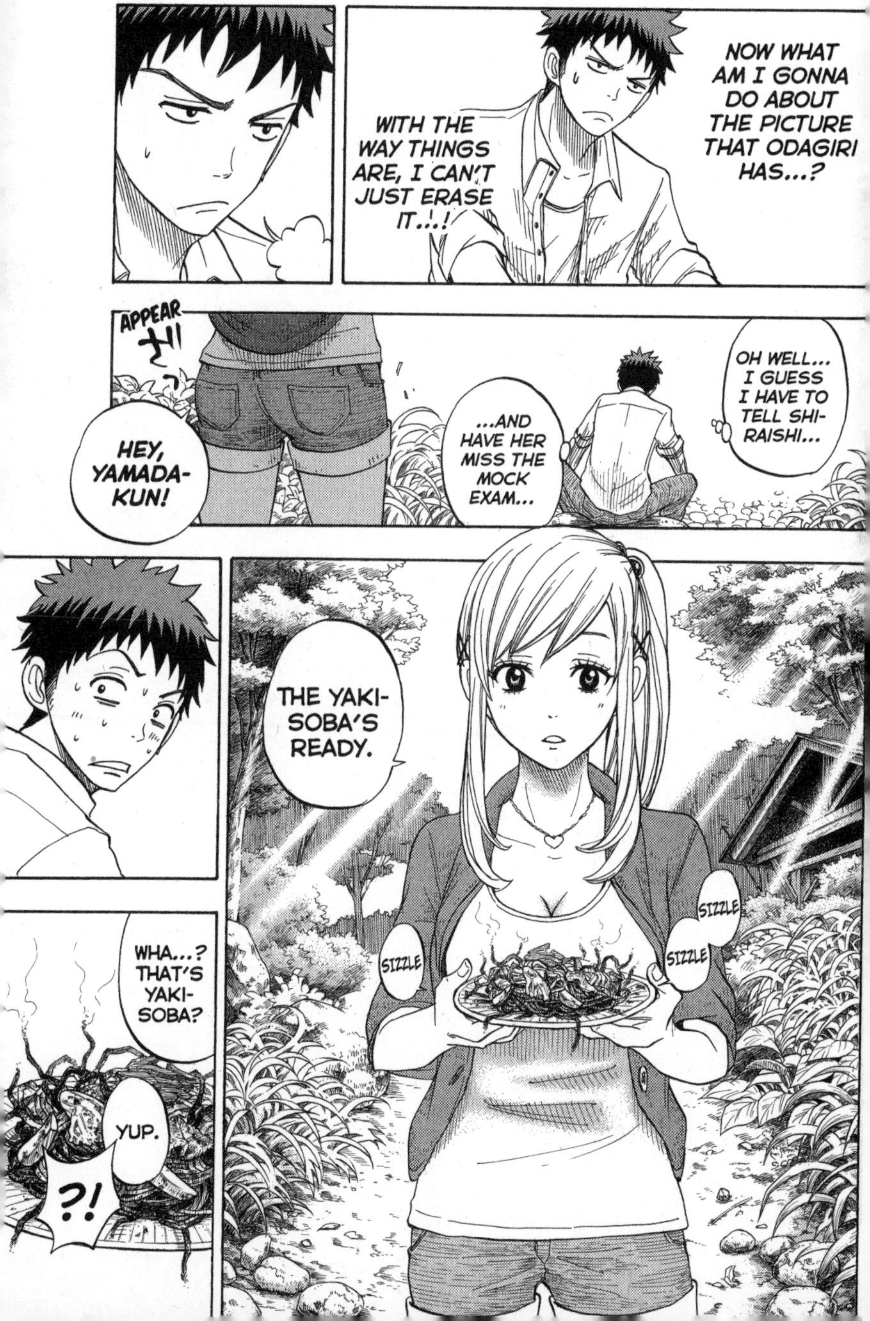
NOW WHAT AM I GONNA DO ABOUT THE PICTURE THAT ODAGIRI HAS...?
WITH THE WAY THINGS ARE, I CAN'T JUST ERASE IT...!!
OH WELL... I GUESS I HAVE TO TELL SHI-RAISHI...
...AND HAVE HER MISS THE MOCK EXAM...
APPEAR
HEY, YAMADA-KUN!
THE YAKI-SOBA'S READY.
SIZZLE
SIZZLE
SIZZLE
WHA...? THAT'S YAKI-SOBA?
YUP.
?!

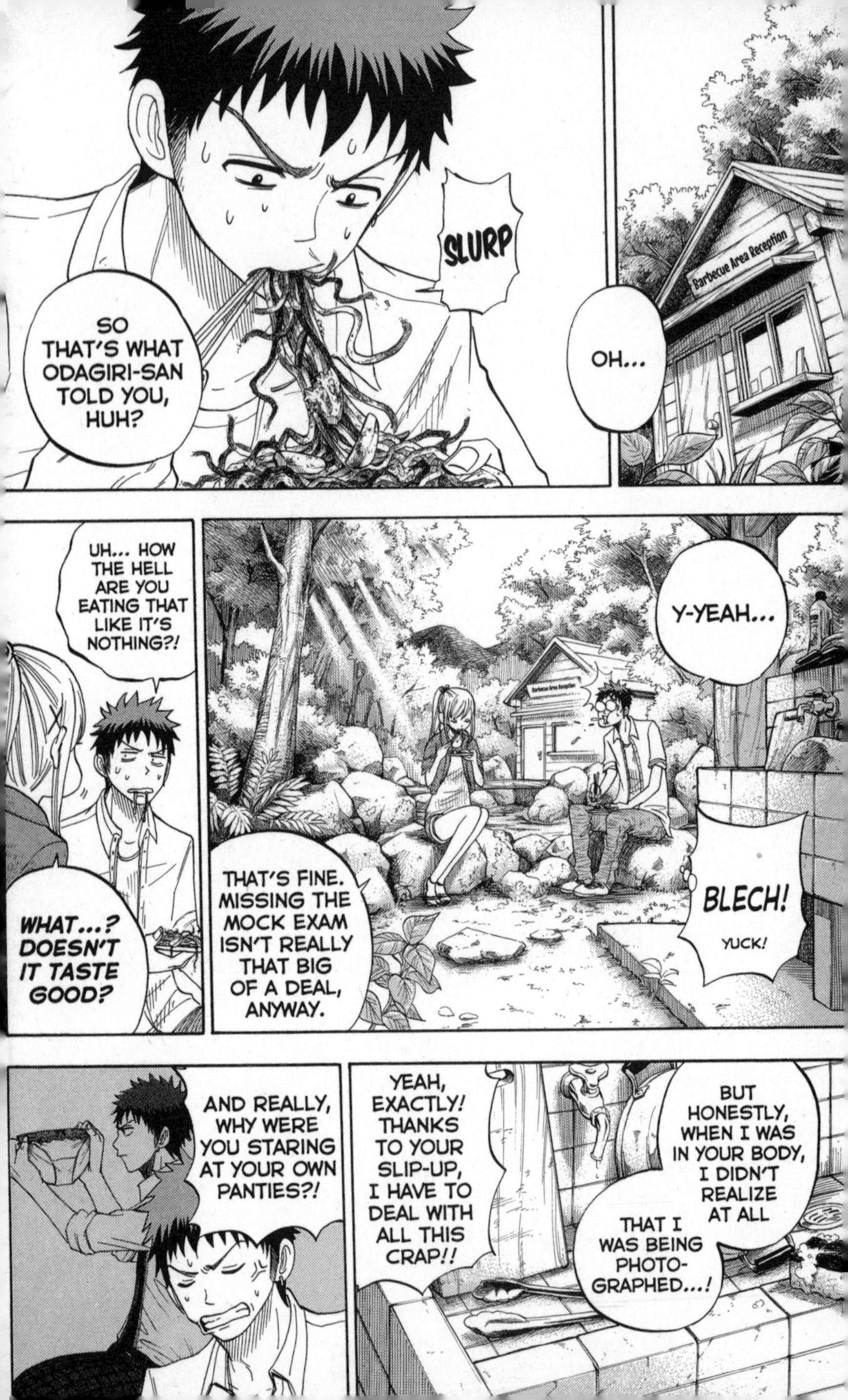
Barbecue Area Reception
OH...
SLURP
SO THAT'S WHAT ODAGIRI-SAN TOLD YOU, HUH?
Y-YEAH...
Barbecue Area Reception
BLECH!
YUCK!
THAT'S FINE. MISSING THE MOCK EXAM ISN'T REALLY THAT BIG OF A DEAL, ANYWAY.
UH... HOW THE HELL ARE YOU EATING THAT LIKE IT'S NOTHING?!
WHAT...? DOESN'T IT TASTE GOOD?
BUT HONESTLY, WHEN I WAS IN YOUR BODY, I DIDN'T REALIZE AT ALL
THAT I WAS BEING PHOTO-GRAPHED...!
YEAH, EXACTLY! THANKS TO YOUR SLIP-UP, I HAVE TO DEAL WITH ALL THIS CRAP!!
AND REALLY, WHY WERE YOU STARING AT YOUR OWN PANTIES?!

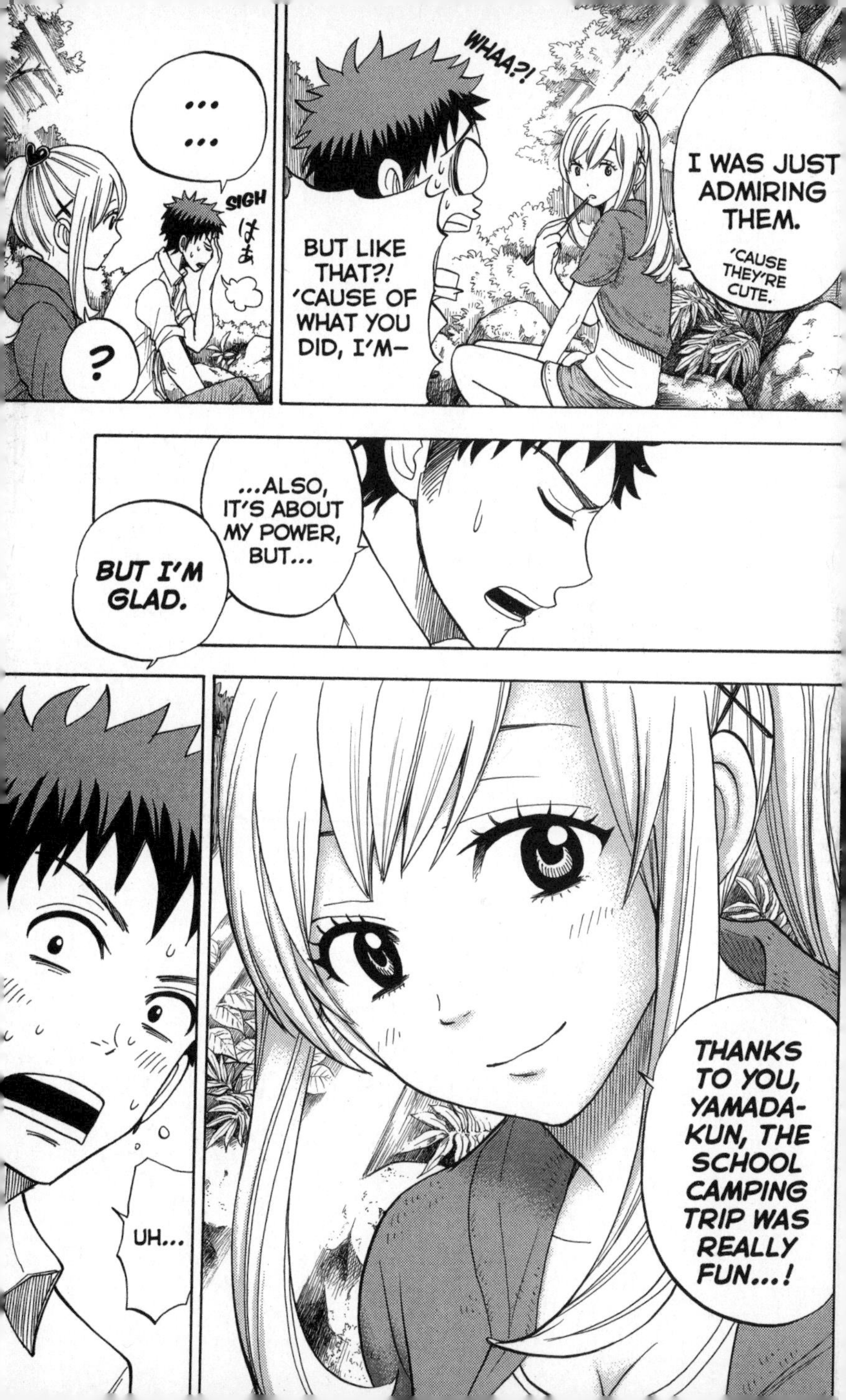
I WAS JUST ADMIRING THEM.
'CAUSE THEY'RE CUTE.
WHAA?!
BUT LIKE THAT?! 'CAUSE OF WHAT YOU DID, I'M–
......
SIGH
はぁ
?
...ALSO, IT'S ABOUT MY POWER, BUT...
BUT I'M GLAD.
THANKS TO YOU, YAMADA-KUN, THE SCHOOL CAMPING TRIP WAS REALLY FUN...!
UH...

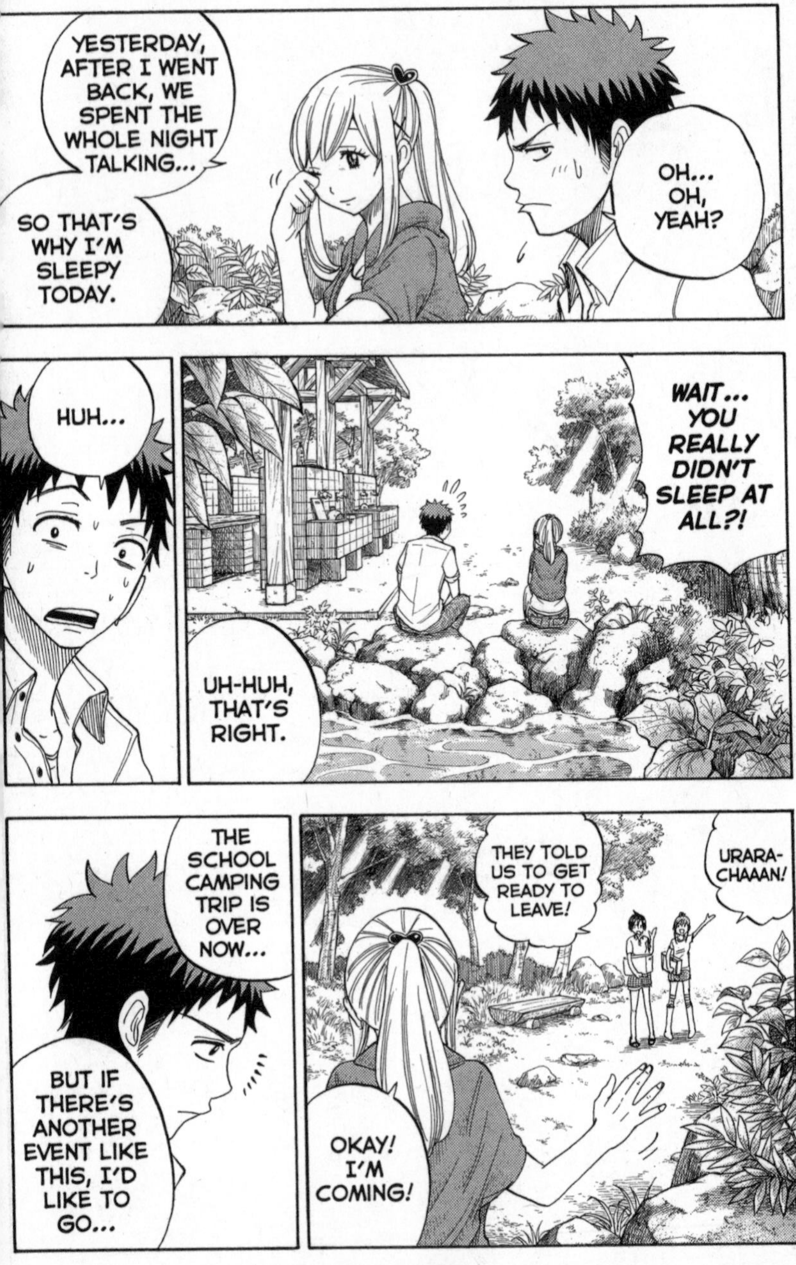
YESTERDAY, AFTER I WENT BACK, WE SPENT THE WHOLE NIGHT TALKING...
SO THAT'S WHY I'M SLEEPY TODAY.
OH... OH, YEAH?
WAIT... YOU REALLY DIDN'T SLEEP AT ALL?!
UH-HUH, THAT'S RIGHT.
HUH...
URARA-CHAAAN!
THEY TOLD US TO GET READY TO LEAVE!
OKAY! I'M COMING!
THE SCHOOL CAMPING TRIP IS OVER NOW...
BUT IF THERE'S ANOTHER EVENT LIKE THIS, I'D LIKE TO GO...

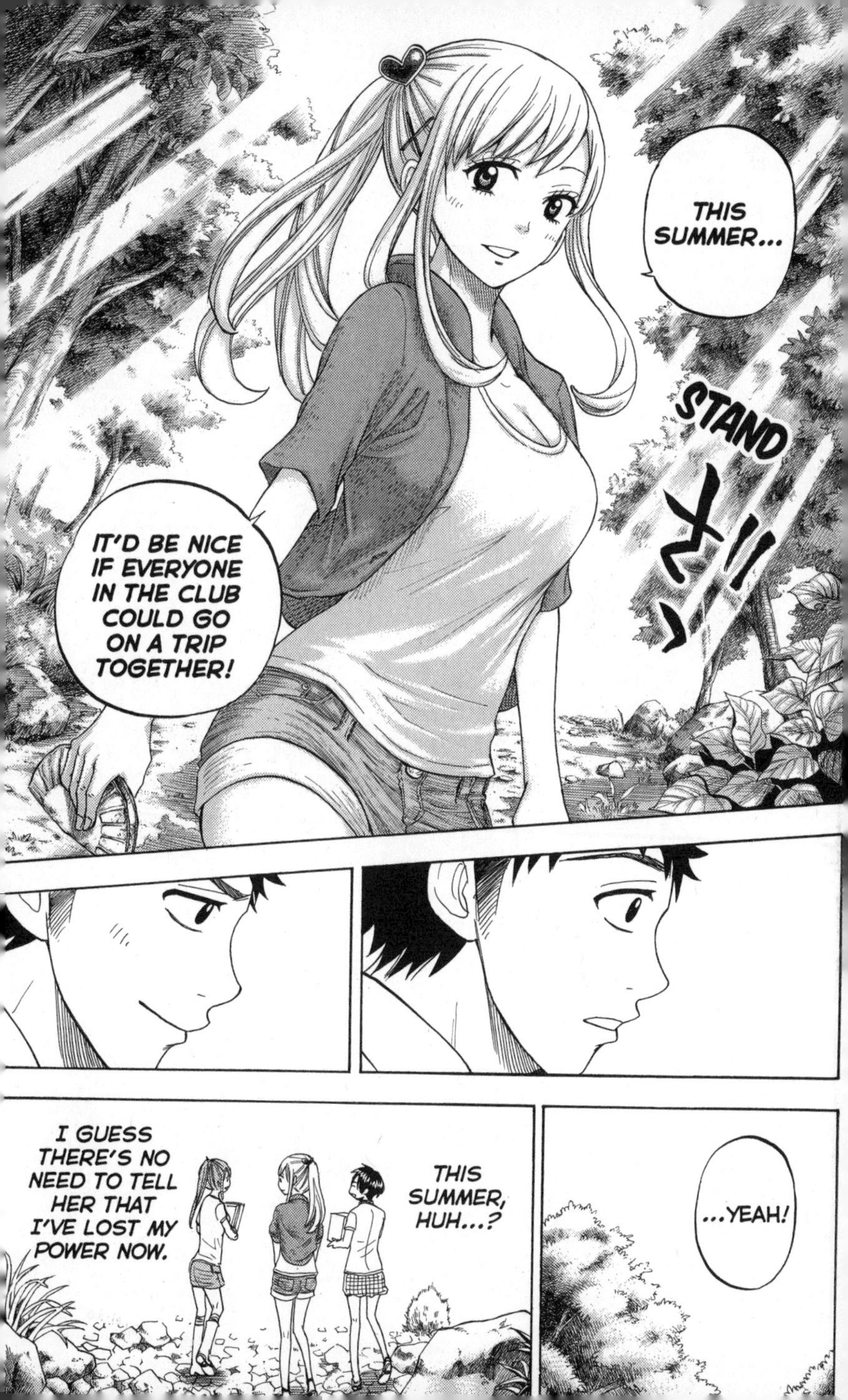
THIS SUMMER...
STAND
IT'D BE NICE IF EVERYONE IN THE CLUB COULD GO ON A TRIP TOGETHER!
...YEAH!
THIS SUMMER, HUH...?
I GUESS THERE'S NO NEED TO TELL HER THAT I'VE LOST MY POWER NOW.

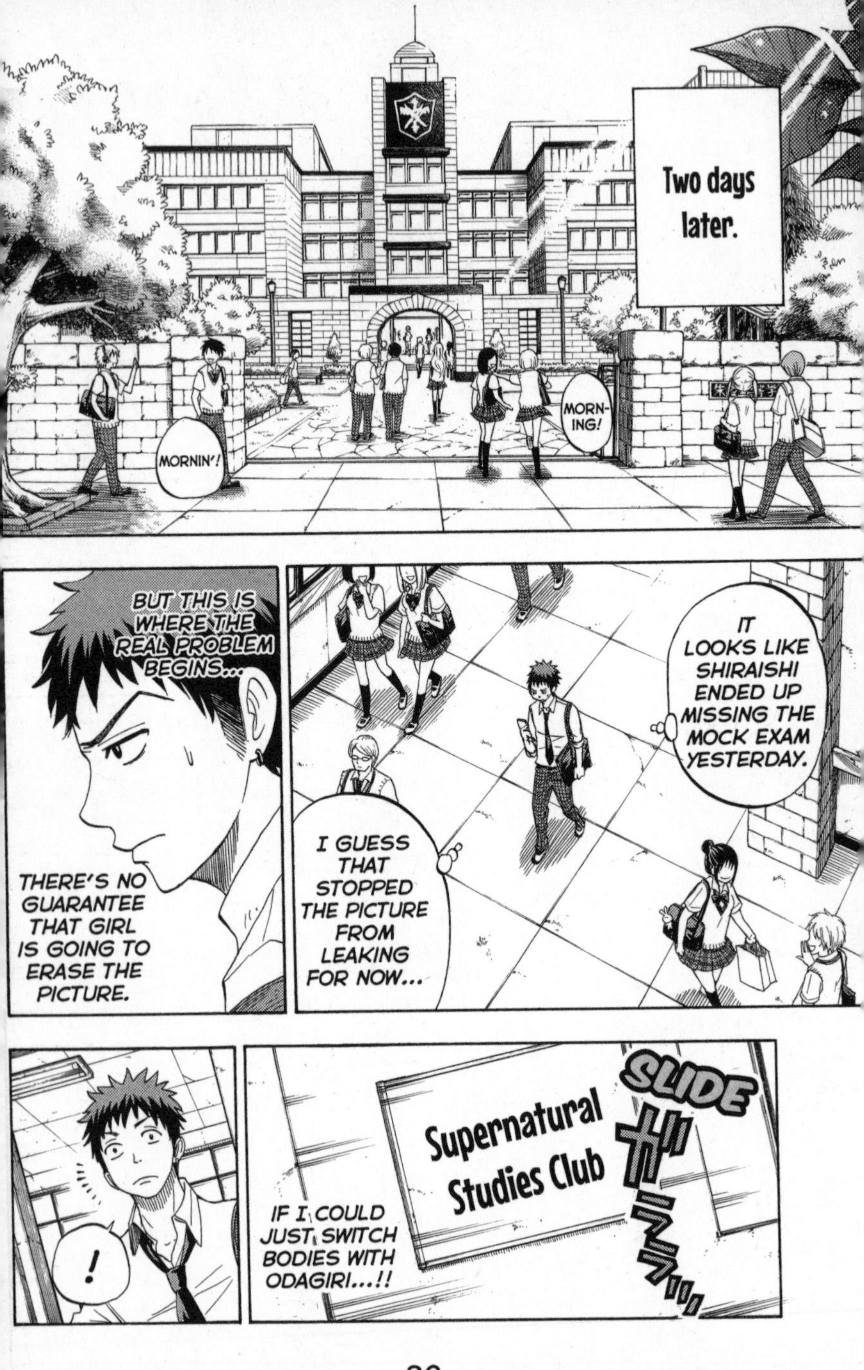
Two days later.
MORN-ING!
MORNIN'!
IT LOOKS LIKE SHIRAISHI ENDED UP MISSING THE MOCK EXAM YESTERDAY.
I GUESS THAT STOPPED THE PICTURE FROM LEAKING FOR NOW...
BUT THIS IS WHERE THE REAL PROBLEM BEGINS...
THERE'S NO GUARANTEE THAT GIRL IS GOING TO ERASE THE PICTURE.
SLIDE
Supernatural Studies Club
IF I COULD JUST SWITCH BODIES WITH ODAGIRI...!!
!

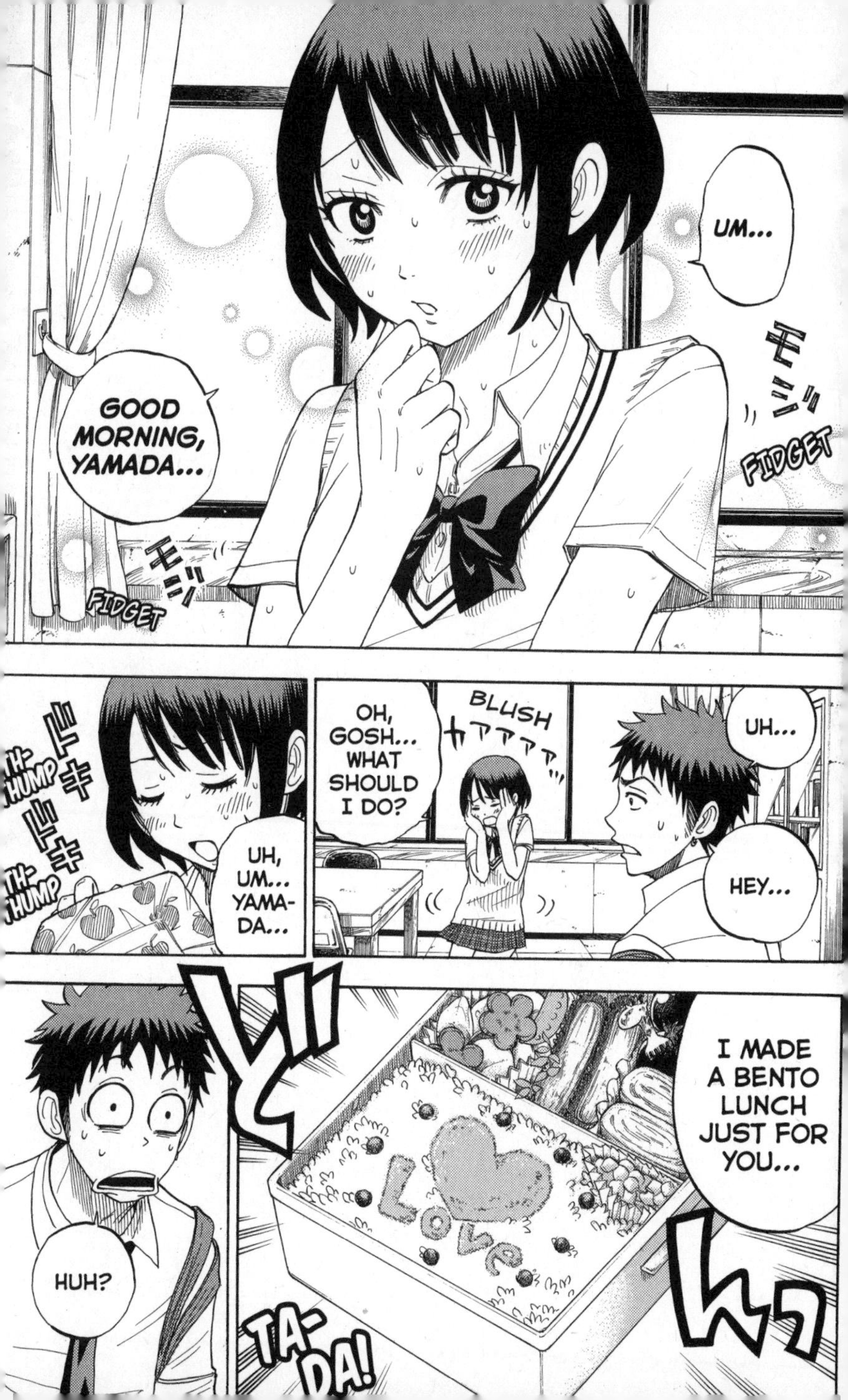
UM...
モジ
FIDGET
GOOD MORNING, YAMADA...
モジ
FIDGET
UH...
HEY...
BLUSH
カアアアア
OH, GOSH... WHAT SHOULD I DO?
ドキ
THUMP
ドキ
THUMP
UH, UM... YAMADA...
I MADE A BENTO LUNCH JUST FOR YOU...
LOVE
TA-DA!
HUH?

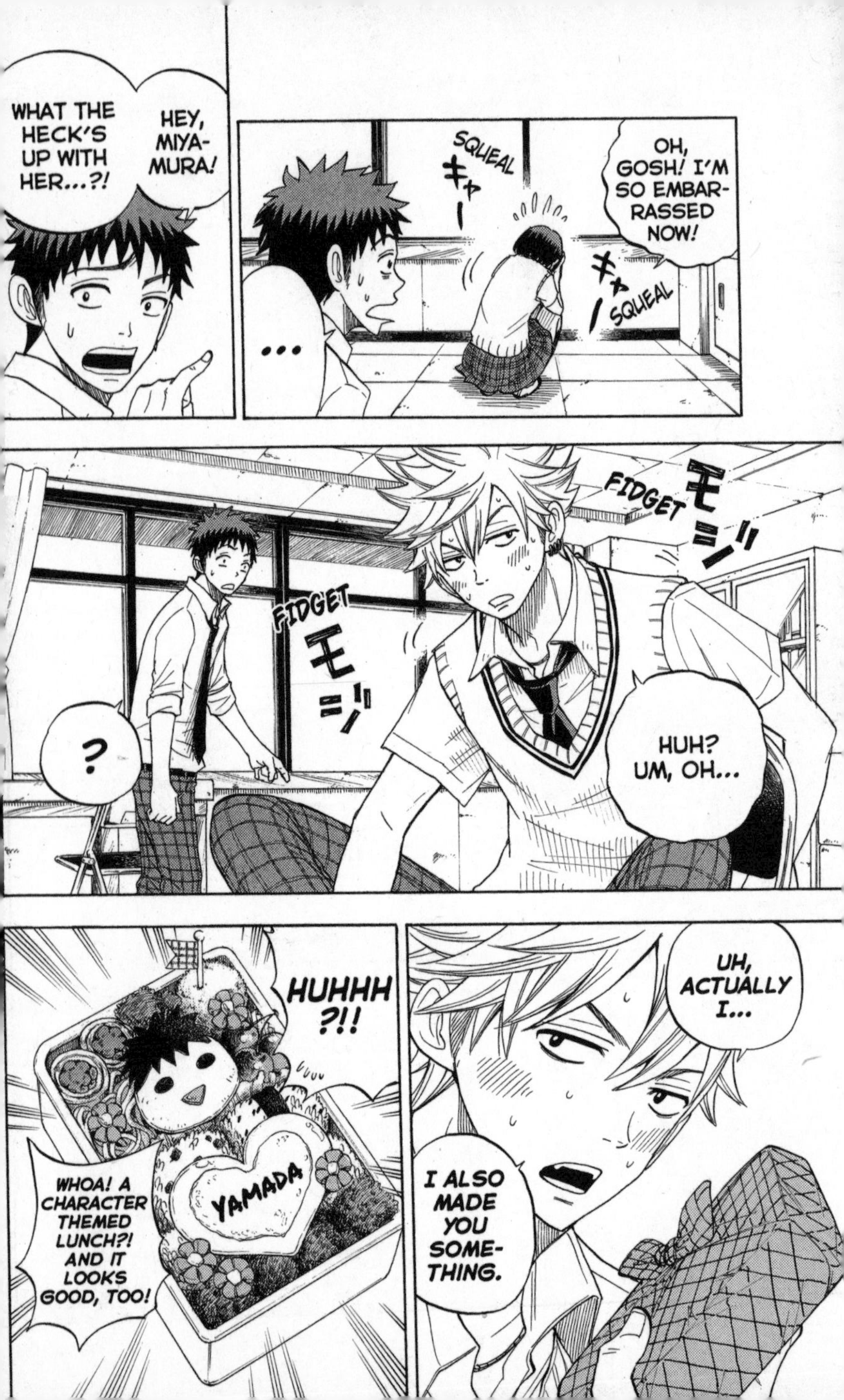
OH, GOSH! I'M SO EMBARRASSED NOW!
SQUEAL
SQUEAL
...
HEY, MIYAMURA!
WHAT THE HECK'S UP WITH HER...?!
FIDGET
HUH? UM, OH...
FIDGET
?
UH, ACTUALLY I...
I ALSO MADE YOU SOMETHING.
HUHHH?!!
YAMADA
WHOA! A CHARACTER THEMED LUNCH?! AND IT LOOKS GOOD, TOO!

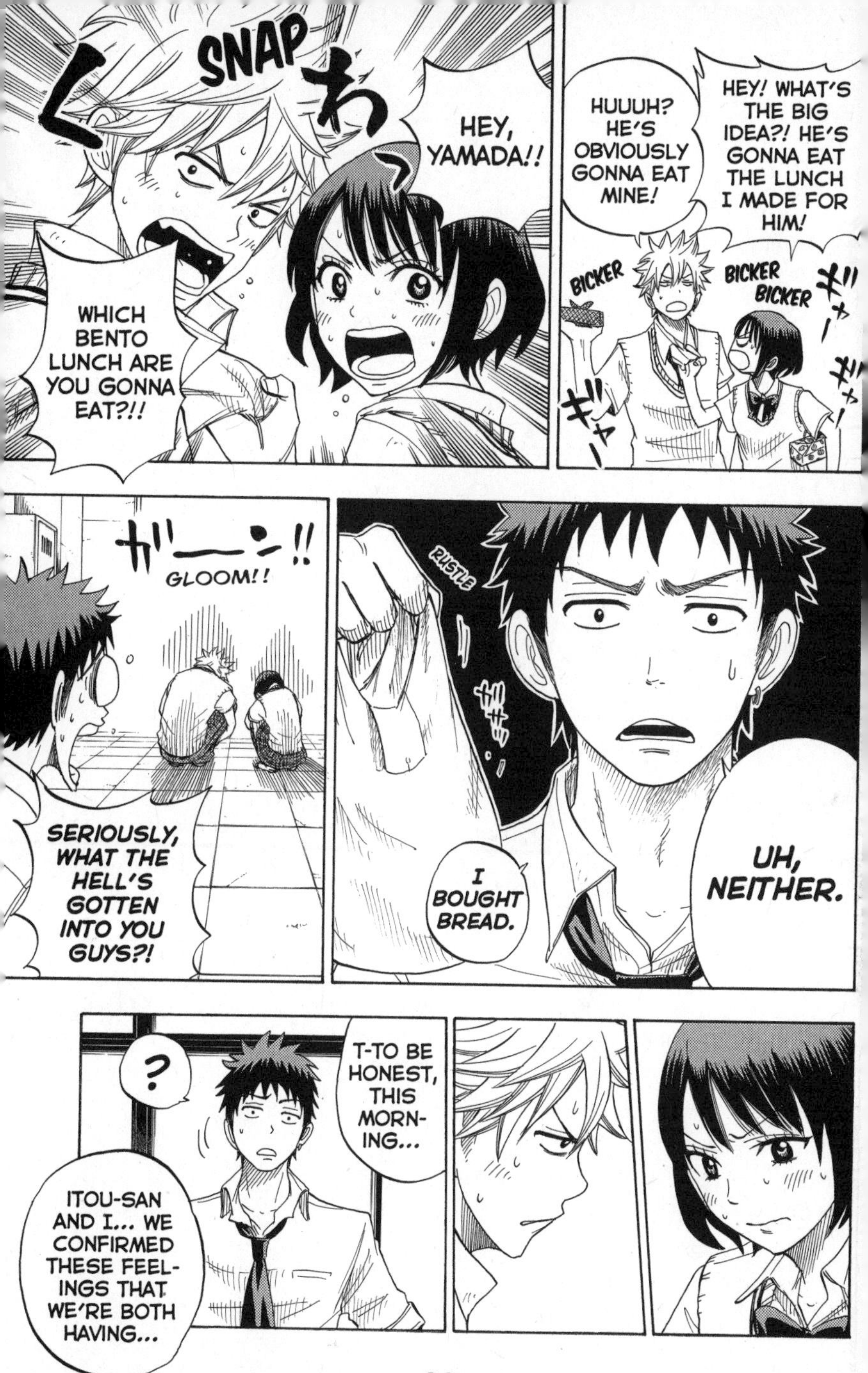
HEY! WHAT'S THE BIG IDEA?! HE'S GONNA EAT THE LUNCH I MADE FOR HIM!
HUUUH? HE'S OBVIOUSLY GONNA EAT MINE!
BICKER BICKER
BICKER
HEY, YAMADA!!
SNAP
WHICH BENTO LUNCH ARE YOU GONNA EAT?!!
UH, NEITHER.
RUSTLE
I BOUGHT BREAD.
GLOOM!!
SERIOUSLY, WHAT THE HELL'S GOTTEN INTO YOU GUYS?!
T-TO BE HONEST, THIS MORN-ING...
?
ITOU-SAN AND I... WE CONFIRMED THESE FEEL-INGS THAT WE'RE BOTH HAVING...

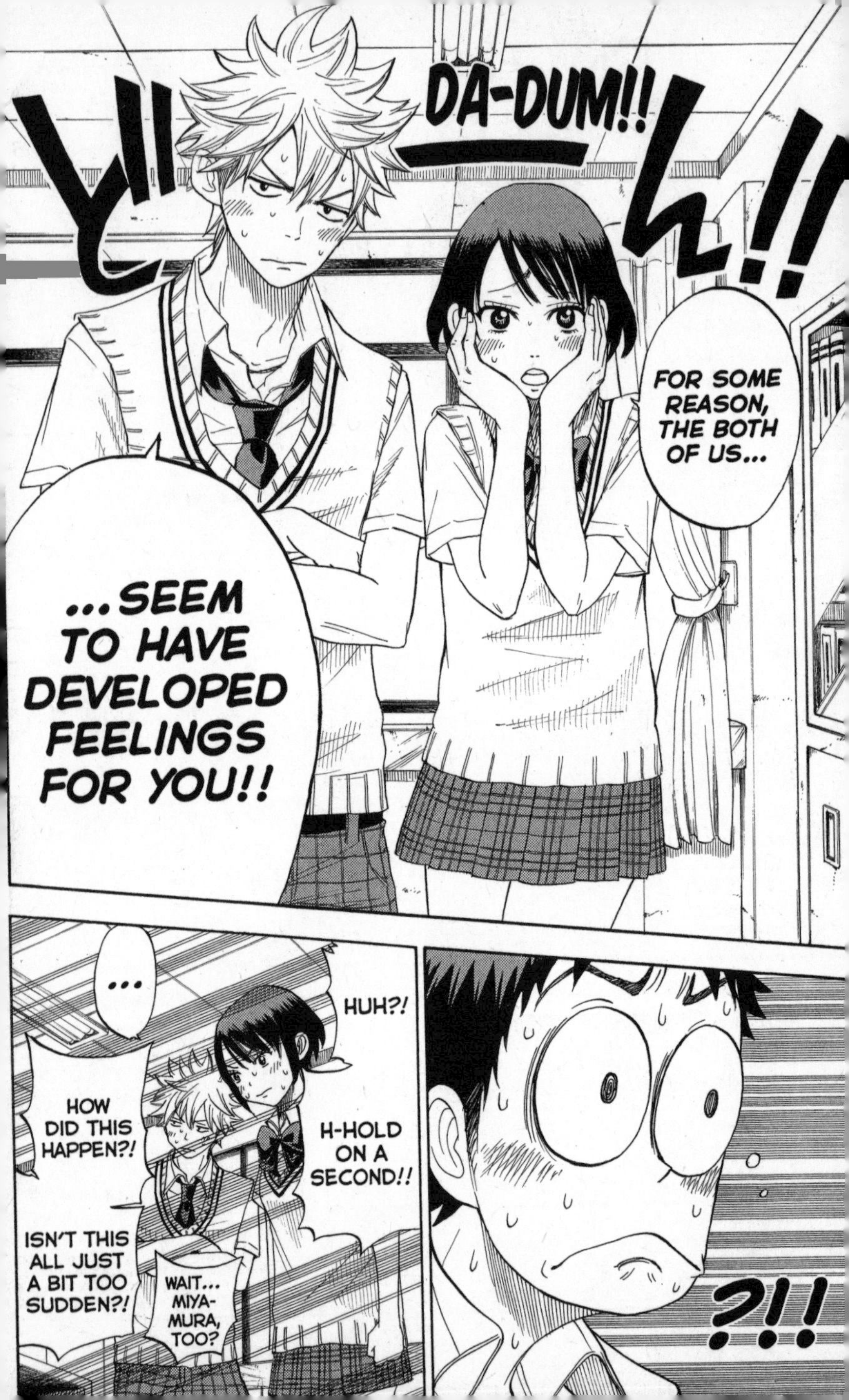
どーん!!
DA-DUM!!
FOR SOME REASON, THE BOTH OF US...
...SEEM TO HAVE DEVELOPED FEELINGS FOR YOU!!
?!!
HUH?!
H-HOLD ON A SECOND!!
...
HOW DID THIS HAPPEN?!
WAIT... MIYAMURA, TOO?
ISN'T THIS ALL JUST A BIT TOO SUDDEN?!

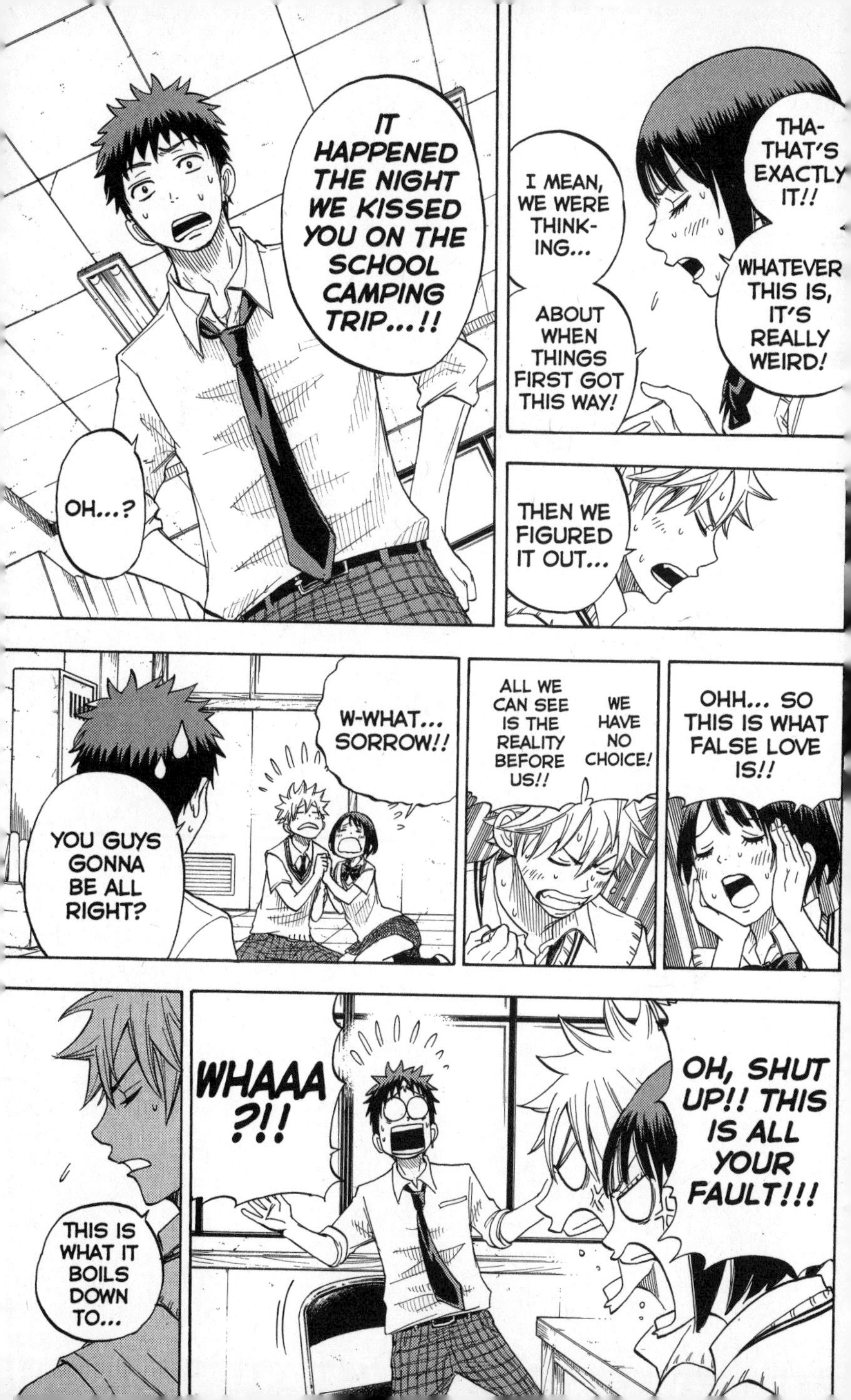
THA-THAT'S EXACTLY IT!!
WHATEVER THIS IS, IT'S REALLY WEIRD!
I MEAN, WE WERE THINK-ING...
ABOUT WHEN THINGS FIRST GOT THIS WAY!
THEN WE FIGURED IT OUT...
IT HAPPENED THE NIGHT WE KISSED YOU ON THE SCHOOL CAMPING TRIP...!!
OH...?
OHH... SO THIS IS WHAT FALSE LOVE IS!!
WE HAVE NO CHOICE!
ALL WE CAN SEE IS THE REALITY BEFORE US!!
W-WHAT... SORROW!!
YOU GUYS GONNA BE ALL RIGHT?
OH, SHUT UP!! THIS IS ALL YOUR FAULT!!!
WHAAA ?!!
THIS IS WHAT IT BOILS DOWN TO...

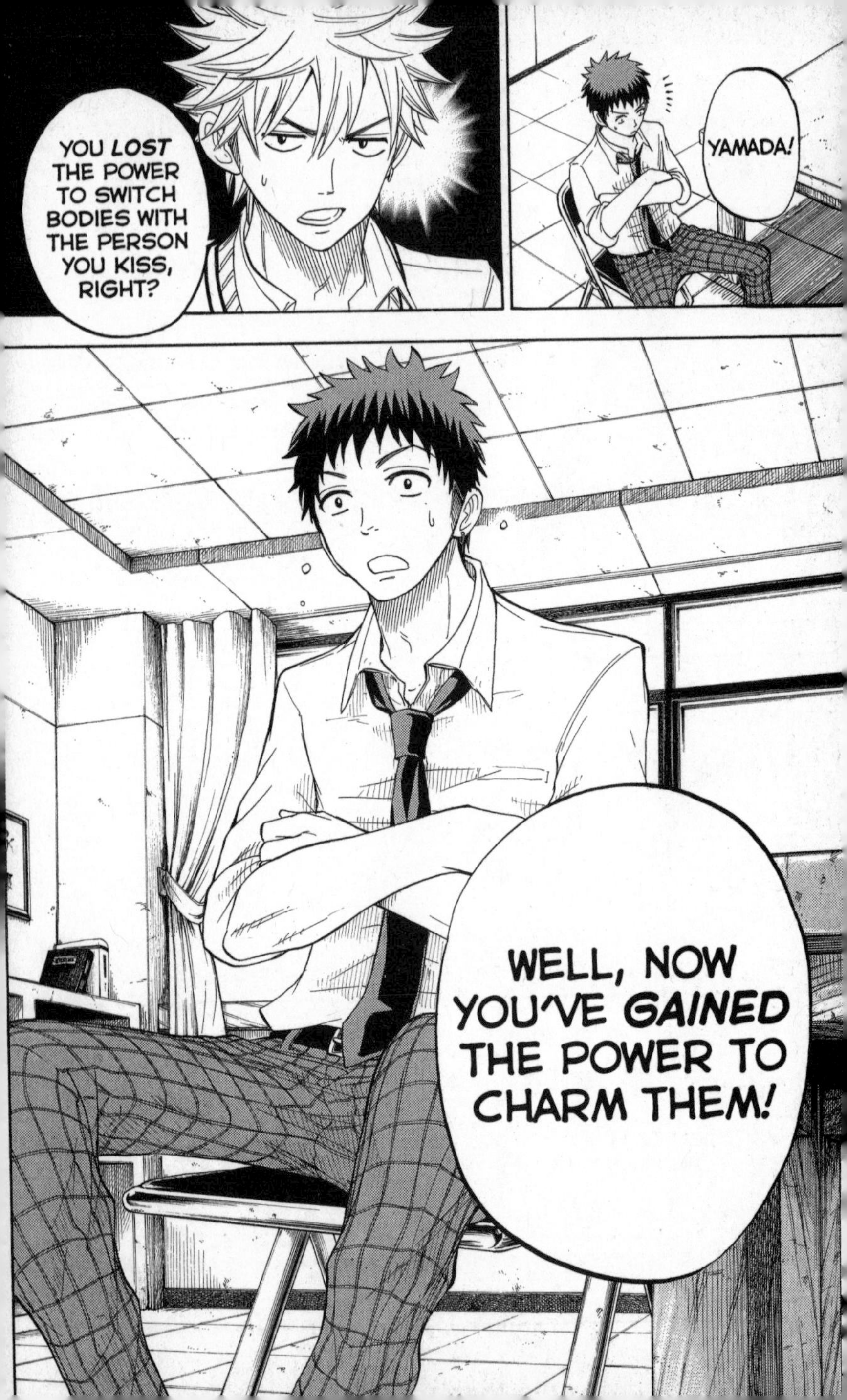
YAMADA!
YOU *LOST* THE POWER TO SWITCH BODIES WITH THE PERSON YOU KISS, RIGHT?
WELL, NOW YOU'VE *GAINED* THE POWER TO CHARM THEM!

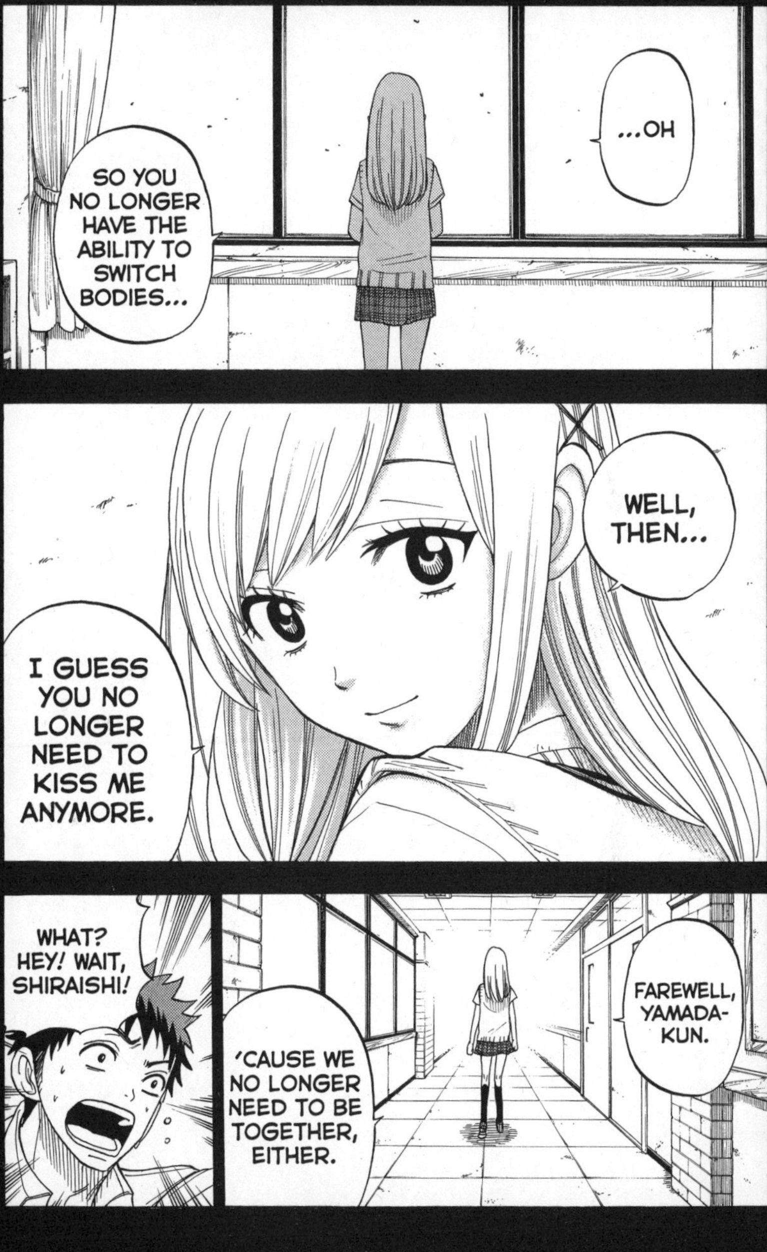
...OH
SO YOU NO LONGER HAVE THE ABILITY TO SWITCH BODIES...
WELL, THEN...
I GUESS YOU NO LONGER NEED TO KISS ME ANYMORE.
FAREWELL, YAMADA-KUN.
'CAUSE WE NO LONGER NEED TO BE TOGETHER, EITHER.
WHAT? HEY! WAIT, SHIRAISHI!

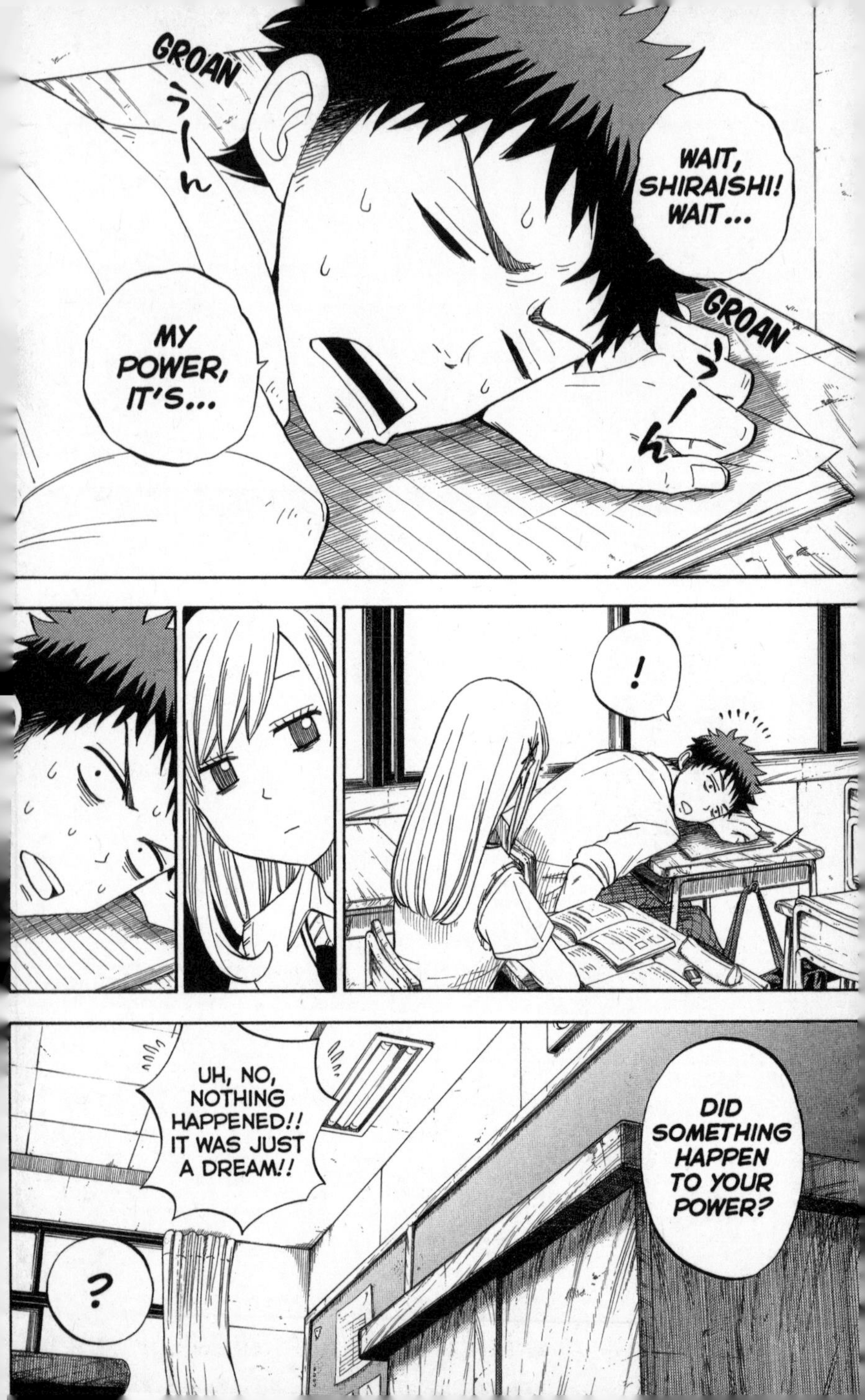
WAIT, SHIRAISHI! WAIT...
GROAN
うーん
GROAN
うーん
MY POWER, IT'S...
!
DID SOMETHING HAPPEN TO YOUR POWER?
UH, NO, NOTHING HAPPENED!! IT WAS JUST A DREAM!!
?

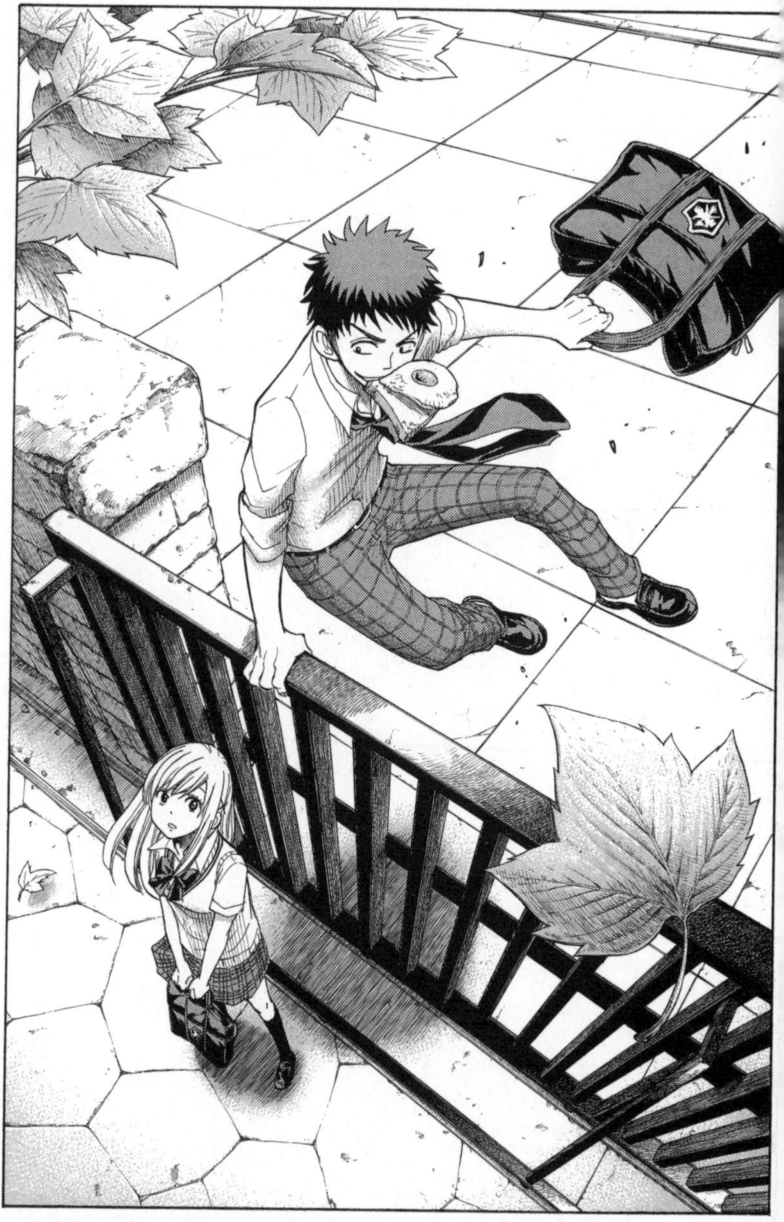

CHAPTER 19: Do whatever you want to me...

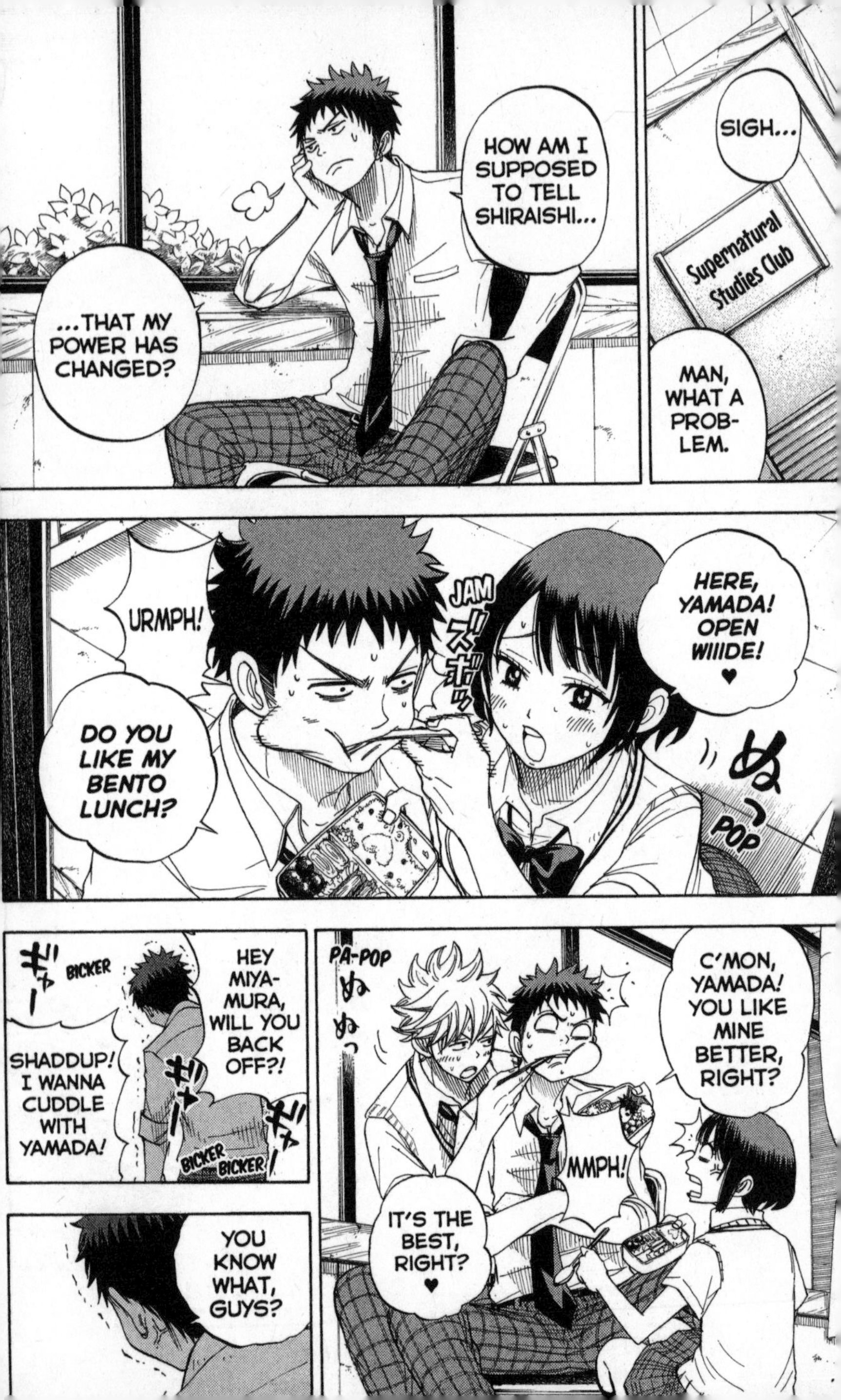
SIGH...
Supernatural Studies Club
MAN, WHAT A PROB-LEM.
HOW AM I SUPPOSED TO TELL SHIRAISHI...
...THAT MY POWER HAS CHANGED?
HERE, YAMADA! OPEN WIIIDE! ♥
POP
JAM
URMPH!
DO YOU LIKE MY BENTO LUNCH?
C'MON, YAMADA! YOU LIKE MINE BETTER, RIGHT?
PA-POP
MMPH!
IT'S THE BEST, RIGHT? ♥
HEY MIYA-MURA, WILL YOU BACK OFF?!
BICKER
SHADDUP! I WANNA CUDDLE WITH YAMADA!
BICKER BICKER
YOU KNOW WHAT, GUYS?

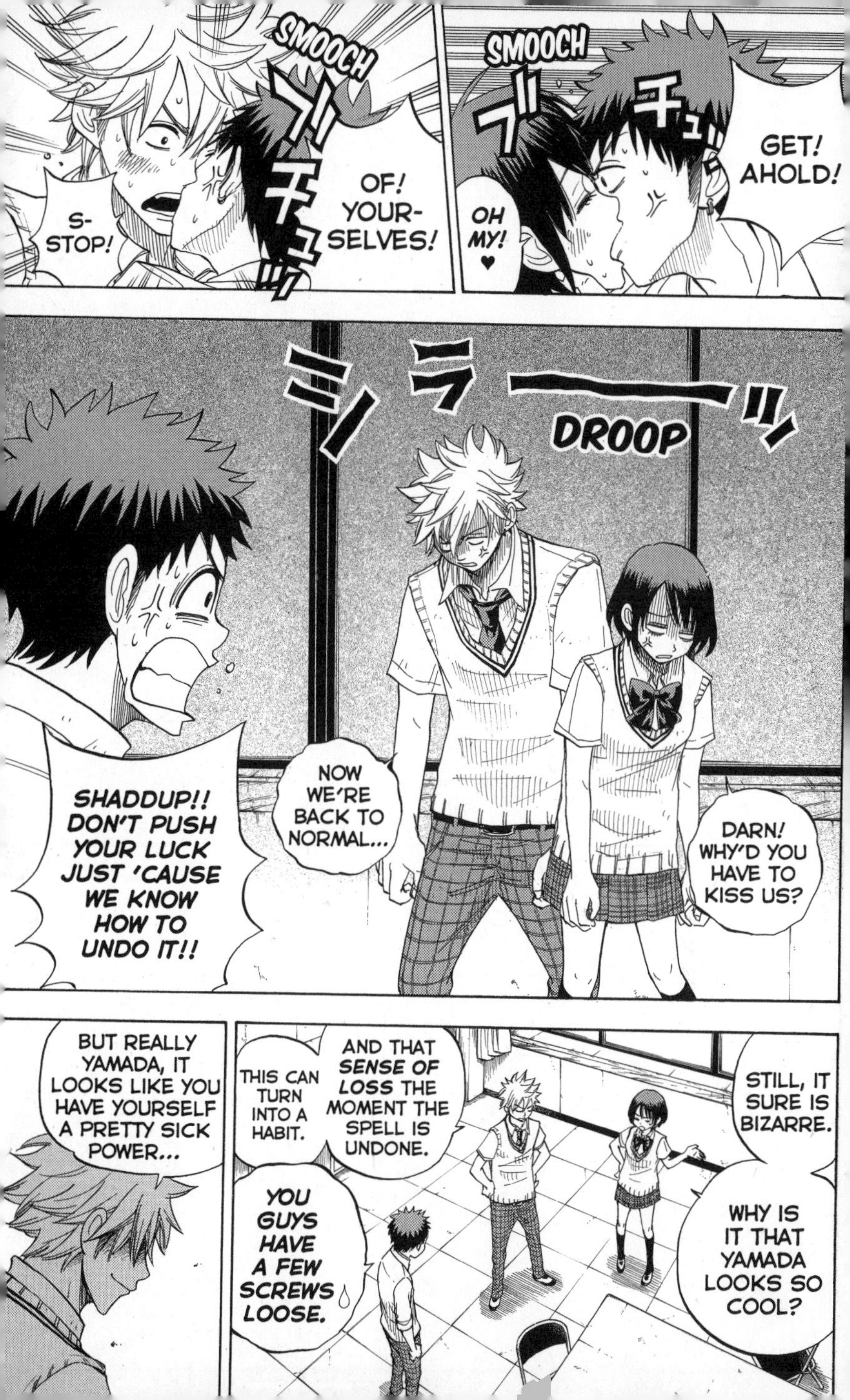
SMOOCH
GET! AHOLD!
OH MY! ♥
SMOOCH
OF! YOUR-SELVES!
S-STOP!
DROOP
DARN! WHY'D YOU HAVE TO KISS US?
NOW WE'RE BACK TO NORMAL...
SHADDUP!! DON'T PUSH YOUR LUCK JUST 'CAUSE WE KNOW HOW TO UNDO IT!!
STILL, IT SURE IS BIZARRE.
AND THAT SENSE OF LOSS THE MOMENT THE SPELL IS UNDONE.
THIS CAN TURN INTO A HABIT.
WHY IS IT THAT YAMADA LOOKS SO COOL?
YOU GUYS HAVE A FEW SCREWS LOOSE.
BUT REALLY YAMADA, IT LOOKS LIKE YOU HAVE YOURSELF A PRETTY SICK POWER...

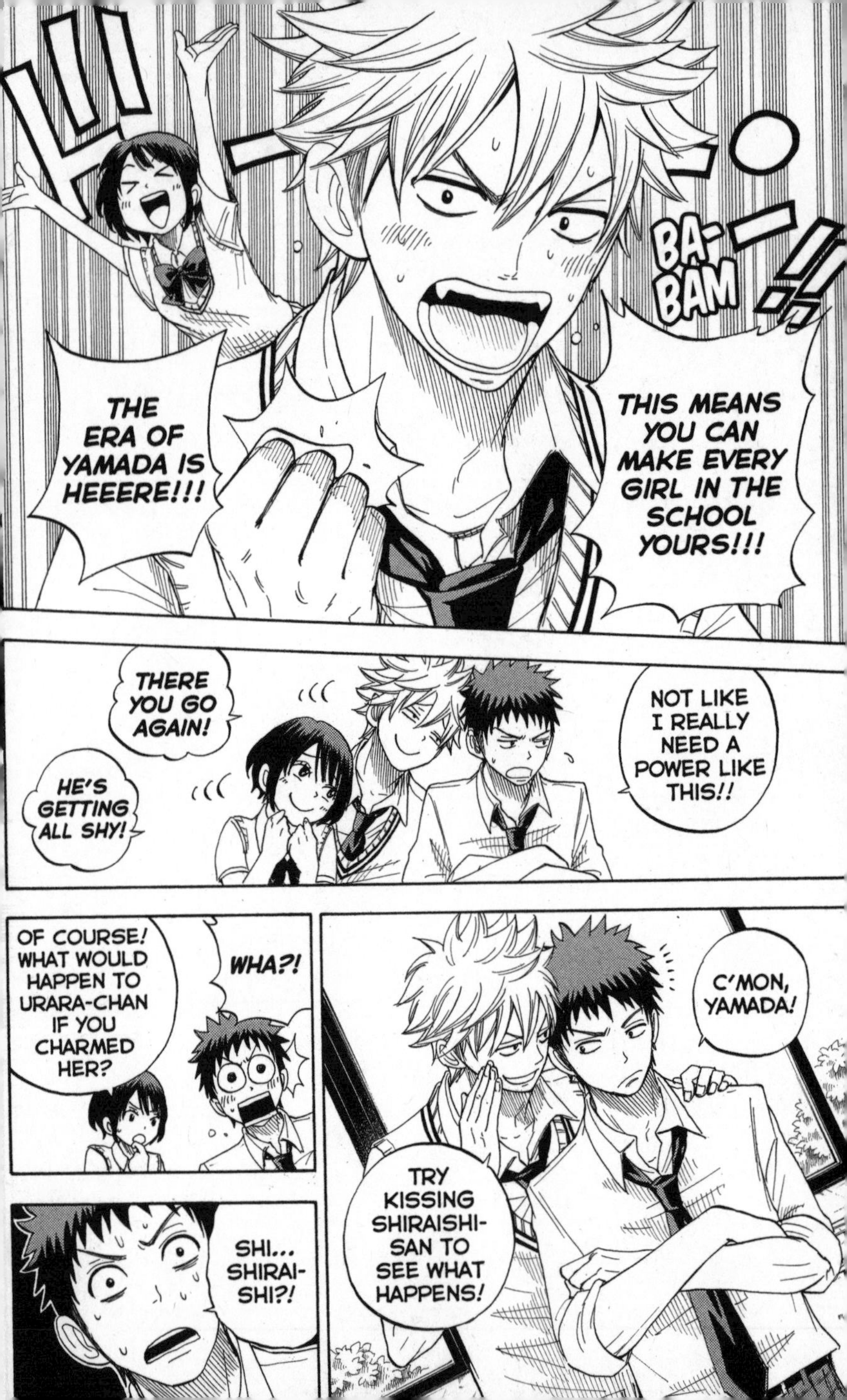
BA-BAM
THIS MEANS YOU CAN MAKE EVERY GIRL IN THE SCHOOL YOURS!!!
THE ERA OF YAMADA IS HEEERE!!!
NOT LIKE I REALLY NEED A POWER LIKE THIS!!
THERE YOU GO AGAIN!
HE'S GETTING ALL SHY!
C'MON, YAMADA!
TRY KISSING SHIRAISHI-SAN TO SEE WHAT HAPPENS!
WHA?!
OF COURSE! WHAT WOULD HAPPEN TO URARA-CHAN IF YOU CHARMED HER?
SHI... SHIRAI-SHI?!

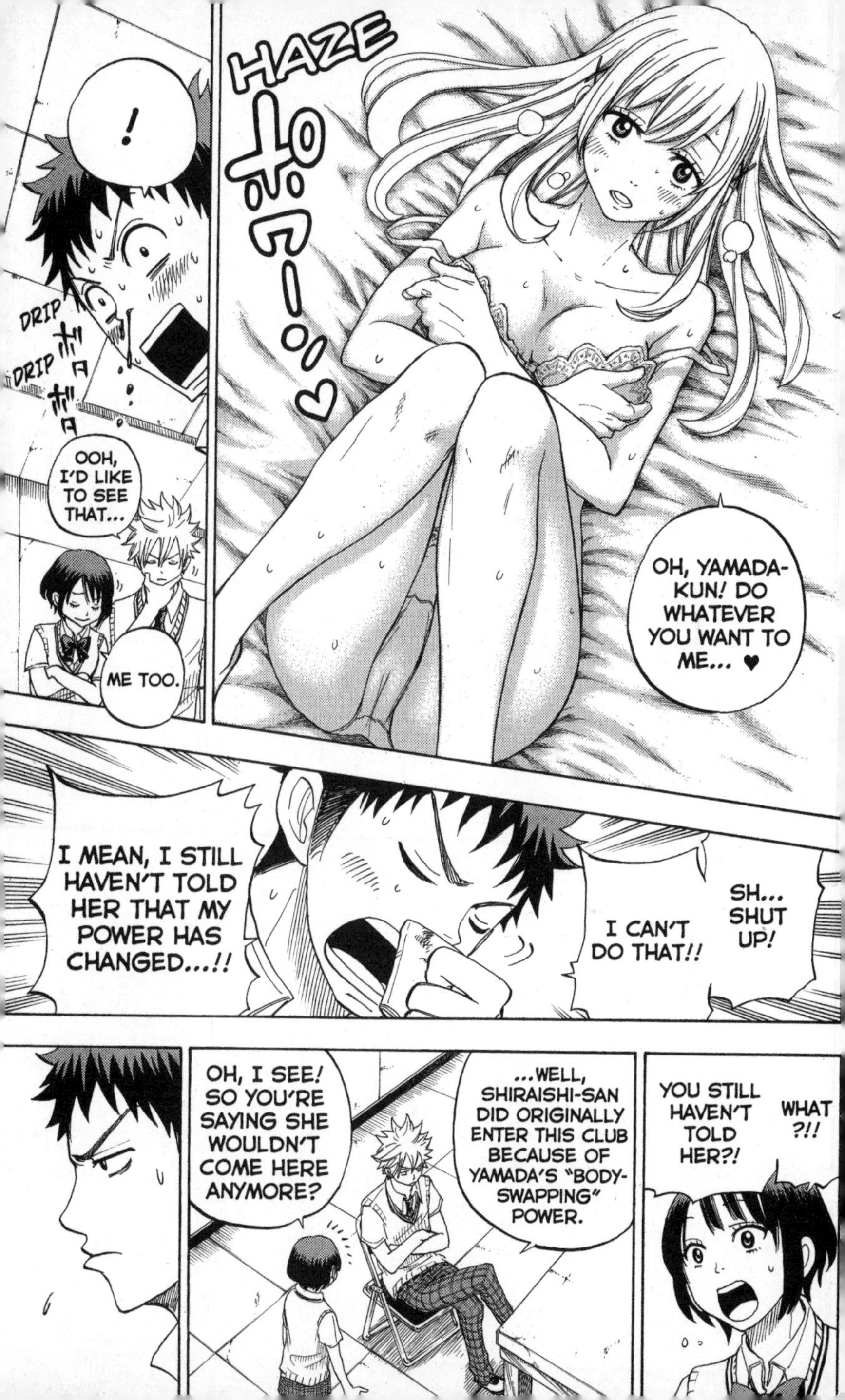
HAZE
OH, YAMADA-KUN! DO WHATEVER YOU WANT TO ME... ♥
!
DRIP
DRIP
OOH, I'D LIKE TO SEE THAT...
ME TOO.
SH... SHUT UP!
I CAN'T DO THAT!!
I MEAN, I STILL HAVEN'T TOLD HER THAT MY POWER HAS CHANGED...!!
WHAT ?!!
YOU STILL HAVEN'T TOLD HER?!
...WELL, SHIRAISHI-SAN DID ORIGINALLY ENTER THIS CLUB BECAUSE OF YAMADA'S "BODY-SWAPPING" POWER.
OH, I SEE! SO YOU'RE SAYING SHE WOULDN'T COME HERE ANYMORE?

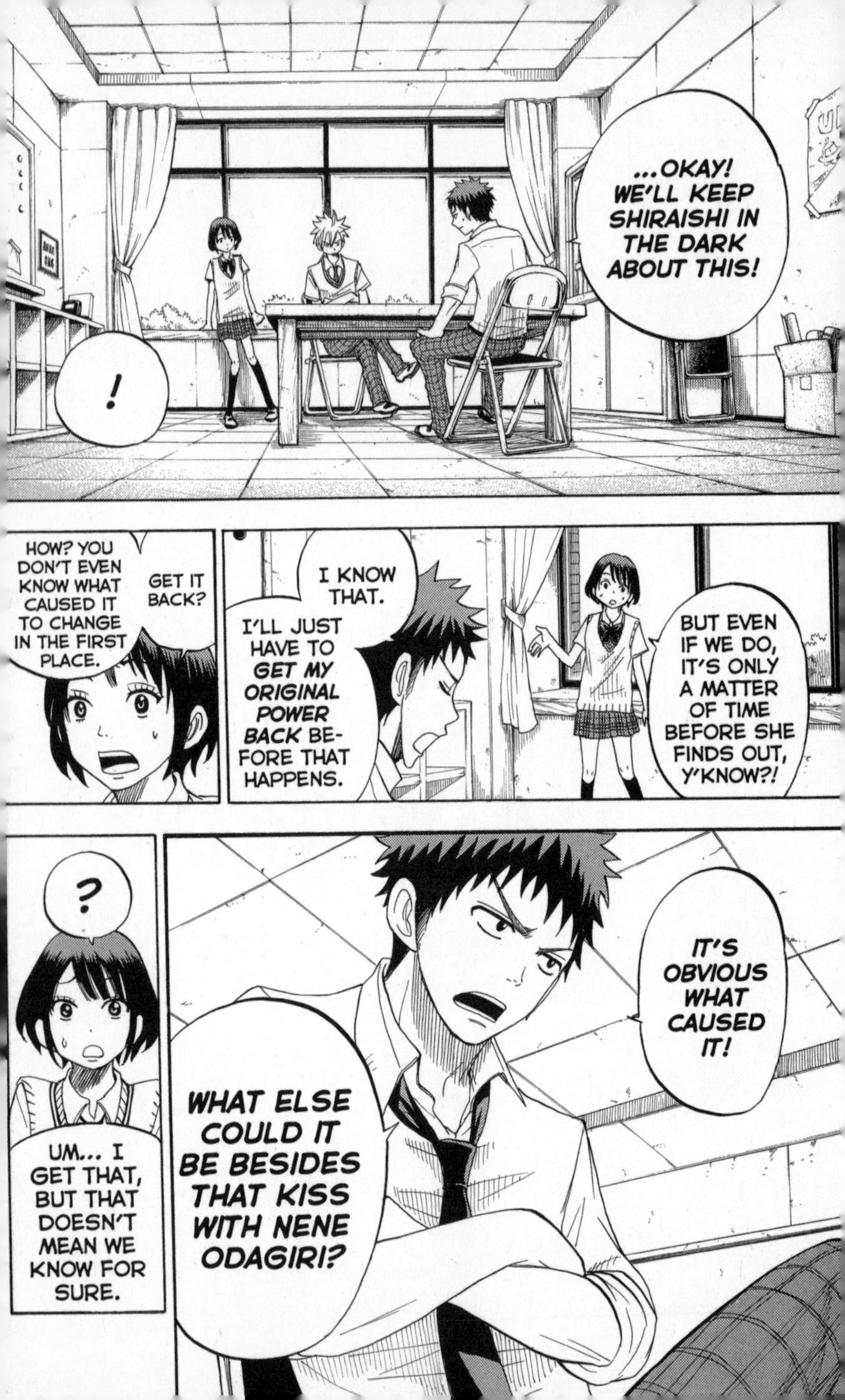
...OKAY! WE'LL KEEP SHIRAISHI IN THE DARK ABOUT THIS!
!
BUT EVEN IF WE DO, IT'S ONLY A MATTER OF TIME BEFORE SHE FINDS OUT, Y'KNOW?!
I KNOW THAT.
I'LL JUST HAVE TO GET MY ORIGINAL POWER BACK BEFORE THAT HAPPENS.
GET IT BACK?
HOW? YOU DON'T EVEN KNOW WHAT CAUSED IT TO CHANGE IN THE FIRST PLACE.
IT'S OBVIOUS WHAT CAUSED IT!
WHAT ELSE COULD IT BE BESIDES THAT KISS WITH NENE ODAGIRI?
?
UM... I GET THAT, BUT THAT DOESN'T MEAN WE KNOW FOR SURE.

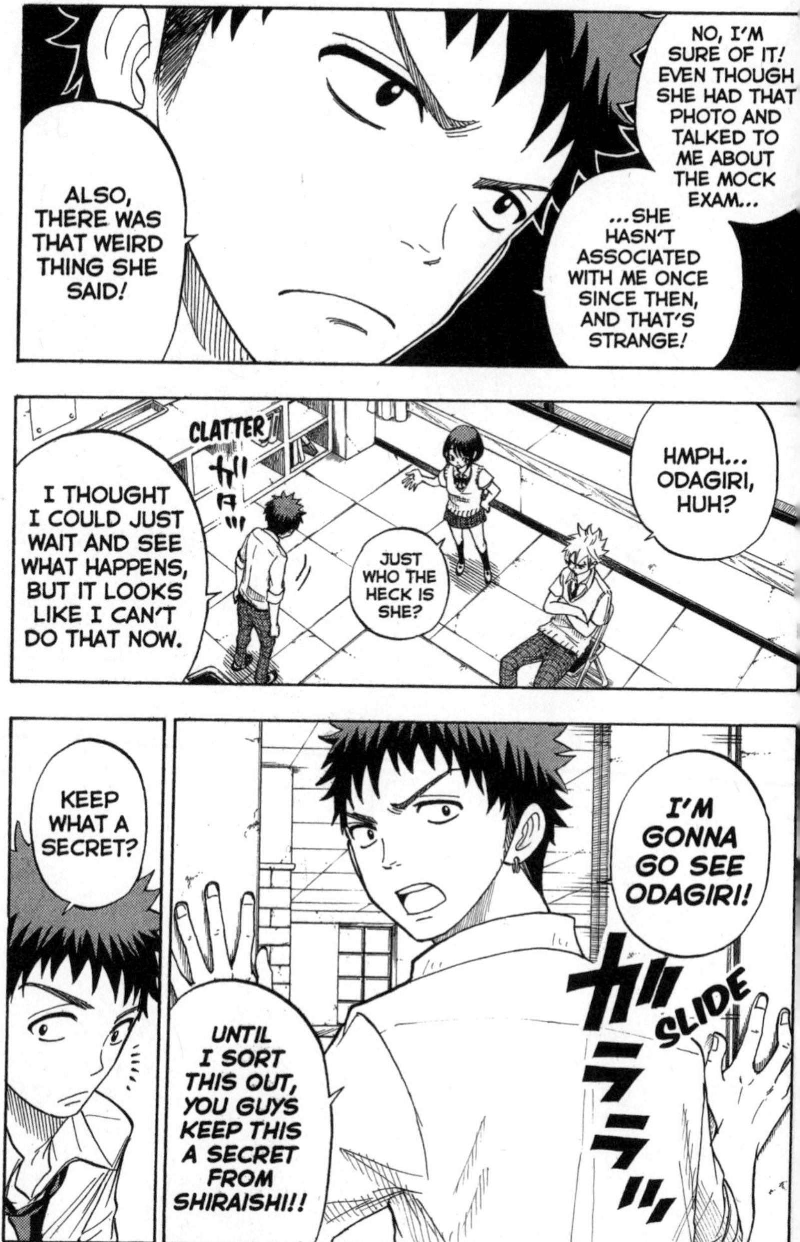
NO, I'M SURE OF IT! EVEN THOUGH SHE HAD THAT PHOTO AND TALKED TO ME ABOUT THE MOCK EXAM...
...SHE HASN'T ASSOCIATED WITH ME ONCE SINCE THEN, AND THAT'S STRANGE!
ALSO, THERE WAS THAT WEIRD THING SHE SAID!
HMPH... ODAGIRI, HUH?
JUST WHO THE HECK IS SHE?
CLATTER
I THOUGHT I COULD JUST WAIT AND SEE WHAT HAPPENS, BUT IT LOOKS LIKE I CAN'T DO THAT NOW.
I'M GONNA GO SEE ODAGIRI!
SLIDE
UNTIL I SORT THIS OUT, YOU GUYS KEEP THIS A SECRET FROM SHIRAISHI!!
KEEP WHAT A SECRET?

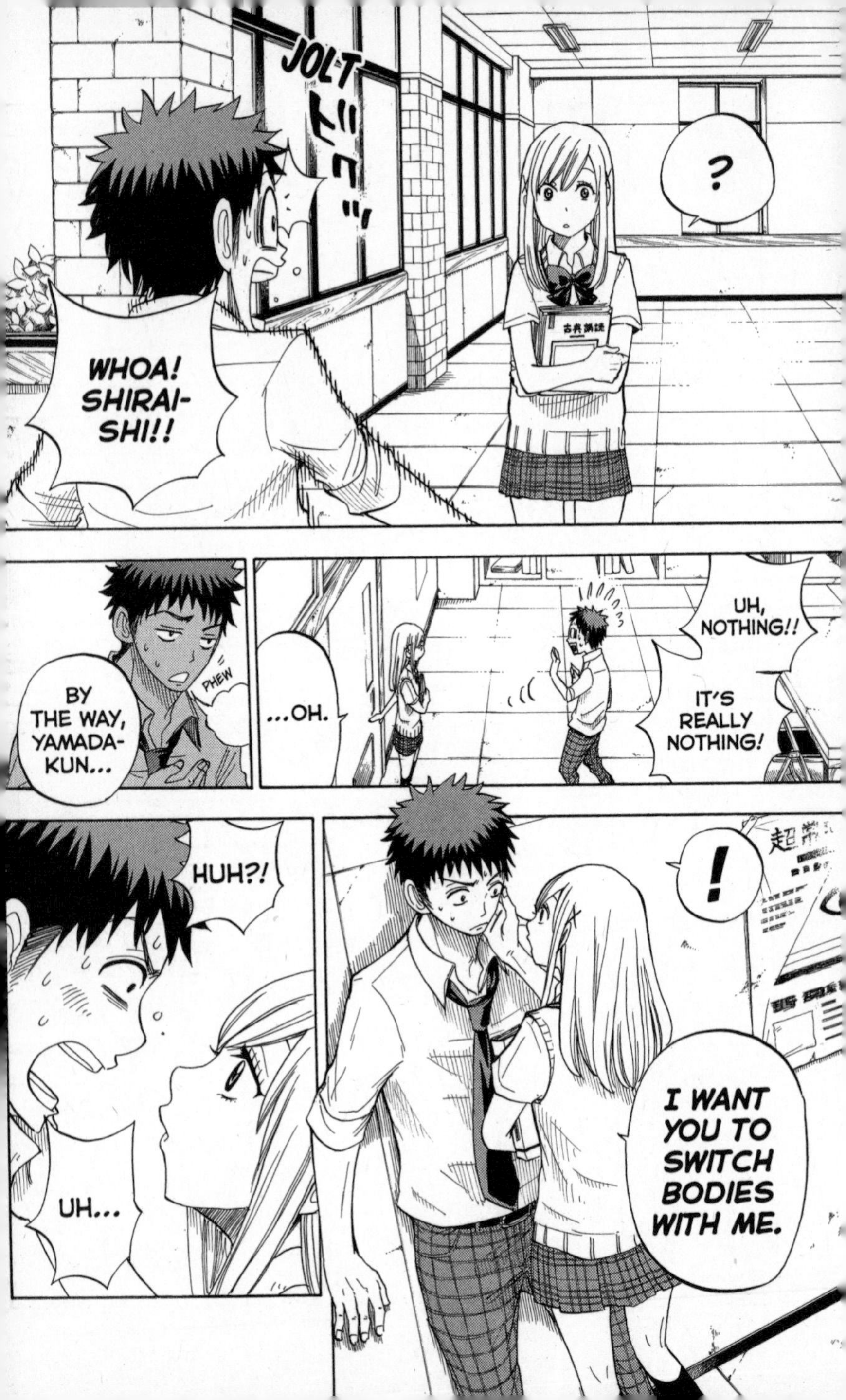
?
JOLT
ビクッ
WHOA! SHIRAI-SHI!!
UH, NOTHING!!
IT'S REALLY NOTHING!
...OH.
PHEW
BY THE WAY, YAMADA-KUN...
!
I WANT YOU TO SWITCH BODIES WITH ME.
HUH?!
UH...

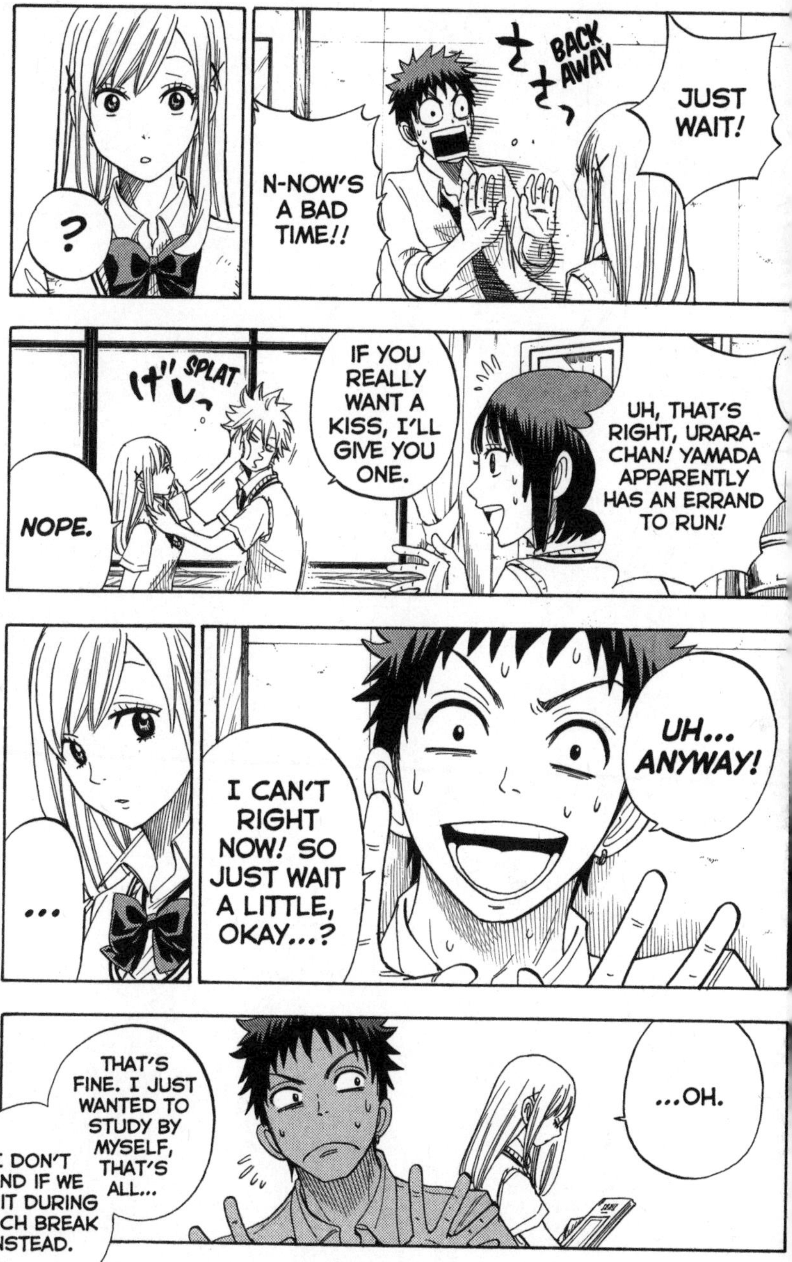
JUST WAIT!
BACK AWAY
N-NOW'S A BAD TIME!!
?
UH, THAT'S RIGHT, URARA-CHAN! YAMADA APPARENTLY HAS AN ERRAND TO RUN!
IF YOU REALLY WANT A KISS, I'LL GIVE YOU ONE.
SPLAT
NOPE.
UH... ANYWAY!
I CAN'T RIGHT NOW! SO JUST WAIT A LITTLE, OKAY...?
...
...OH.
THAT'S FINE. I JUST WANTED TO STUDY BY MYSELF, THAT'S ALL...
I DON'T MIND IF WE DO IT DURING LUNCH BREAK INSTEAD.

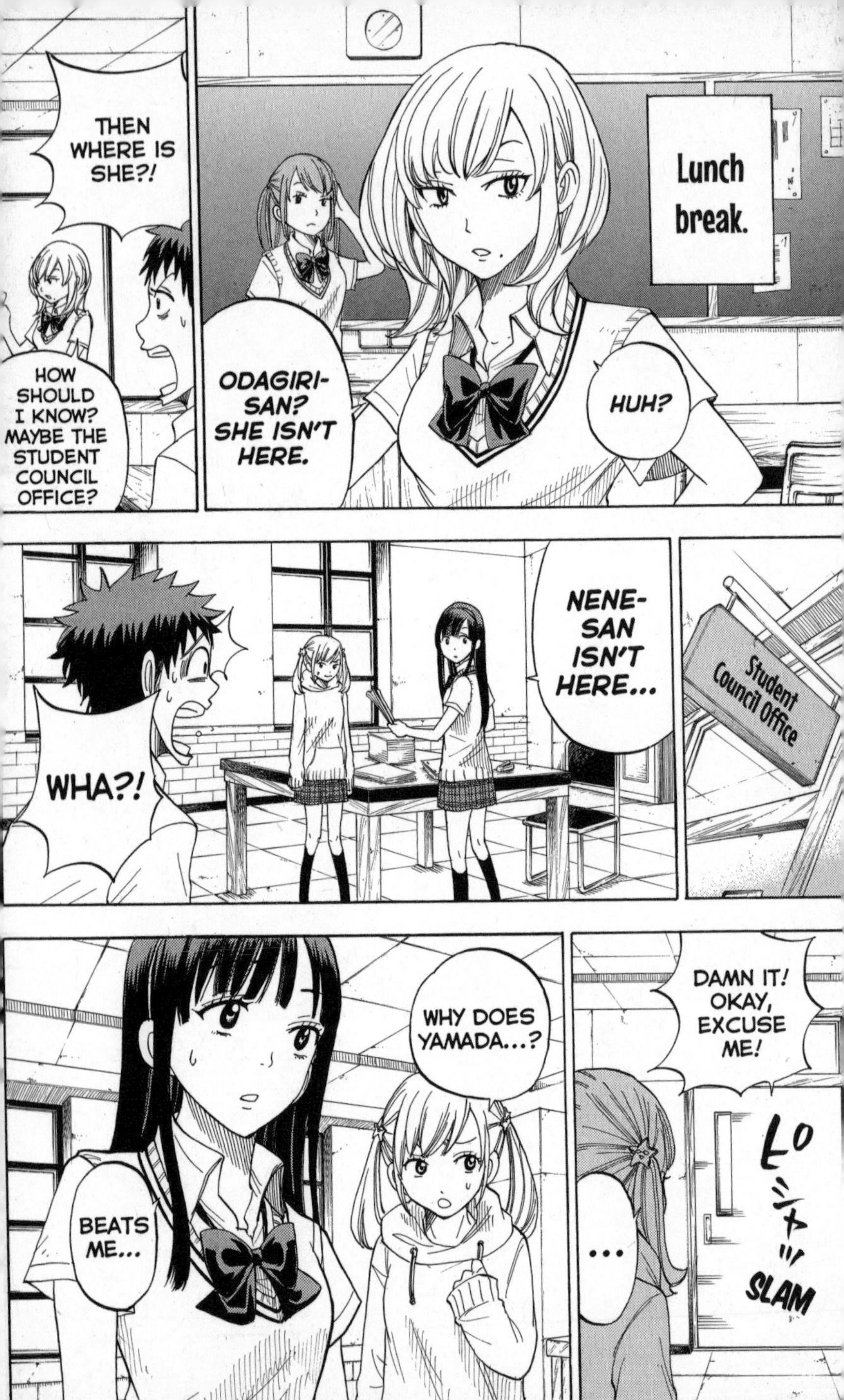
Lunch break.
HUH?
ODAGIRI-SAN? SHE ISN'T HERE.
THEN WHERE IS SHE?!
HOW SHOULD I KNOW? MAYBE THE STUDENT COUNCIL OFFICE?
Student Council Office
NENE-SAN ISN'T HERE...
WHA?!
DAMN IT! OKAY, EXCUSE ME!
ピシャッ
SLAM
...
WHY DOES YAMADA...?
BEATS ME...

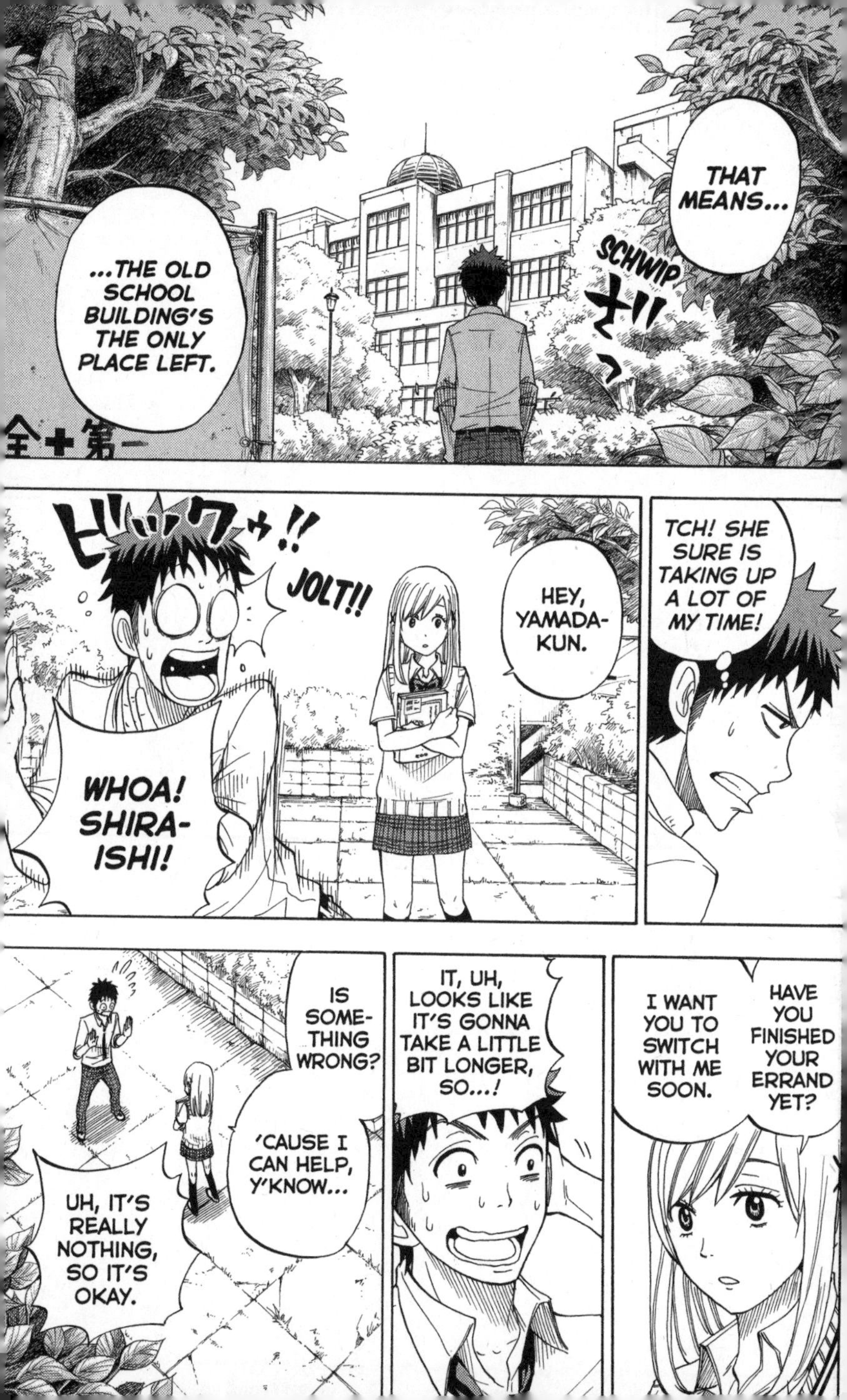
THAT MEANS...
SCHWIP
...THE OLD SCHOOL BUILDING'S THE ONLY PLACE LEFT.
TCH! SHE SURE IS TAKING UP A LOT OF MY TIME!
HEY, YAMADA-KUN.
JOLT!!
WHOA! SHIRA-ISHI!
HAVE YOU FINISHED YOUR ERRAND YET?
I WANT YOU TO SWITCH WITH ME SOON.
IT, UH, LOOKS LIKE IT'S GONNA TAKE A LITTLE BIT LONGER, SO...!
IS SOMETHING WRONG?
'CAUSE I CAN HELP, Y'KNOW...
UH, IT'S REALLY NOTHING, SO IT'S OKAY.

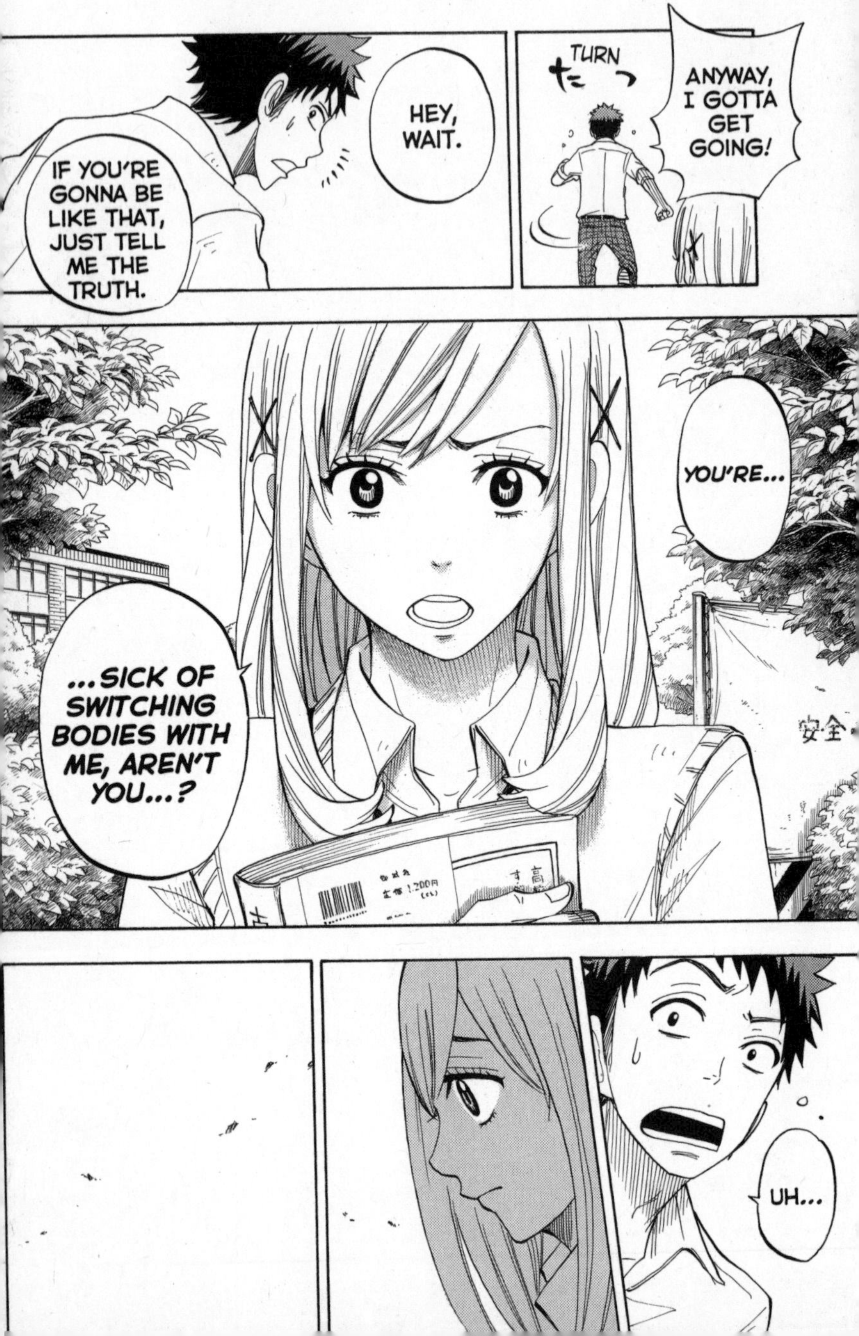
TURN
ANYWAY, I GOTTA GET GOING!
HEY, WAIT.
IF YOU'RE GONNA BE LIKE THAT, JUST TELL ME THE TRUTH.
YOU'RE...
...SICK OF SWITCHING BODIES WITH ME, AREN'T YOU...?
UH...

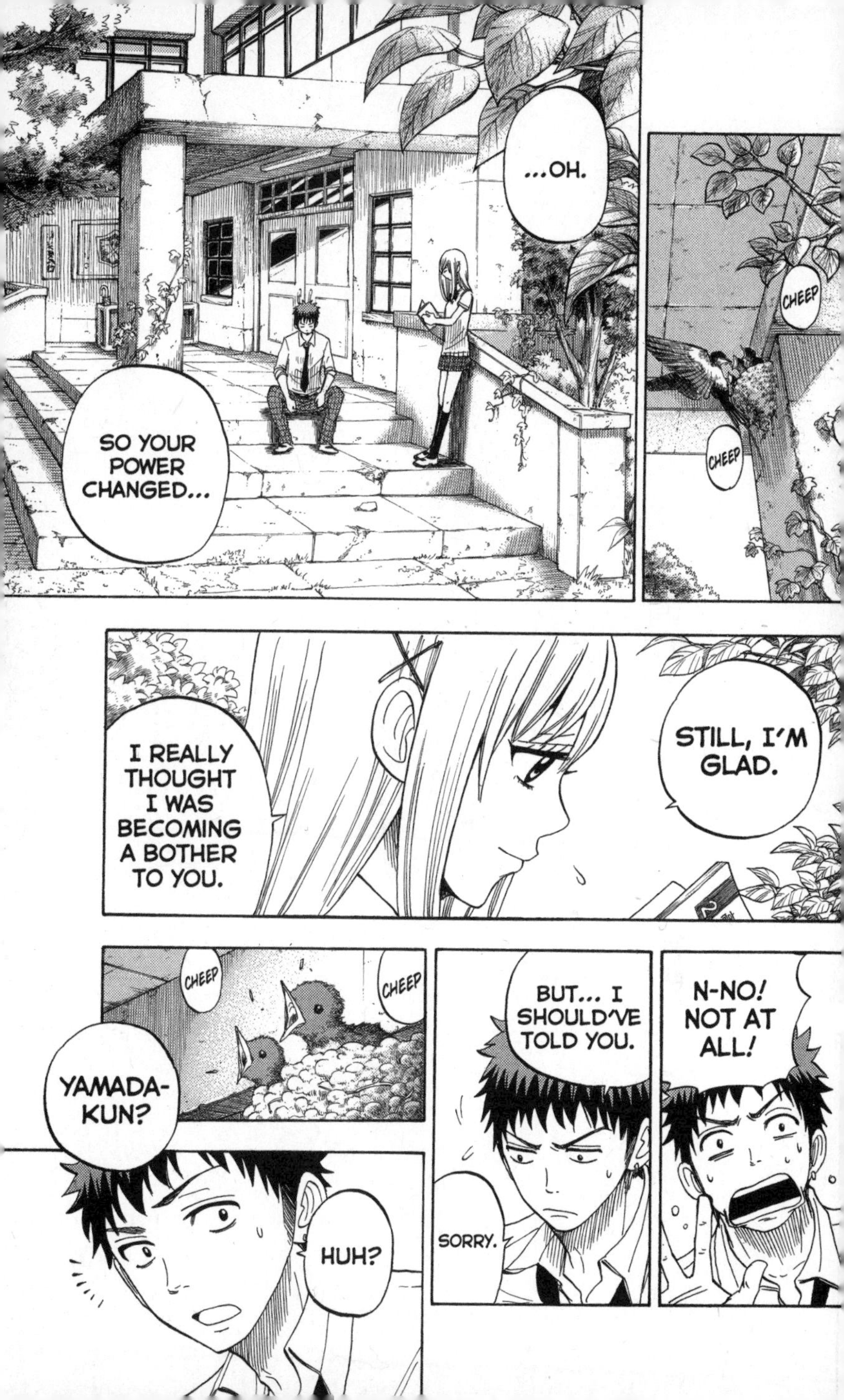
CHEEP
CHEEP
...OH.
SO YOUR POWER CHANGED...
STILL, I'M GLAD.
I REALLY THOUGHT I WAS BECOMING A BOTHER TO YOU.
N-NO! NOT AT ALL!
BUT... I SHOULD'VE TOLD YOU.
SORRY.
CHEEP
CHEEP
YAMADA-KUN?
HUH?

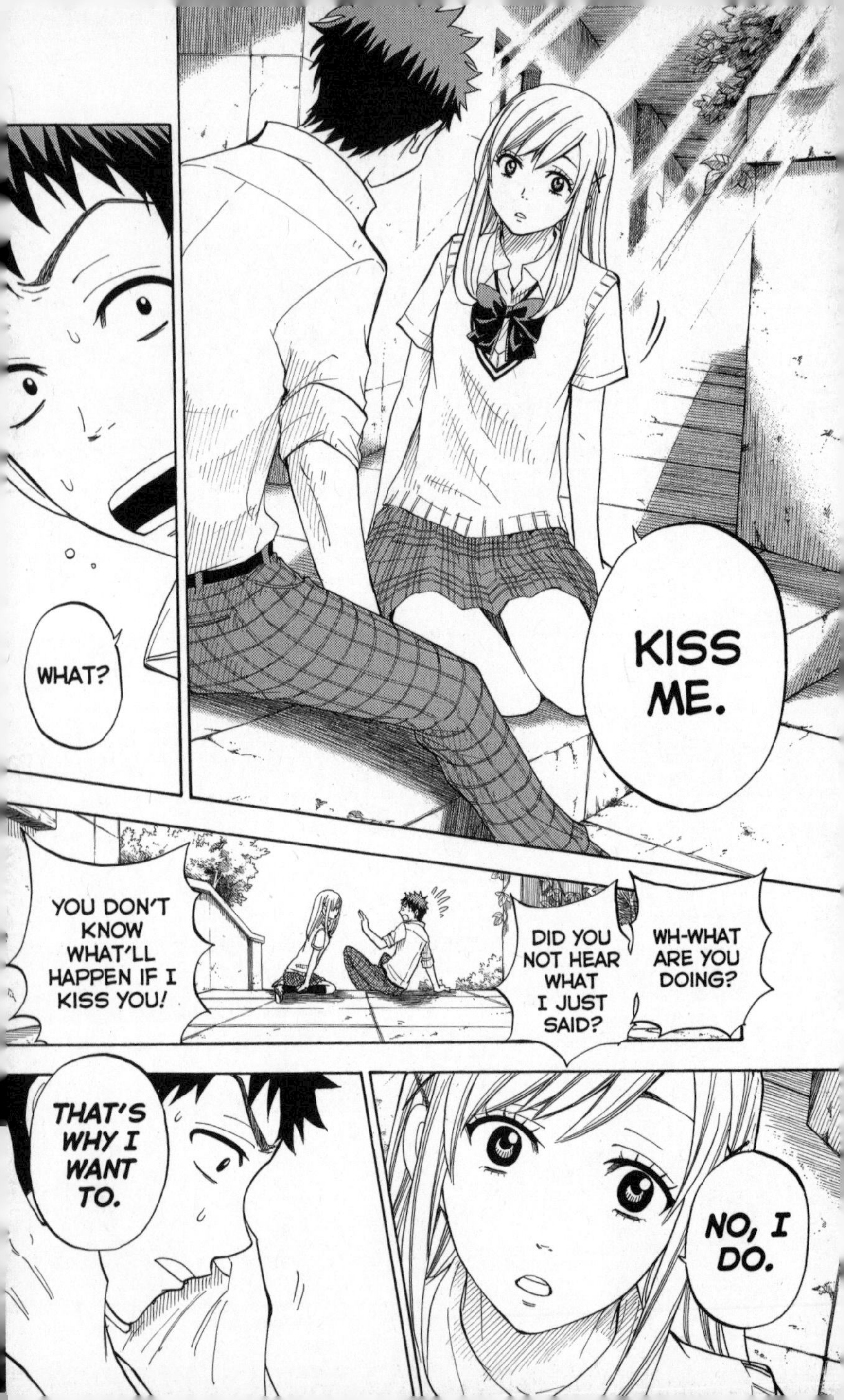
KISS ME.
WHAT?
WH-WHAT ARE YOU DOING?
DID YOU NOT HEAR WHAT I JUST SAID?
YOU DON'T KNOW WHAT'LL HAPPEN IF I KISS YOU!
NO, I DO.
THAT'S WHY I WANT TO.

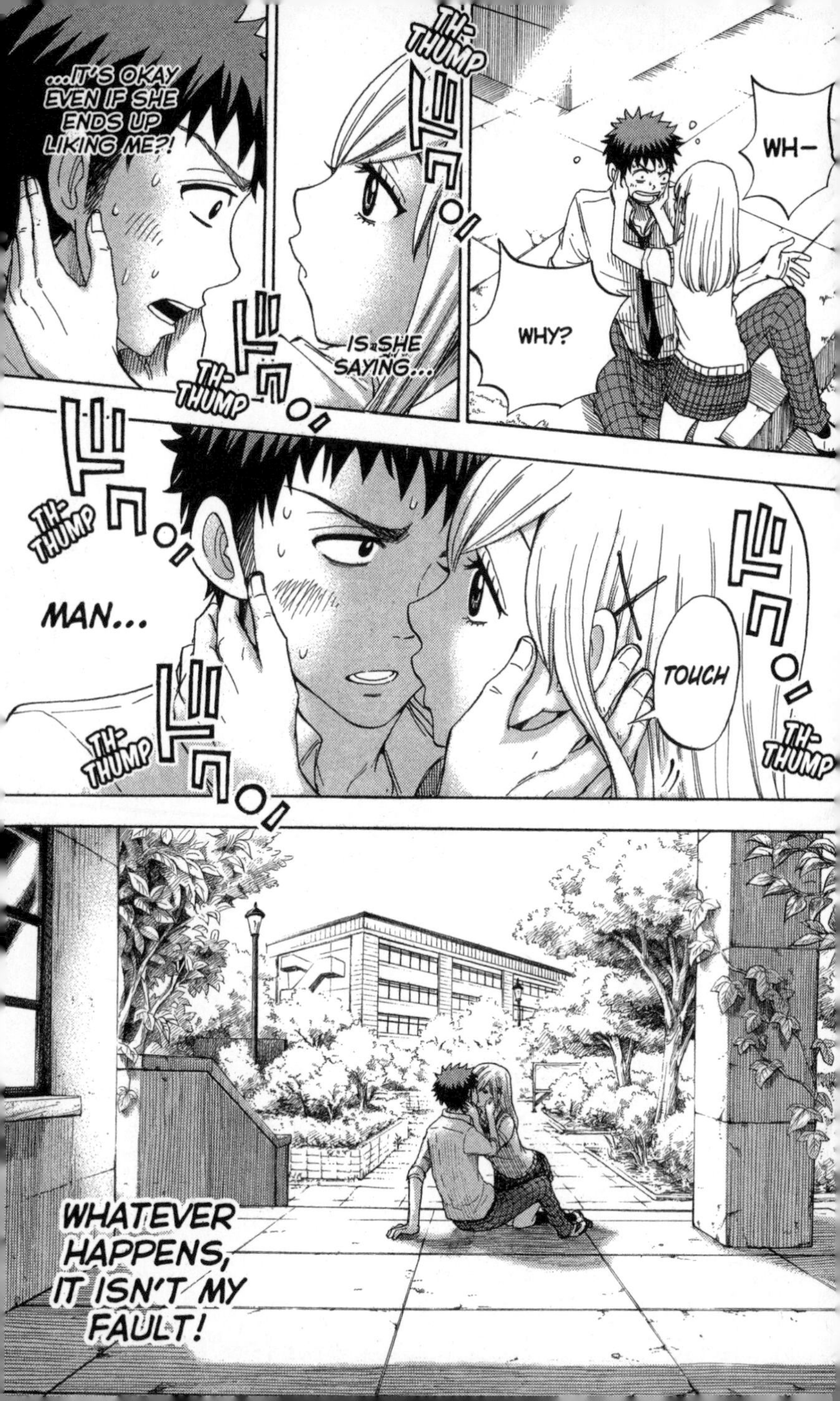
WH–
WHY?
TH-THUMP
IS SHE SAYING...
TH-THUMP
...IT'S OKAY EVEN IF SHE ENDS UP LIKING ME?!
TH-THUMP
TOUCH
TH-THUMP
MAN...
TH-THUMP
WHATEVER HAPPENS, IT ISN'T MY FAULT!

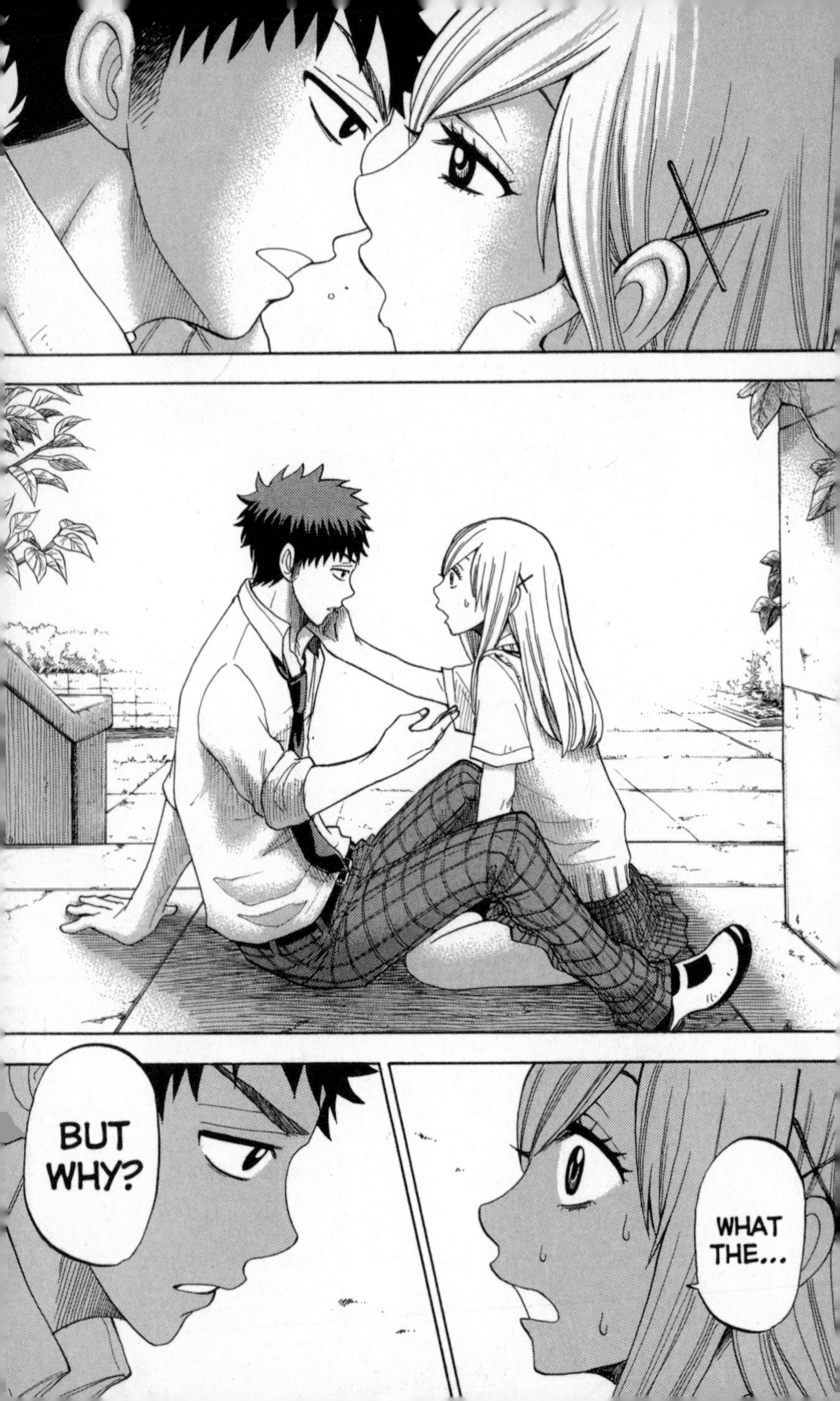
WHAT THE...
BUT WHY?

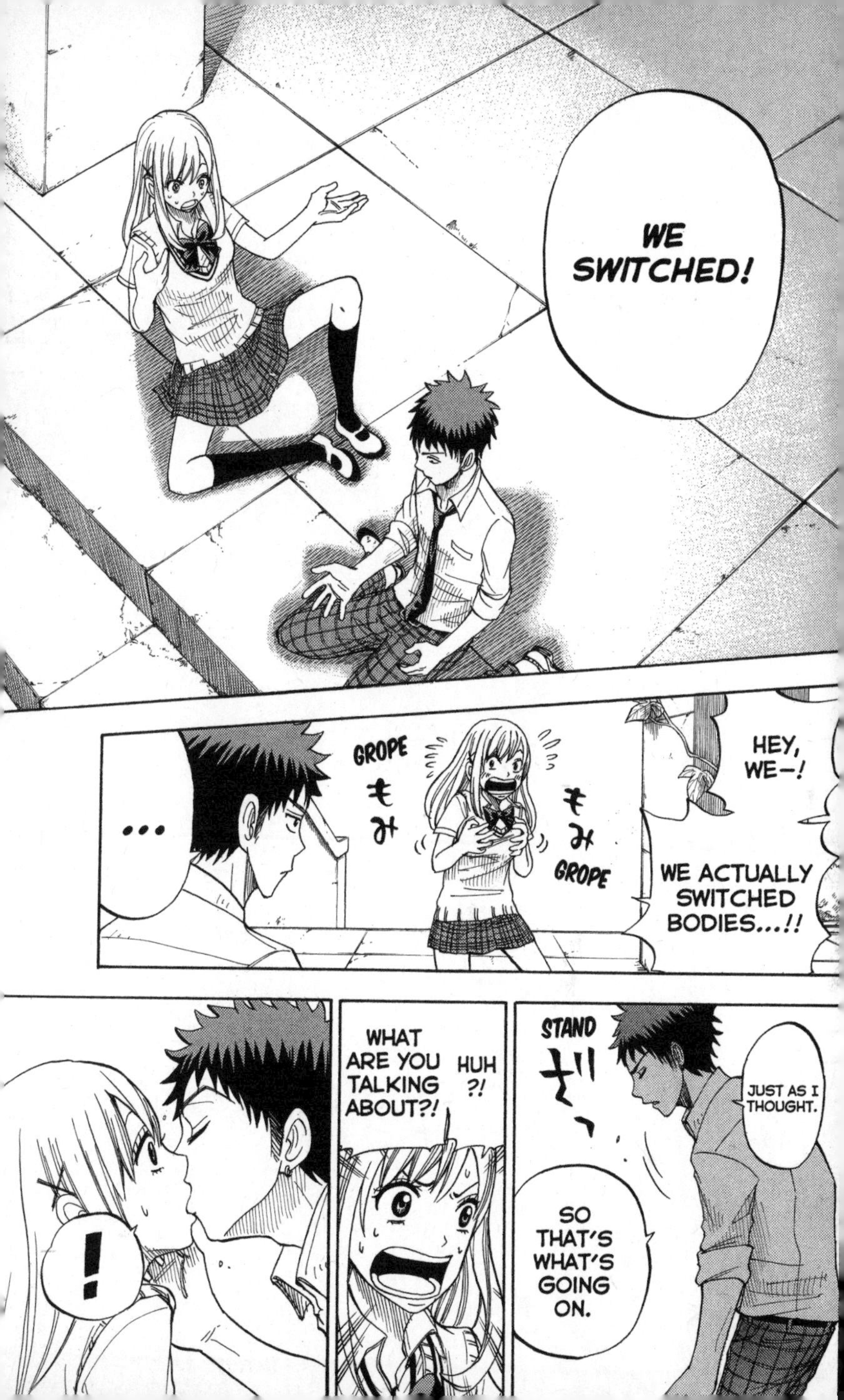
WE SWITCHED!
HEY, WE—!
WE ACTUALLY SWITCHED BODIES...!!
GROPE
もみ
GROPE
もみ
...
JUST AS I THOUGHT.
SO THAT'S WHAT'S GOING ON.
STAND
ざっ
HUH ?!
WHAT ARE YOU TALKING ABOUT?!
!

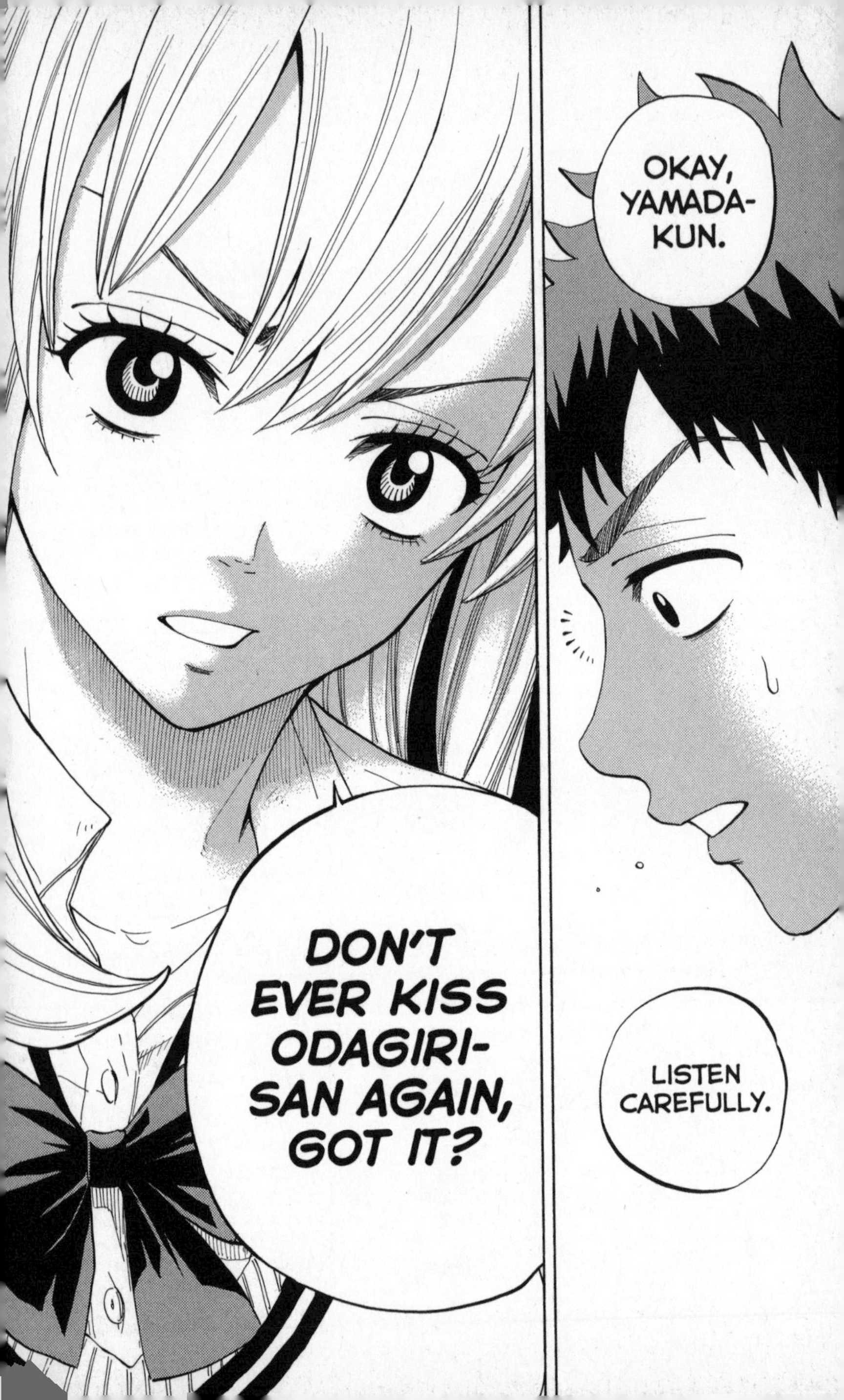
OKAY, YAMADA-KUN.
LISTEN CAREFULLY.
DON'T EVER KISS ODAGIRI-SAN AGAIN, GOT IT?

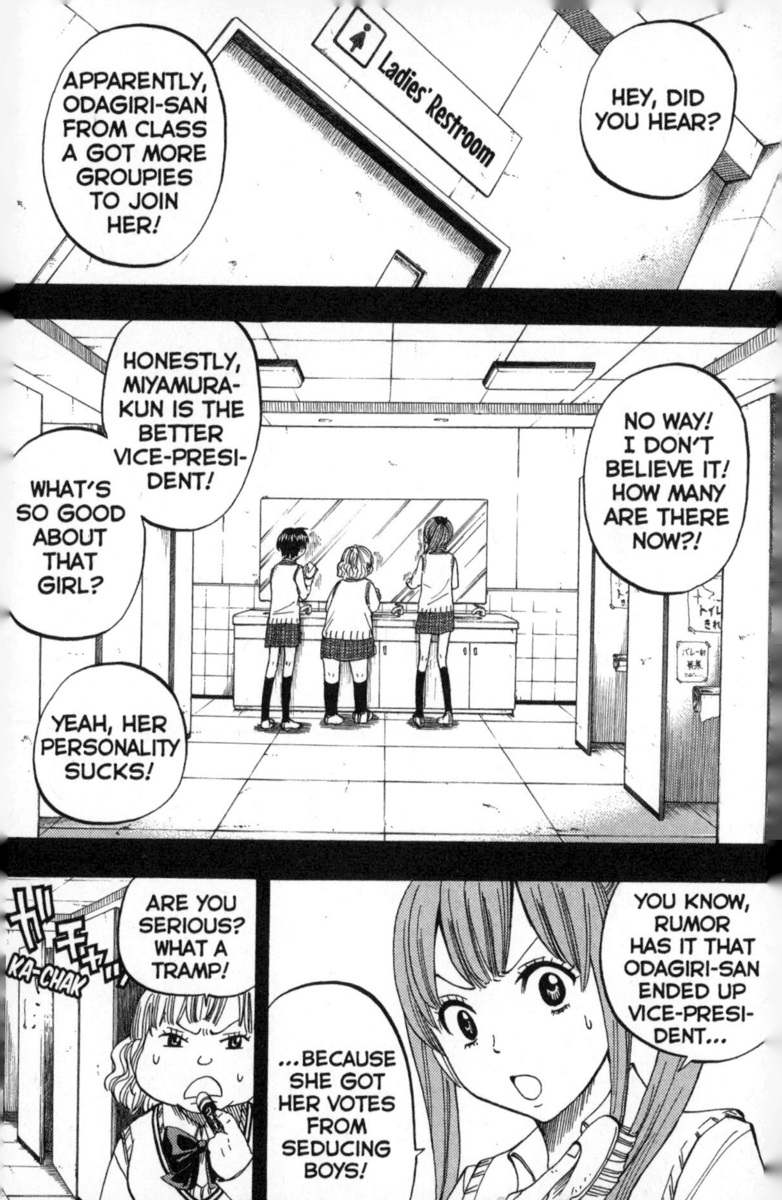
HEY, DID YOU HEAR?
Ladies' Restroom
APPARENTLY, ODAGIRI-SAN FROM CLASS A GOT MORE GROUPIES TO JOIN HER!
NO WAY! I DON'T BELIEVE IT! HOW MANY ARE THERE NOW?!
HONESTLY, MIYAMURA-KUN IS THE BETTER VICE-PRESIDENT!
WHAT'S SO GOOD ABOUT THAT GIRL?
YEAH, HER PERSONALITY SUCKS!
YOU KNOW, RUMOR HAS IT THAT ODAGIRI-SAN ENDED UP VICE-PRESIDENT...
...BECAUSE SHE GOT HER VOTES FROM SEDUCING BOYS!
ARE YOU SERIOUS? WHAT A TRAMP!
KA-CHAK

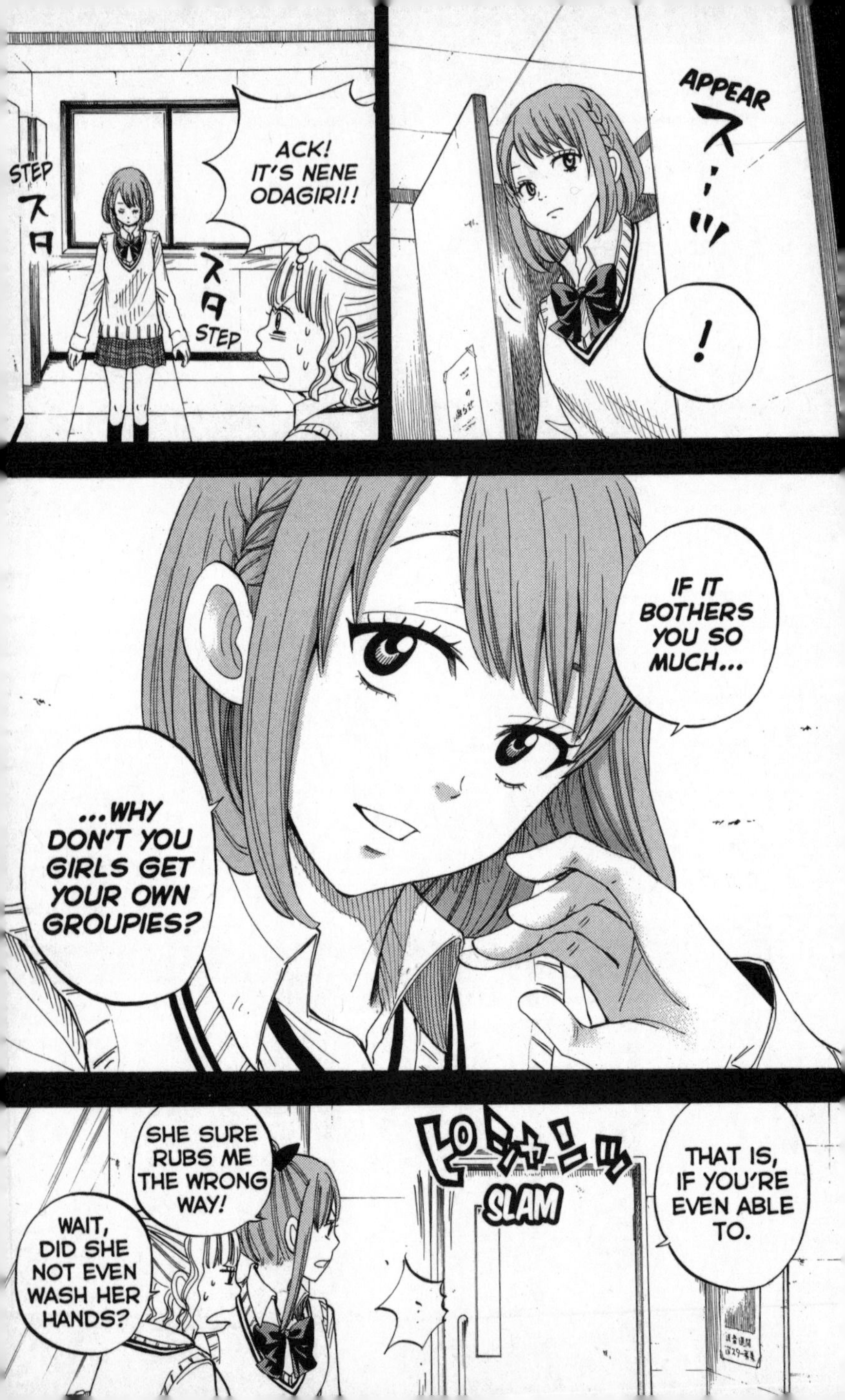
APPEAR
ス…ッ
!
ACK! IT'S NENE ODAGIRI!!
STEP
スタ
スタ
STEP
IF IT BOTHERS YOU SO MUCH...
...WHY DON'T YOU GIRLS GET YOUR OWN GROUPIES?
THAT IS, IF YOU'RE EVEN ABLE TO.
ピシャンッ
SLAM
SHE SURE RUBS ME THE WRONG WAY!
WAIT, DID SHE NOT EVEN WASH HER HANDS?

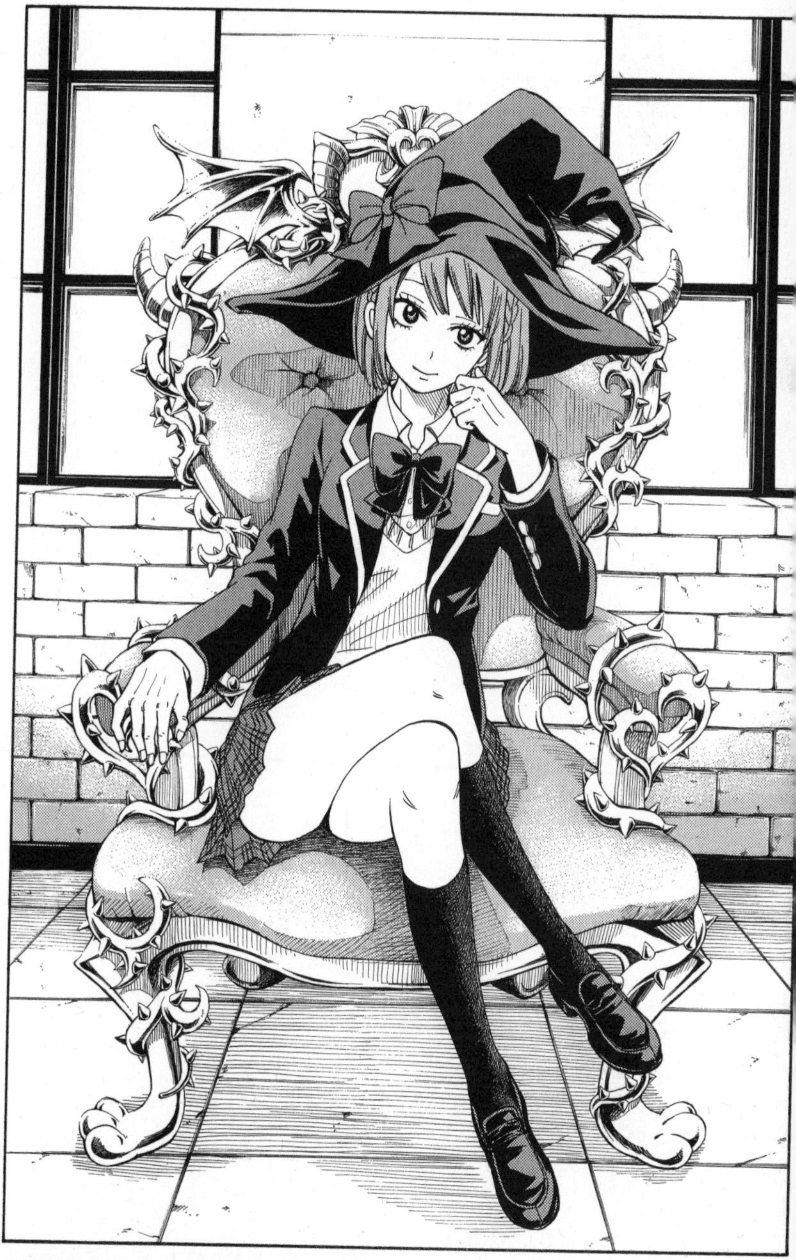

CHAPTER 20: Think about it.

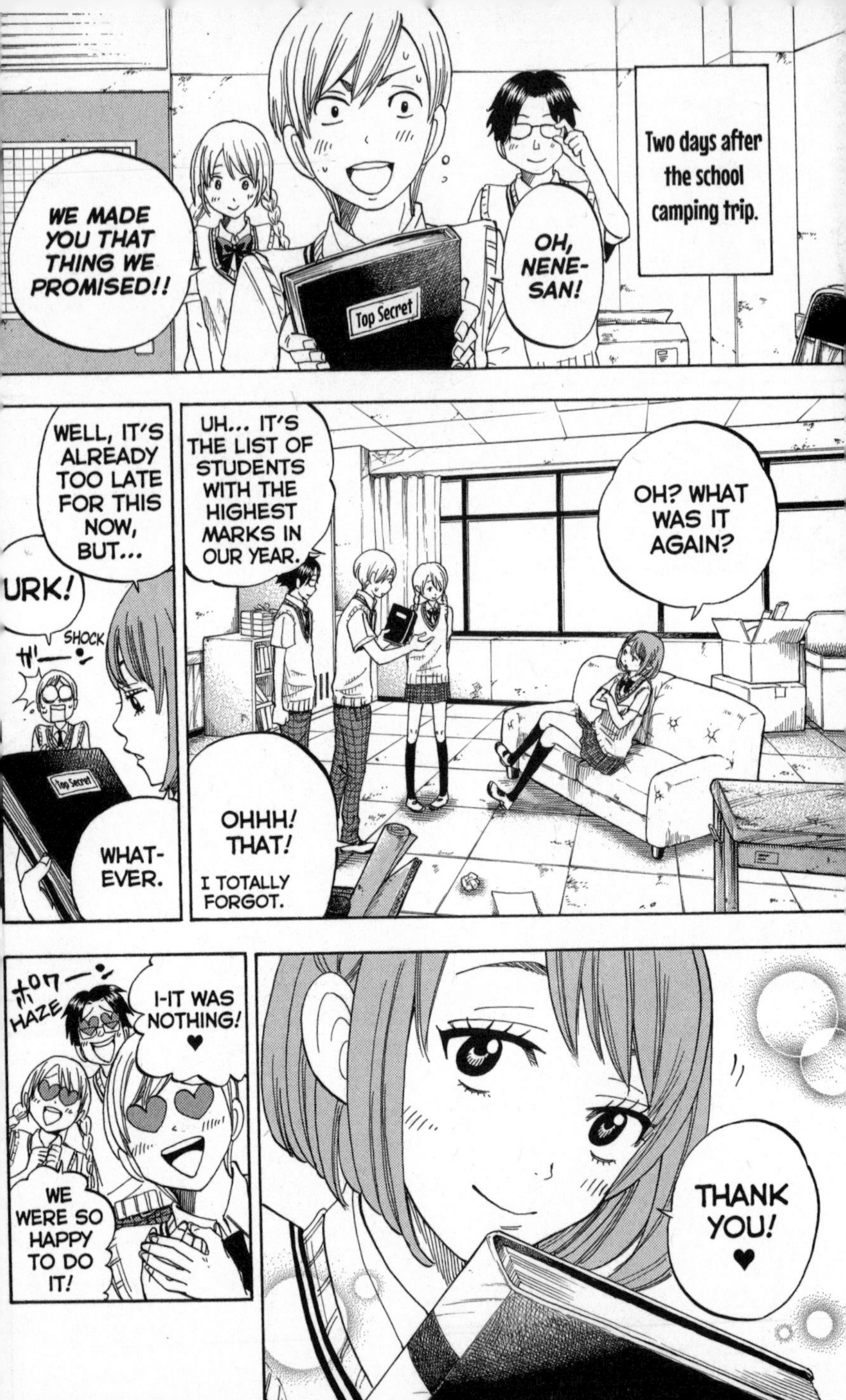
Two days after the school camping trip.
OH, NENE-SAN!
WE MADE YOU THAT THING WE PROMISED!!
OH? WHAT WAS IT AGAIN?
UH... IT'S THE LIST OF STUDENTS WITH THE HIGHEST MARKS IN OUR YEAR.
OHHH! THAT!
I TOTALLY FORGOT.
WELL, IT'S ALREADY TOO LATE FOR THIS NOW, BUT...
URK!
SHOCK
WHAT-EVER.
Top Secret
THANK YOU! ♥
I-IT WAS NOTHING! ♥
HAZE
WE WERE SO HAPPY TO DO IT!

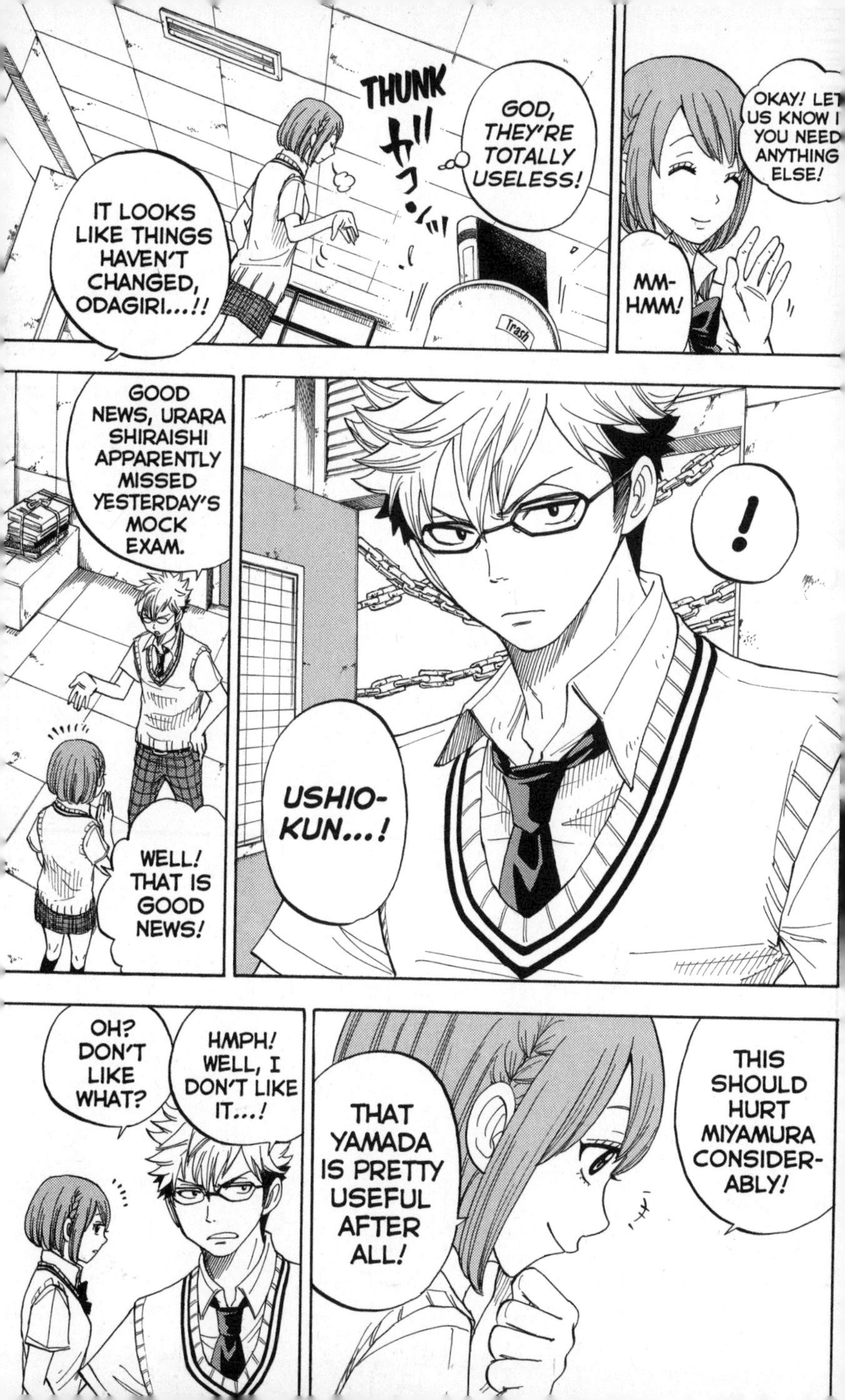
OKAY! LET US KNOW I YOU NEED ANYTHING ELSE!
MM-HMM!
GOD, THEY'RE TOTALLY USELESS!
THUNK
IT LOOKS LIKE THINGS HAVEN'T CHANGED, ODAGIRI...!!
!
USHIO-KUN...!
GOOD NEWS, URARA SHIRAISHI APPARENTLY MISSED YESTERDAY'S MOCK EXAM.
WELL! THAT IS GOOD NEWS!
THIS SHOULD HURT MIYAMURA CONSIDER-ABLY!
THAT YAMADA IS PRETTY USEFUL AFTER ALL!
HMPH! WELL, I DON'T LIKE IT...!
OH? DON'T LIKE WHAT?

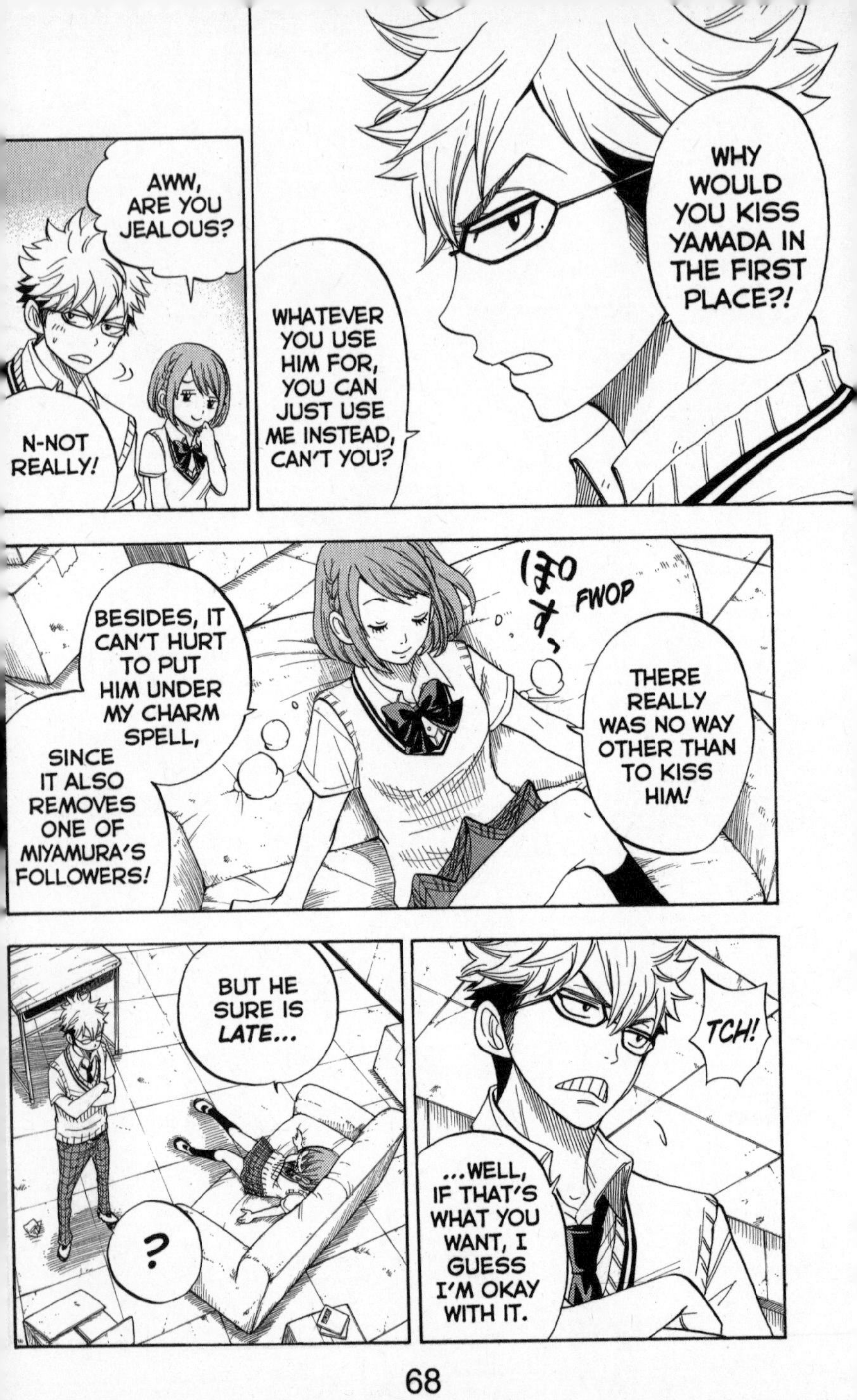
WHY WOULD YOU KISS YAMADA IN THE FIRST PLACE?!
WHATEVER YOU USE HIM FOR, YOU CAN JUST USE ME INSTEAD, CAN'T YOU?
AWW, ARE YOU JEALOUS?
N-NOT REALLY!
FWOP
THERE REALLY WAS NO WAY OTHER THAN TO KISS HIM!
BESIDES, IT CAN'T HURT TO PUT HIM UNDER MY CHARM SPELL,
SINCE IT ALSO REMOVES ONE OF MIYAMURA'S FOLLOWERS!
TCH!
...WELL, IF THAT'S WHAT YOU WANT, I GUESS I'M OKAY WITH IT.
BUT HE SURE IS LATE...
?

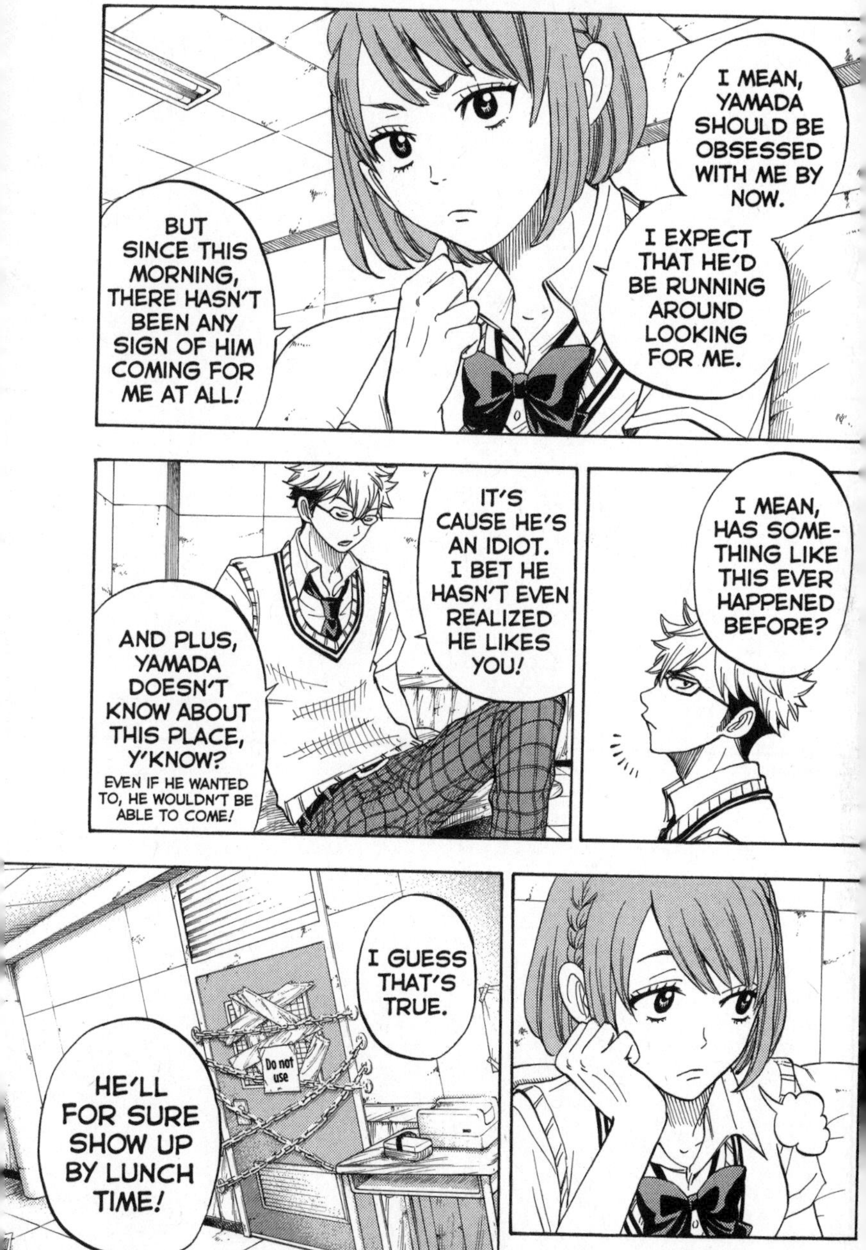
I MEAN, YAMADA SHOULD BE OBSESSED WITH ME BY NOW.
I EXPECT THAT HE'D BE RUNNING AROUND LOOKING FOR ME.
BUT SINCE THIS MORNING, THERE HASN'T BEEN ANY SIGN OF HIM COMING FOR ME AT ALL!
I MEAN, HAS SOME-THING LIKE THIS EVER HAPPENED BEFORE?
IT'S CAUSE HE'S AN IDIOT. I BET HE HASN'T EVEN REALIZED HE LIKES YOU!
AND PLUS, YAMADA DOESN'T KNOW ABOUT THIS PLACE, Y'KNOW?
EVEN IF HE WANTED TO, HE WOULDN'T BE ABLE TO COME!
I GUESS THAT'S TRUE.
Do not use
HE'LL FOR SURE SHOW UP BY LUNCH TIME!

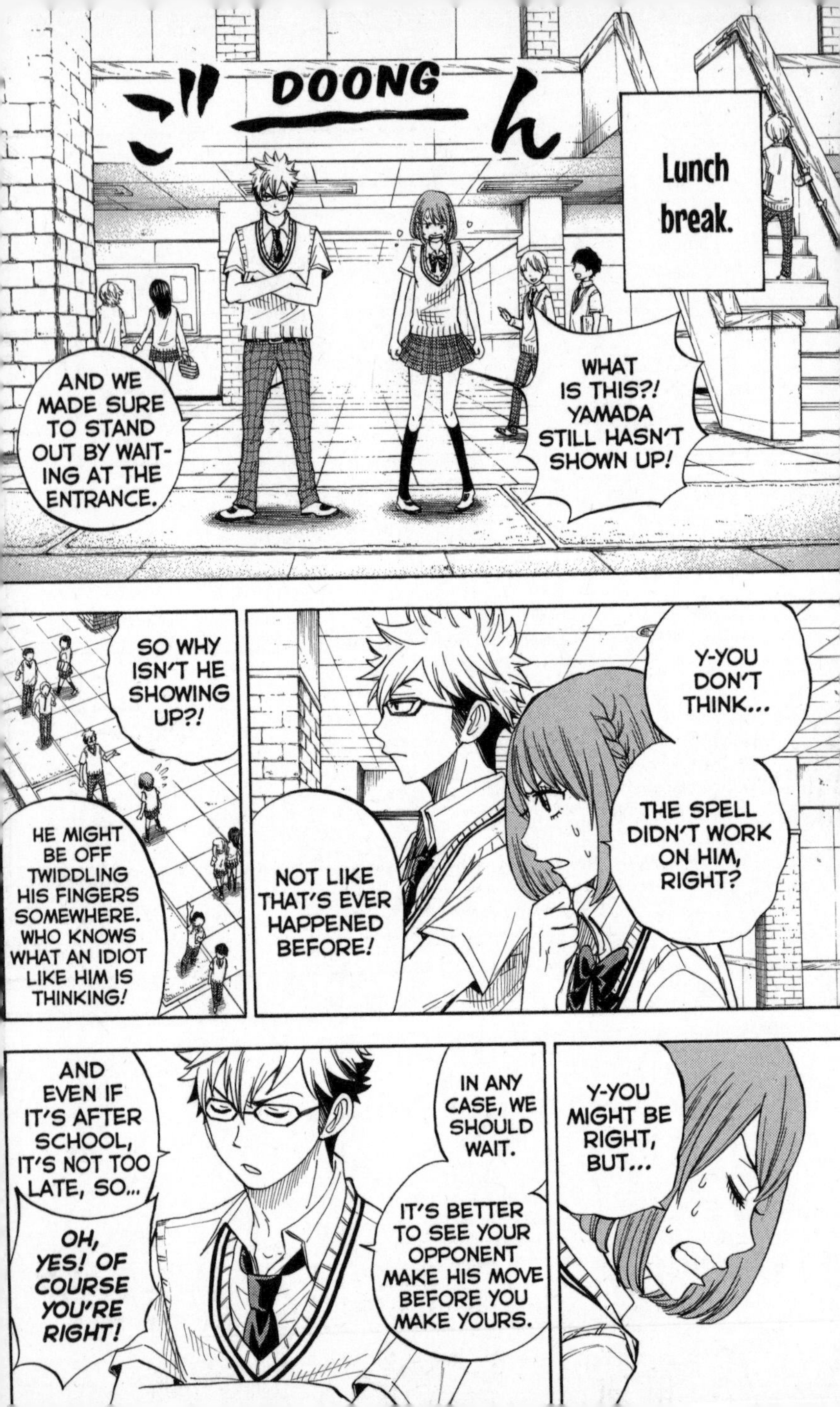
Lunch break.
DOONG
WHAT IS THIS?! YAMADA STILL HASN'T SHOWN UP!
AND WE MADE SURE TO STAND OUT BY WAIT-ING AT THE ENTRANCE.
Y-YOU DON'T THINK...
THE SPELL DIDN'T WORK ON HIM, RIGHT?
NOT LIKE THAT'S EVER HAPPENED BEFORE!
SO WHY ISN'T HE SHOWING UP?!
HE MIGHT BE OFF TWIDDLING HIS FINGERS SOMEWHERE. WHO KNOWS WHAT AN IDIOT LIKE HIM IS THINKING!
Y-YOU MIGHT BE RIGHT, BUT...
IN ANY CASE, WE SHOULD WAIT.
IT'S BETTER TO SEE YOUR OPPONENT MAKE HIS MOVE BEFORE YOU MAKE YOURS.
AND EVEN IF IT'S AFTER SCHOOL, IT'S NOT TOO LATE, SO...
OH, YES! OF COURSE YOU'RE RIGHT!

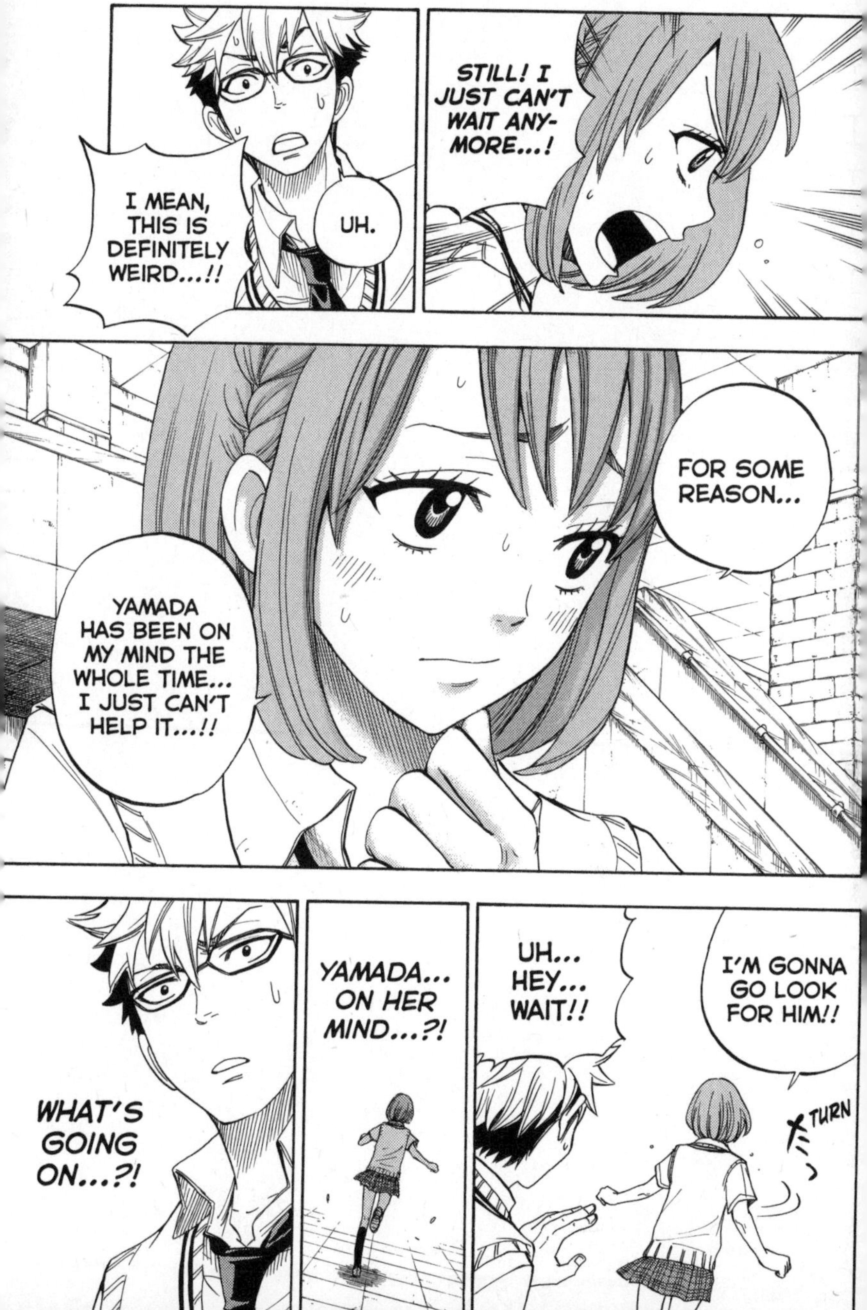
STILL! I JUST CAN'T WAIT ANY-MORE...!
UH.
I MEAN, THIS IS DEFINITELY WEIRD...!!
FOR SOME REASON...
YAMADA HAS BEEN ON MY MIND THE WHOLE TIME... I JUST CAN'T HELP IT...!!
I'M GONNA GO LOOK FOR HIM!!
TURN
UH... HEY... WAIT!!
YAMADA... ON HER MIND...?!
WHAT'S GOING ON...?!

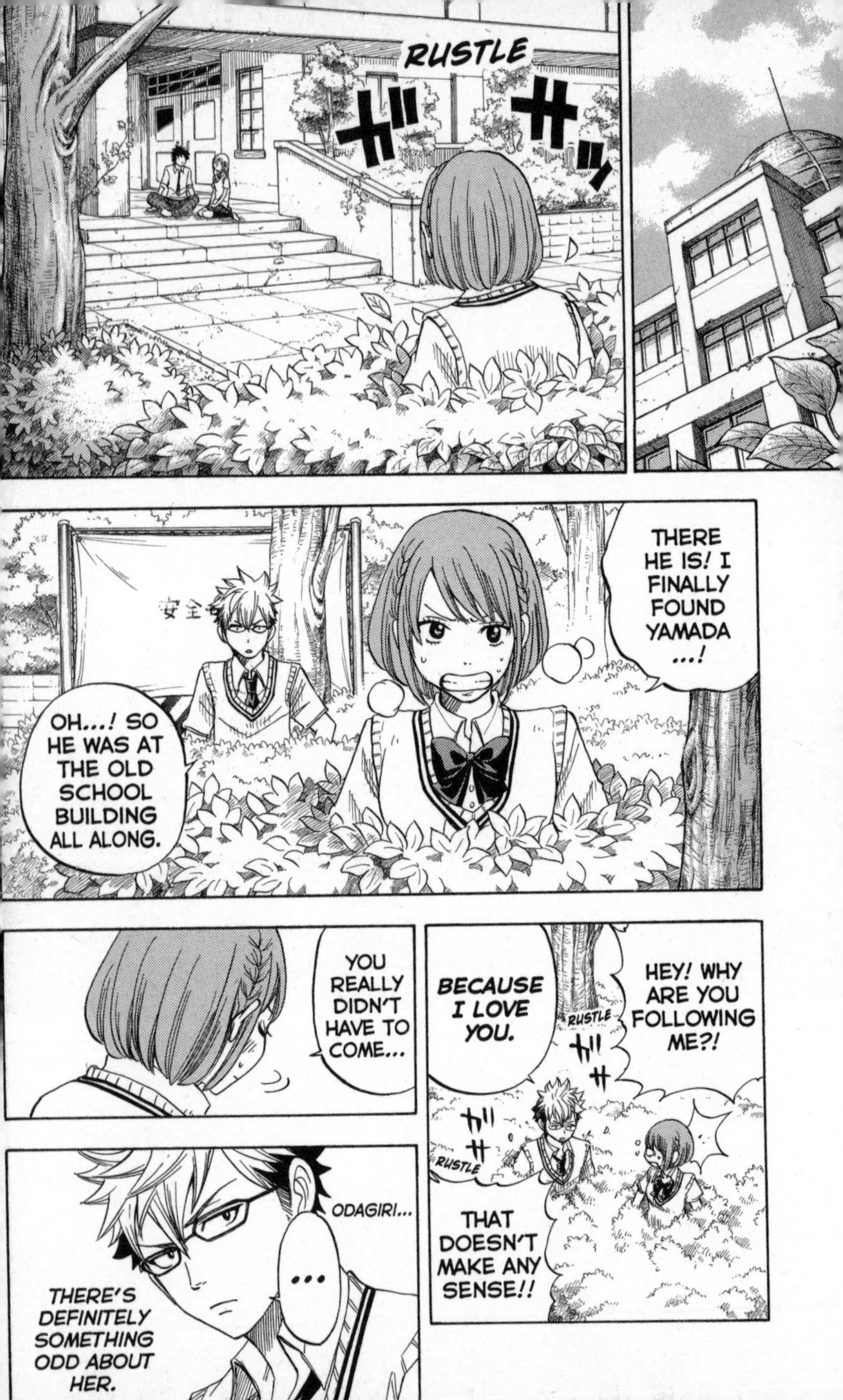
RUSTLE
THERE HE IS! I FINALLY FOUND YAMADA ...!
OH...! SO HE WAS AT THE OLD SCHOOL BUILDING ALL ALONG.
HEY! WHY ARE YOU FOLLOWING ME?!
RUSTLE
BECAUSE I LOVE YOU.
RUSTLE
THAT DOESN'T MAKE ANY SENSE!!
YOU REALLY DIDN'T HAVE TO COME...
ODAGIRI...
...
THERE'S DEFINITELY SOMETHING ODD ABOUT HER.

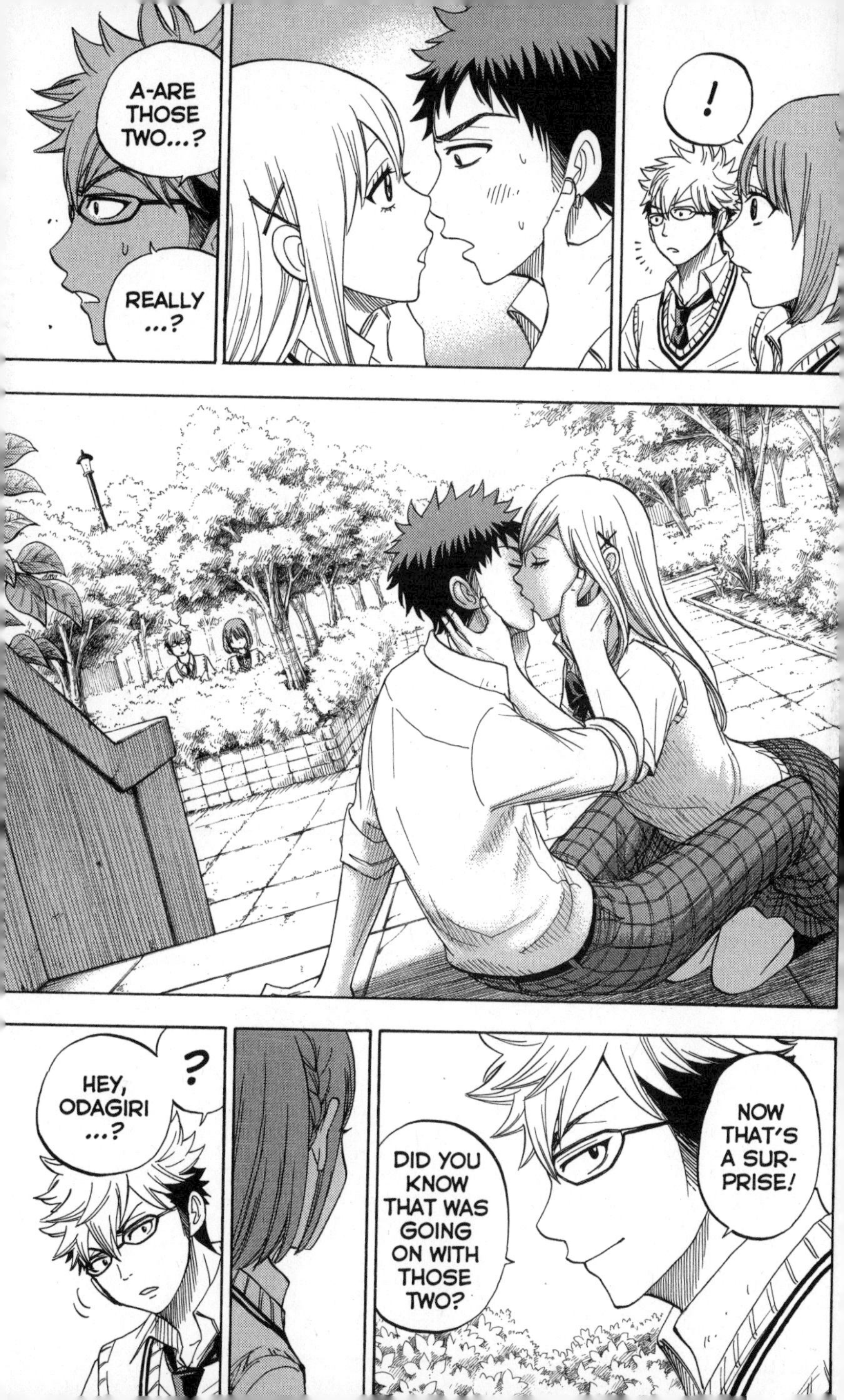
!
A-ARE THOSE TWO...?
REALLY ...?
NOW THAT'S A SUR-PRISE!
DID YOU KNOW THAT WAS GOING ON WITH THOSE TWO?
?
HEY, ODAGIRI ...?

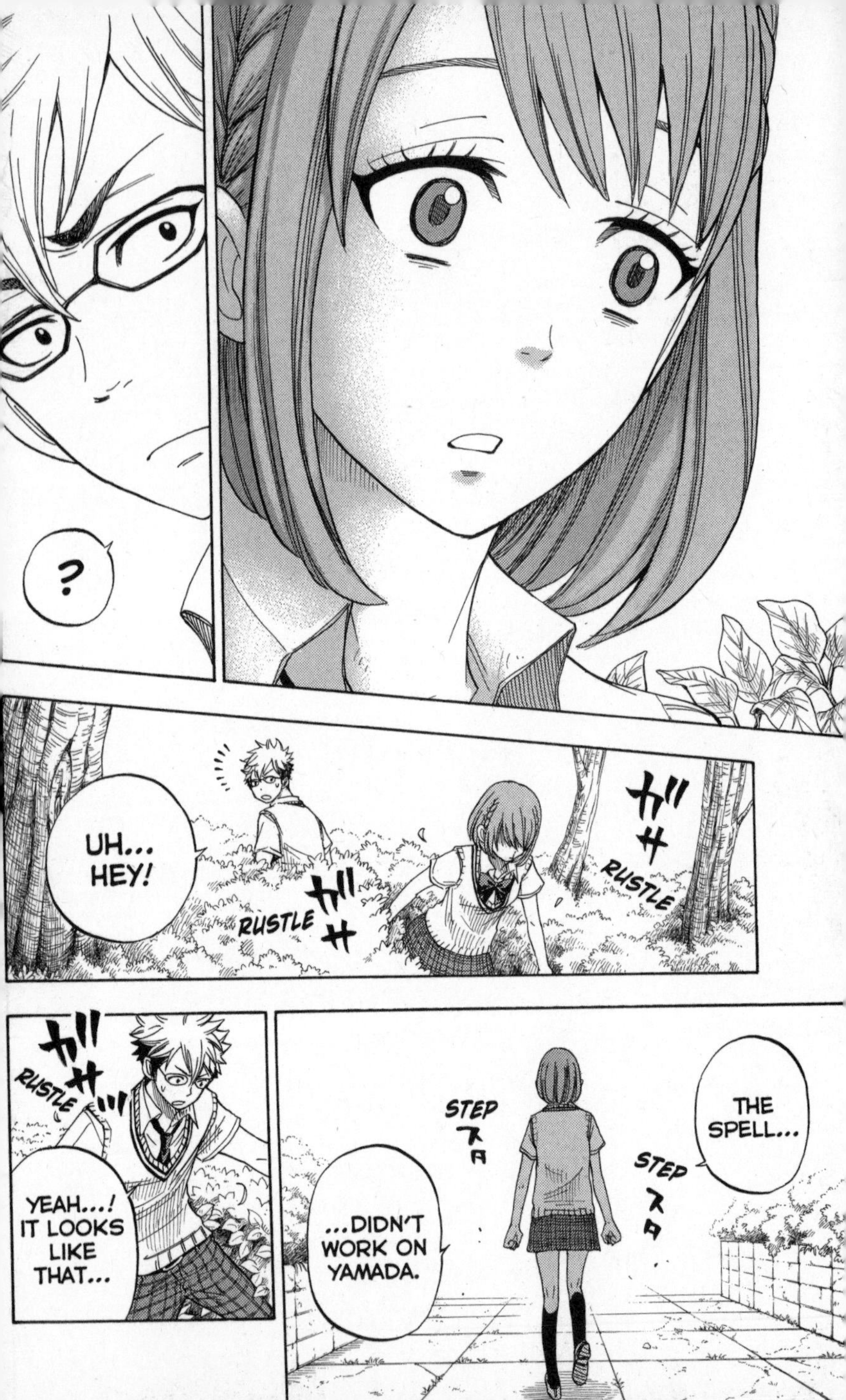
?
ガサ
RUSTLE
UH... HEY!
ガサ
RUSTLE
THE SPELL...
STEP
スタ
STEP
スタ
...DIDN'T WORK ON YAMADA.
ガサ
RUSTLE
YEAH...! IT LOOKS LIKE THAT...

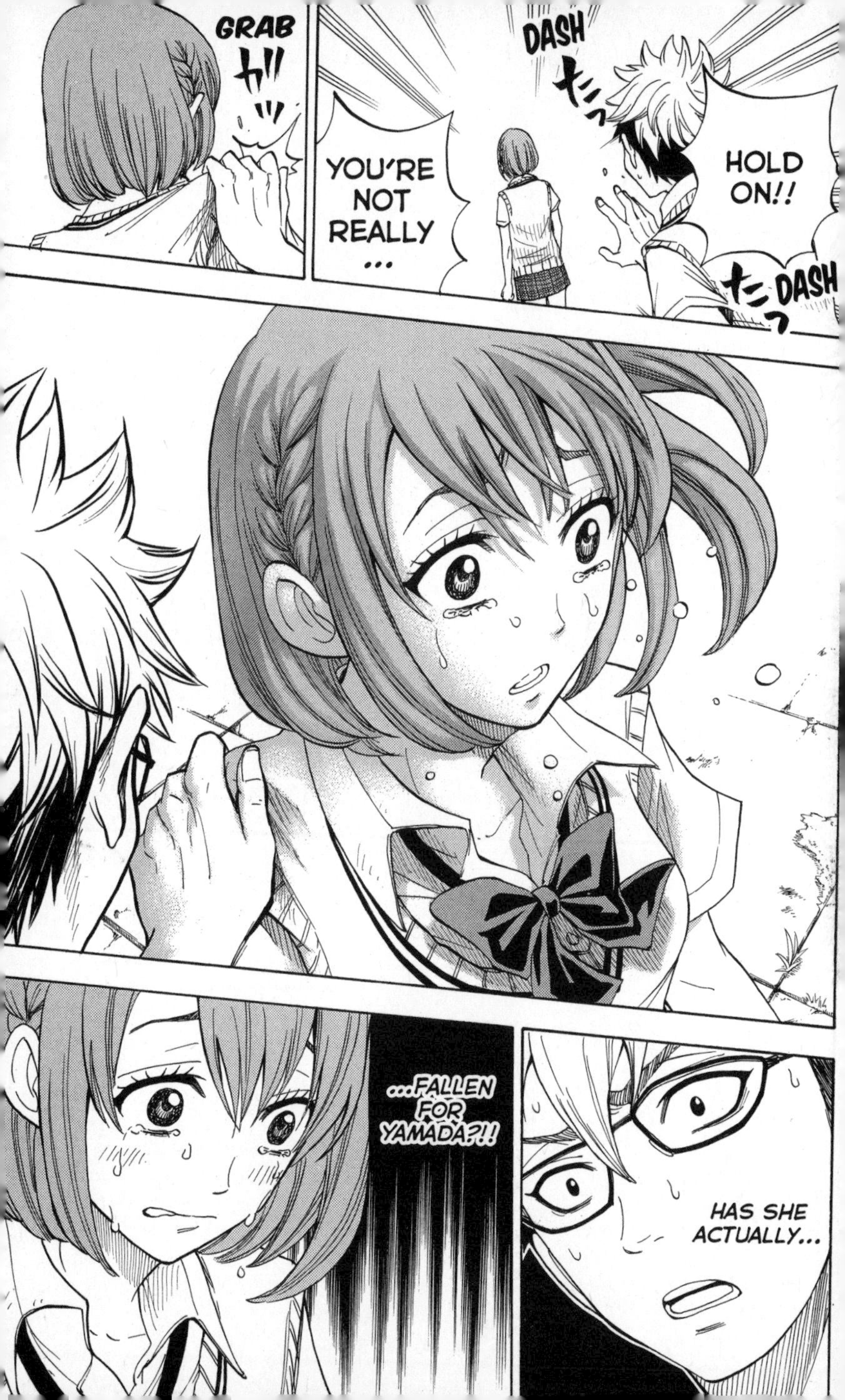
DASH
たっ
HOLD ON!!
たっ
DASH
YOU'RE NOT REALLY...
GRAB
ガッ
HAS SHE ACTUALLY...
...FALLEN FOR YAMADA?!!

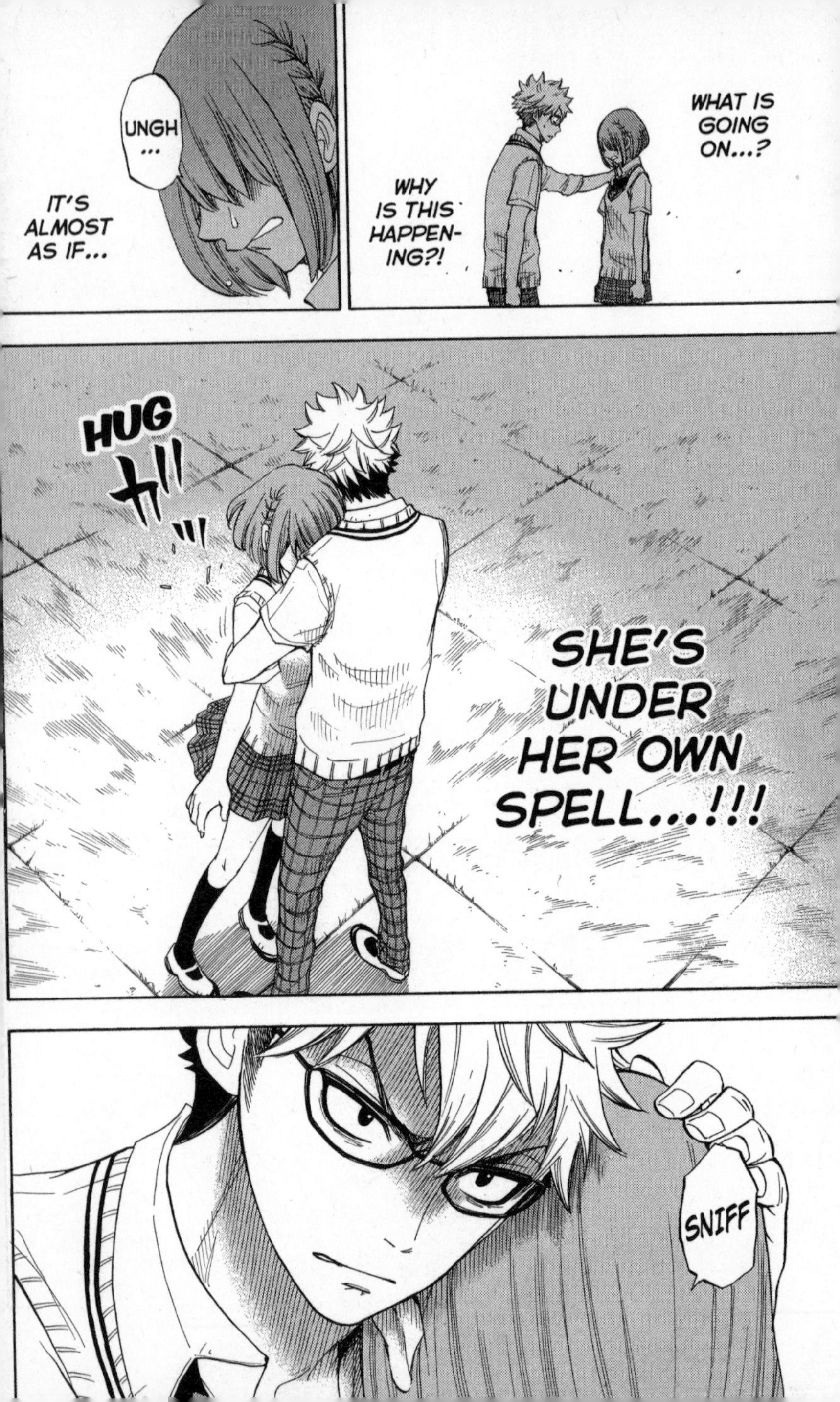
WHAT IS GOING ON...?
WHY IS THIS HAPPENING?!
UNGH ...
IT'S ALMOST AS IF...
HUG
SHE'S UNDER HER OWN SPELL...!!!
SNIFF

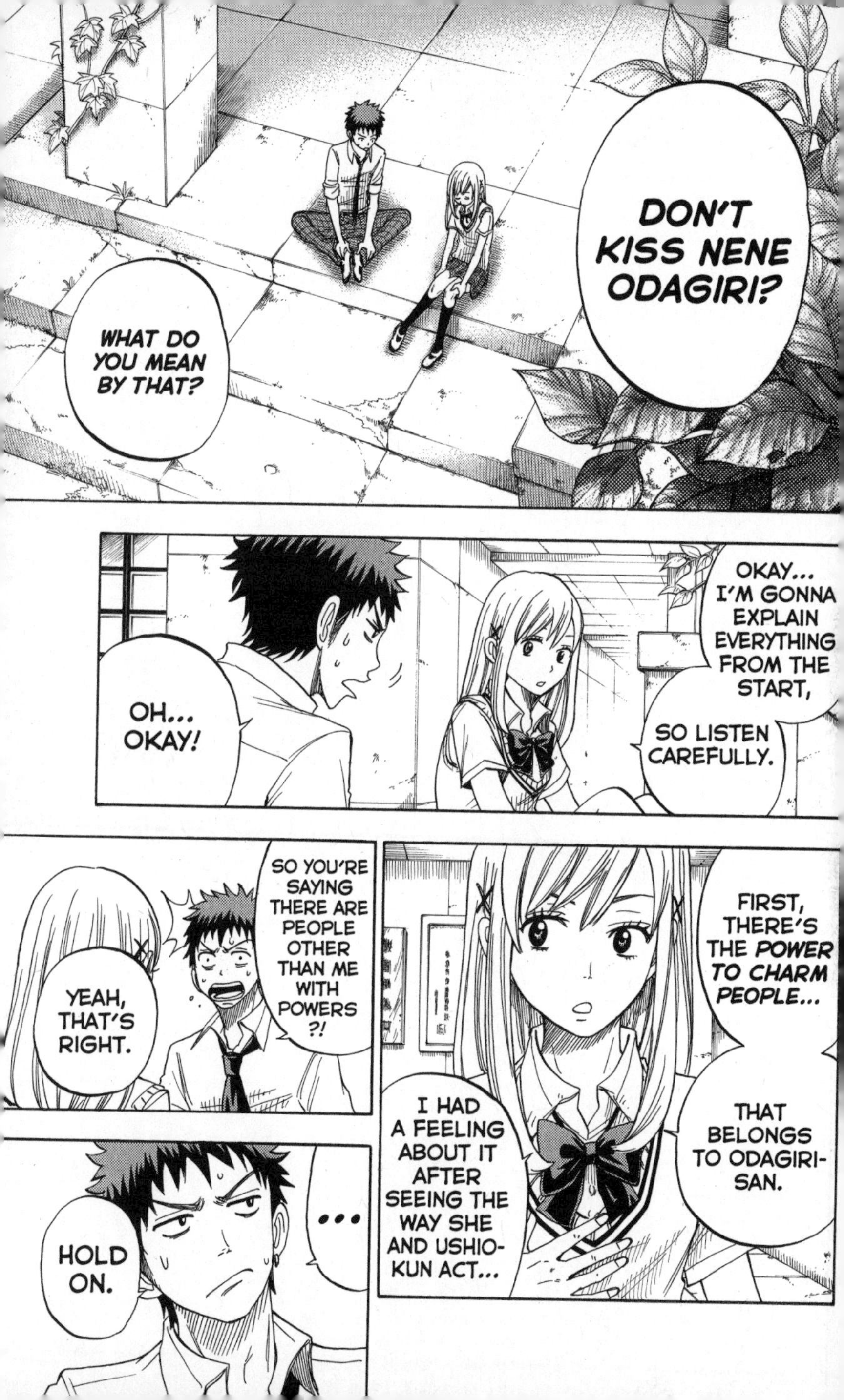
DON'T KISS NENE ODAGIRI?
WHAT DO YOU MEAN BY THAT?
OKAY... I'M GONNA EXPLAIN EVERYTHING FROM THE START,
SO LISTEN CAREFULLY.
OH... OKAY!
FIRST, THERE'S THE *POWER TO CHARM PEOPLE*...
THAT BELONGS TO ODAGIRI-SAN.
I HAD A FEELING ABOUT IT AFTER SEEING THE WAY SHE AND USHIO-KUN ACT...
SO YOU'RE SAYING THERE ARE PEOPLE OTHER THAN ME WITH POWERS ?!
YEAH, THAT'S RIGHT.
...
HOLD ON.

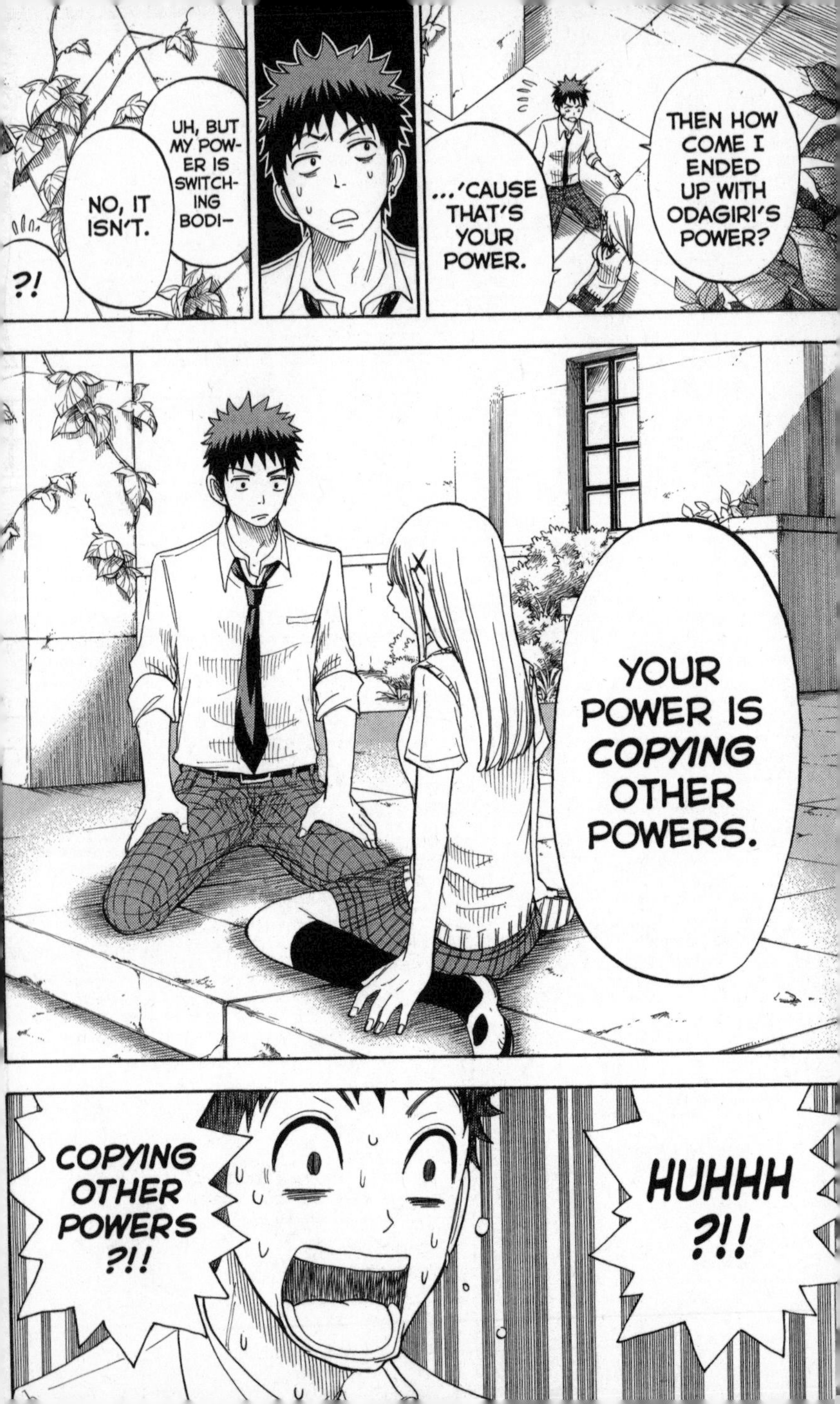
THEN HOW COME I ENDED UP WITH ODAGIRI'S POWER?
...'CAUSE THAT'S YOUR POWER.
UH, BUT MY POW-ER IS SWITCH-ING BODI—
NO, IT ISN'T.
?!
YOUR POWER IS *COPYING* OTHER POWERS.
HUHHH ?!!
COPYING OTHER POWERS ?!!

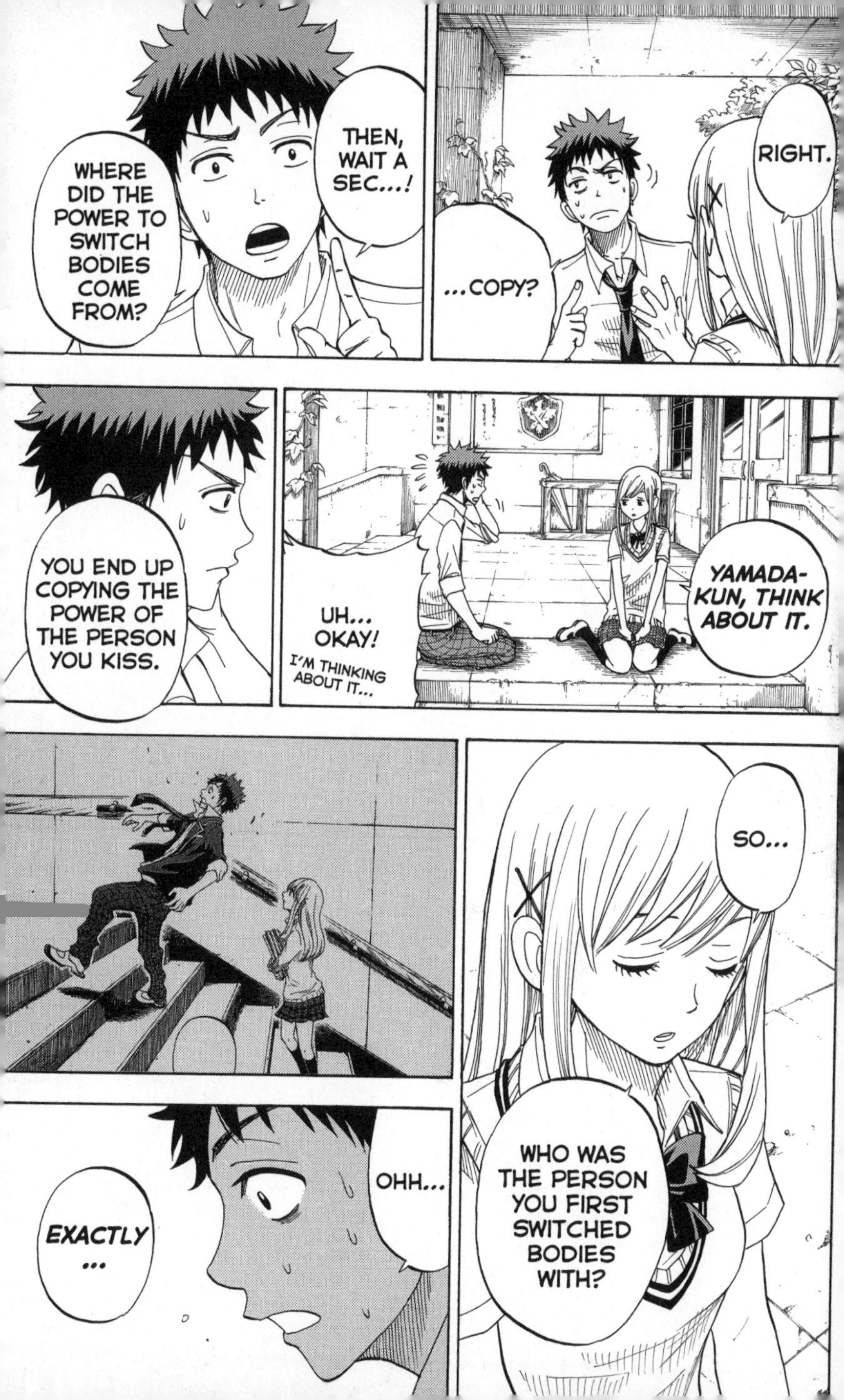
RIGHT.
...COPY?
THEN, WAIT A SEC...!
WHERE DID THE POWER TO SWITCH BODIES COME FROM?
YAMADA-KUN, THINK ABOUT IT.
UH... OKAY!
I'M THINKING ABOUT IT...
YOU END UP COPYING THE POWER OF THE PERSON YOU KISS.
SO...
WHO WAS THE PERSON YOU FIRST SWITCHED BODIES WITH?
OHH...
EXACTLY...

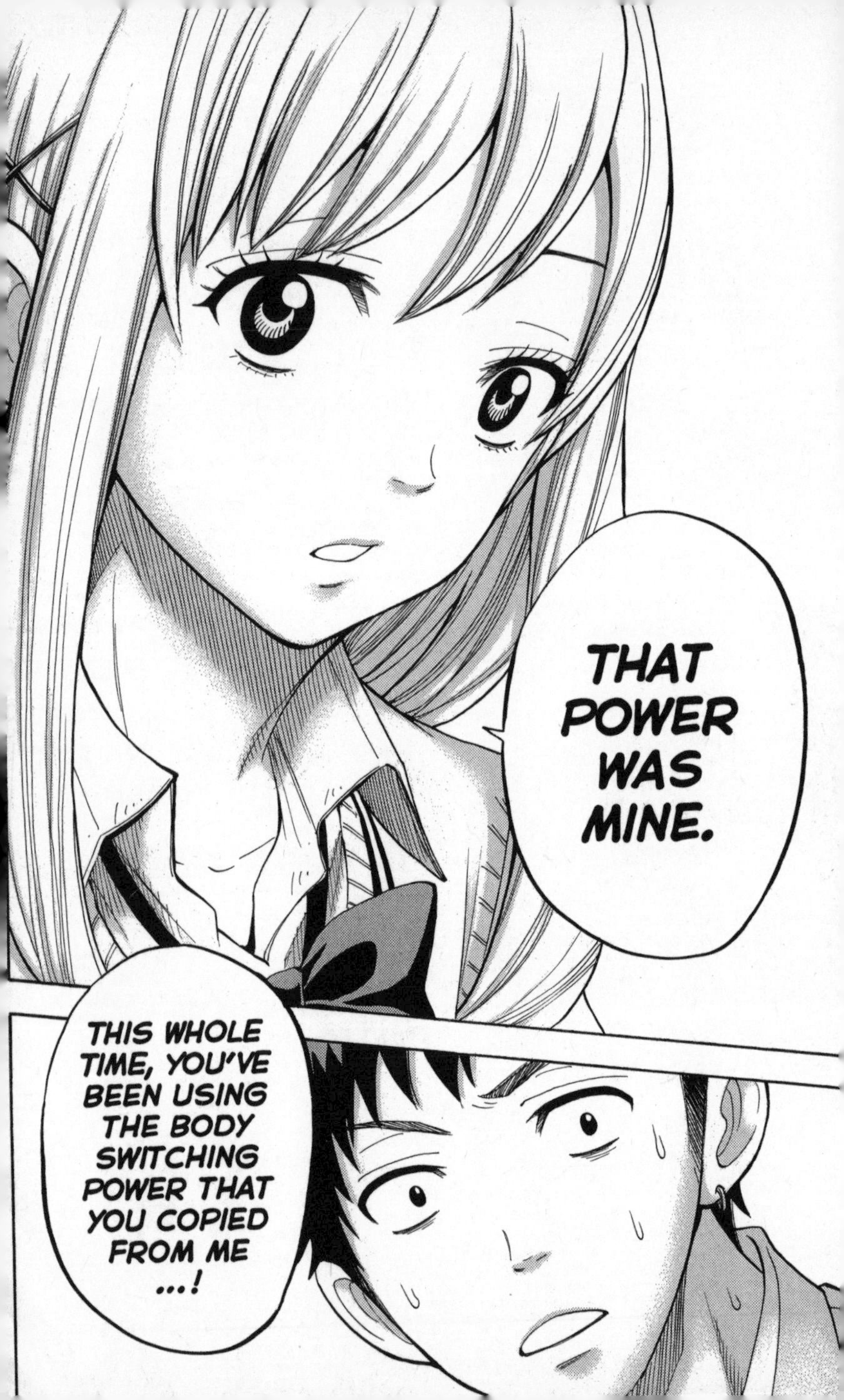
THAT POWER WAS MINE.
THIS WHOLE TIME, YOU'VE BEEN USING THE BODY SWITCHING POWER THAT YOU COPIED FROM ME ...!

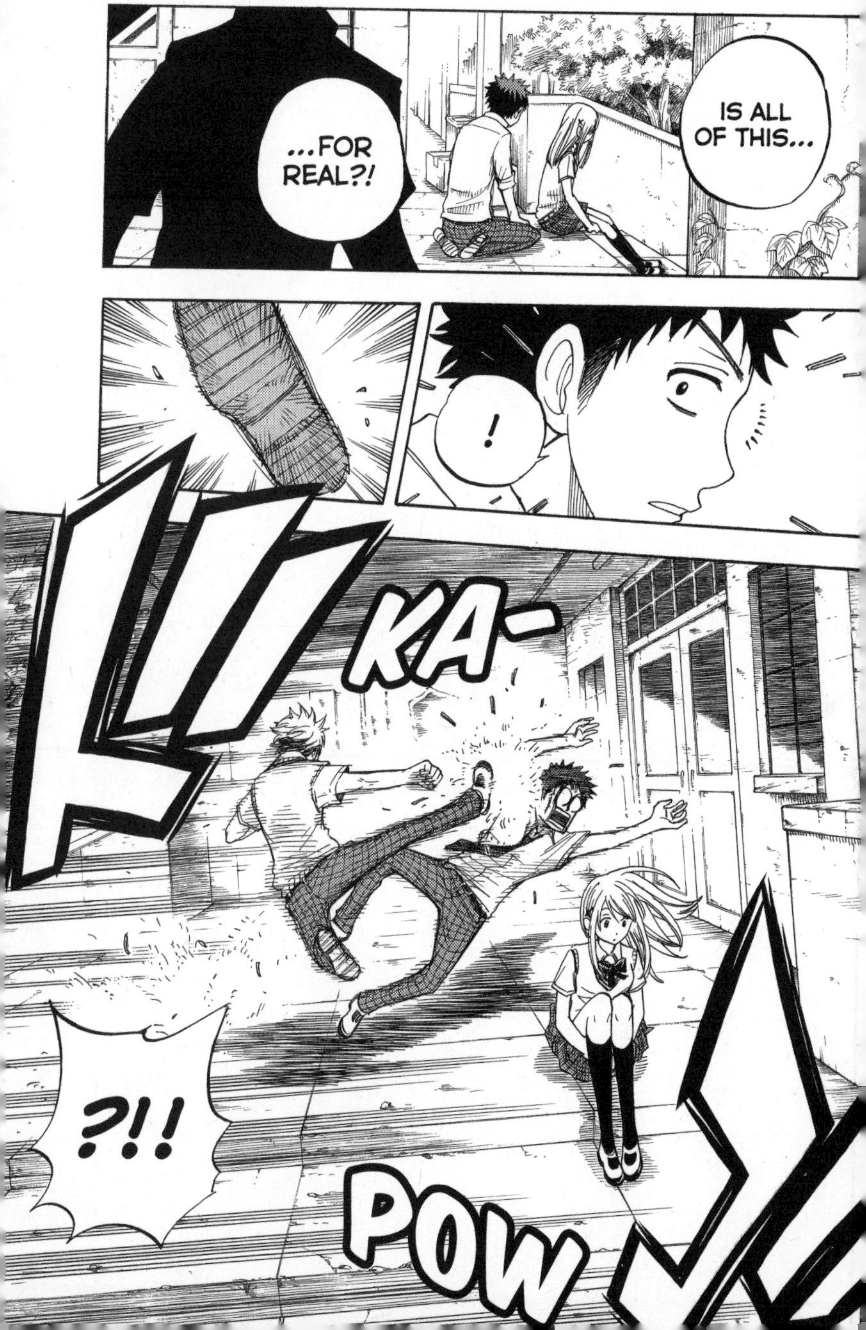
IS ALL OF THIS...
...FOR REAL?!
!
KA-
POW
?!!

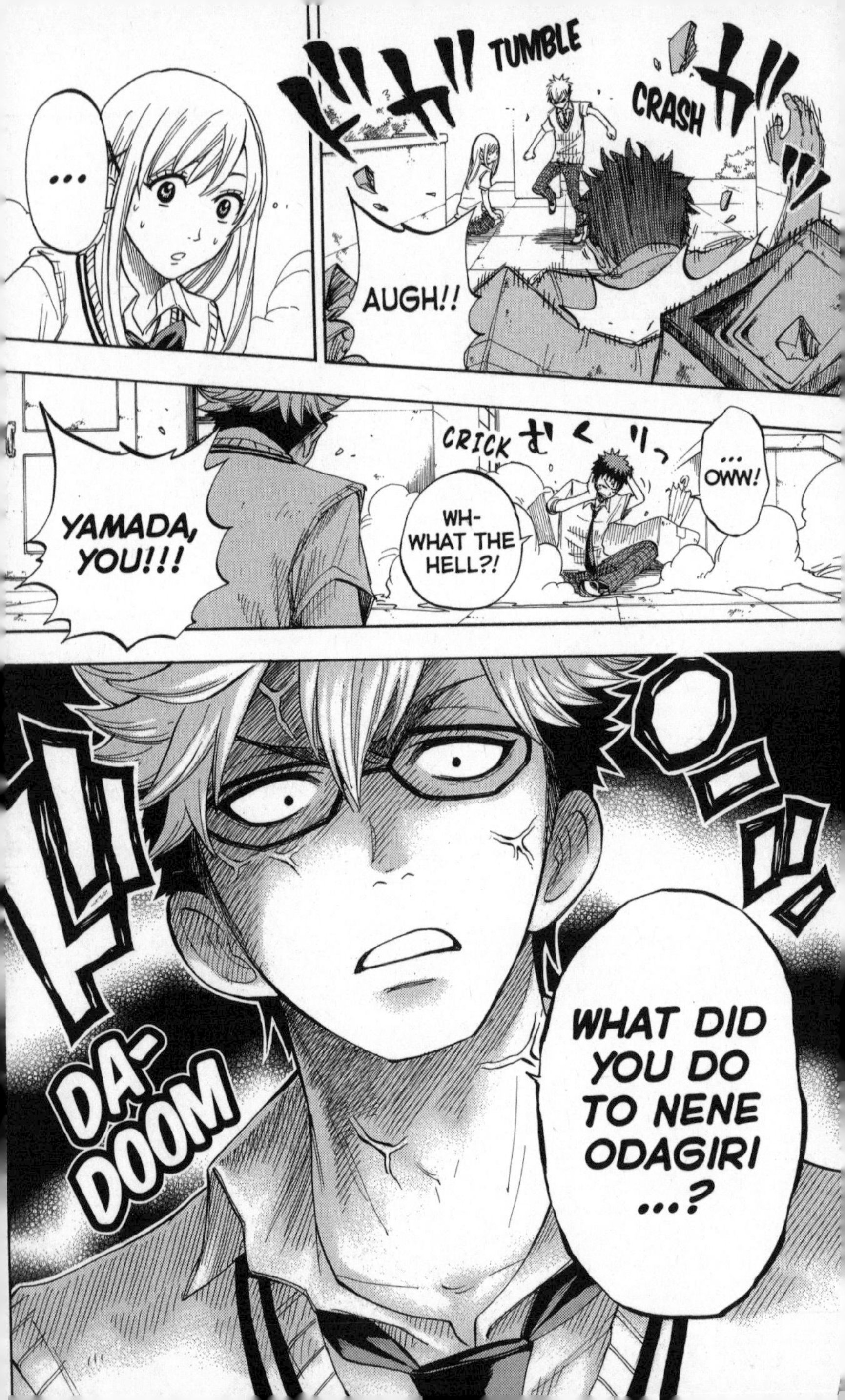
CRASH
TUMBLE
AUGH!!
...
... OWW!
CRICK
WH- WHAT THE HELL?!
YAMADA, YOU!!!
WHAT DID YOU DO TO NENE ODAGIRI ...?
DA-DOOM

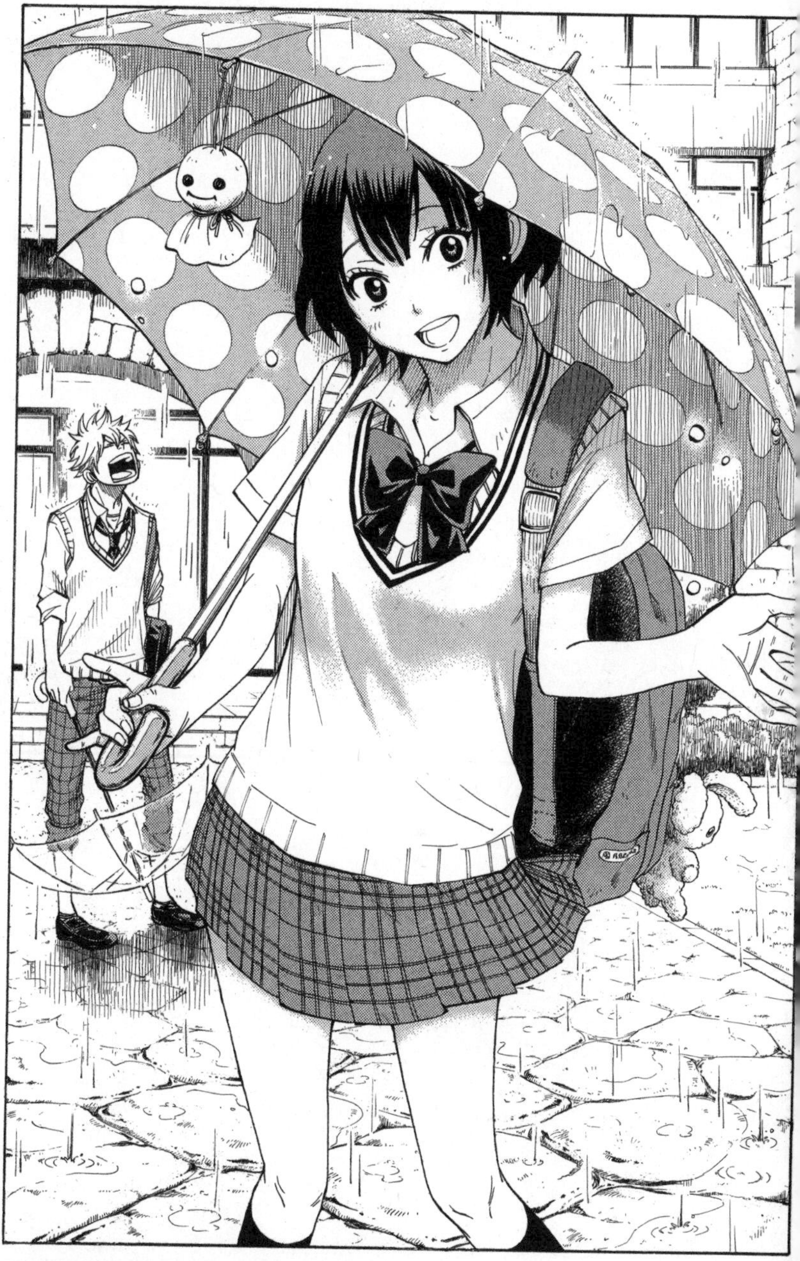

CHAPTER 21: Wow, that hurt.

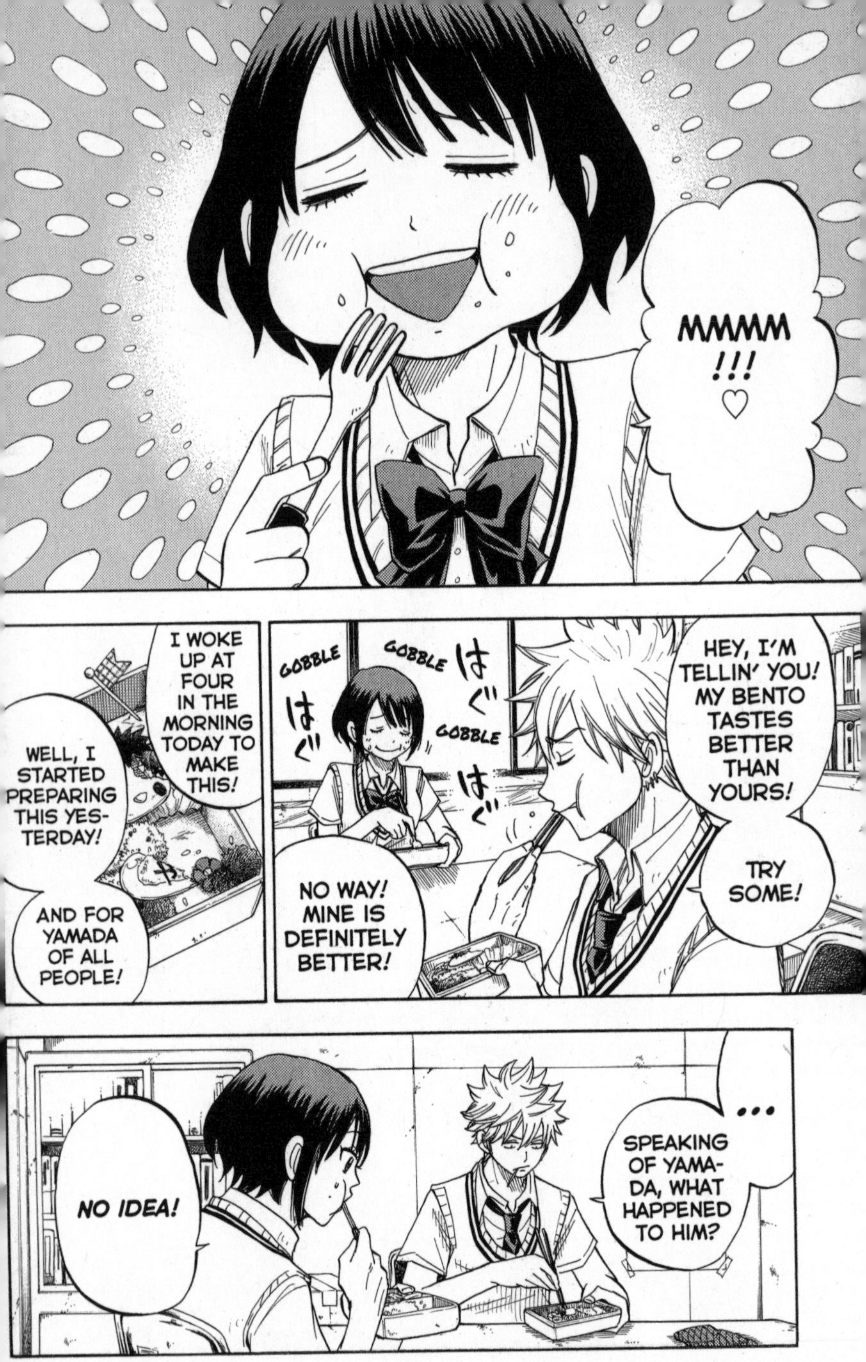
MMMM !!! ♡
HEY, I'M TELLIN' YOU! MY BENTO TASTES BETTER THAN YOURS!
TRY SOME!
GOBBLE
はぐ
GOBBLE
はぐ
GOBBLE
はぐ
NO WAY! MINE IS DEFINITELY BETTER!
I WOKE UP AT FOUR IN THE MORNING TODAY TO MAKE THIS!
WELL, I STARTED PREPARING THIS YES-TERDAY!
AND FOR YAMADA OF ALL PEOPLE!
...
SPEAKING OF YAMA-DA, WHAT HAPPENED TO HIM?
NO IDEA!

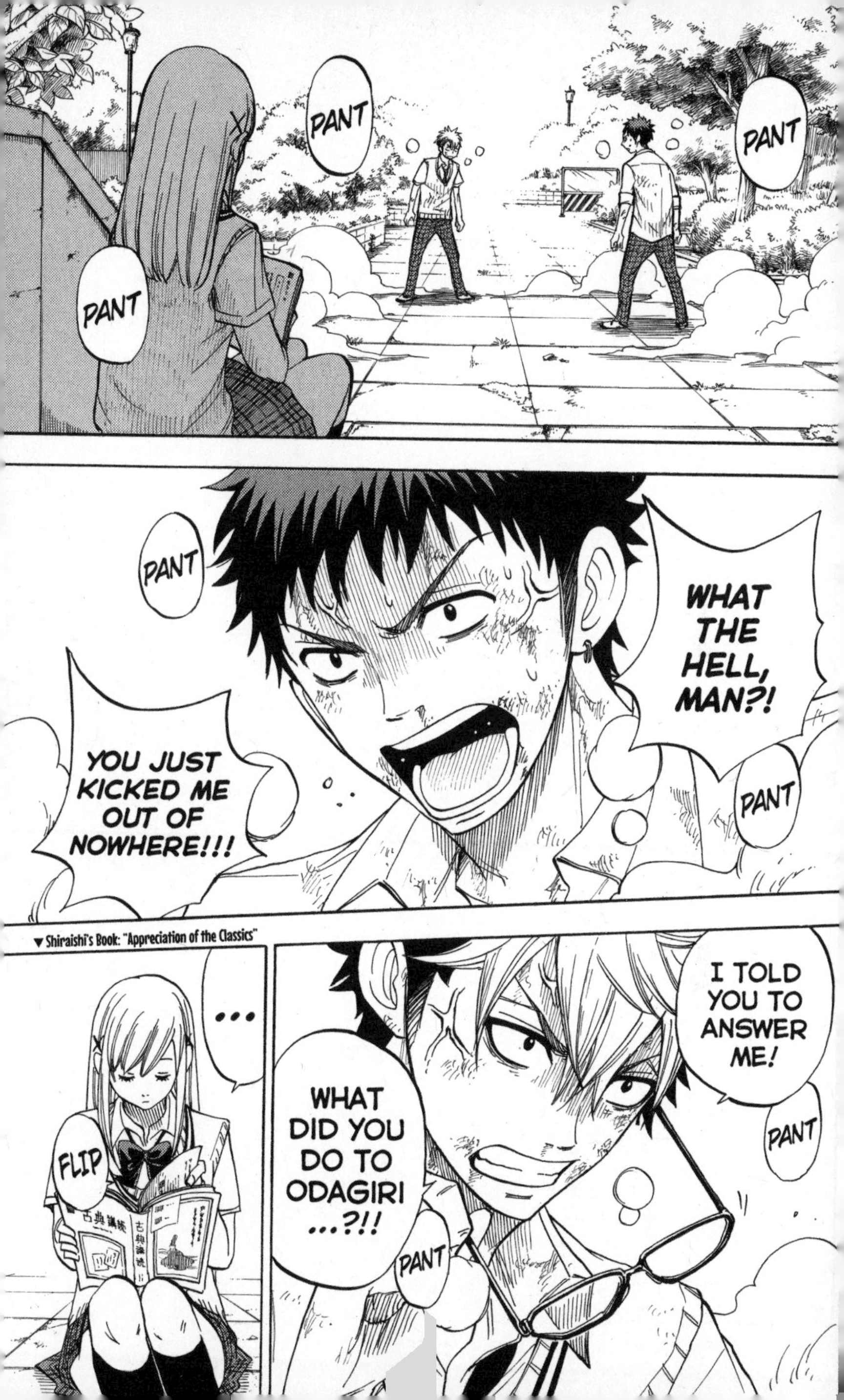
PANT
PANT
PANT
WHAT THE HELL, MAN?!
PANT
YOU JUST KICKED ME OUT OF NOWHERE!!!
PANT
I TOLD YOU TO ANSWER ME!
PANT
WHAT DID YOU DO TO ODAGIRI ...?!!
PANT
...
FLIP

▼ Shiraishi's Book: "Appreciation of the Classics"

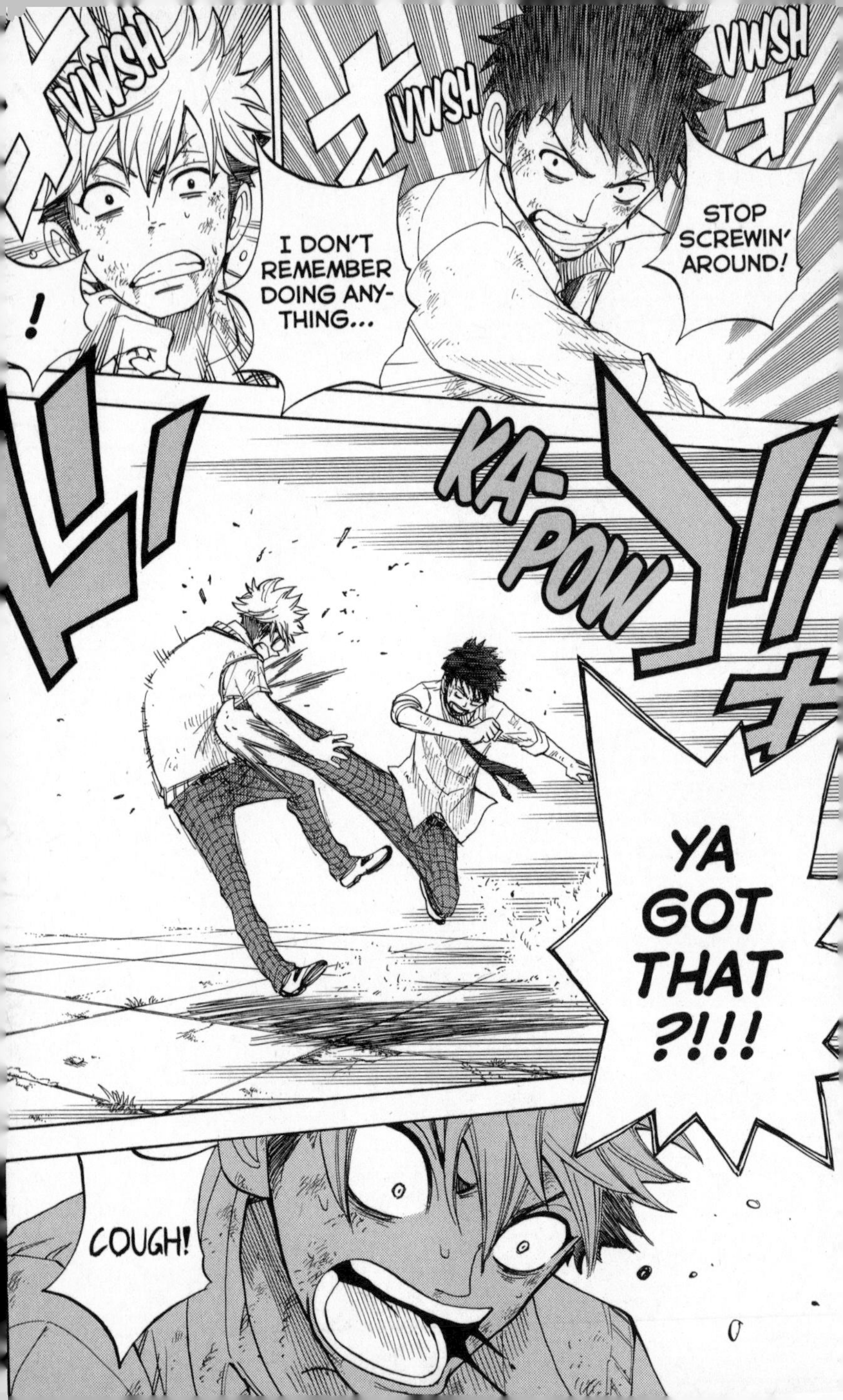

VWSH
STOP SCREWIN' AROUND!
VWSH
I DON'T REMEMBER DOING ANY-THING...
VWSH
!
KA-POW
YA GOT THAT?!!!
COUGH!

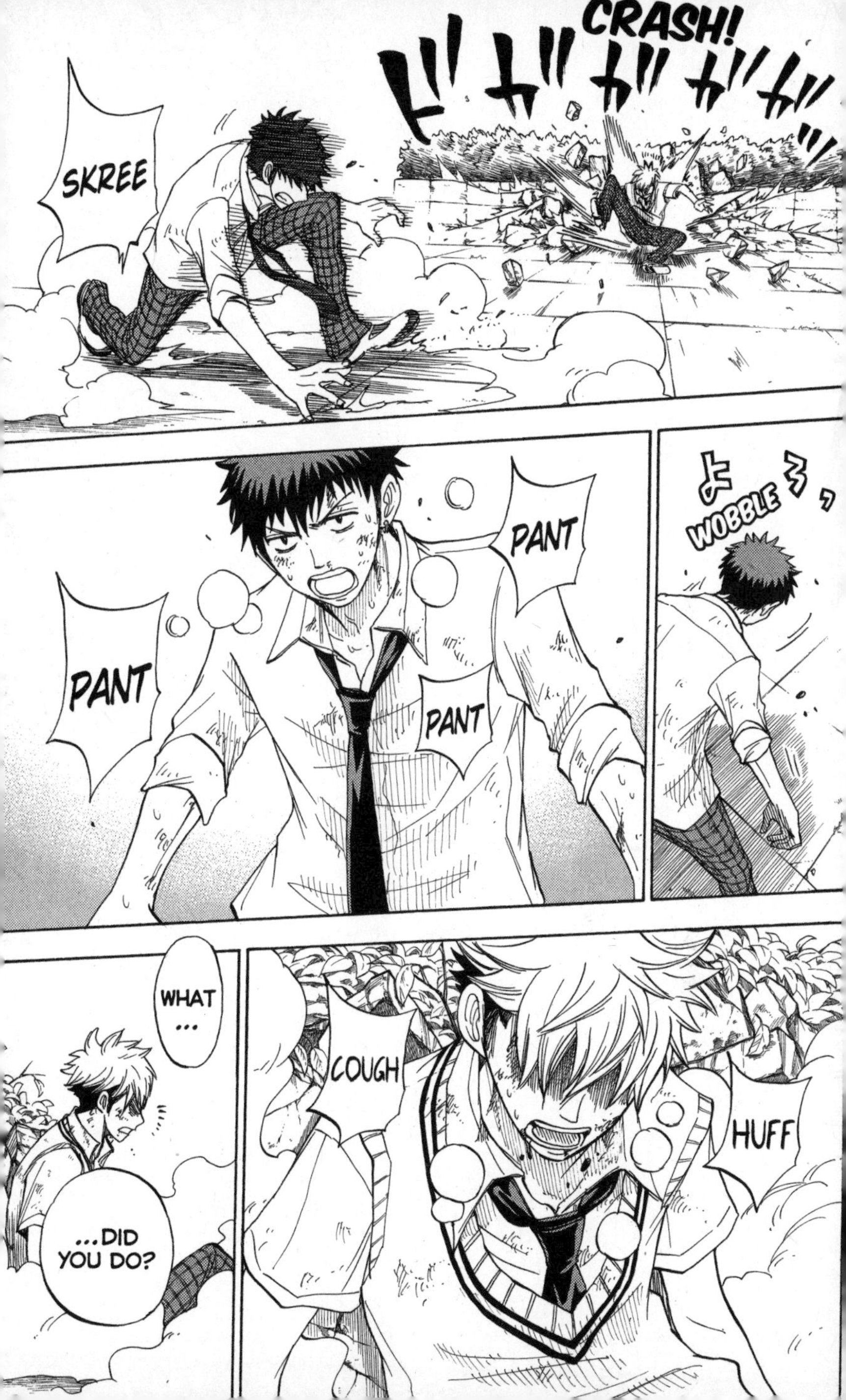
CRASH!
ドガガガガ
SKREE
よろっ
WOBBLE
PANT
PANT
PANT
HUFF
COUGH
WHAT ...
...DID YOU DO?

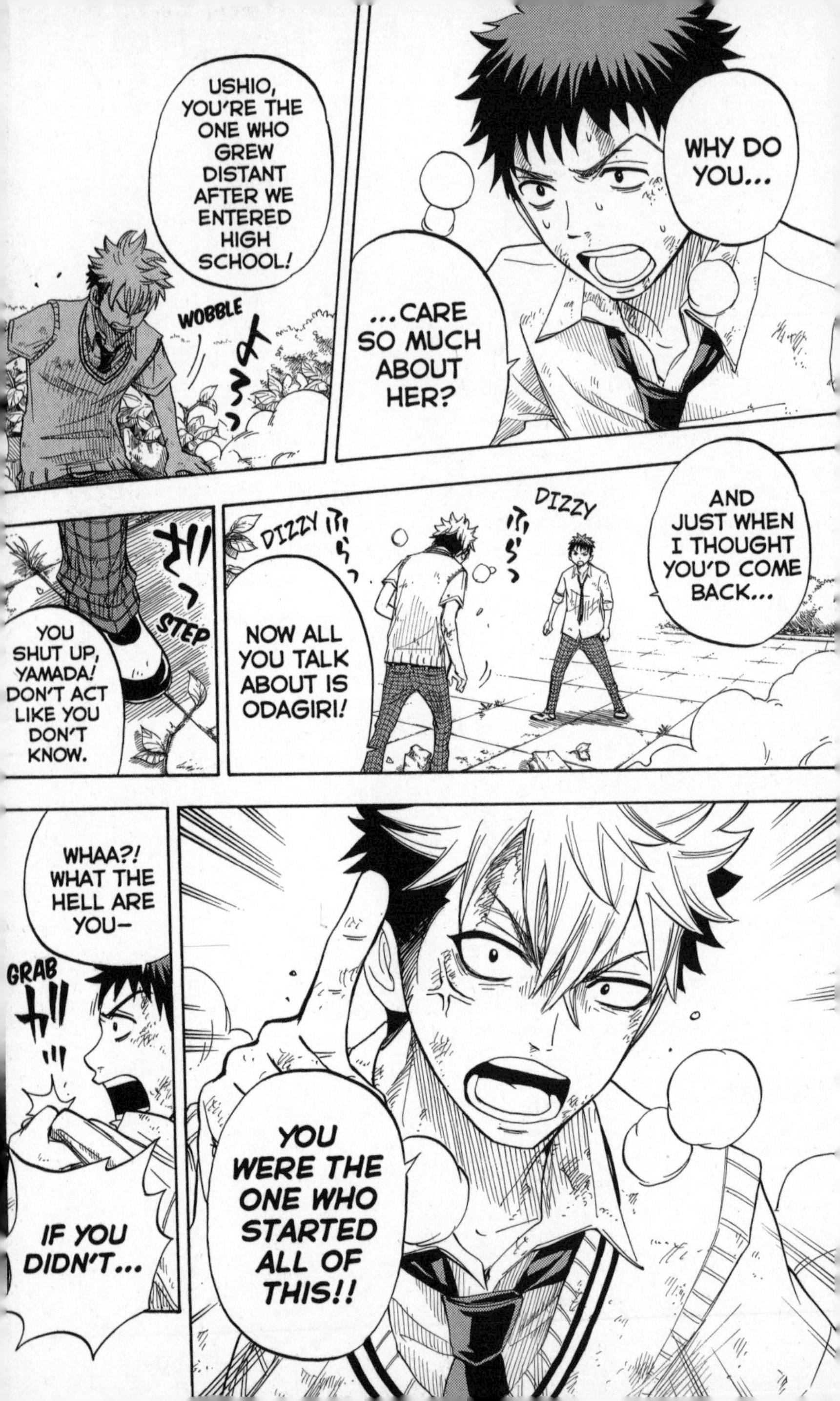
WHY DO YOU...
...CARE SO MUCH ABOUT HER?
USHIO, YOU'RE THE ONE WHO GREW DISTANT AFTER WE ENTERED HIGH SCHOOL!
WOBBLE
AND JUST WHEN I THOUGHT YOU'D COME BACK...
DIZZY
DIZZY
NOW ALL YOU TALK ABOUT IS ODAGIRI!
STEP
YOU SHUT UP, YAMADA! DON'T ACT LIKE YOU DON'T KNOW.
YOU WERE THE ONE WHO STARTED ALL OF THIS!!
WHAA?! WHAT THE HELL ARE YOU—
GRAB
IF YOU DIDN'T...

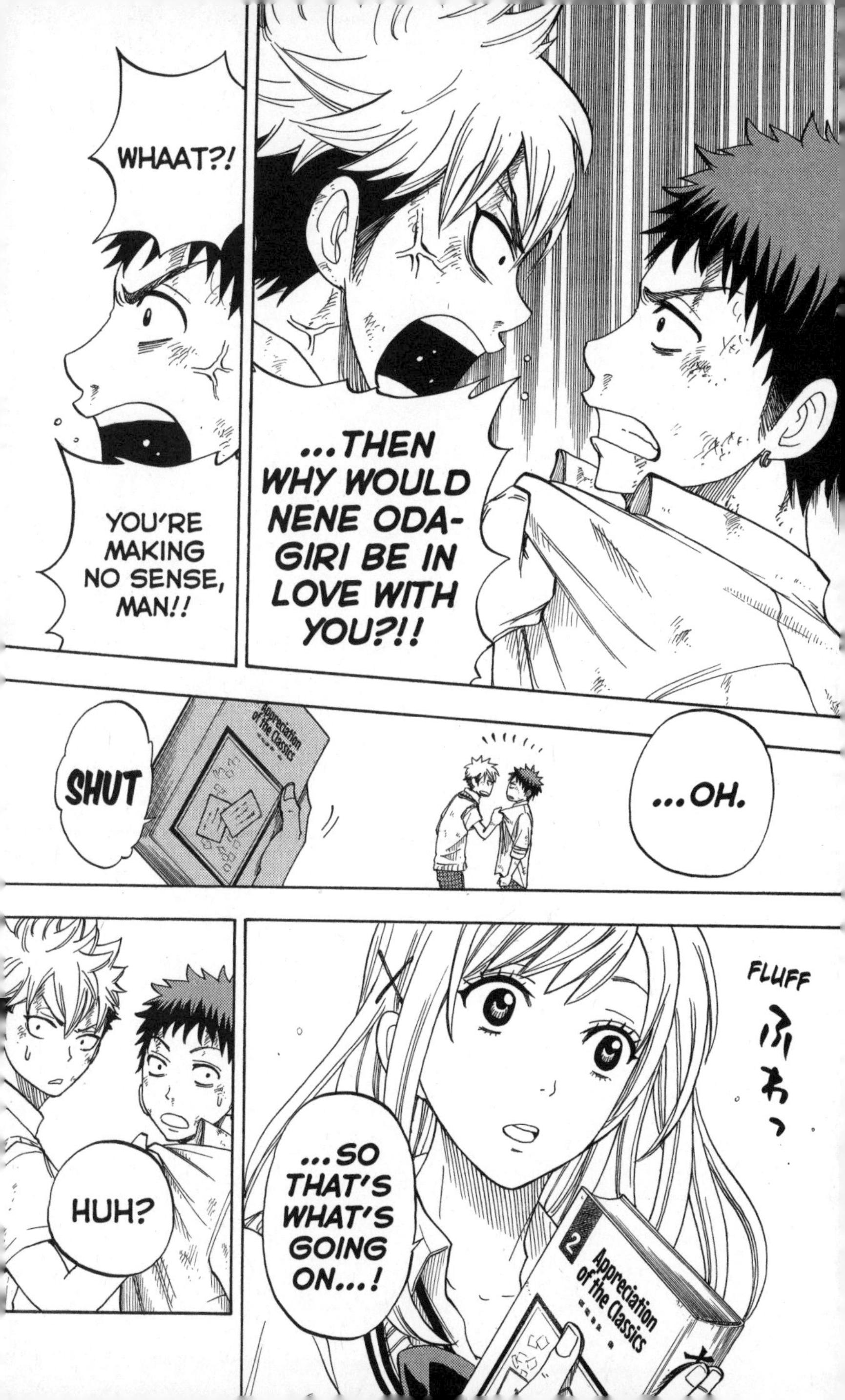
...THEN WHY WOULD NENE ODA-GIRI BE IN LOVE WITH YOU?!!
WHAAT?!
YOU'RE MAKING NO SENSE, MAN!!
...OH.
Appreciation of the Classics
SHUT
FLUFF
ふわっ
...SO THAT'S WHAT'S GOING ON...!
2 Appreciation of the Classics
HUH?

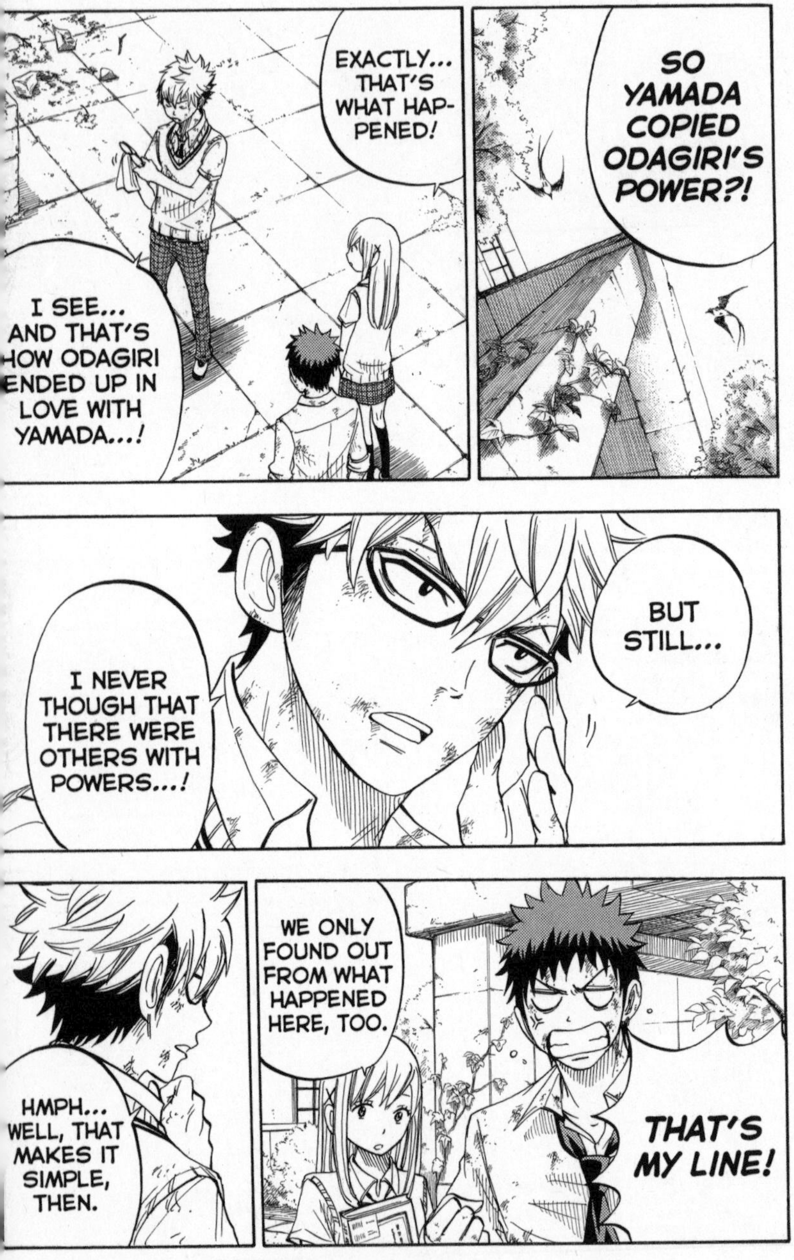
SO YAMADA COPIED ODAGIRI'S POWER?!
EXACTLY... THAT'S WHAT HAP-PENED!
I SEE... AND THAT'S HOW ODAGIRI ENDED UP IN LOVE WITH YAMADA...!
BUT STILL...
I NEVER THOUGH THAT THERE WERE OTHERS WITH POWERS...!
THAT'S MY LINE!
WE ONLY FOUND OUT FROM WHAT HAPPENED HERE, TOO.
HMPH... WELL, THAT MAKES IT SIMPLE, THEN.

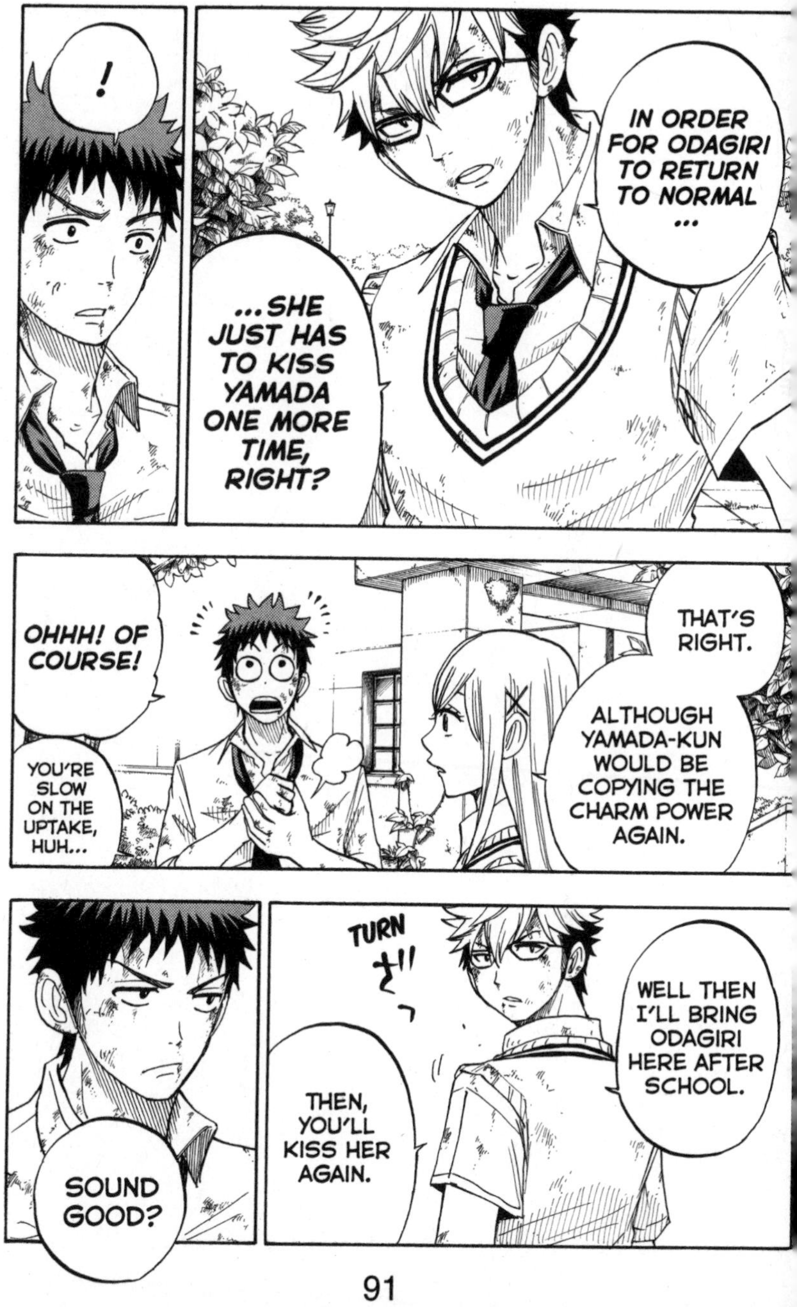
IN ORDER FOR ODAGIRI TO RETURN TO NORMAL ...
...SHE JUST HAS TO KISS YAMADA ONE MORE TIME, RIGHT?
!
THAT'S RIGHT.
ALTHOUGH YAMADA-KUN WOULD BE COPYING THE CHARM POWER AGAIN.
OHHH! OF COURSE!
YOU'RE SLOW ON THE UPTAKE, HUH...
TURN
WELL THEN I'LL BRING ODAGIRI HERE AFTER SCHOOL.
THEN, YOU'LL KISS HER AGAIN.
SOUND GOOD?

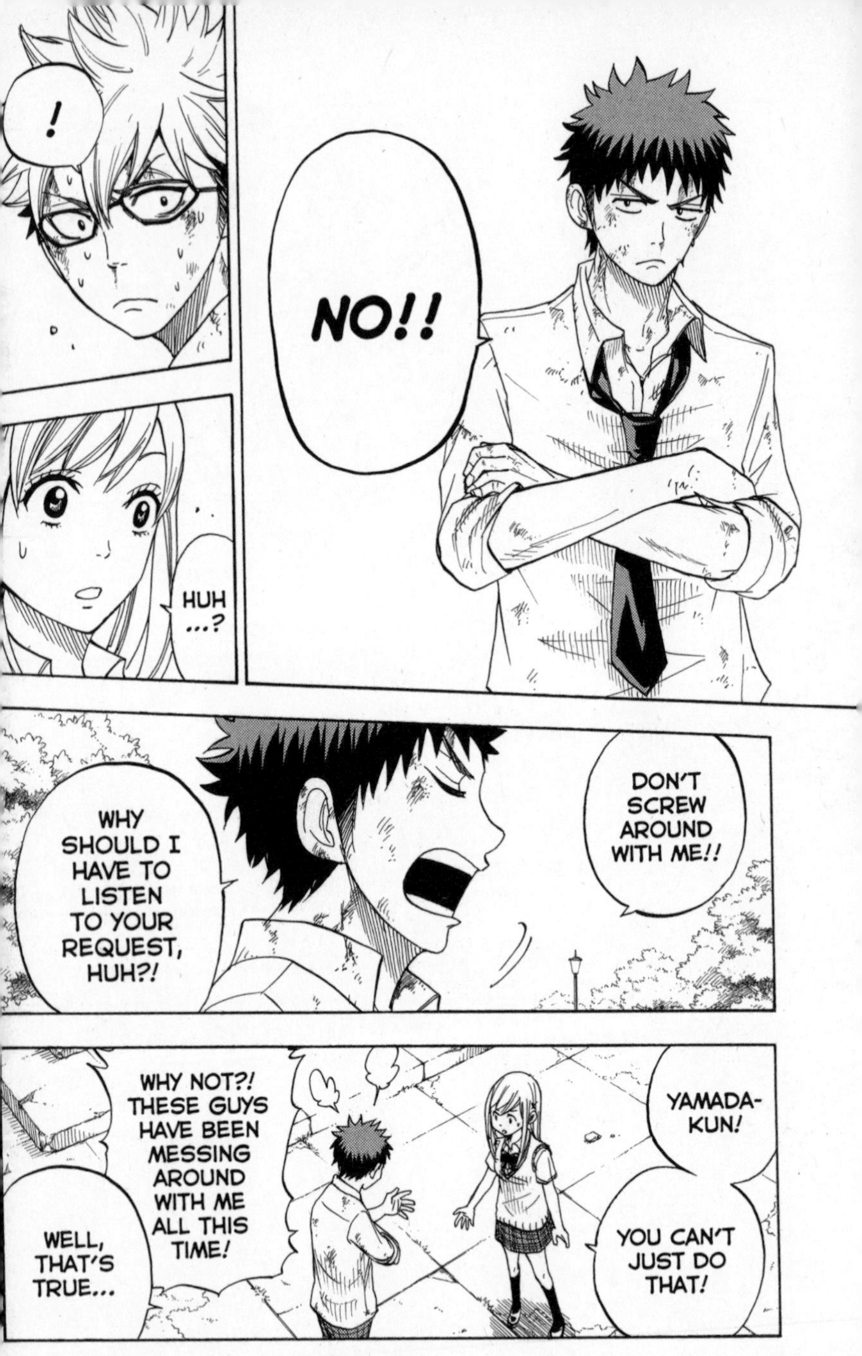
NO!!
!
HUH ...?
DON'T SCREW AROUND WITH ME!!
WHY SHOULD I HAVE TO LISTEN TO YOUR REQUEST, HUH?!
YAMADA-KUN!
YOU CAN'T JUST DO THAT!
WHY NOT?! THESE GUYS HAVE BEEN MESSING AROUND WITH ME ALL THIS TIME!
WELL, THAT'S TRUE...

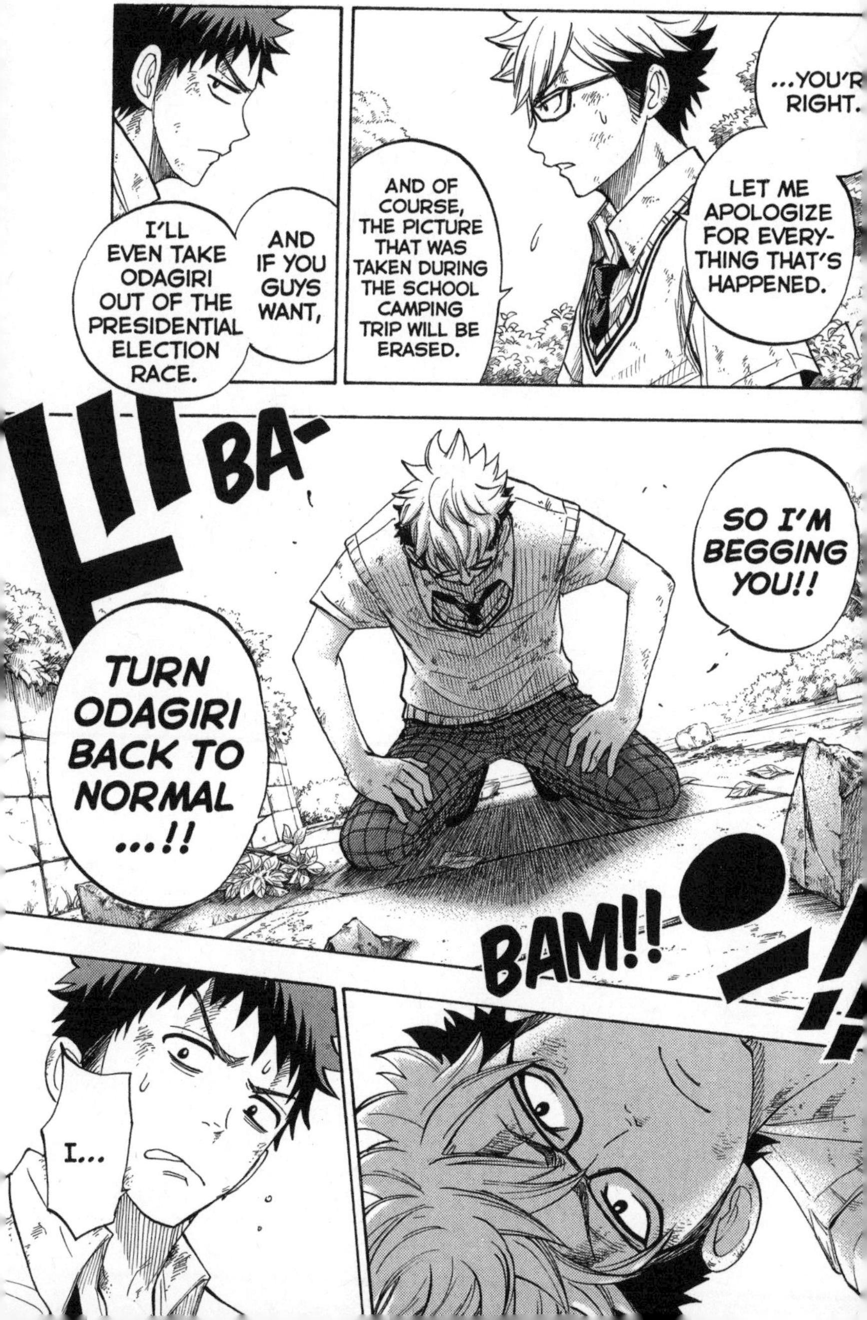
...YOU'R RIGHT.
LET ME APOLOGIZE FOR EVERYTHING THAT'S HAPPENED.
AND OF COURSE, THE PICTURE THAT WAS TAKEN DURING THE SCHOOL CAMPING TRIP WILL BE ERASED.
AND IF YOU GUYS WANT,
I'LL EVEN TAKE ODAGIRI OUT OF THE PRESIDENTIAL ELECTION RACE.
BA-
SO I'M BEGGING YOU!!
TURN ODAGIRI BACK TO NORMAL ...!!
BAM!!
I...

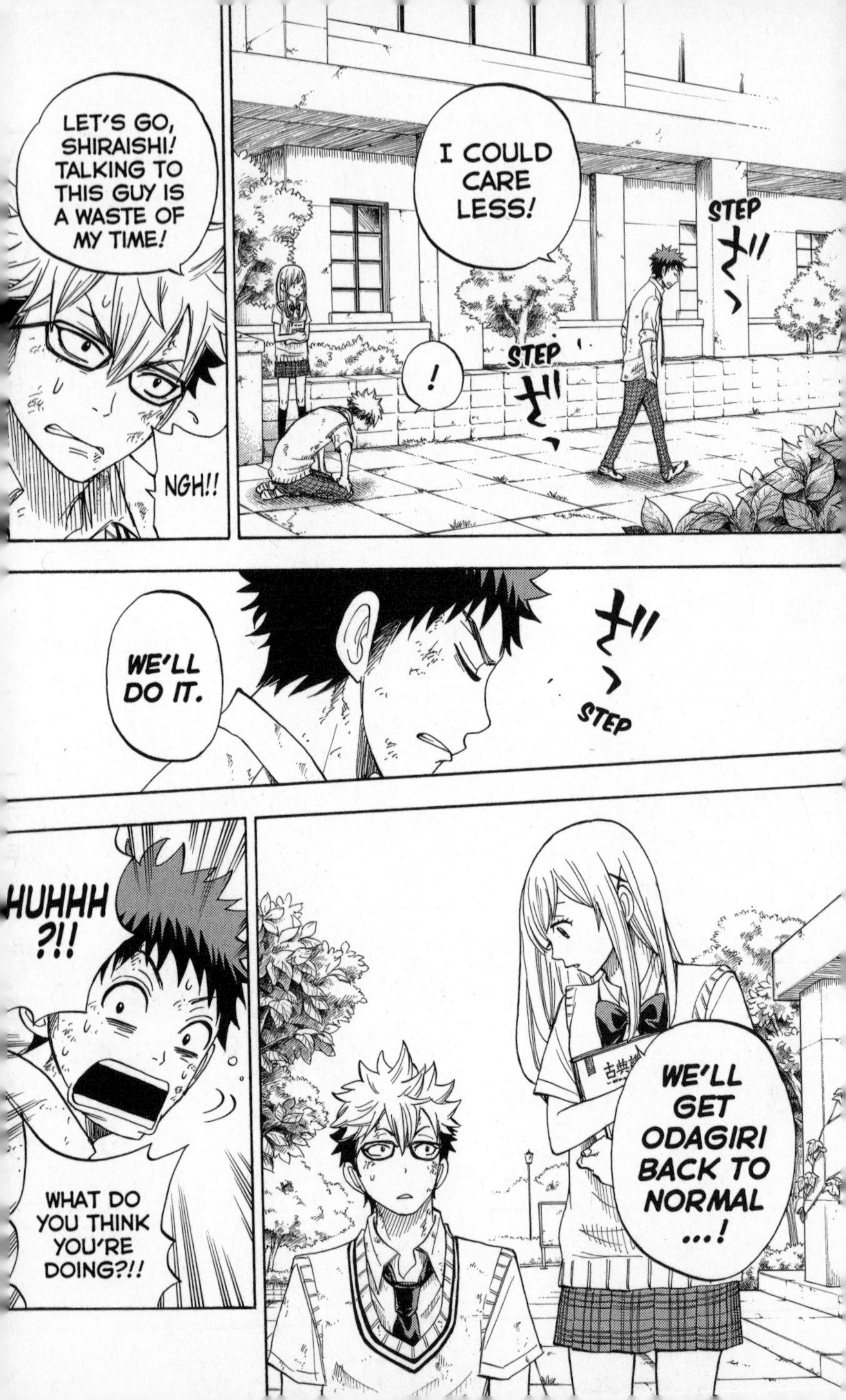
STEP
I COULD CARE LESS!
STEP
!
LET'S GO, SHIRAISHI! TALKING TO THIS GUY IS A WASTE OF MY TIME!
NGH!!
STEP
WE'LL DO IT.
WE'LL GET ODAGIRI BACK TO NORMAL ...!
HUHHH ?!!
WHAT DO YOU THINK YOU'RE DOING?!!

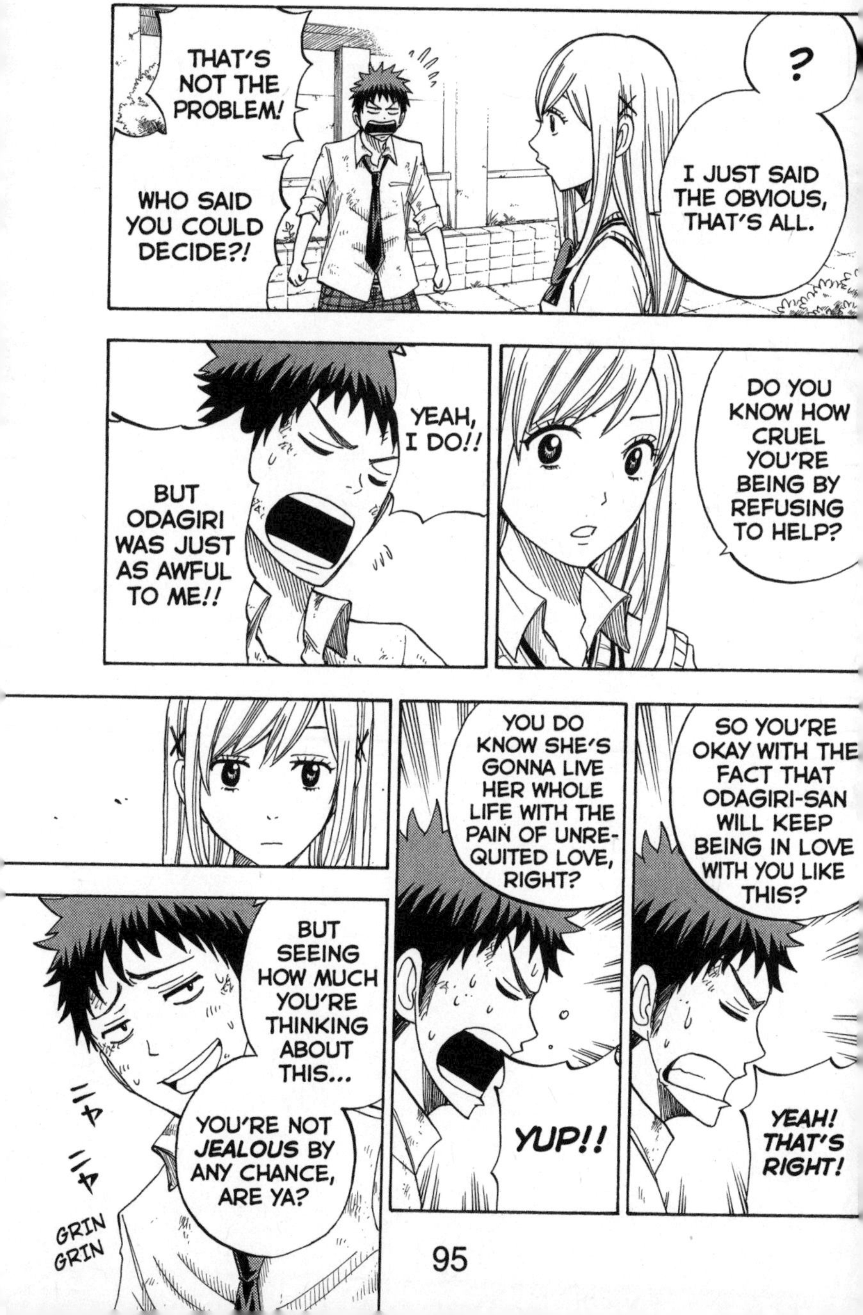
?
I JUST SAID THE OBVIOUS, THAT'S ALL.
THAT'S NOT THE PROBLEM!
WHO SAID YOU COULD DECIDE?!
DO YOU KNOW HOW CRUEL YOU'RE BEING BY REFUSING TO HELP?
YEAH, I DO!!
BUT ODAGIRI WAS JUST AS AWFUL TO ME!!
SO YOU'RE OKAY WITH THE FACT THAT ODAGIRI-SAN WILL KEEP BEING IN LOVE WITH YOU LIKE THIS?
YEAH! THAT'S RIGHT!
YOU DO KNOW SHE'S GONNA LIVE HER WHOLE LIFE WITH THE PAIN OF UNRE-QUITED LOVE, RIGHT?
YUP!!
BUT SEEING HOW MUCH YOU'RE THINKING ABOUT THIS...
YOU'RE NOT *JEALOUS* BY ANY CHANCE, ARE YA?
ニヤ ニヤ
GRIN GRIN

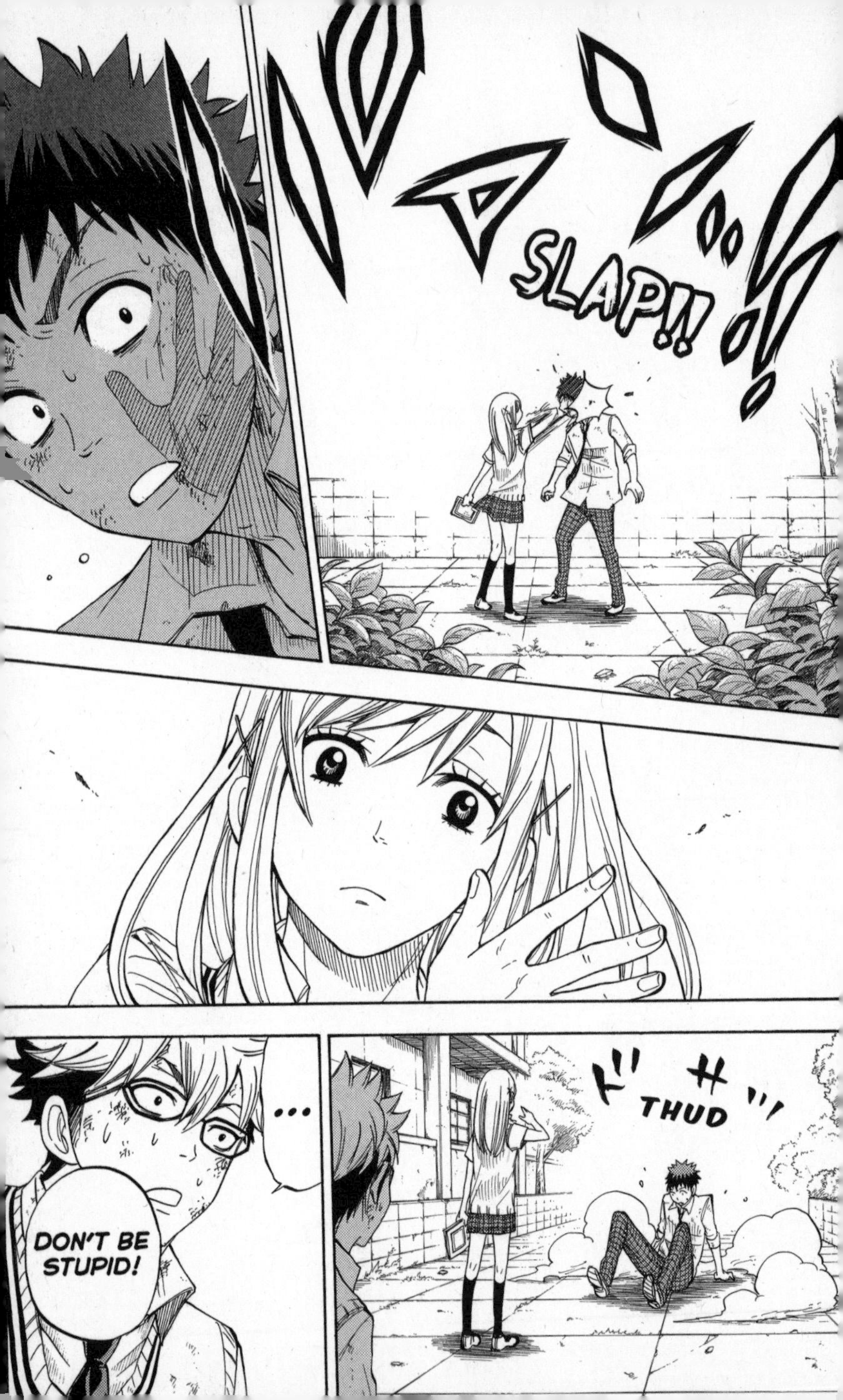
SLAP!!
THUD
...
DON'T BE STUPID!

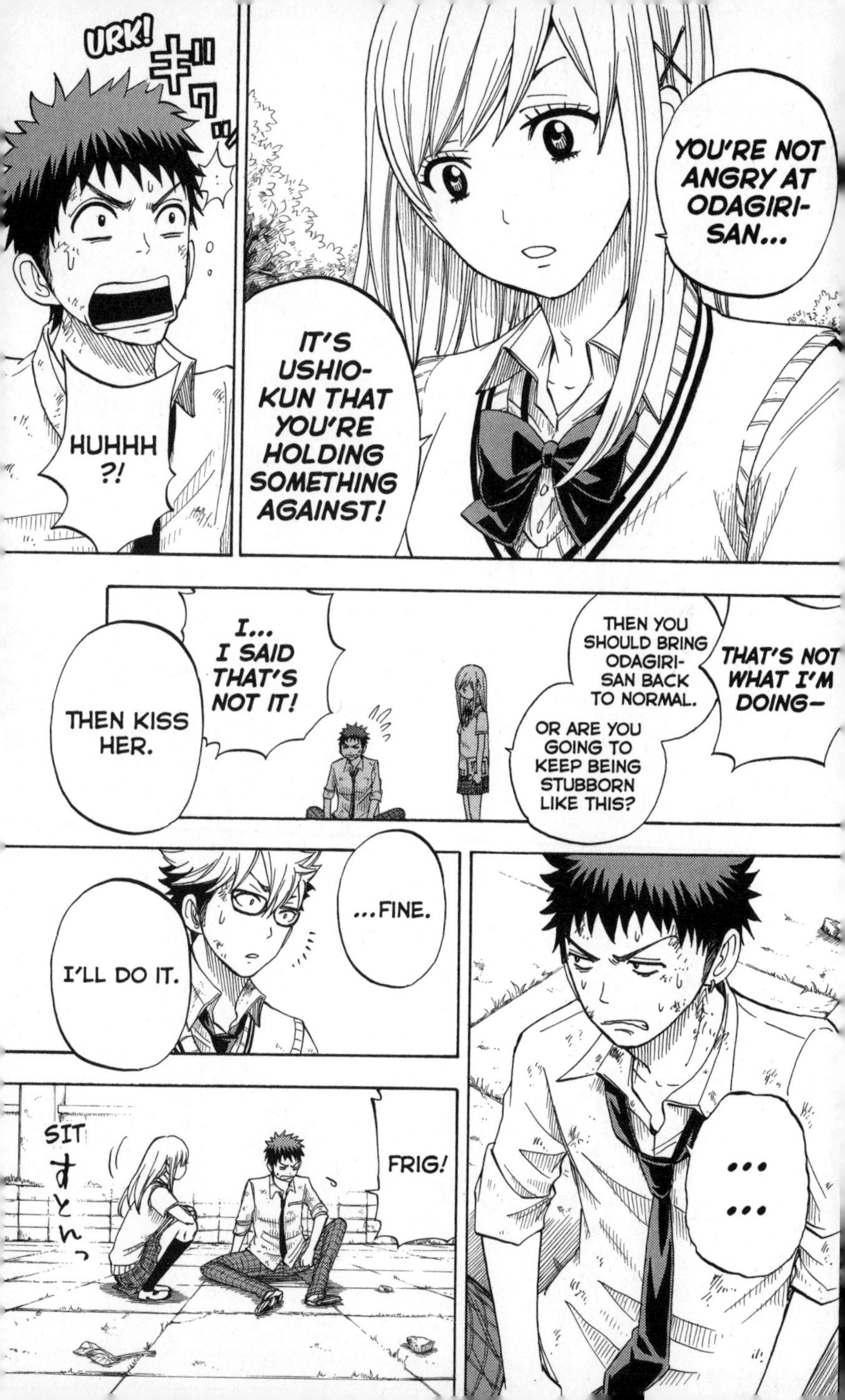
YOU'RE NOT ANGRY AT ODAGIRI-SAN...
IT'S USHIO-KUN THAT YOU'RE HOLDING SOMETHING AGAINST!
URK!
ギクッ
HUHHH ?!
THAT'S NOT WHAT I'M DOING—
THEN YOU SHOULD BRING ODAGIRI-SAN BACK TO NORMAL.
OR ARE YOU GOING TO KEEP BEING STUBBORN LIKE THIS?
I... I SAID THAT'S NOT IT!
THEN KISS HER.
... ...
...FINE.
I'LL DO IT.
FRIG!
SIT
すとんっ

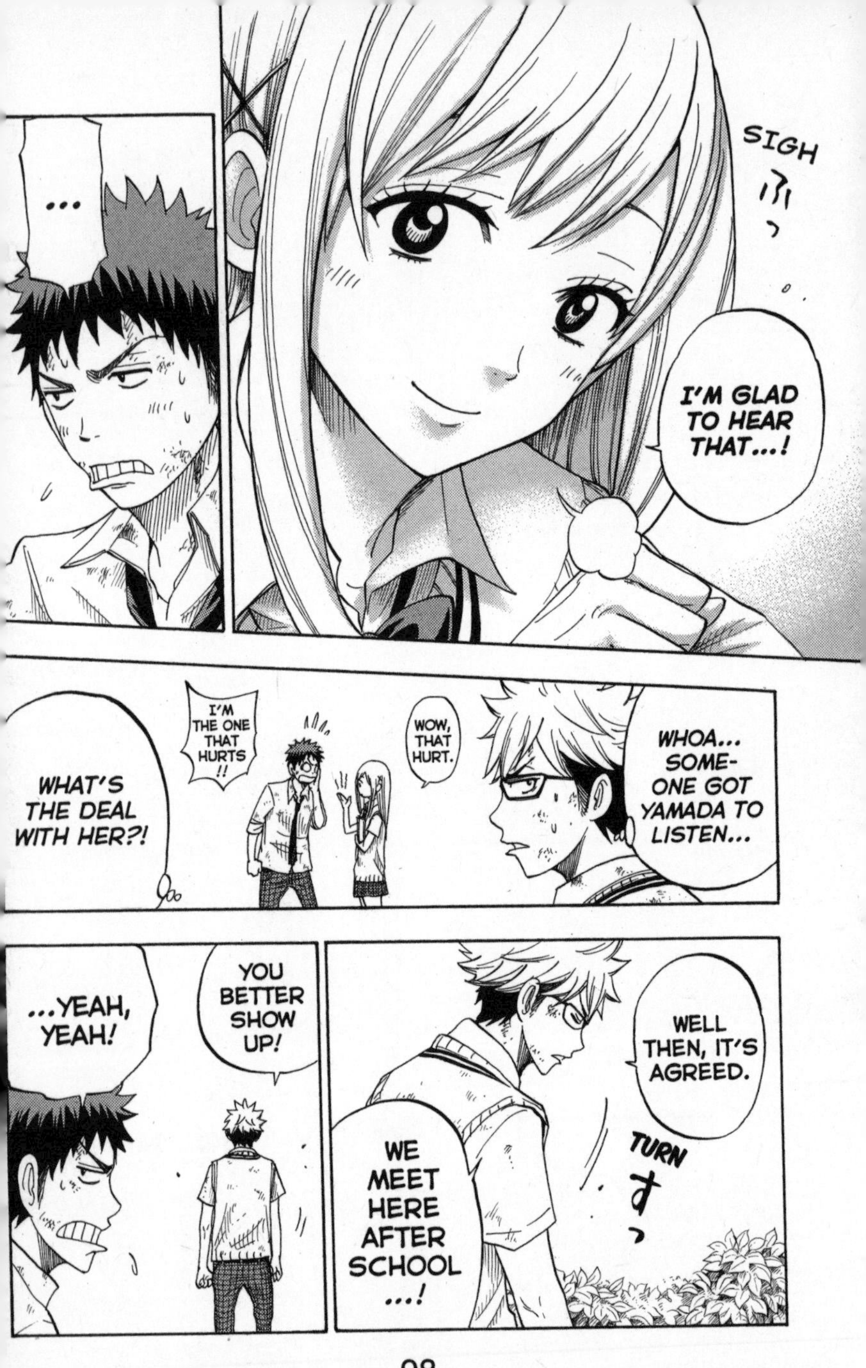
SIGH
ふっ
I'M GLAD TO HEAR THAT...!
...
WHOA... SOME-ONE GOT YAMADA TO LISTEN...
WOW, THAT HURT.
I'M THE ONE THAT HURTS !!
WHAT'S THE DEAL WITH HER?!
WELL THEN, IT'S AGREED.
TURN
すっ
WE MEET HERE AFTER SCHOOL ...!
YOU BETTER SHOW UP!
...YEAH, YEAH!

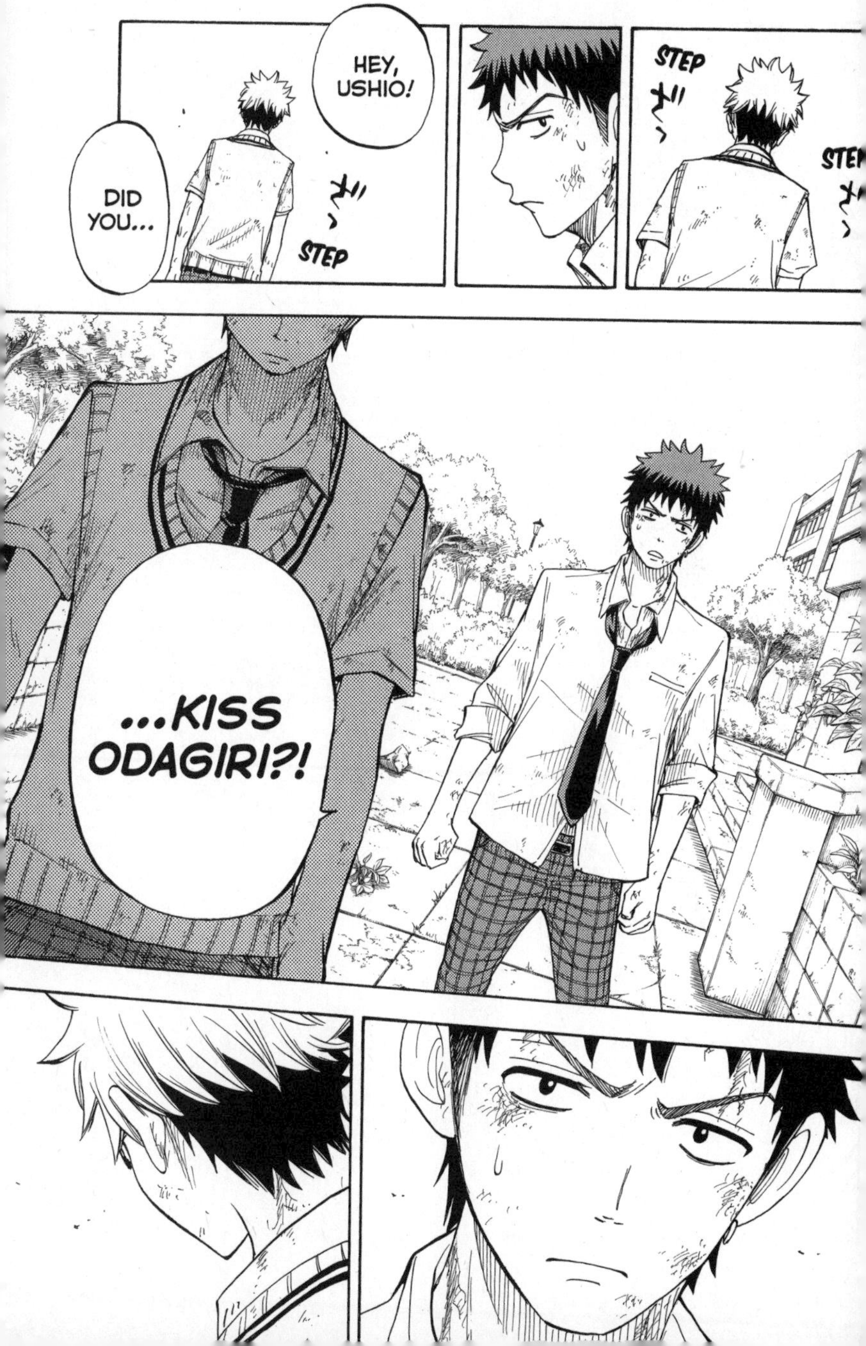
STEP
ざっ
STE
ざっ
HEY, USHIO!
DID YOU...
ざっ
STEP
...KISS ODAGIRI?!

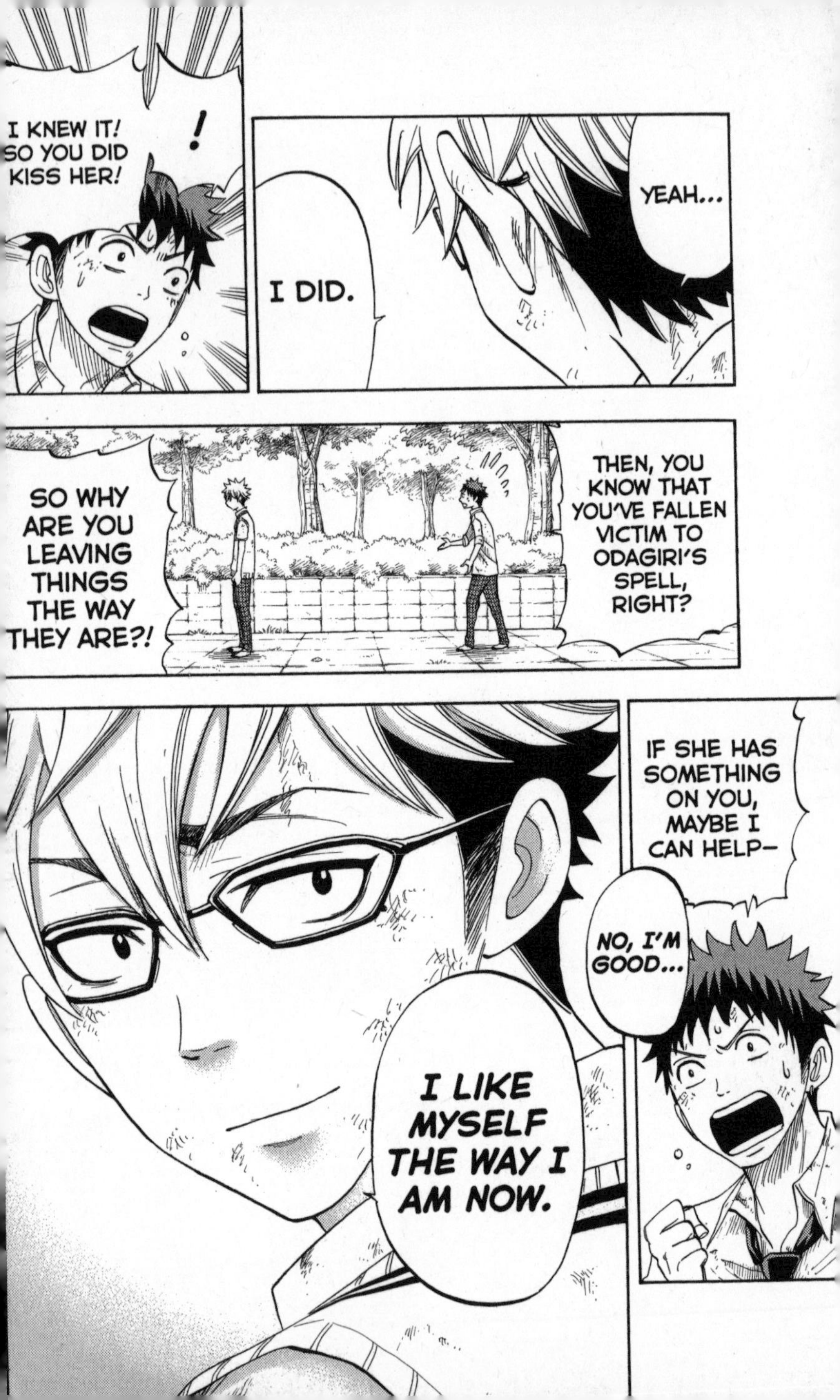
YEAH...
I DID.
!
I KNEW IT! SO YOU DID KISS HER!
THEN, YOU KNOW THAT YOU'VE FALLEN VICTIM TO ODAGIRI'S SPELL, RIGHT?
SO WHY ARE YOU LEAVING THINGS THE WAY THEY ARE?!
IF SHE HAS SOMETHING ON YOU, MAYBE I CAN HELP–
NO, I'M GOOD...
I LIKE MYSELF THE WAY I AM NOW.

STEP

I'M SORRY.

HUHHH?!! WHAT'S THAT SUPPOSED TO MEAN ?!!

WELL...

RAWR

WHO WOULD'VE THOUGHT YOU HAD FRIENDS AT THIS SCHOOL ...?

WASN'T EXPECT-ING THAT.

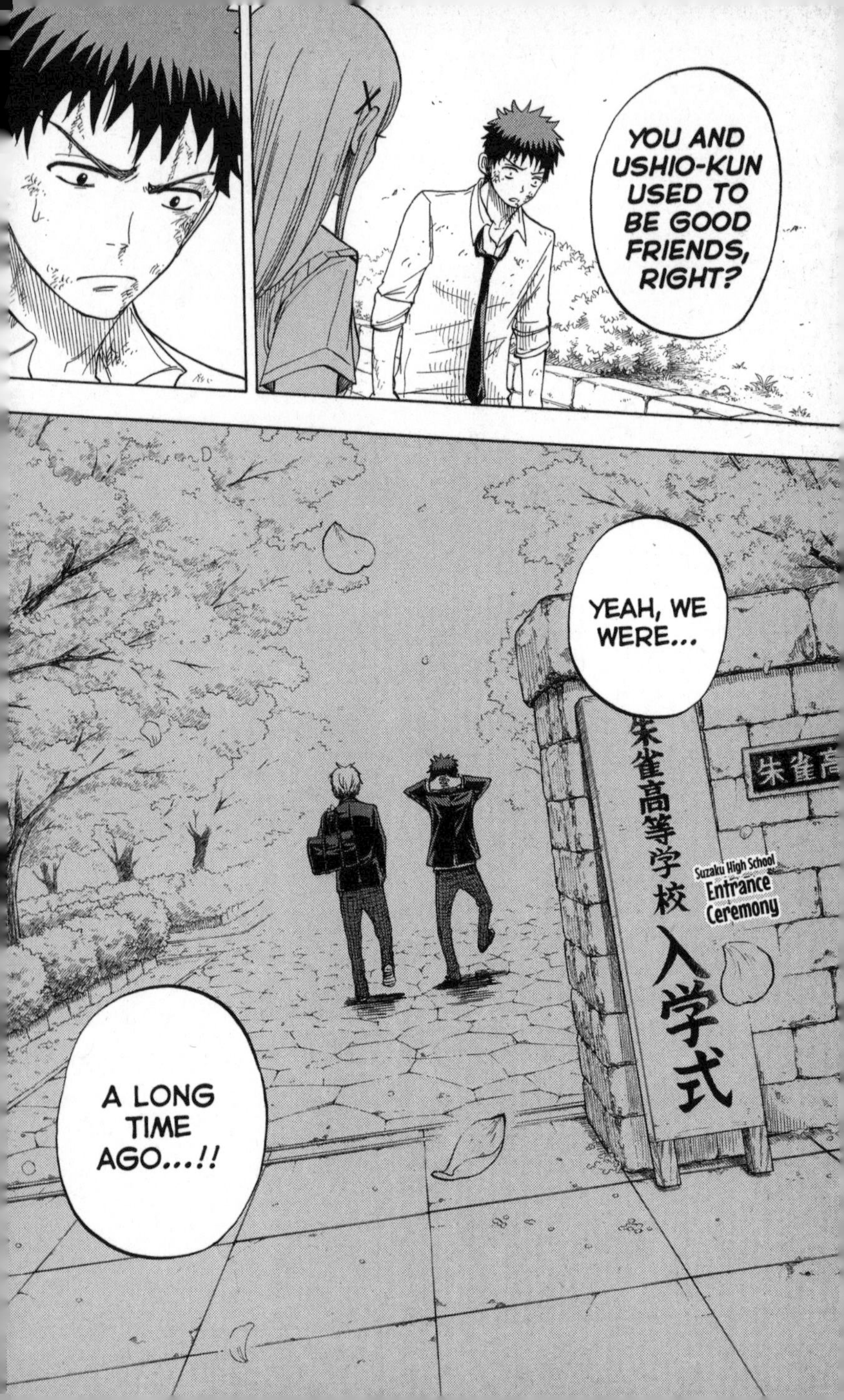
YOU AND USHIO-KUN USED TO BE GOOD FRIENDS, RIGHT?
YEAH, WE WERE...
朱雀高等学校 入学式
Suzaku High School Entrance Ceremony
A LONG TIME AGO...!!

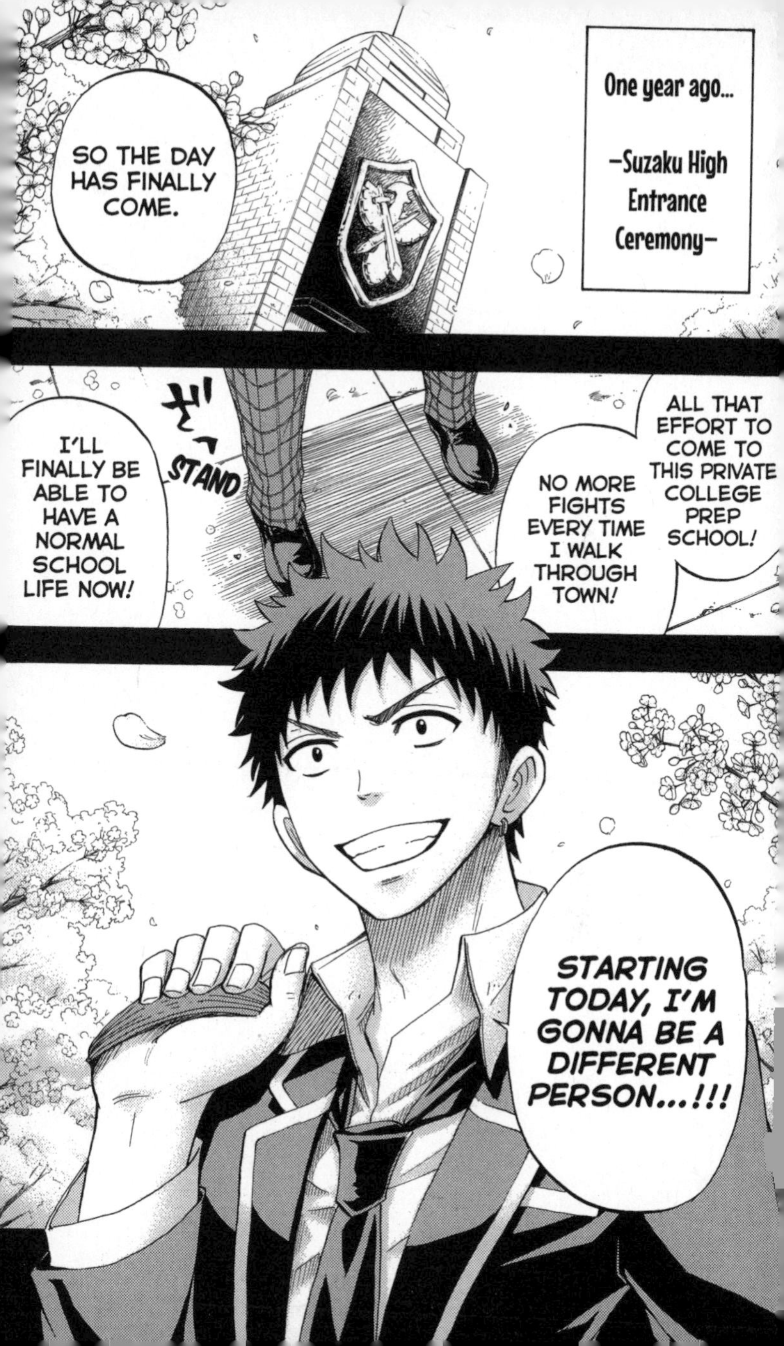
One year ago...
—Suzaku High Entrance Ceremony—
SO THE DAY HAS FINALLY COME.
ALL THAT EFFORT TO COME TO THIS PRIVATE COLLEGE PREP SCHOOL!
NO MORE FIGHTS EVERY TIME I WALK THROUGH TOWN!
STAND
I'LL FINALLY BE ABLE TO HAVE A NORMAL SCHOOL LIFE NOW!
STARTING TODAY, I'M GONNA BE A DIFFERENT PERSON...!!!

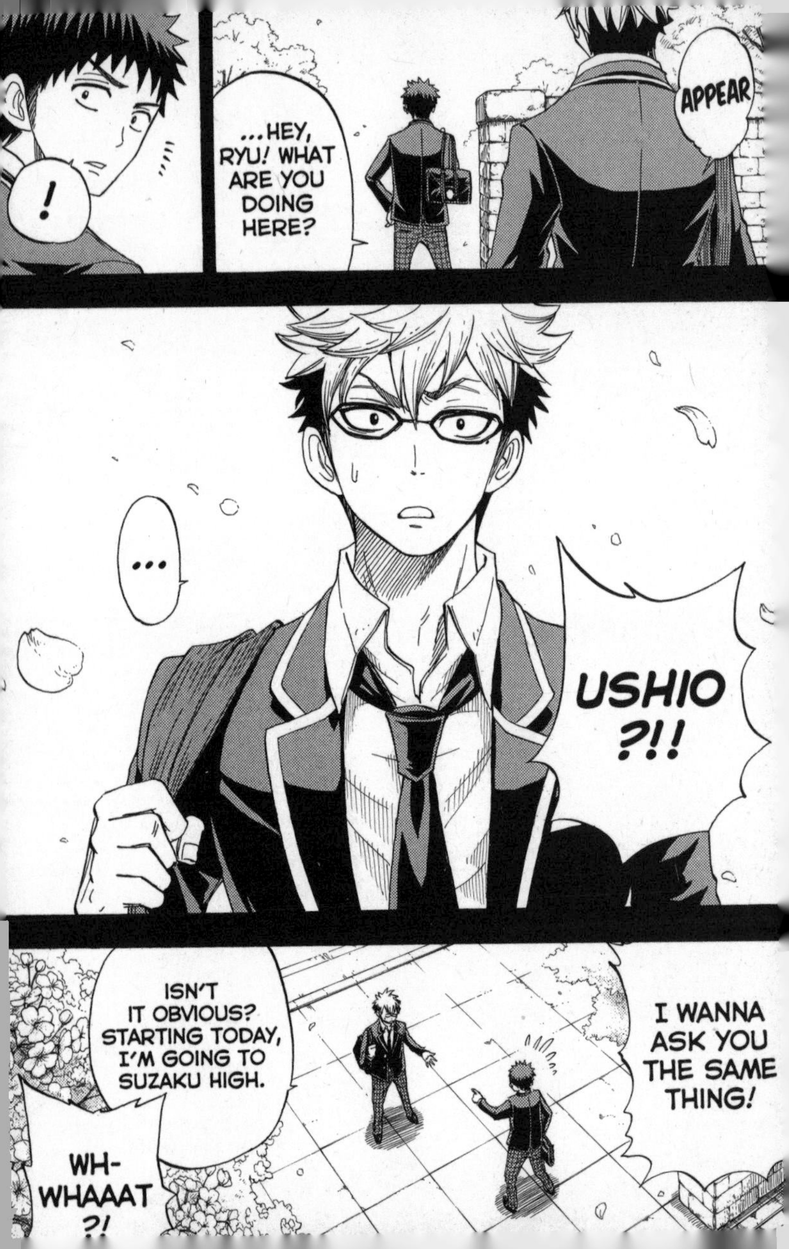
APPEAR
...HEY, RYU! WHAT ARE YOU DOING HERE?
!
USHIO ?!!
...
I WANNA ASK YOU THE SAME THING!
ISN'T IT OBVIOUS? STARTING TODAY, I'M GOING TO SUZAKU HIGH.
WH-WHAAAT ?!

CHAPTER 22: Such a tragedy.

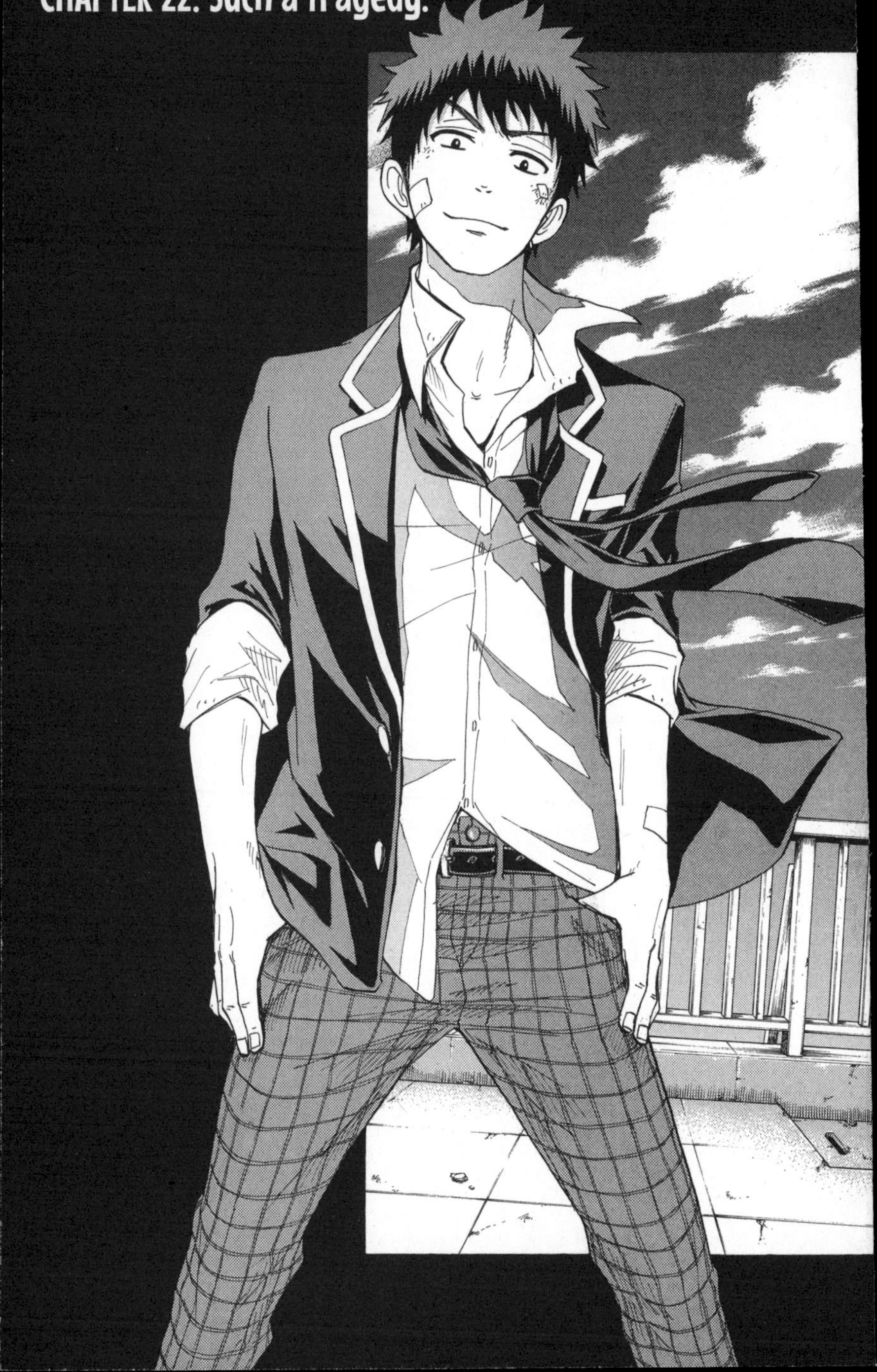

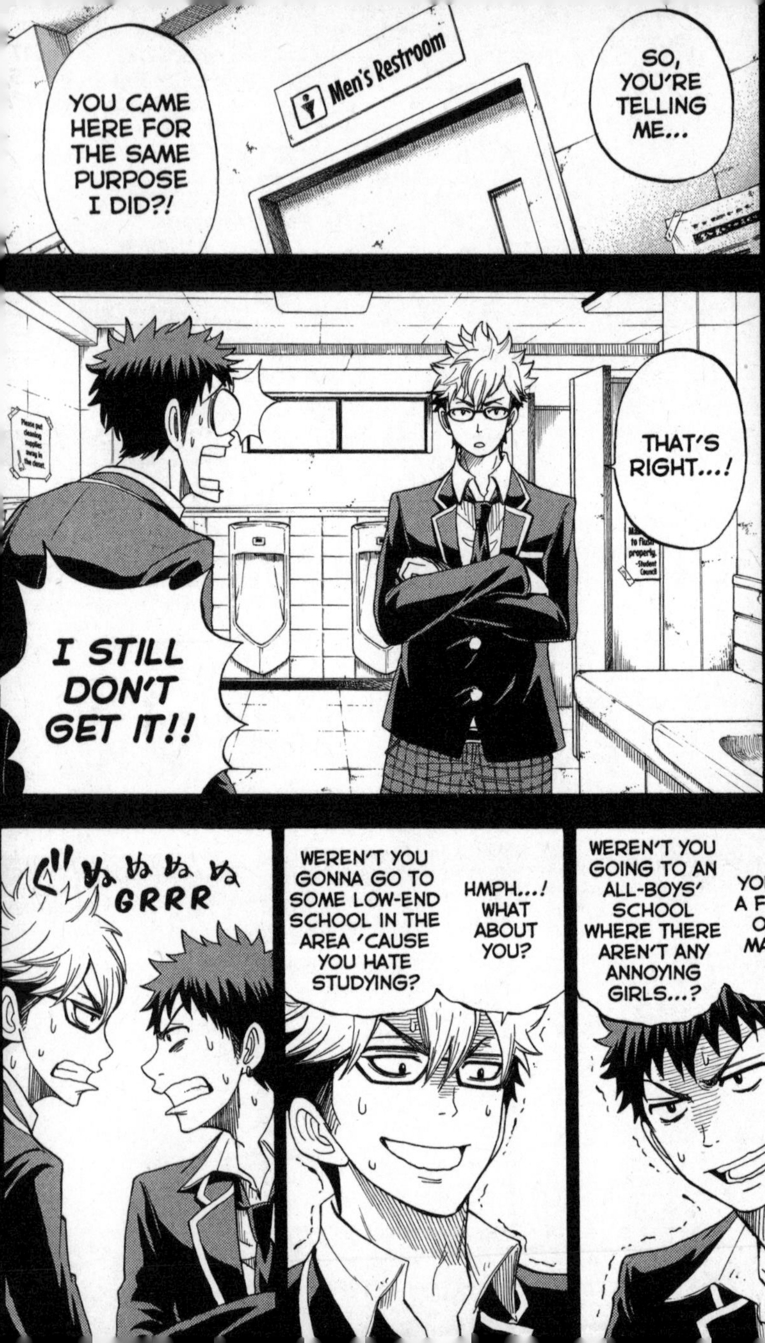
Men's Restroom
SO, YOU'RE TELLING ME...
YOU CAME HERE FOR THE SAME PURPOSE I DID?!
THAT'S RIGHT...!
I STILL DON'T GET IT!!
YOU'RE A FUNNY ONE, MAN...
WEREN'T YOU GOING TO AN ALL-BOYS' SCHOOL WHERE THERE AREN'T ANY ANNOYING GIRLS...?
HMPH...! WHAT ABOUT YOU?
WEREN'T YOU GONNA GO TO SOME LOW-END SCHOOL IN THE AREA 'CAUSE YOU HATE STUDYING?
ぐぬぬぬぬ
GRRR

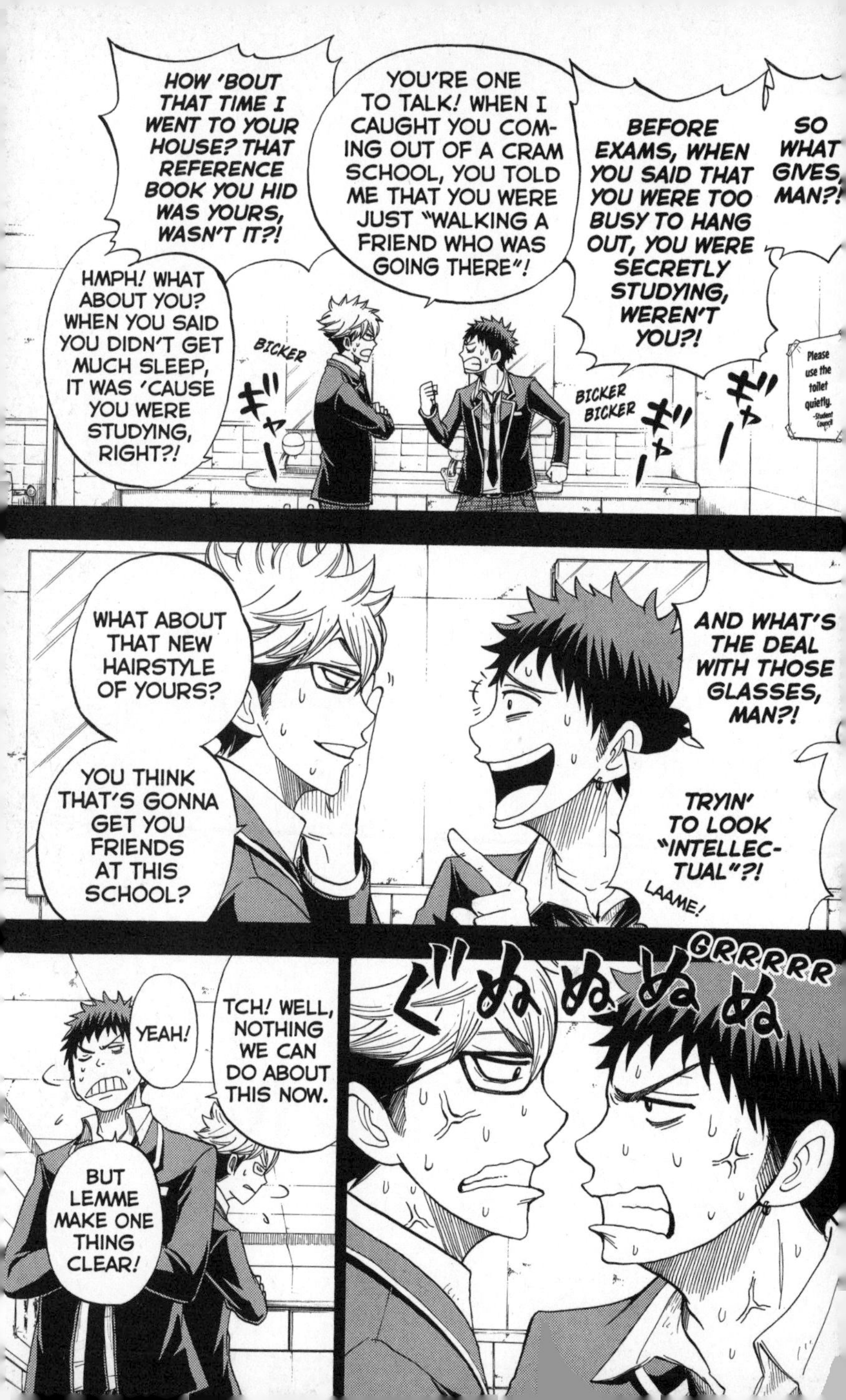
SO WHAT GIVES, MAN?!
BEFORE EXAMS, WHEN YOU SAID THAT YOU WERE TOO BUSY TO HANG OUT, YOU WERE SECRETLY STUDYING, WEREN'T YOU?!
ギャー
BICKER BICKER
ギャー
Please use the toilet quietly. -Student Council
YOU'RE ONE TO TALK! WHEN I CAUGHT YOU COMING OUT OF A CRAM SCHOOL, YOU TOLD ME THAT YOU WERE JUST "WALKING A FRIEND WHO WAS GOING THERE"!
HOW 'BOUT THAT TIME I WENT TO YOUR HOUSE? THAT REFERENCE BOOK YOU HID WAS YOURS, WASN'T IT?!
BICKER
ギャー
HMPH! WHAT ABOUT YOU? WHEN YOU SAID YOU DIDN'T GET MUCH SLEEP, IT WAS 'CAUSE YOU WERE STUDYING, RIGHT?!
AND WHAT'S THE DEAL WITH THOSE GLASSES, MAN?!
TRYIN' TO LOOK "INTELLECTUAL"?!
LAAME!
WHAT ABOUT THAT NEW HAIRSTYLE OF YOURS?
YOU THINK THAT'S GONNA GET YOU FRIENDS AT THIS SCHOOL?
GRRRRRR
ぐぬぬぬぬ
TCH! WELL, NOTHING WE CAN DO ABOUT THIS NOW.
YEAH!
BUT LEMME MAKE ONE THING CLEAR!

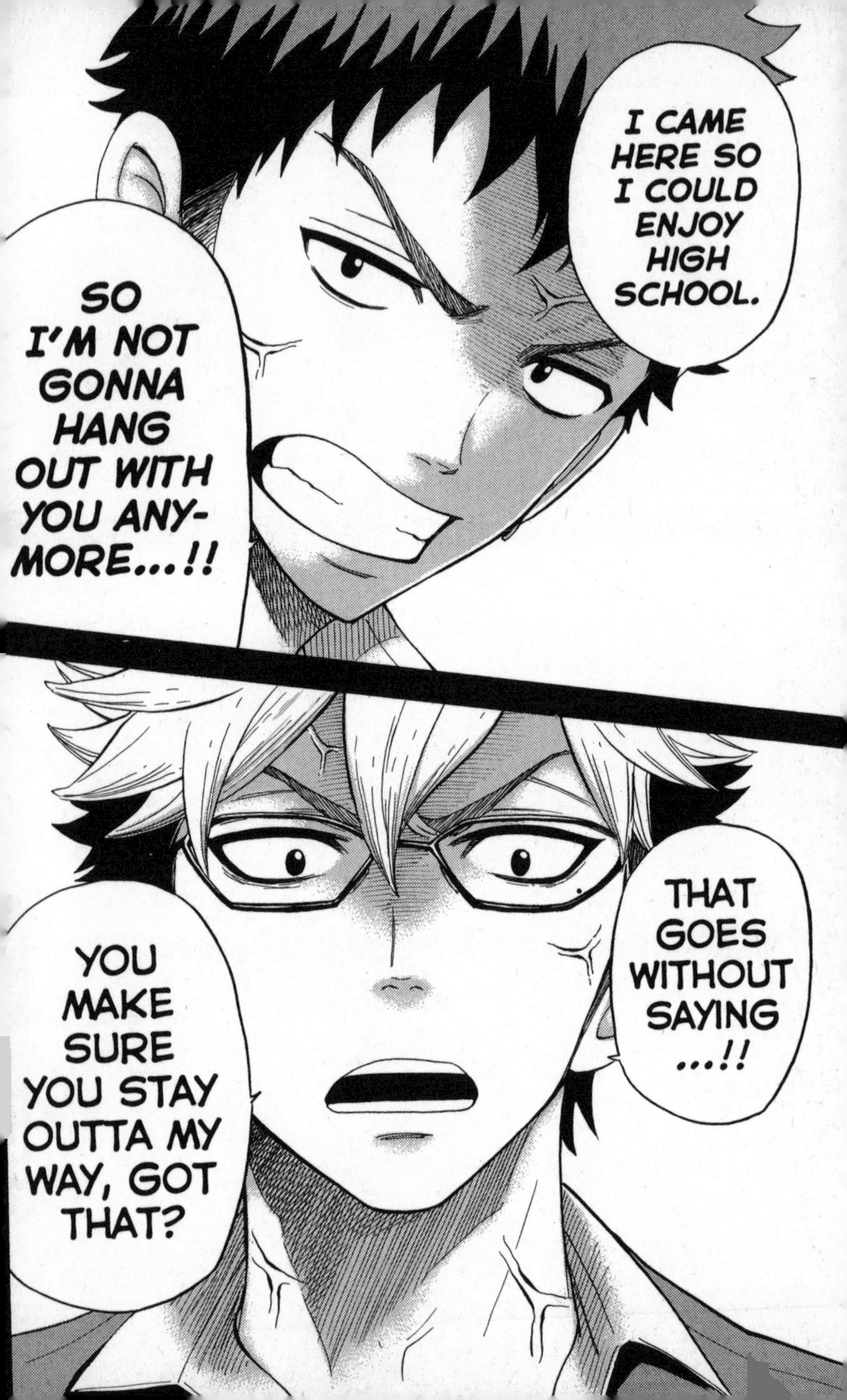
I CAME HERE SO I COULD ENJOY HIGH SCHOOL.
SO I'M NOT GONNA HANG OUT WITH YOU ANY-MORE...!!
THAT GOES WITHOUT SAYING ...!!
YOU MAKE SURE YOU STAY OUTTA MY WAY, GOT THAT?

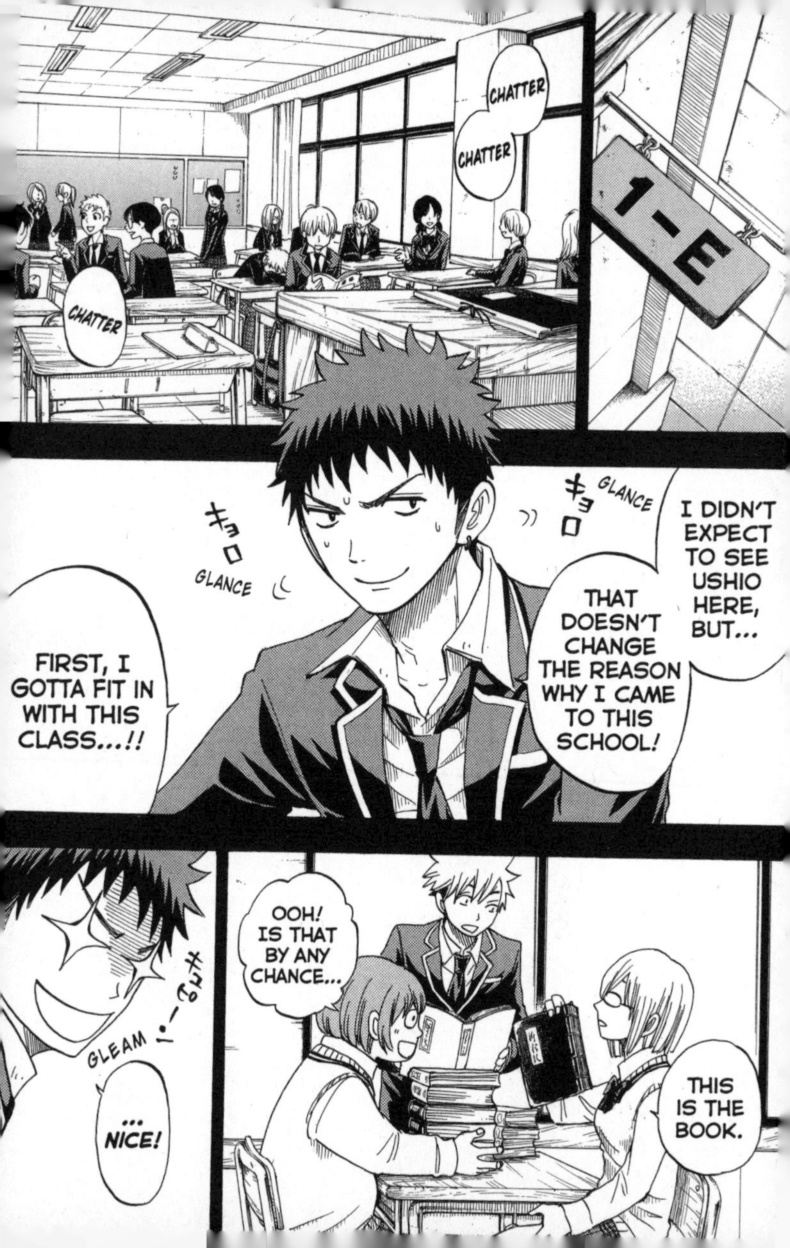
1-E
CHATTER
CHATTER
CHATTER
I DIDN'T EXPECT TO SEE USHIO HERE, BUT...
THAT DOESN'T CHANGE THE REASON WHY I CAME TO THIS SCHOOL!
キョロ
GLANCE
キョロ
GLANCE
FIRST, I GOTTA FIT IN WITH THIS CLASS...!!
THIS IS THE BOOK.
OOH! IS THAT BY ANY CHANCE...
キラーン!
GLEAM
...NICE!

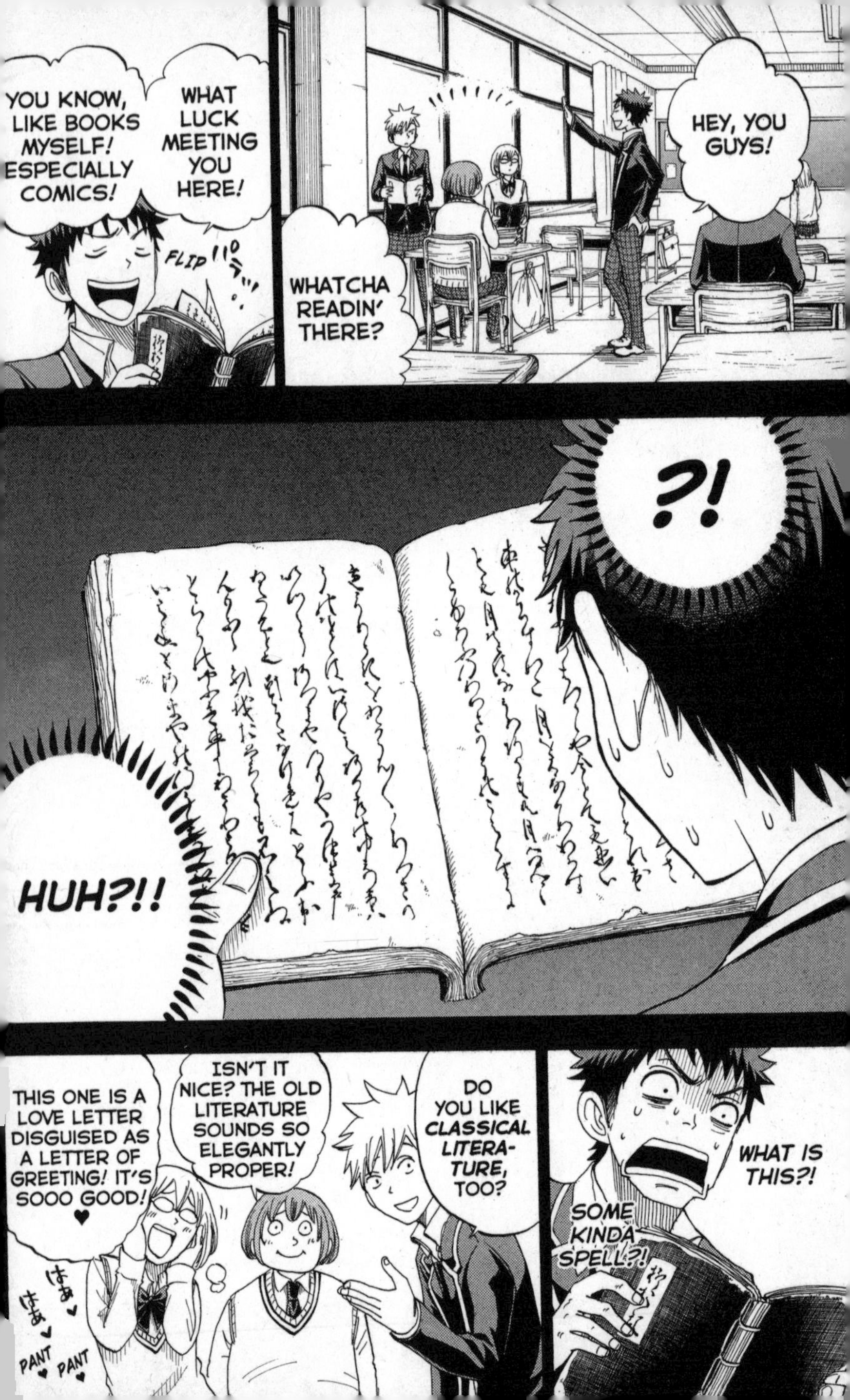
HEY, YOU GUYS!
WHATCHA READIN' THERE?
WHAT LUCK MEETING YOU HERE!
YOU KNOW, LIKE BOOKS MYSELF! ESPECIALLY COMICS!
FLIP
?!
HUH?!!
WHAT IS THIS?!
SOME KINDA SPELL?!
DO YOU LIKE CLASSICAL LITERA-TURE, TOO?
ISN'T IT NICE? THE OLD LITERATURE SOUNDS SO ELEGANTLY PROPER!
THIS ONE IS A LOVE LETTER DISGUISED AS A LETTER OF GREETING! IT'S SOOO GOOD! ♥
はあ♥ はあ♥
PANT♥ PANT♥

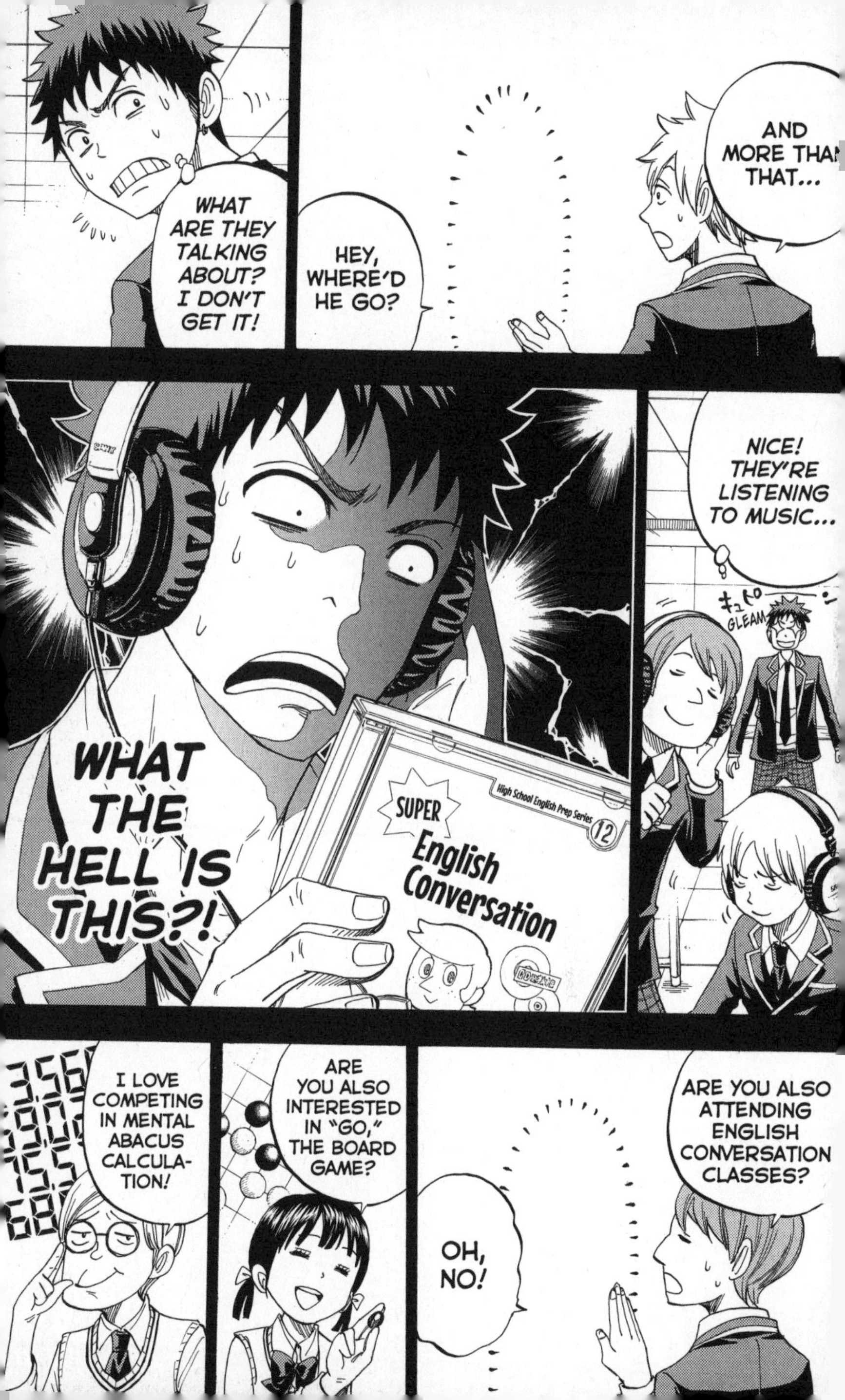

AND MORE THAN THAT...
HEY, WHERE'D HE GO?
WHAT ARE THEY TALKING ABOUT? I DON'T GET IT!
NICE! THEY'RE LISTENING TO MUSIC...
GLEAM
High School English Prep Series 12
SUPER English Conversation
WHAT THE HELL IS THIS?!
ARE YOU ALSO ATTENDING ENGLISH CONVERSATION CLASSES?
OH, NO!
ARE YOU ALSO INTERESTED IN "GO," THE BOARD GAME?
I LOVE COMPETING IN MENTAL ABACUS CALCULATION!

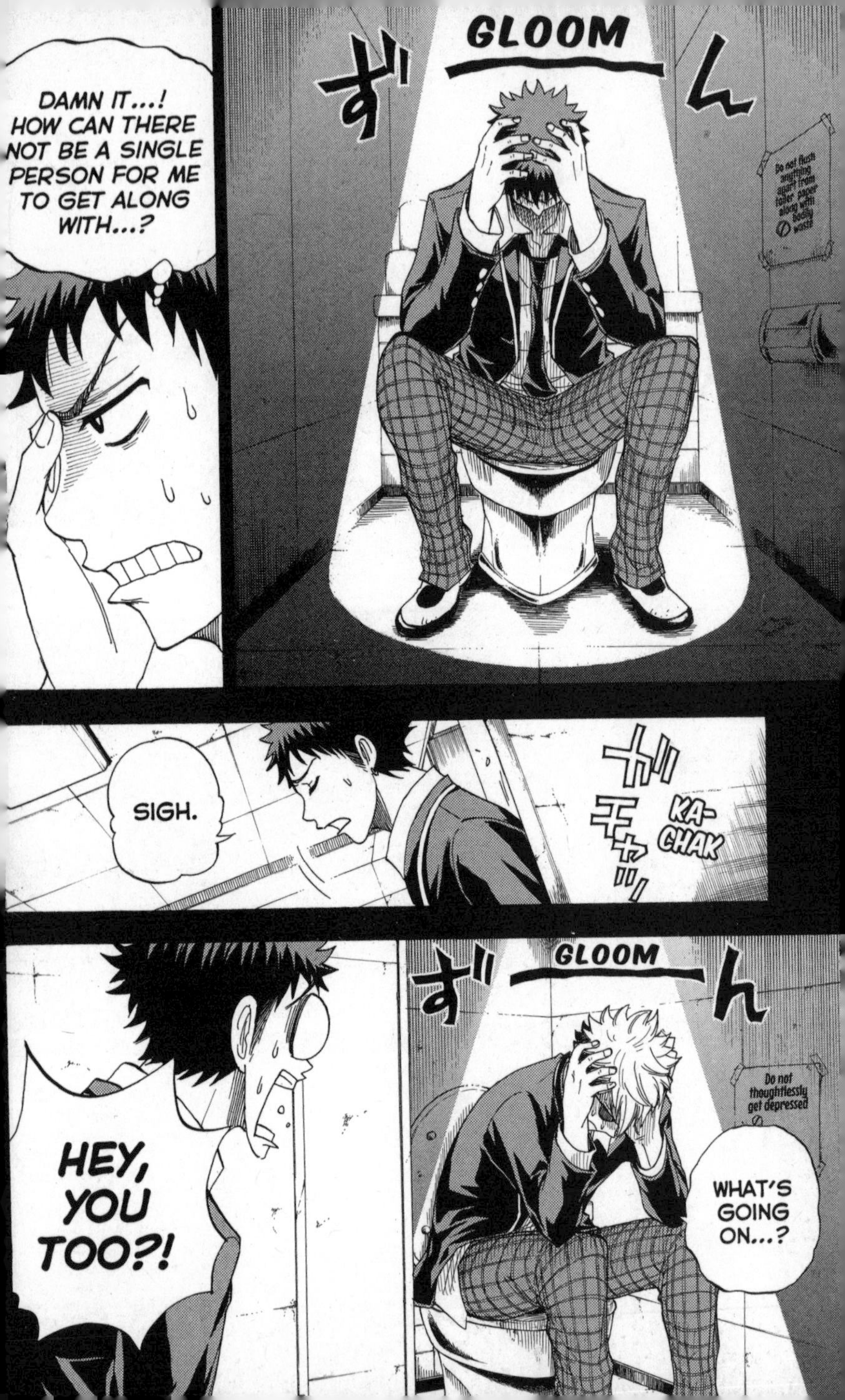
GLOOM
Do not flush anything apart from toilet paper along with bodily waste
DAMN IT...! HOW CAN THERE NOT BE A SINGLE PERSON FOR ME TO GET ALONG WITH...?
KA-CHAK
SIGH.
GLOOM
Do not thoughtlessly get depressed
WHAT'S GOING ON...?
HEY, YOU TOO?!

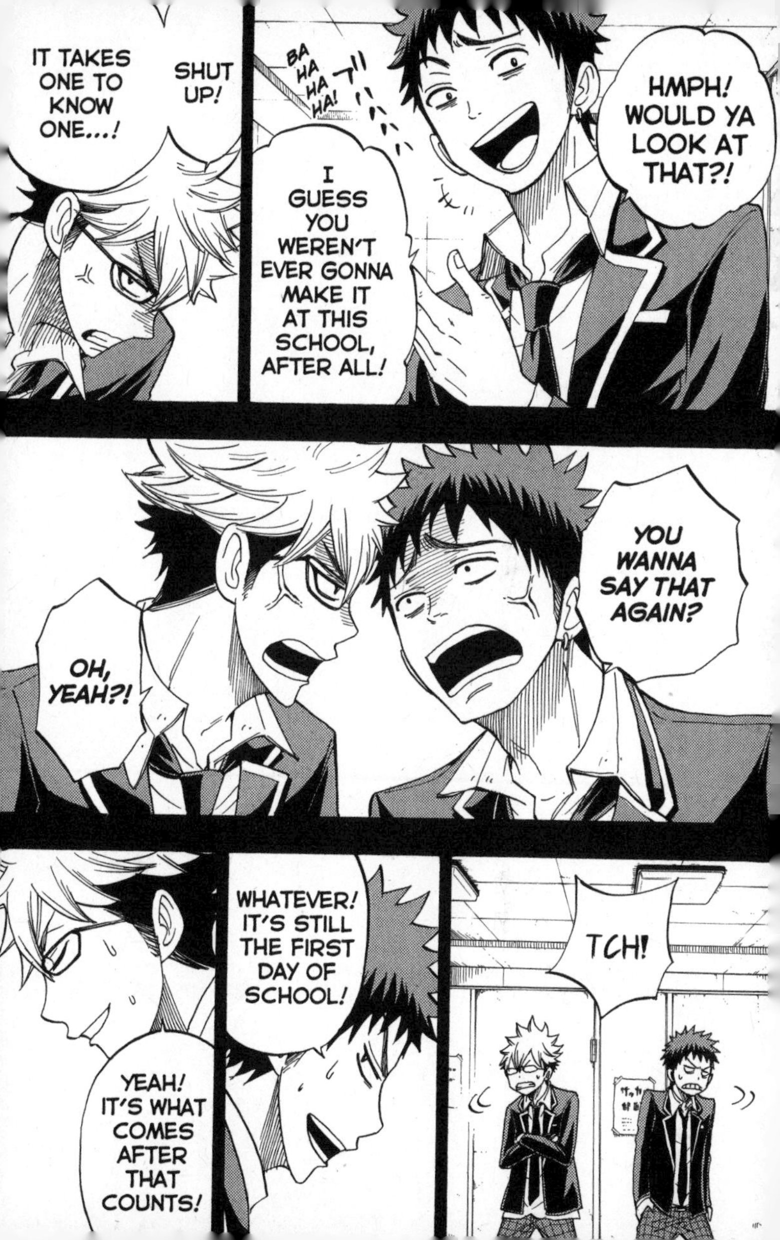
HMPH! WOULD YA LOOK AT THAT?!
BA HA HA HA!
I GUESS YOU WEREN'T EVER GONNA MAKE IT AT THIS SCHOOL, AFTER ALL!
SHUT UP!
IT TAKES ONE TO KNOW ONE...!
YOU WANNA SAY THAT AGAIN?
OH, YEAH?!
TCH!
WHATEVER! IT'S STILL THE FIRST DAY OF SCHOOL!
YEAH! IT'S WHAT COMES AFTER THAT COUNTS!

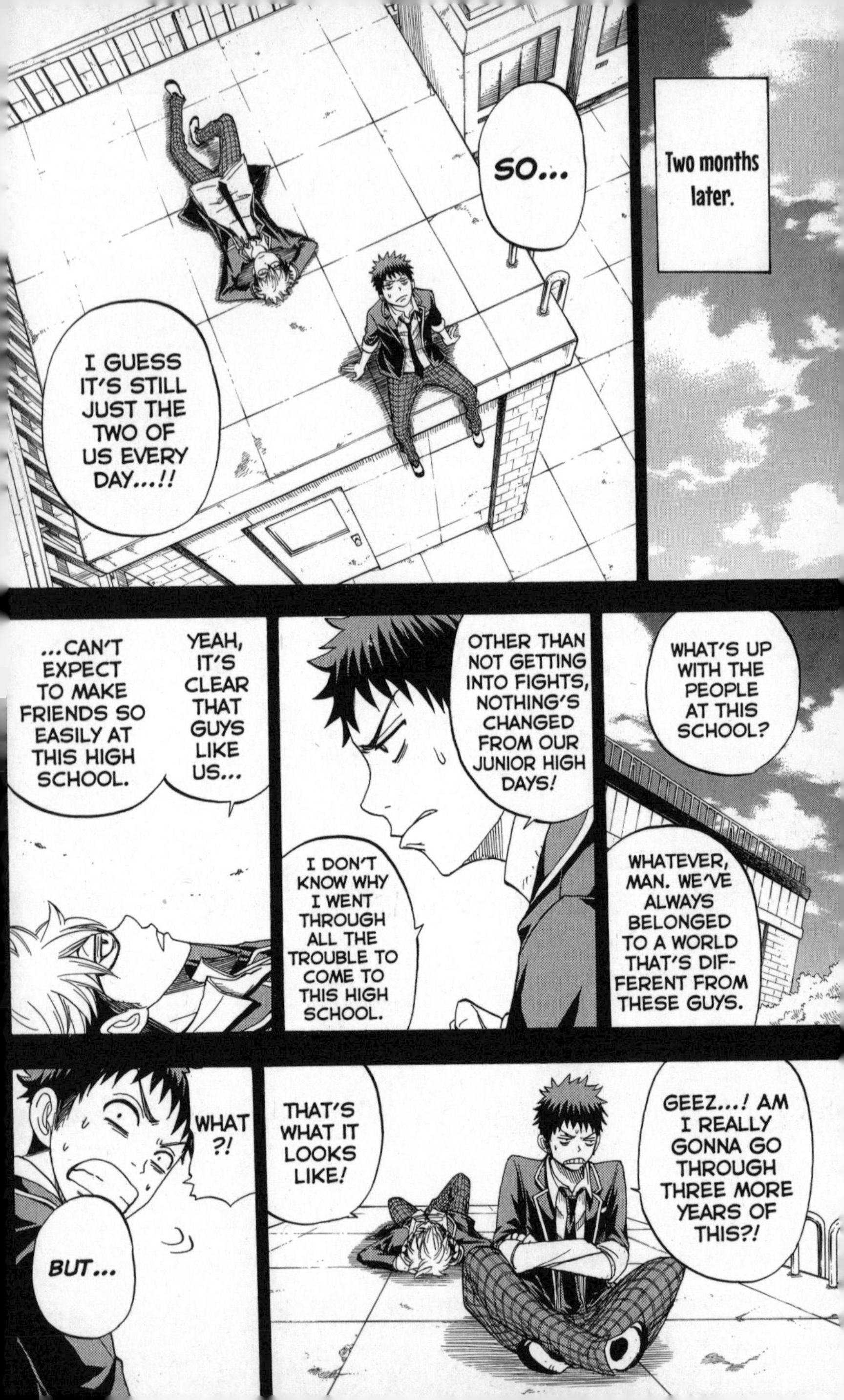
Two months later.
SO...
I GUESS IT'S STILL JUST THE TWO OF US EVERY DAY...!!
WHAT'S UP WITH THE PEOPLE AT THIS SCHOOL?
WHATEVER, MAN. WE'VE ALWAYS BELONGED TO A WORLD THAT'S DIF-FERENT FROM THESE GUYS.
OTHER THAN NOT GETTING INTO FIGHTS, NOTHING'S CHANGED FROM OUR JUNIOR HIGH DAYS!
I DON'T KNOW WHY I WENT THROUGH ALL THE TROUBLE TO COME TO THIS HIGH SCHOOL.
YEAH, IT'S CLEAR THAT GUYS LIKE US...
...CAN'T EXPECT TO MAKE FRIENDS SO EASILY AT THIS HIGH SCHOOL.
GEEZ...! AM I REALLY GONNA GO THROUGH THREE MORE YEARS OF THIS?!
THAT'S WHAT IT LOOKS LIKE!
BUT...
WHAT?!

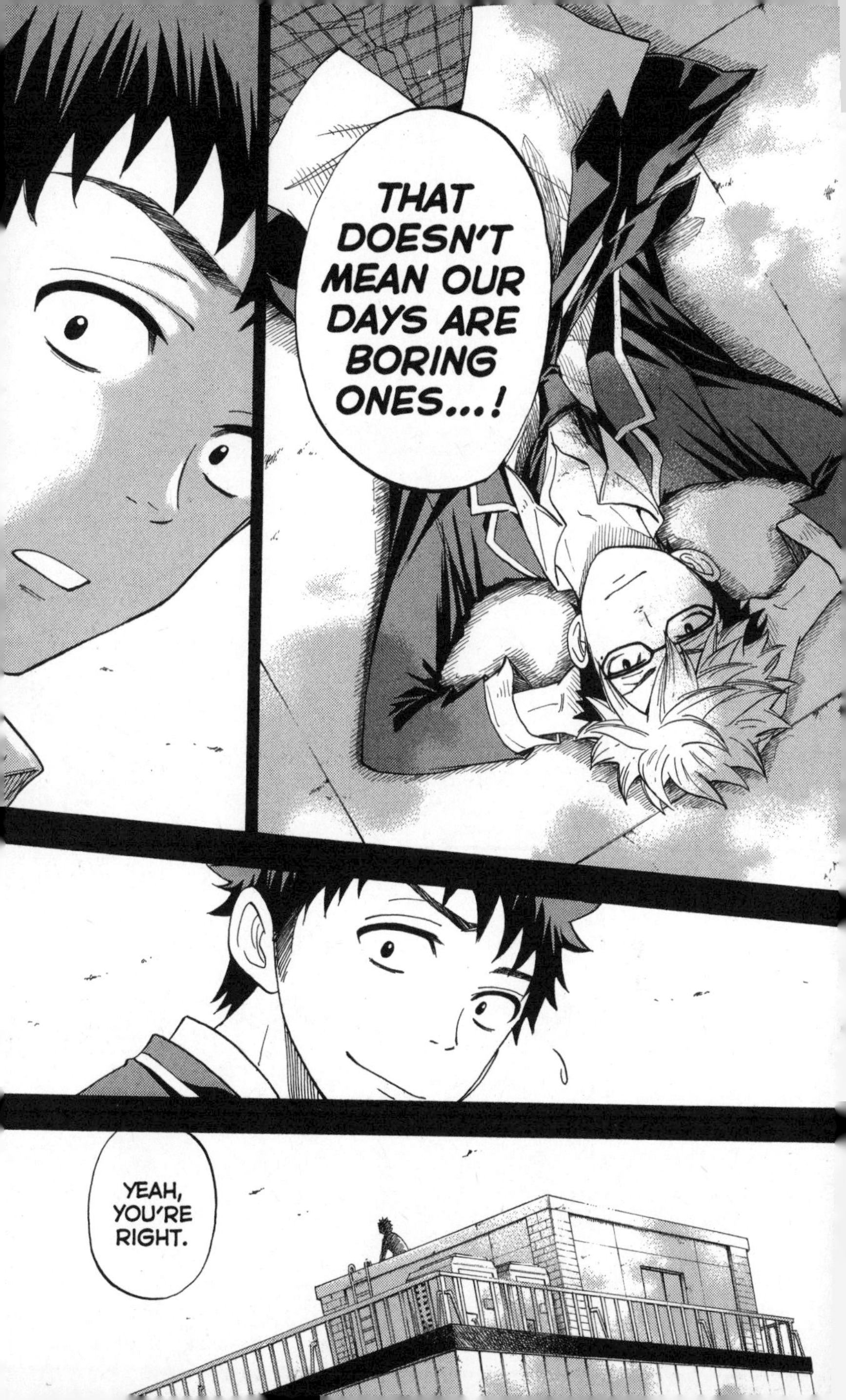
THAT DOESN'T MEAN OUR DAYS ARE BORING ONES...!
YEAH, YOU'RE RIGHT.

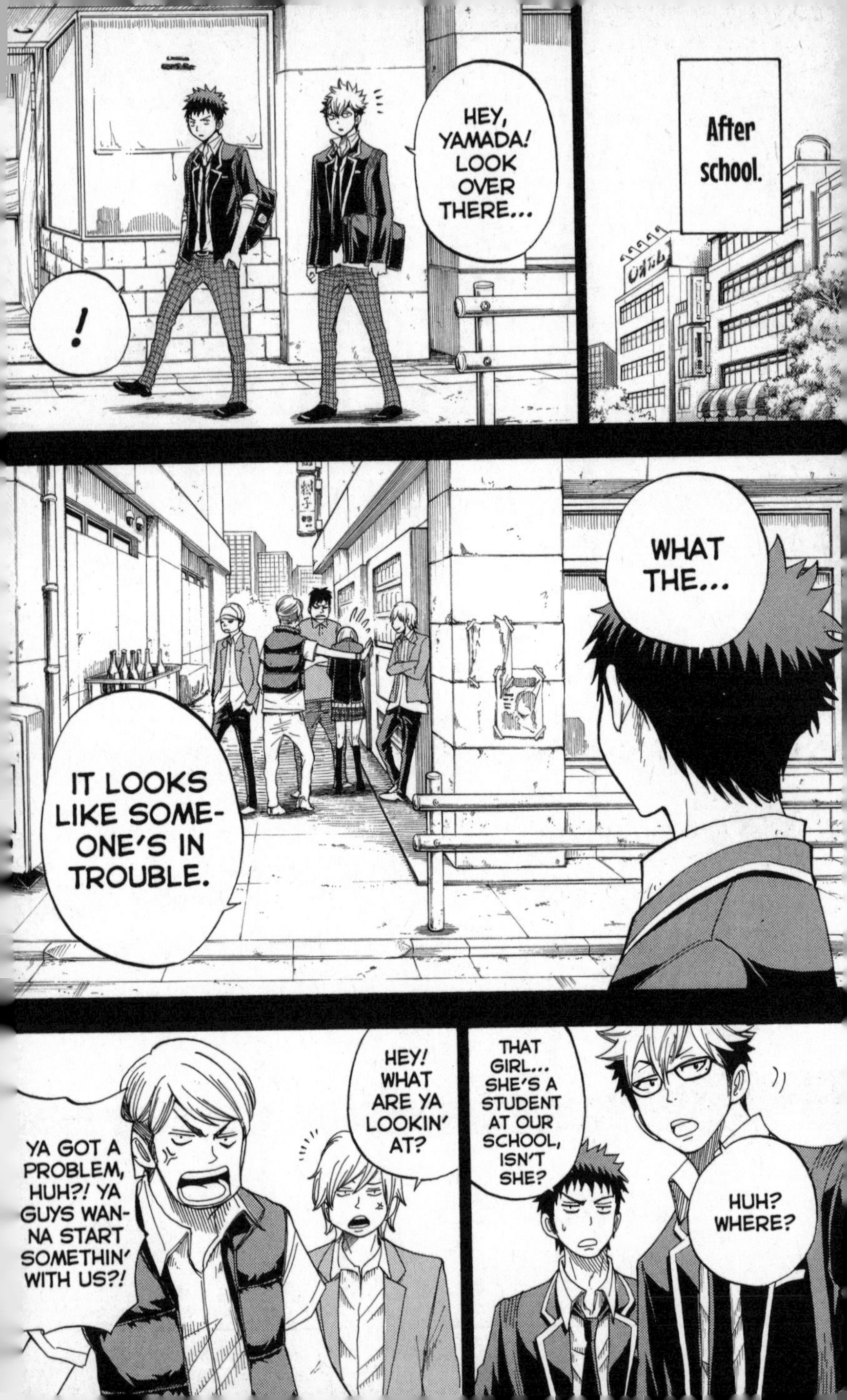
After school.
HEY, YAMADA! LOOK OVER THERE...
!
WHAT THE...
IT LOOKS LIKE SOME-ONE'S IN TROUBLE.
THAT GIRL... SHE'S A STUDENT AT OUR SCHOOL, ISN'T SHE?
HUH? WHERE?
HEY! WHAT ARE YA LOOKIN' AT?
YA GOT A PROBLEM, HUH?! YA GUYS WAN-NA START SOMETHIN' WITH US?!

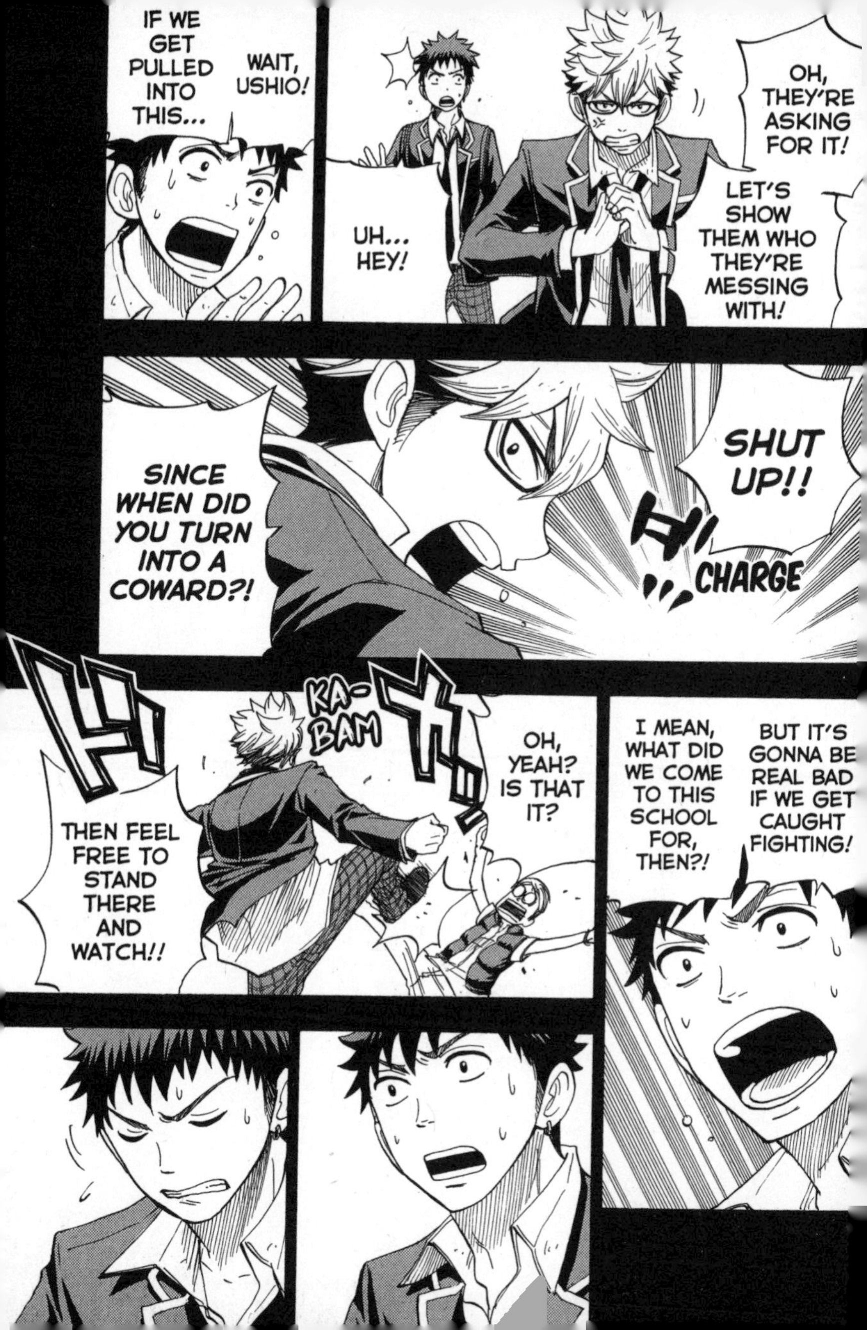
OH, THEY'RE ASKING FOR IT!
LET'S SHOW THEM WHO THEY'RE MESSING WITH!
UH... HEY!
WAIT, USHIO!
IF WE GET PULLED INTO THIS...
SHUT UP!!
CHARGE
SINCE WHEN DID YOU TURN INTO A COWARD?!
BUT IT'S GONNA BE REAL BAD IF WE GET CAUGHT FIGHTING!
I MEAN, WHAT DID WE COME TO THIS SCHOOL FOR, THEN?!
OH, YEAH? IS THAT IT?
KA-BAM
THEN FEEL FREE TO STAND THERE AND WATCH!!

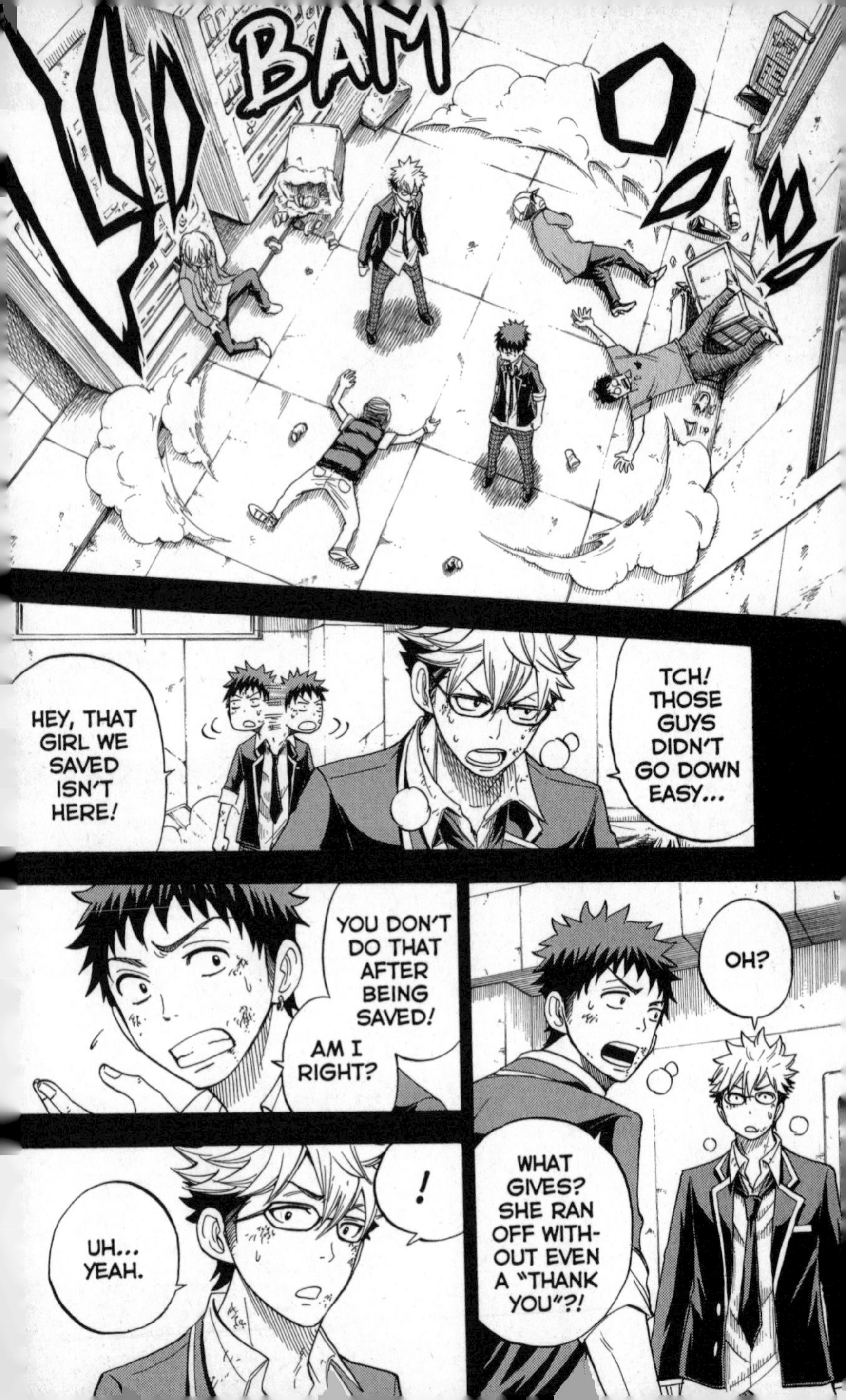
BAM
TCH! THOSE GUYS DIDN'T GO DOWN EASY...
HEY, THAT GIRL WE SAVED ISN'T HERE!
OH?
WHAT GIVES? SHE RAN OFF WITH-OUT EVEN A "THANK YOU"?!
YOU DON'T DO THAT AFTER BEING SAVED!
AM I RIGHT?
!
UH... YEAH.

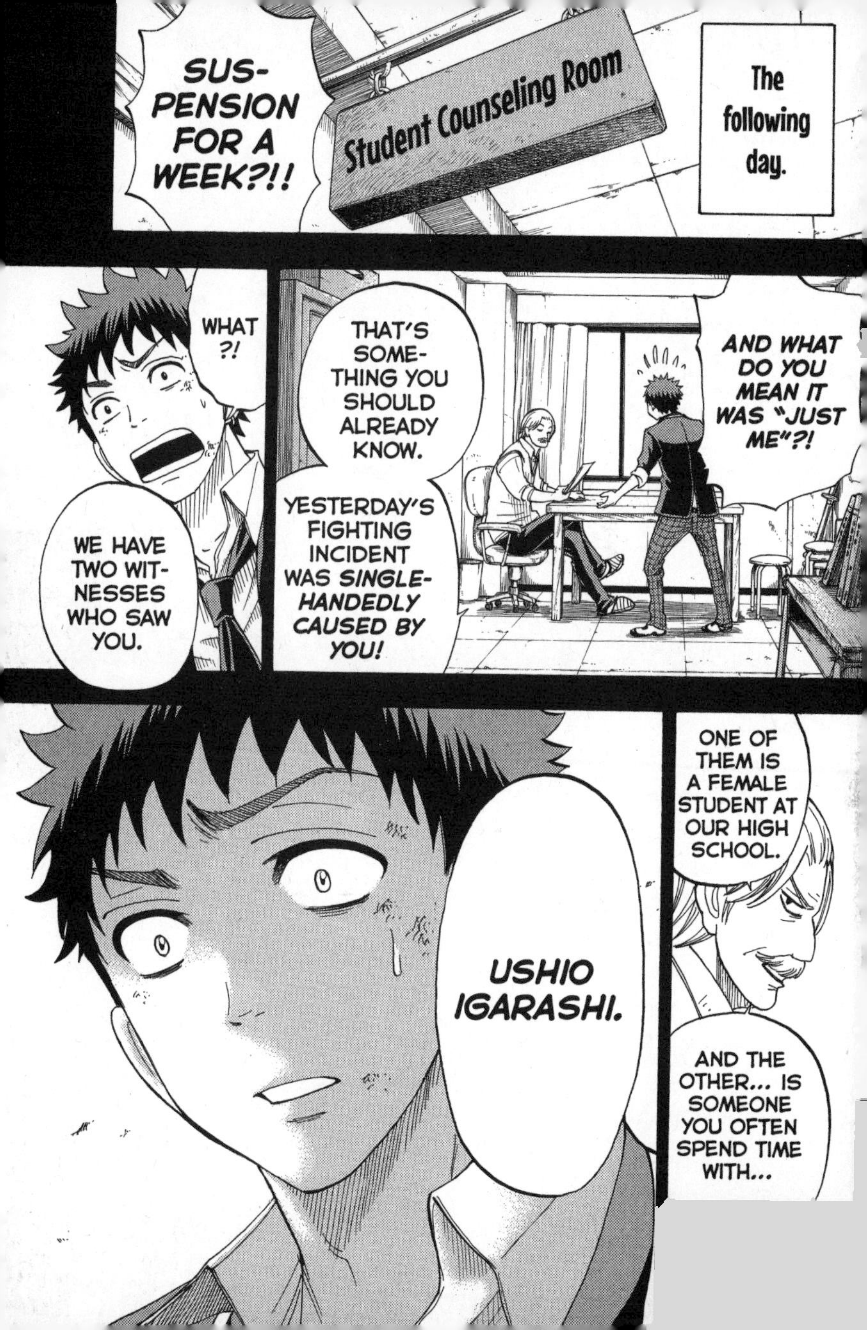
The following day.
Student Counseling Room
SUS-PENSION FOR A WEEK?!!
AND WHAT DO YOU MEAN IT WAS "JUST ME"?!
THAT'S SOME-THING YOU SHOULD ALREADY KNOW.
YESTERDAY'S FIGHTING INCIDENT WAS SINGLE-HANDEDLY CAUSED BY YOU!
WHAT?!
WE HAVE TWO WIT-NESSES WHO SAW YOU.
ONE OF THEM IS A FEMALE STUDENT AT OUR HIGH SCHOOL.
AND THE OTHER... IS SOMEONE YOU OFTEN SPEND TIME WITH...
USHIO IGARASHI.

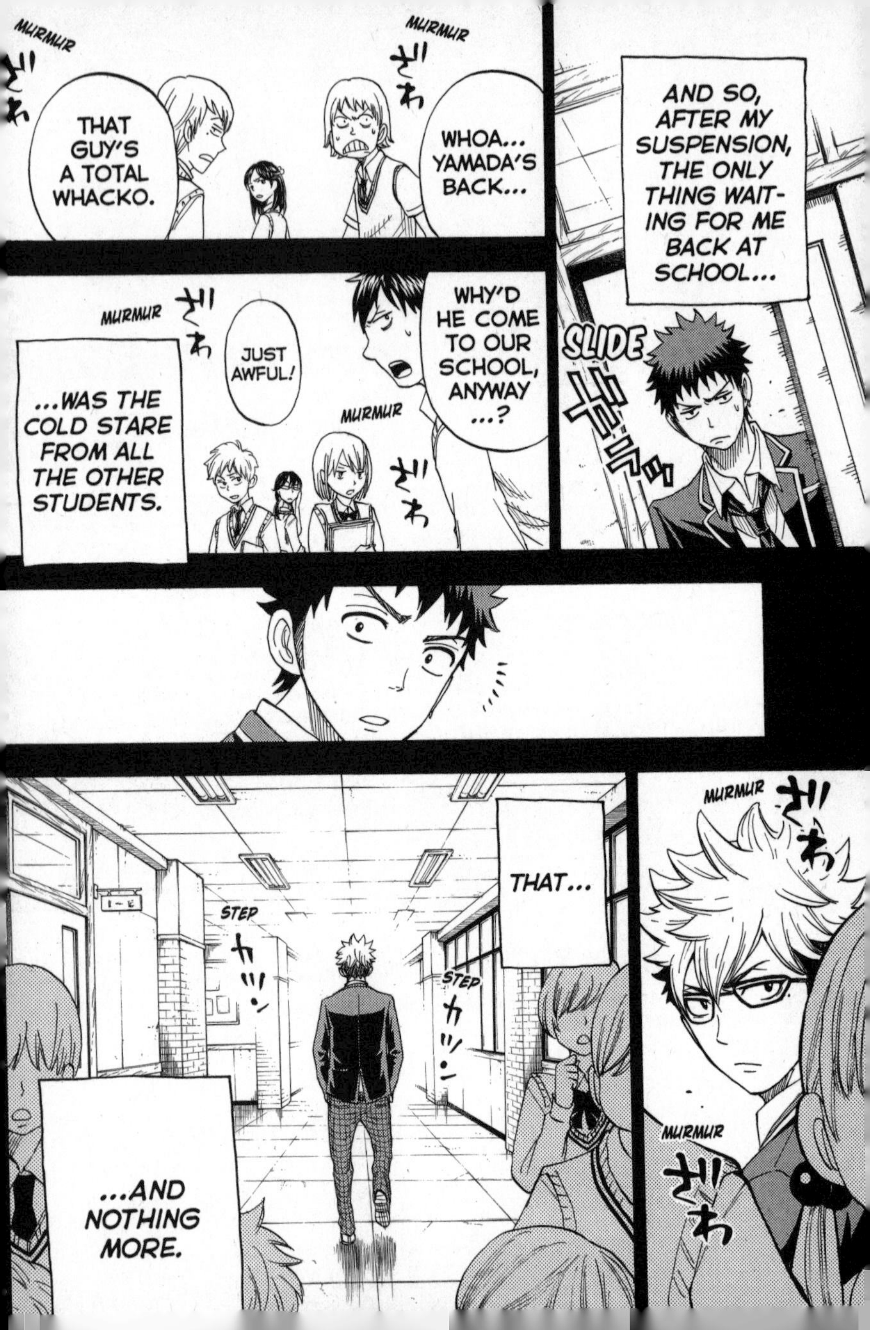
AND SO, AFTER MY SUSPENSION, THE ONLY THING WAITING FOR ME BACK AT SCHOOL...
SLIDE
MURMUR
ざわ
WHOA... YAMADA'S BACK...
THAT GUY'S A TOTAL WHACKO.
MURMUR
ざわ
WHY'D HE COME TO OUR SCHOOL, ANYWAY ...?
MURMUR
ざわ
JUST AWFUL!
MURMUR
ざわ
...WAS THE COLD STARE FROM ALL THE OTHER STUDENTS.
MURMUR
ざわ
MURMUR
ざわ
THAT...
STEP
STEP
...AND NOTHING MORE.

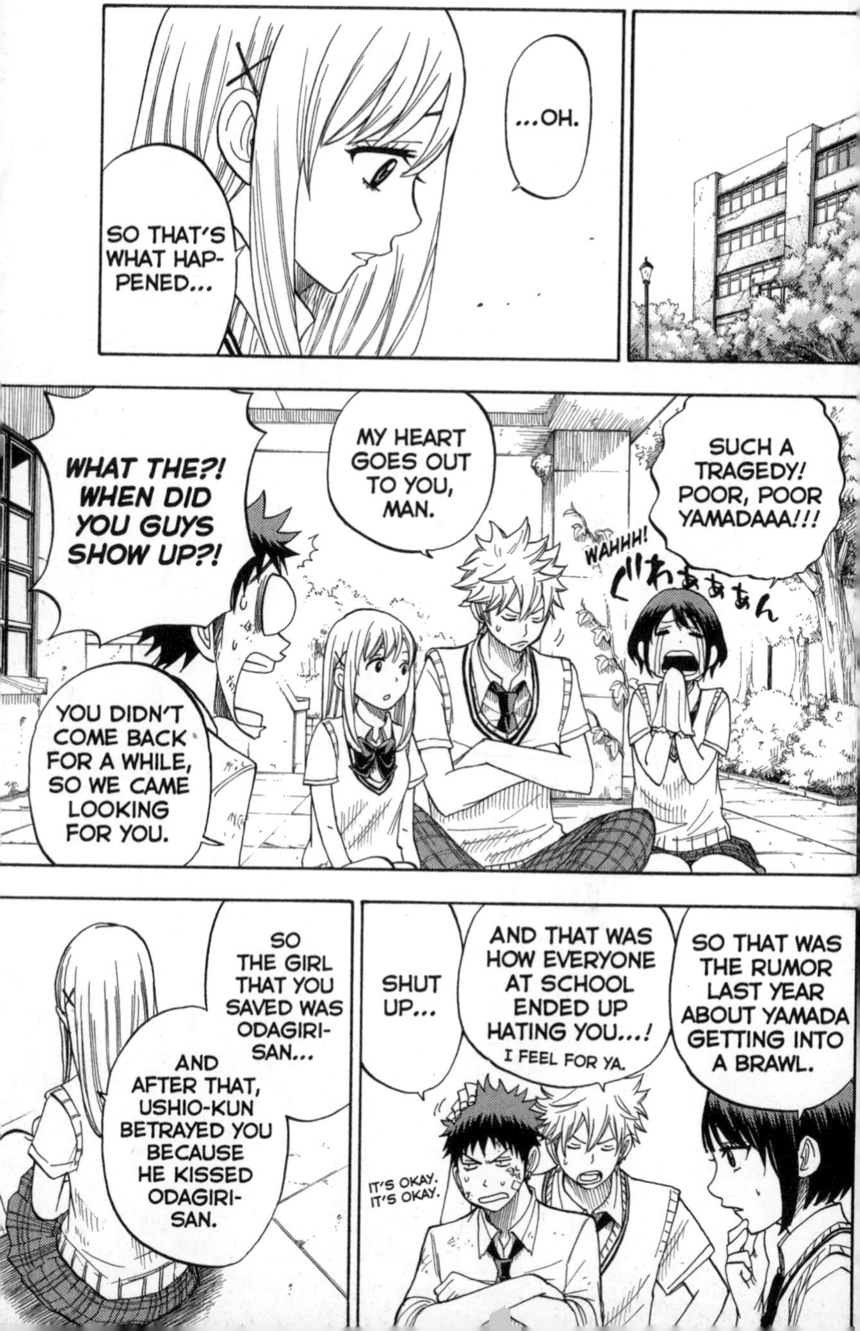
...OH.
SO THAT'S WHAT HAPPENED...
SUCH A TRAGEDY! POOR, POOR YAMADAAA!!!
WAHHH!
ぐわあああん
MY HEART GOES OUT TO YOU, MAN.
WHAT THE?! WHEN DID YOU GUYS SHOW UP?!
YOU DIDN'T COME BACK FOR A WHILE, SO WE CAME LOOKING FOR YOU.
SO THAT WAS THE RUMOR LAST YEAR ABOUT YAMADA GETTING INTO A BRAWL.
AND THAT WAS HOW EVERYONE AT SCHOOL ENDED UP HATING YOU...!
I FEEL FOR YA.
SHUT UP...
IT'S OKAY. IT'S OKAY.
SO THE GIRL THAT YOU SAVED WAS ODAGIRI-SAN...
AND AFTER THAT, USHIO-KUN BETRAYED YOU BECAUSE HE KISSED ODAGIRI-SAN.

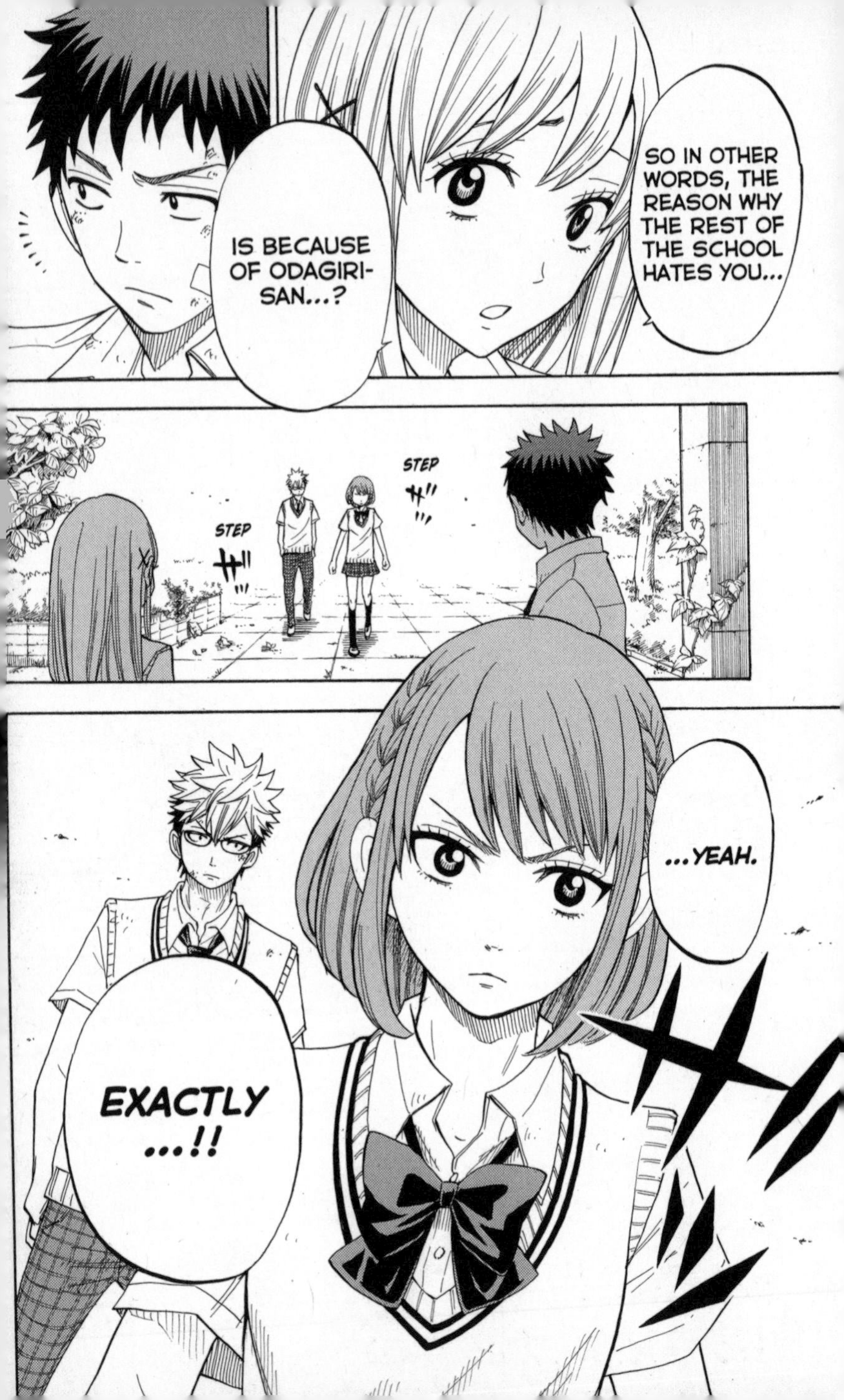
SO IN OTHER WORDS, THE REASON WHY THE REST OF THE SCHOOL HATES YOU...
IS BECAUSE OF ODAGIRI-SAN...?
STEP
STEP
...YEAH.
EXACTLY ...!!

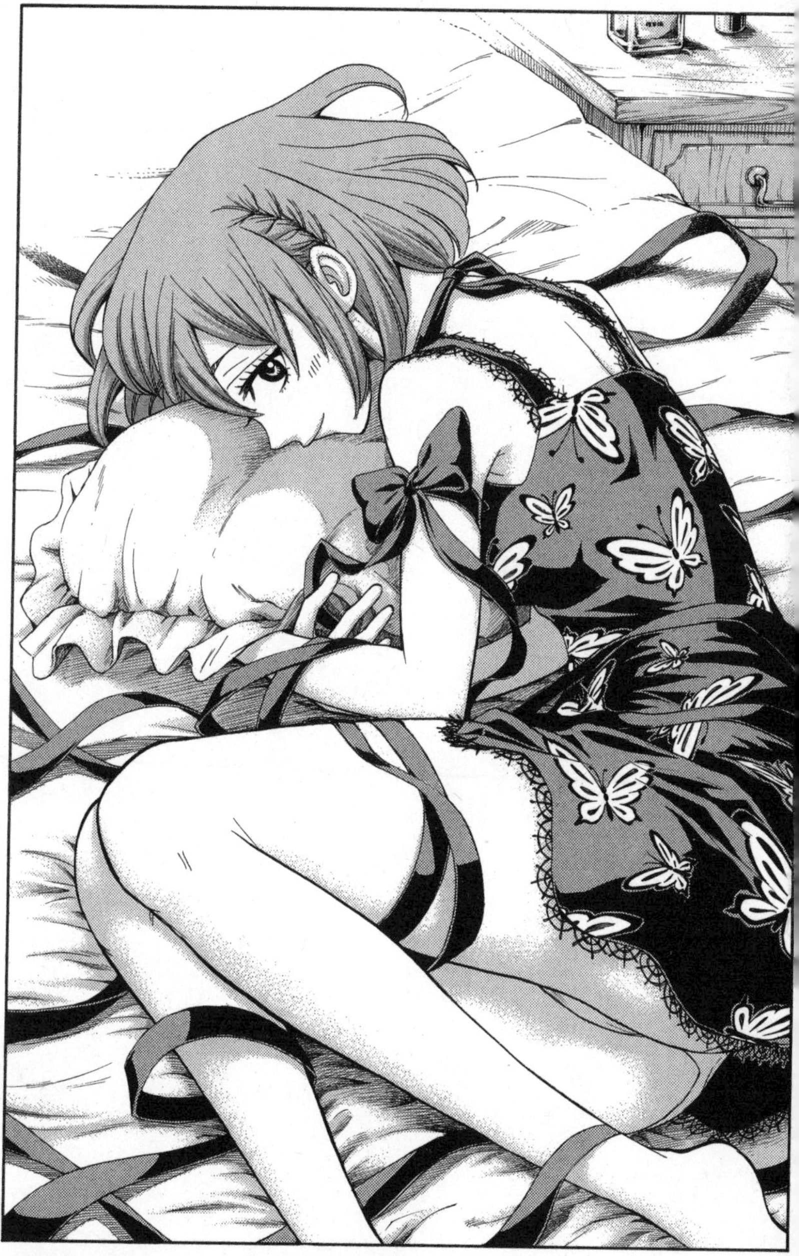

CHAPTER 23: Do you dislike me...?

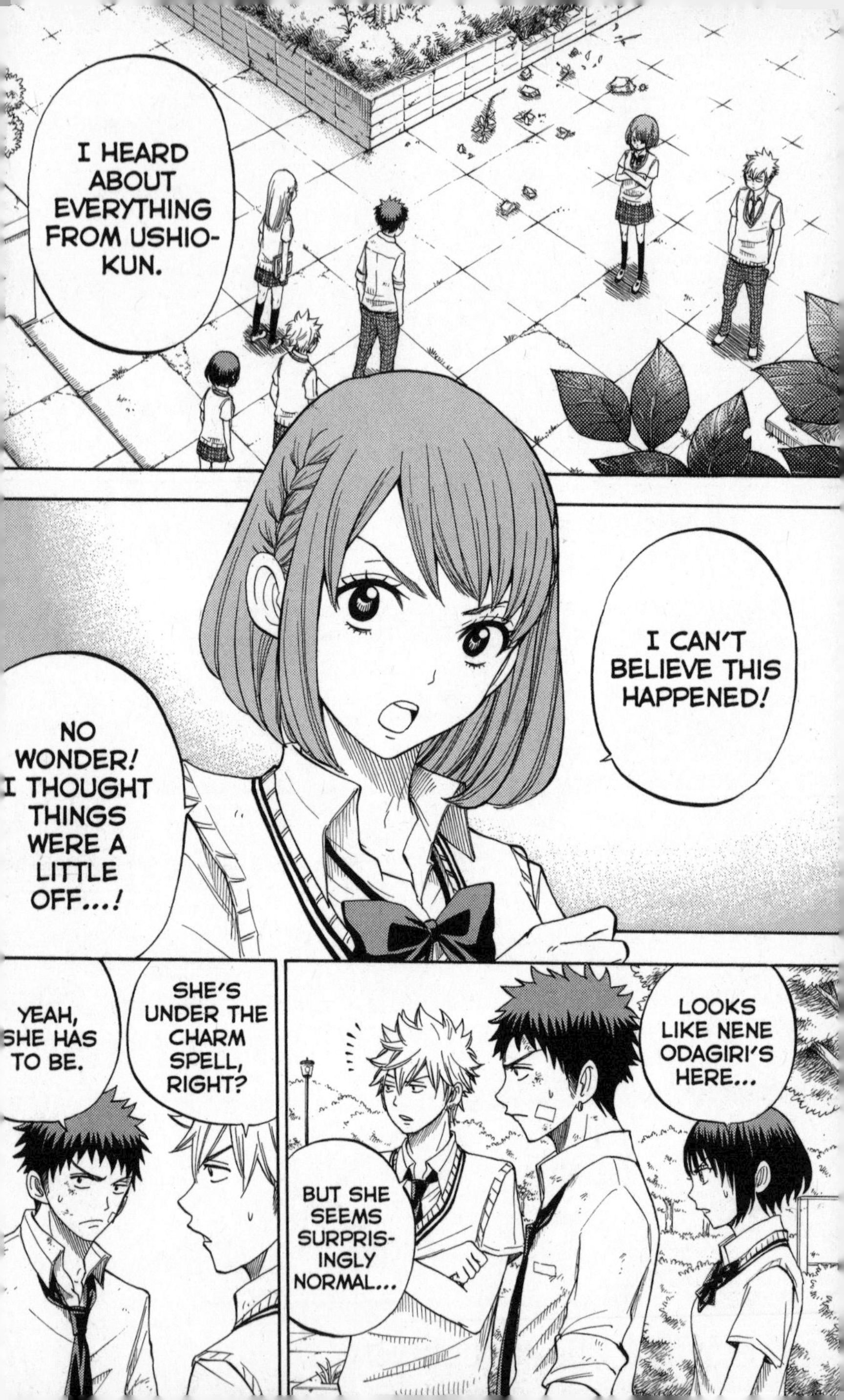
I HEARD ABOUT EVERYTHING FROM USHIO-KUN.
I CAN'T BELIEVE THIS HAPPENED!
NO WONDER! I THOUGHT THINGS WERE A LITTLE OFF...!
LOOKS LIKE NENE ODAGIRI'S HERE...
BUT SHE SEEMS SURPRISINGLY NORMAL...
SHE'S UNDER THE CHARM SPELL, RIGHT?
YEAH, SHE HAS TO BE.

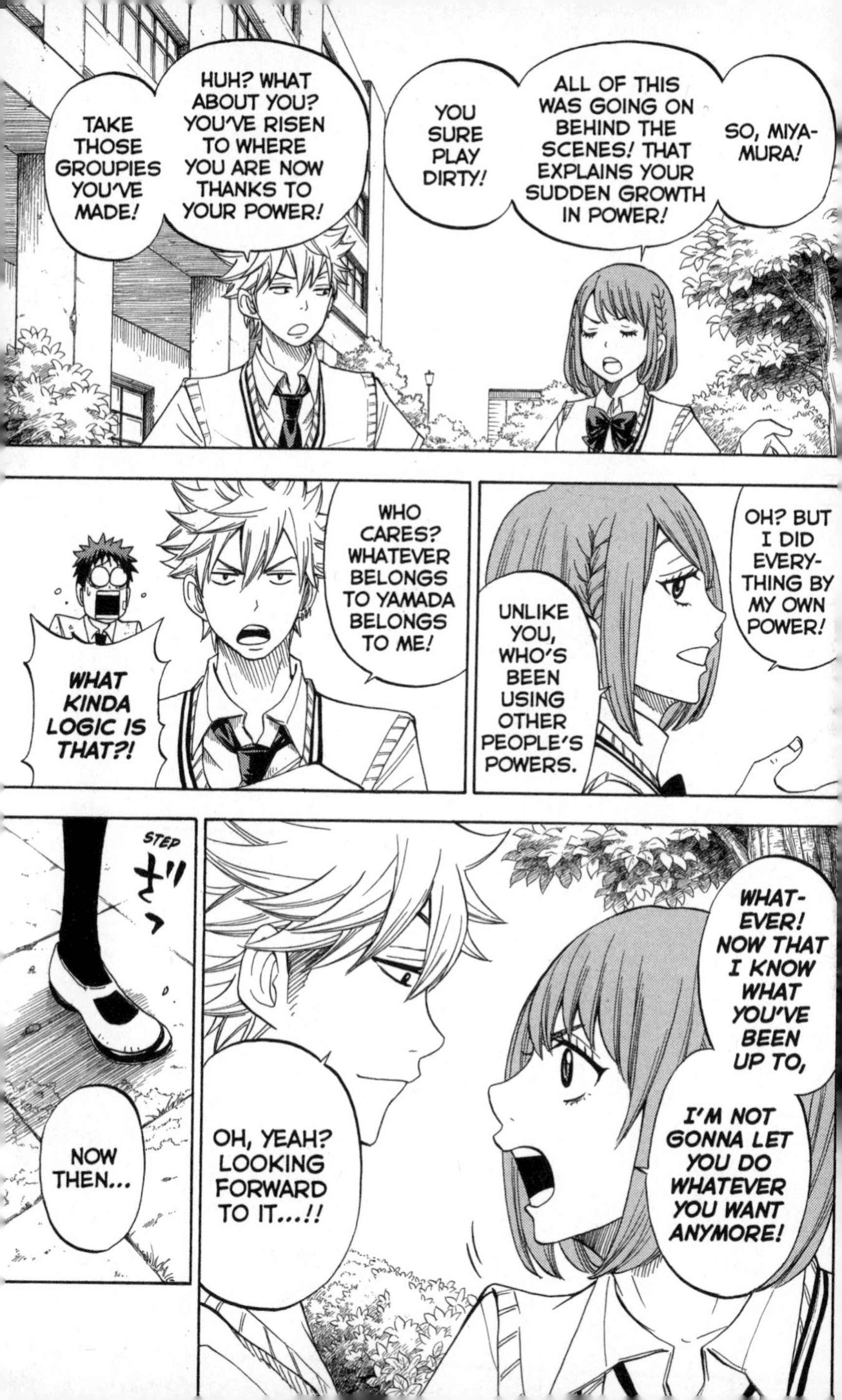
SO, MIYA-MURA!
ALL OF THIS WAS GOING ON BEHIND THE SCENES! THAT EXPLAINS YOUR SUDDEN GROWTH IN POWER!
YOU SURE PLAY DIRTY!
HUH? WHAT ABOUT YOU? YOU'VE RISEN TO WHERE YOU ARE NOW THANKS TO YOUR POWER!
TAKE THOSE GROUPIES YOU'VE MADE!
OH? BUT I DID EVERY-THING BY MY OWN POWER!
UNLIKE YOU, WHO'S BEEN USING OTHER PEOPLE'S POWERS.
WHO CARES? WHATEVER BELONGS TO YAMADA BELONGS TO ME!
WHAT KINDA LOGIC IS THAT?!
WHAT-EVER! NOW THAT I KNOW WHAT YOU'VE BEEN UP TO,
I'M NOT GONNA LET YOU DO WHATEVER YOU WANT ANYMORE!
OH, YEAH? LOOKING FORWARD TO IT...!!
STEP
ざっ
NOW THEN...

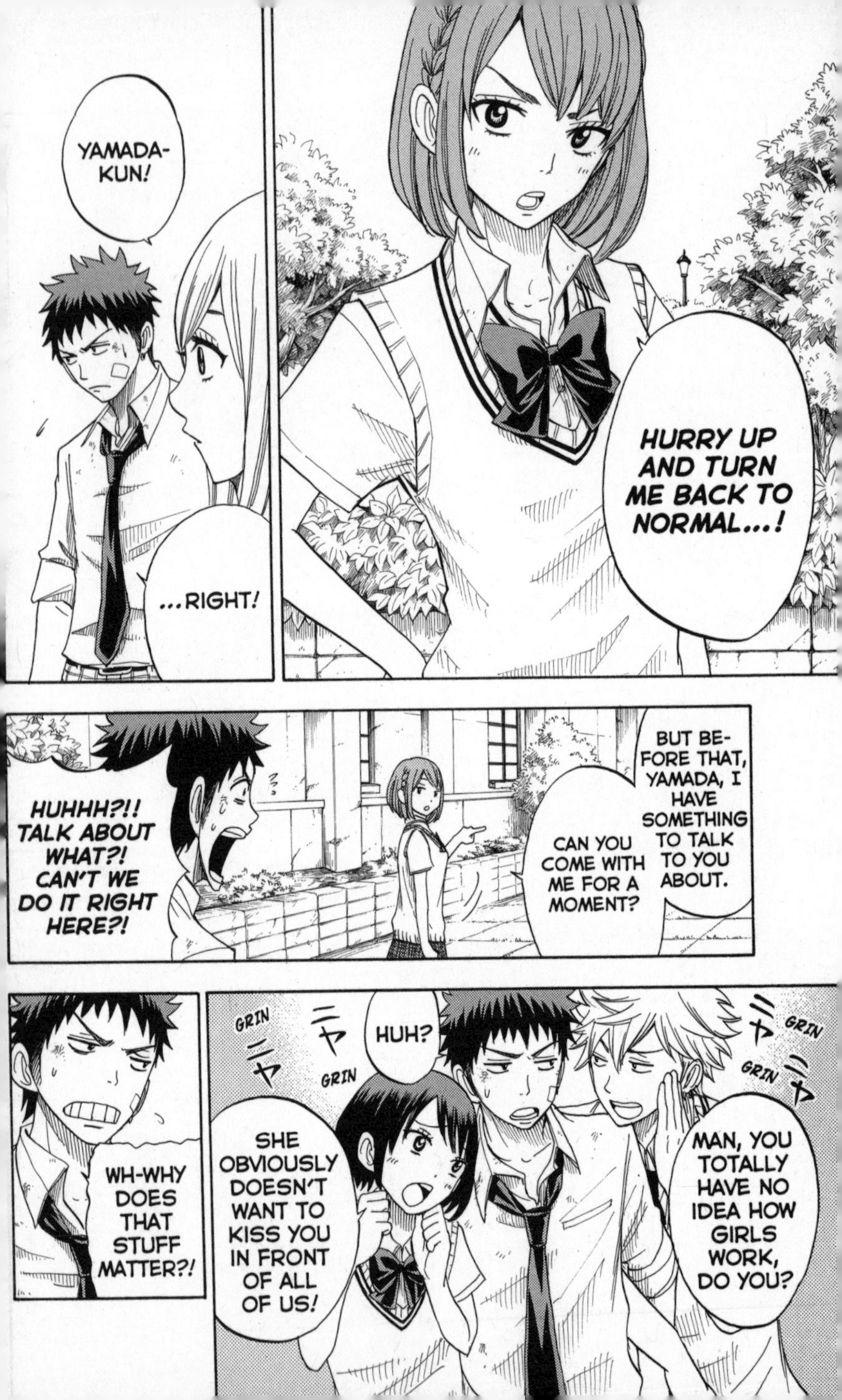
HURRY UP AND TURN ME BACK TO NORMAL...!
YAMADA-KUN!
...RIGHT!
BUT BE-FORE THAT, YAMADA, I HAVE SOMETHING TO TALK TO YOU ABOUT.
CAN YOU COME WITH ME FOR A MOMENT?
HUHHH?!! TALK ABOUT WHAT?! CAN'T WE DO IT RIGHT HERE?!
ニヤ GRIN
ニヤ GRIN
MAN, YOU TOTALLY HAVE NO IDEA HOW GIRLS WORK, DO YOU?
HUH?
ニヤ GRIN
ニヤ GRIN
SHE OBVIOUSLY DOESN'T WANT TO KISS YOU IN FRONT OF ALL OF US!
WH-WHY DOES THAT STUFF MATTER?!

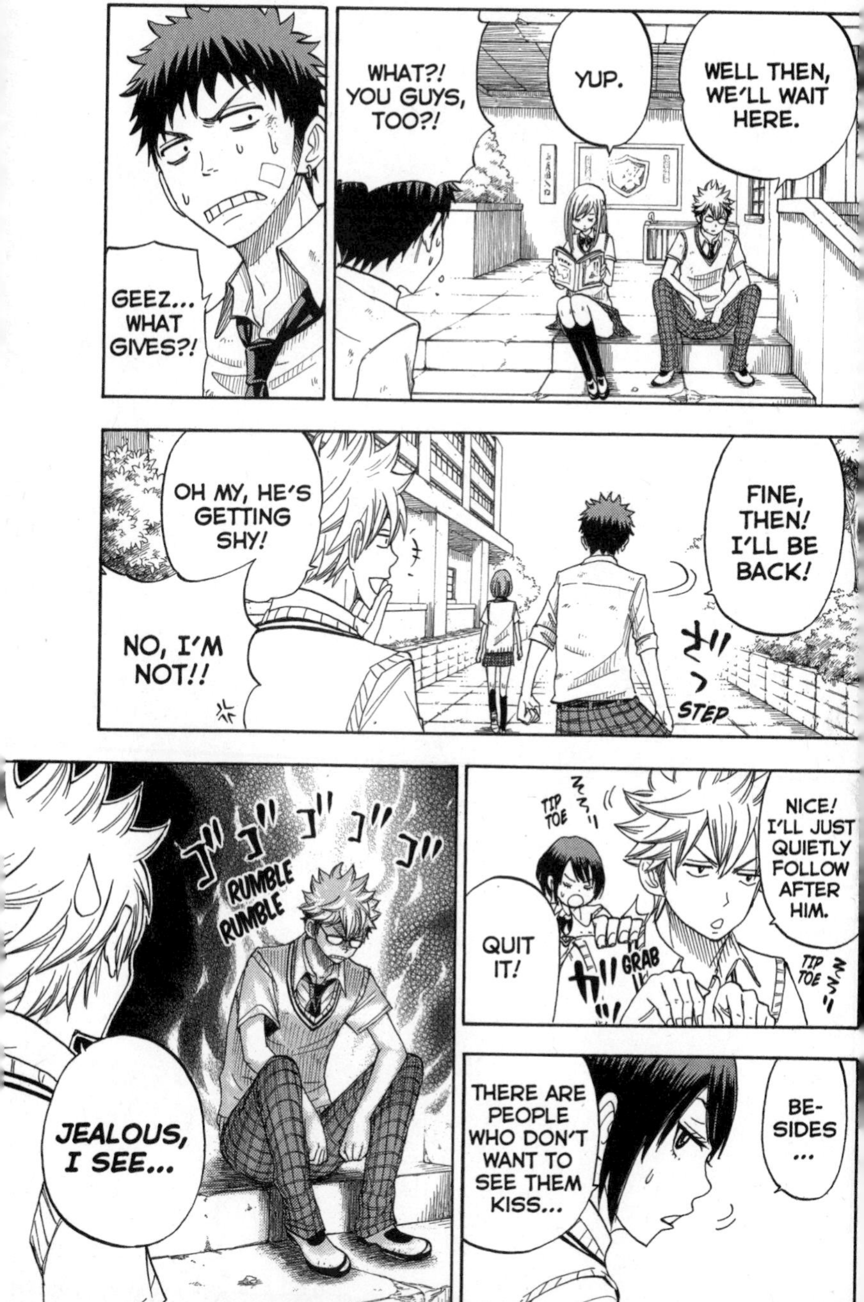

WELL THEN, WE'LL WAIT HERE.
YUP.
WHAT?! YOU GUYS, TOO?!
GEEZ... WHAT GIVES?!
FINE, THEN! I'LL BE BACK!
STEP
OH MY, HE'S GETTING SHY!
NO, I'M NOT!!
NICE! I'LL JUST QUIETLY FOLLOW AFTER HIM.
TIP TOE
TIP TOE
GRAB
QUIT IT!
BE-SIDES...
THERE ARE PEOPLE WHO DON'T WANT TO SEE THEM KISS...
RUMBLE RUMBLE
JEALOUS, I SEE...

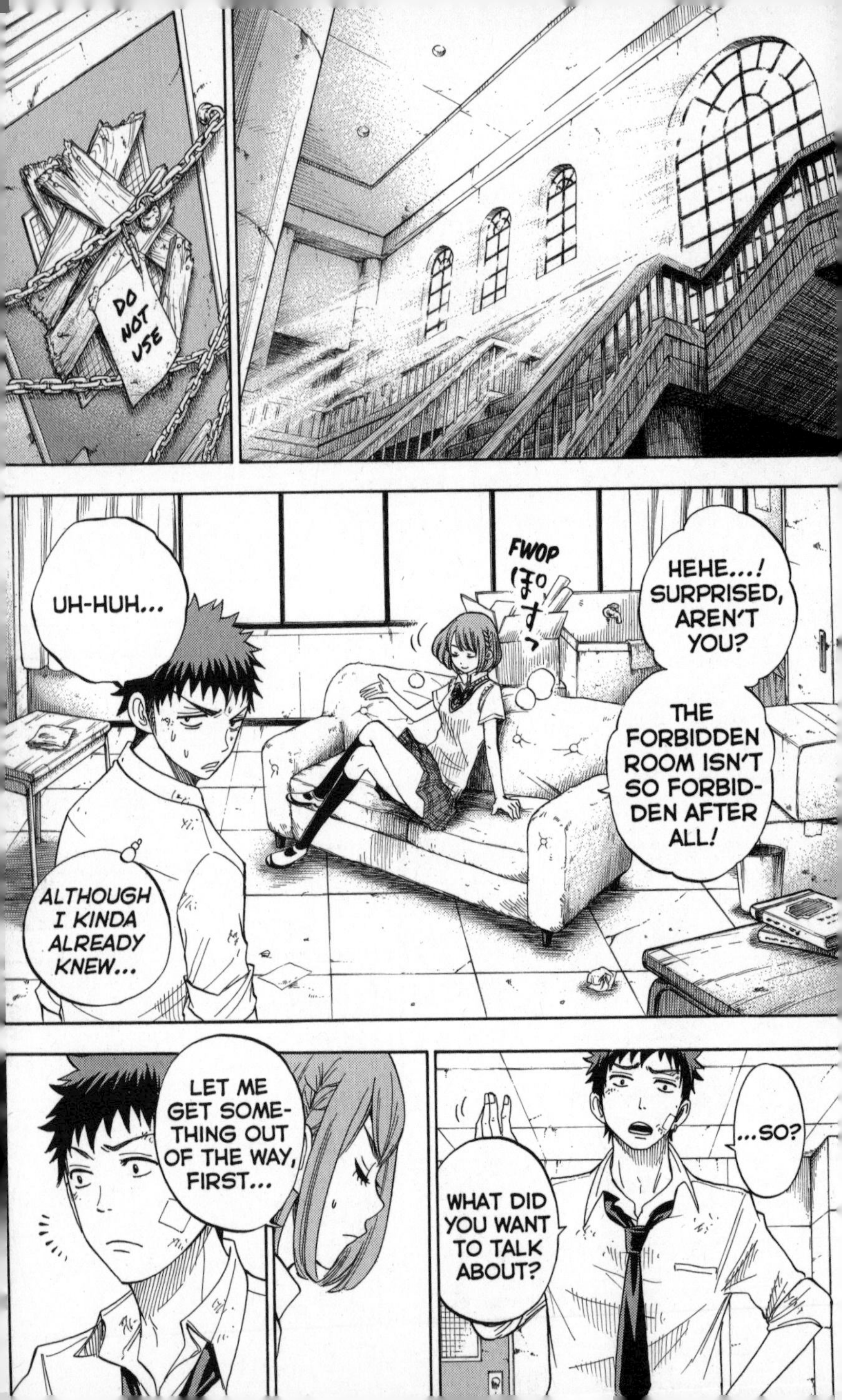
DO NOT USE
HEHE...! SURPRISED, AREN'T YOU?
THE FORBIDDEN ROOM ISN'T SO FORBID-DEN AFTER ALL!
FWOP
ぽすっ
UH-HUH...
ALTHOUGH I KINDA ALREADY KNEW...
...SO?
WHAT DID YOU WANT TO TALK ABOUT?
LET ME GET SOME-THING OUT OF THE WAY, FIRST...

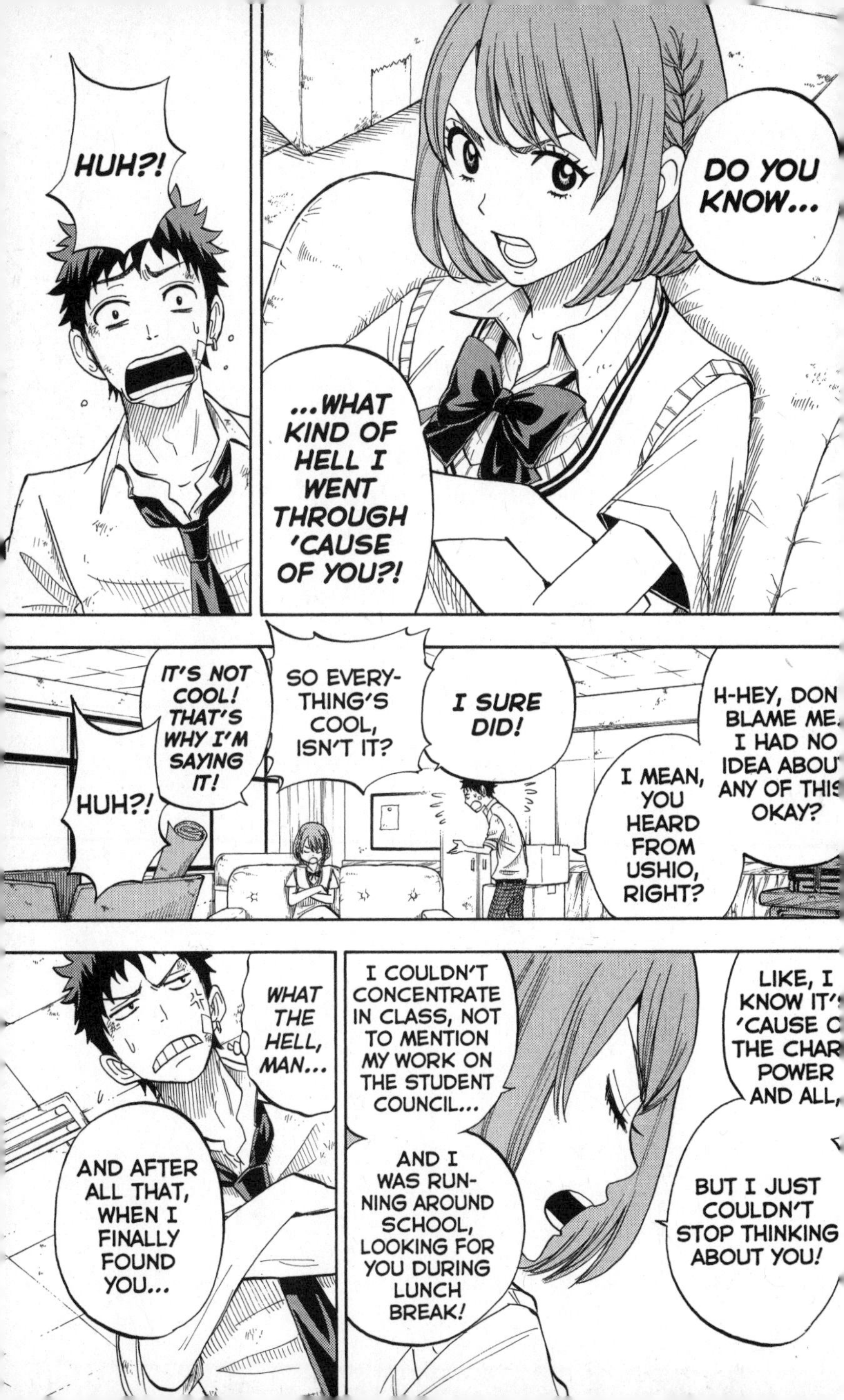
DO YOU KNOW...
...WHAT KIND OF HELL I WENT THROUGH 'CAUSE OF YOU?!
HUH?!
H-HEY, DON BLAME ME. I HAD NO IDEA ABOU ANY OF THIS OKAY?
I MEAN, YOU HEARD FROM USHIO, RIGHT?
I SURE DID!
SO EVERY-THING'S COOL, ISN'T IT?
IT'S NOT COOL! THAT'S WHY I'M SAYING IT!
HUH?!
LIKE, I KNOW IT'S 'CAUSE O THE CHAR POWER AND ALL,
BUT I JUST COULDN'T STOP THINKING ABOUT YOU!
I COULDN'T CONCENTRATE IN CLASS, NOT TO MENTION MY WORK ON THE STUDENT COUNCIL...
AND I WAS RUN-NING AROUND SCHOOL, LOOKING FOR YOU DURING LUNCH BREAK!
WHAT THE HELL, MAN...
AND AFTER ALL THAT, WHEN I FINALLY FOUND YOU...

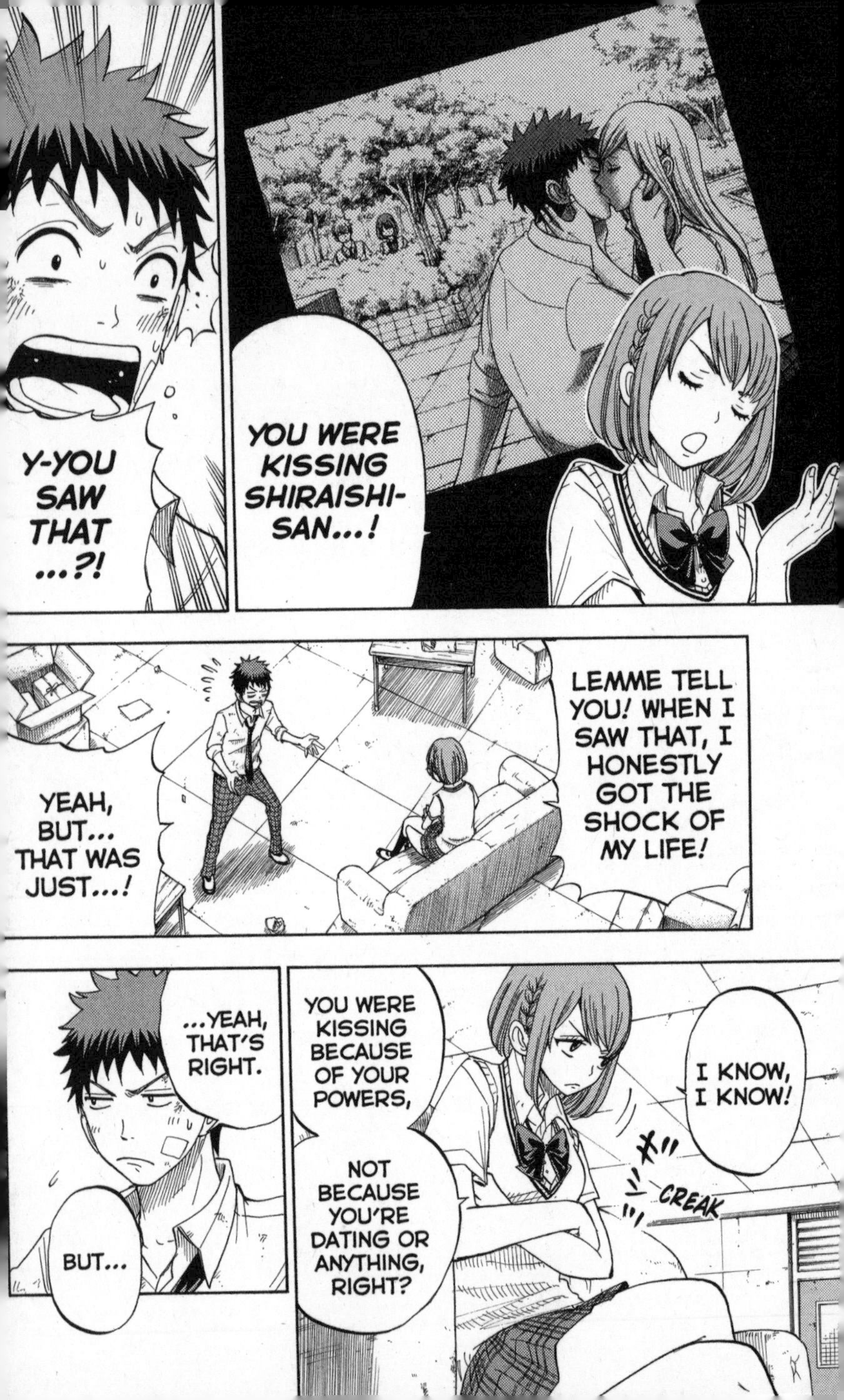

YOU WERE KISSING SHIRAISHI-SAN...!
Y-YOU SAW THAT...?!
LEMME TELL YOU! WHEN I SAW THAT, I HONESTLY GOT THE SHOCK OF MY LIFE!
YEAH, BUT... THAT WAS JUST...!
I KNOW, I KNOW!
YOU WERE KISSING BECAUSE OF YOUR POWERS,
NOT BECAUSE YOU'RE DATING OR ANYTHING, RIGHT?
CREAK
...YEAH, THAT'S RIGHT.
BUT...

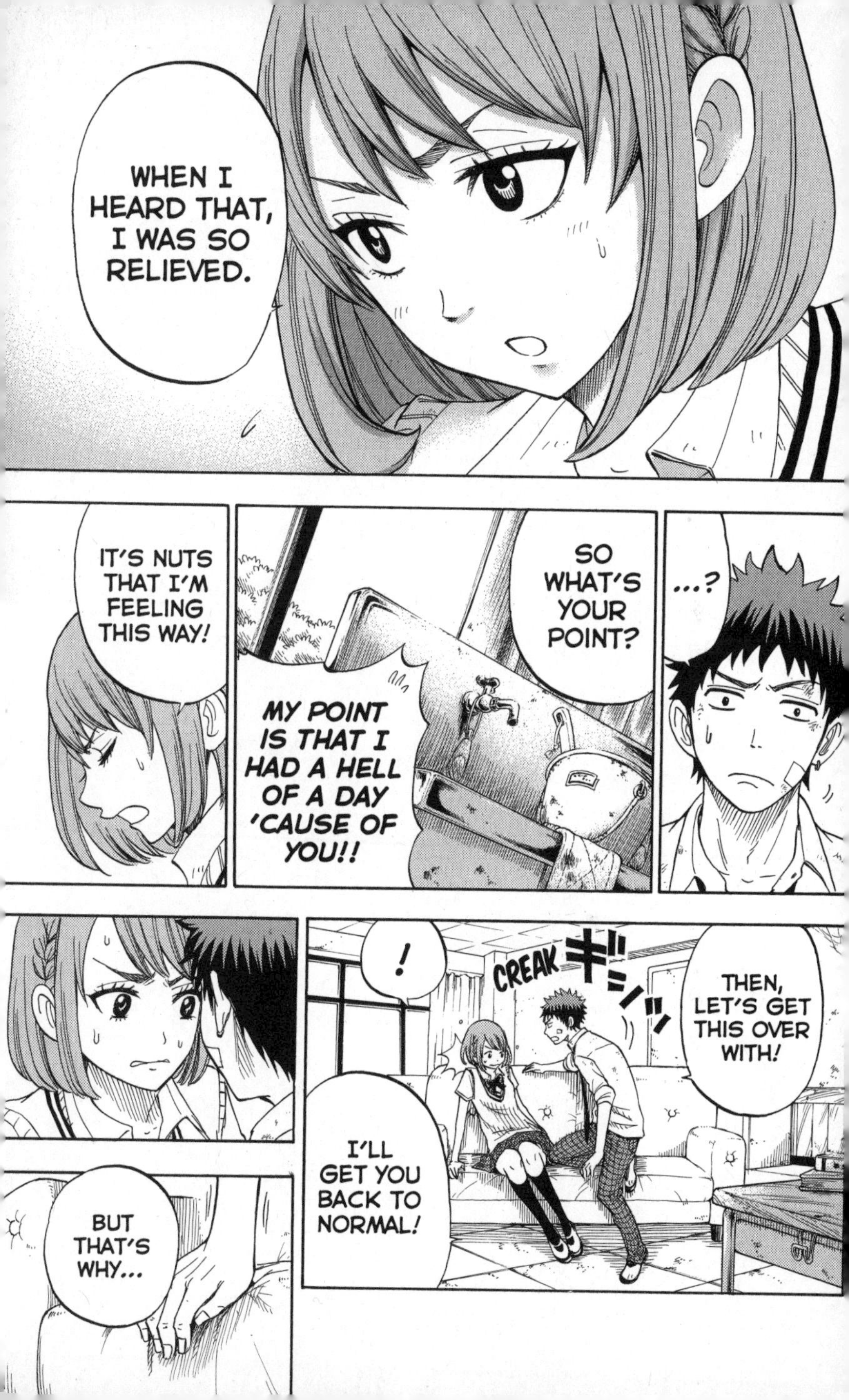
WHEN I HEARD THAT, I WAS SO RELIEVED.
...?
SO WHAT'S YOUR POINT?
MY POINT IS THAT I HAD A HELL OF A DAY 'CAUSE OF YOU!!
IT'S NUTS THAT I'M FEELING THIS WAY!
THEN, LET'S GET THIS OVER WITH!
CREAK
!
I'LL GET YOU BACK TO NORMAL!
BUT THAT'S WHY...

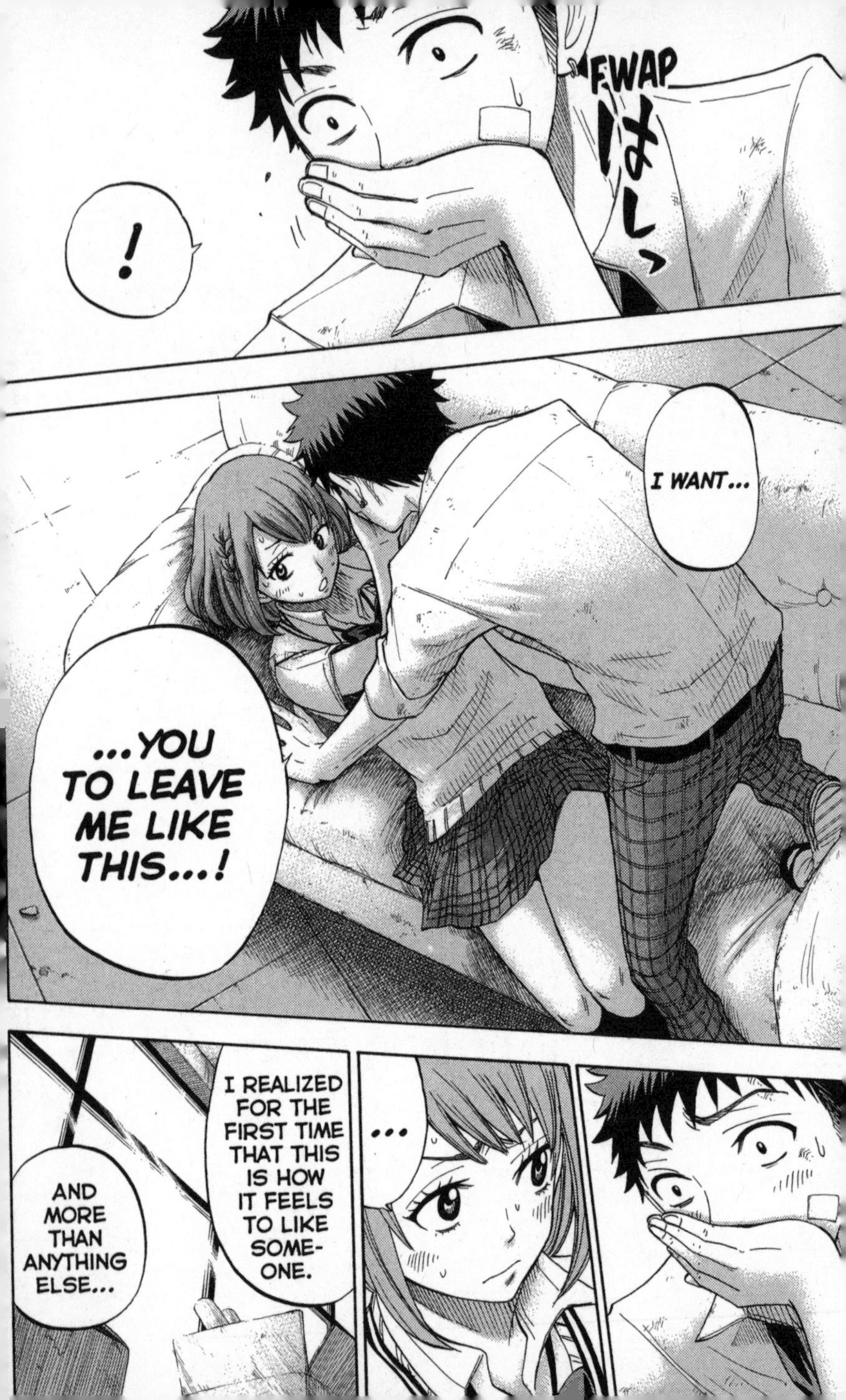
FWAP
はしっ
!
I WANT...
...YOU TO LEAVE ME LIKE THIS...!
...
I REALIZED FOR THE FIRST TIME THAT THIS IS HOW IT FEELS TO LIKE SOME-ONE.
AND MORE THAN ANYTHING ELSE...

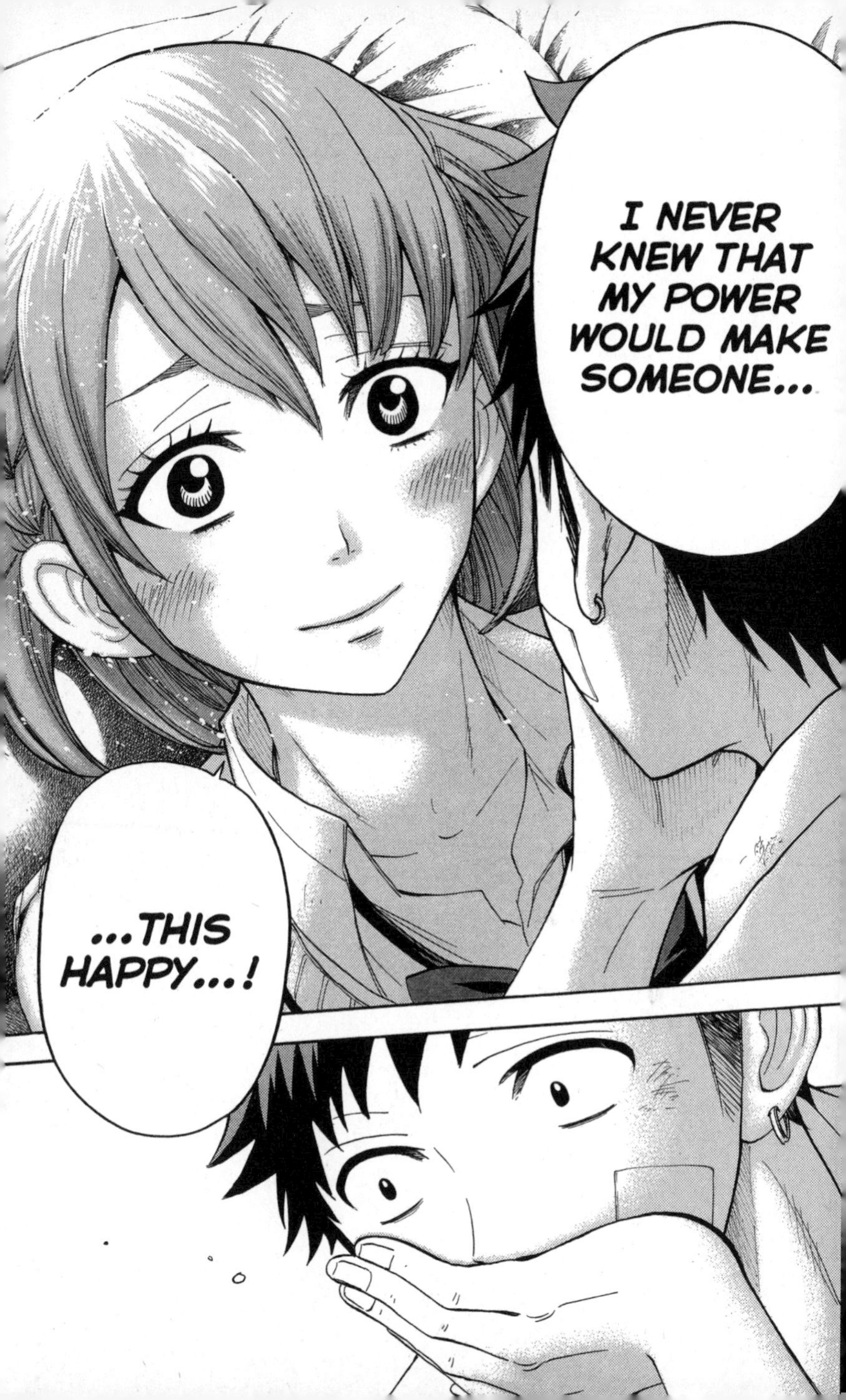
I NEVER KNEW THAT MY POWER WOULD MAKE SOMEONE...
...THIS HAPPY...!

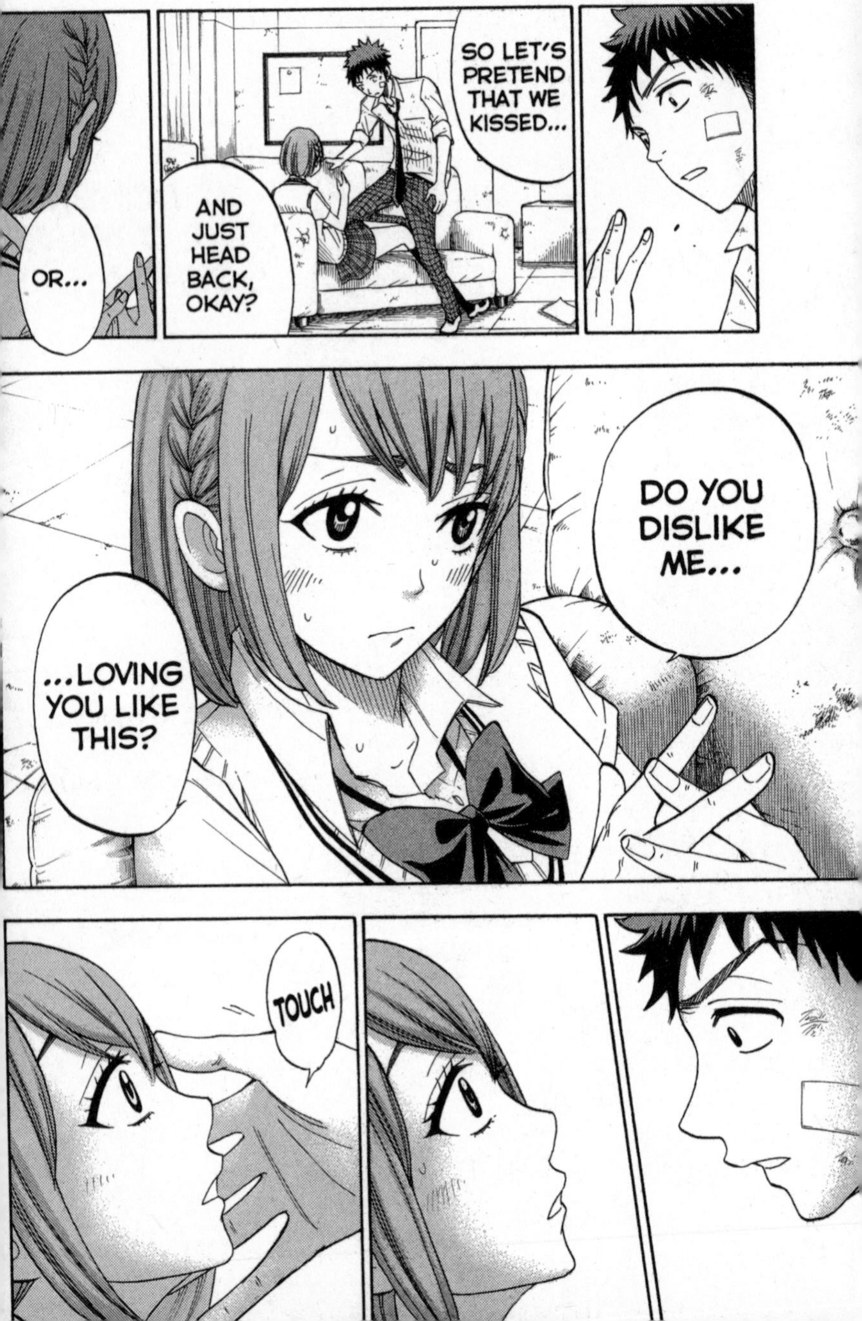
SO LET'S PRETEND THAT WE KISSED...
AND JUST HEAD BACK, OKAY?
OR...
DO YOU DISLIKE ME...
...LOVING YOU LIKE THIS?
TOUCH

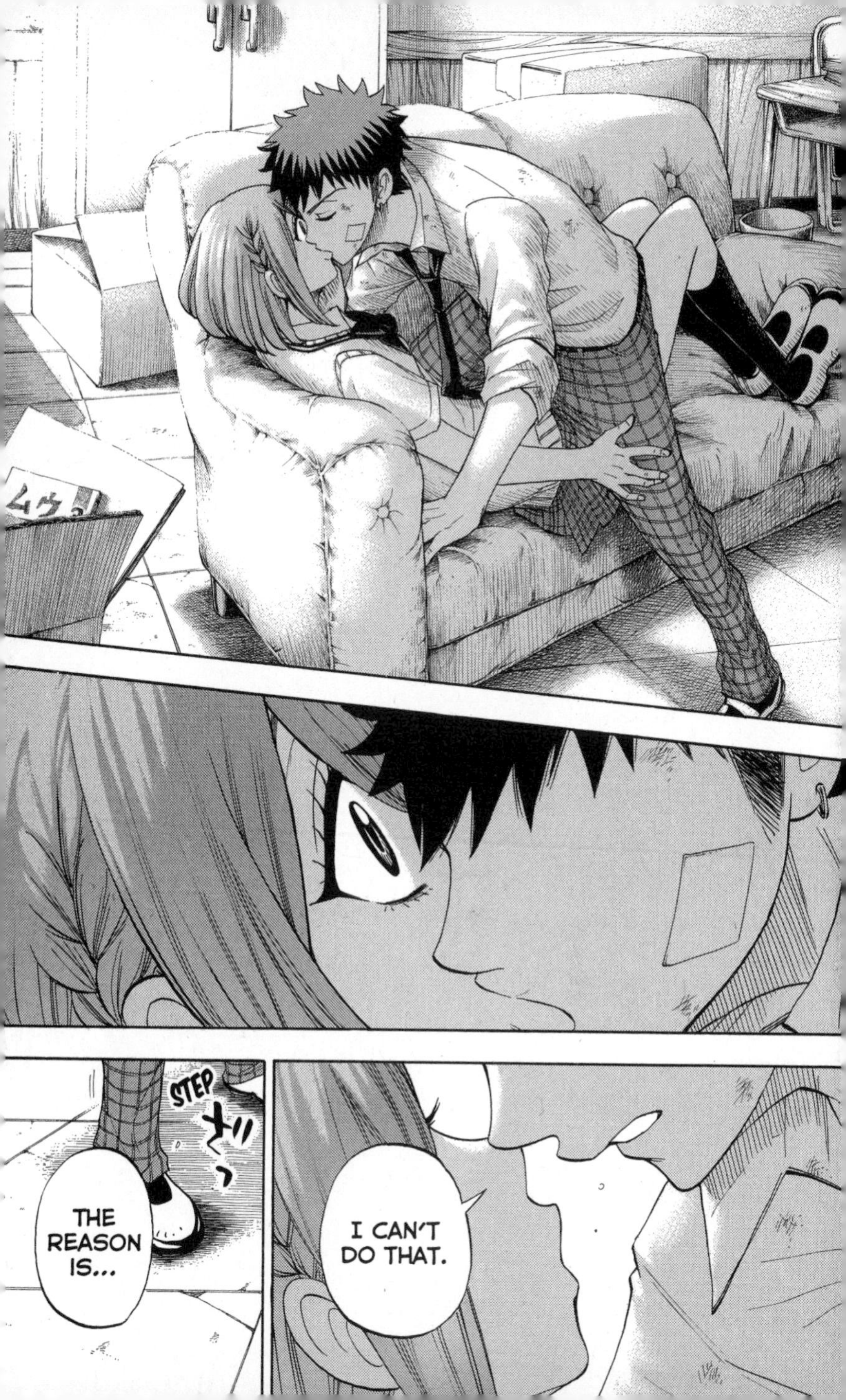
I CAN'T DO THAT.
STEP
THE REASON IS...

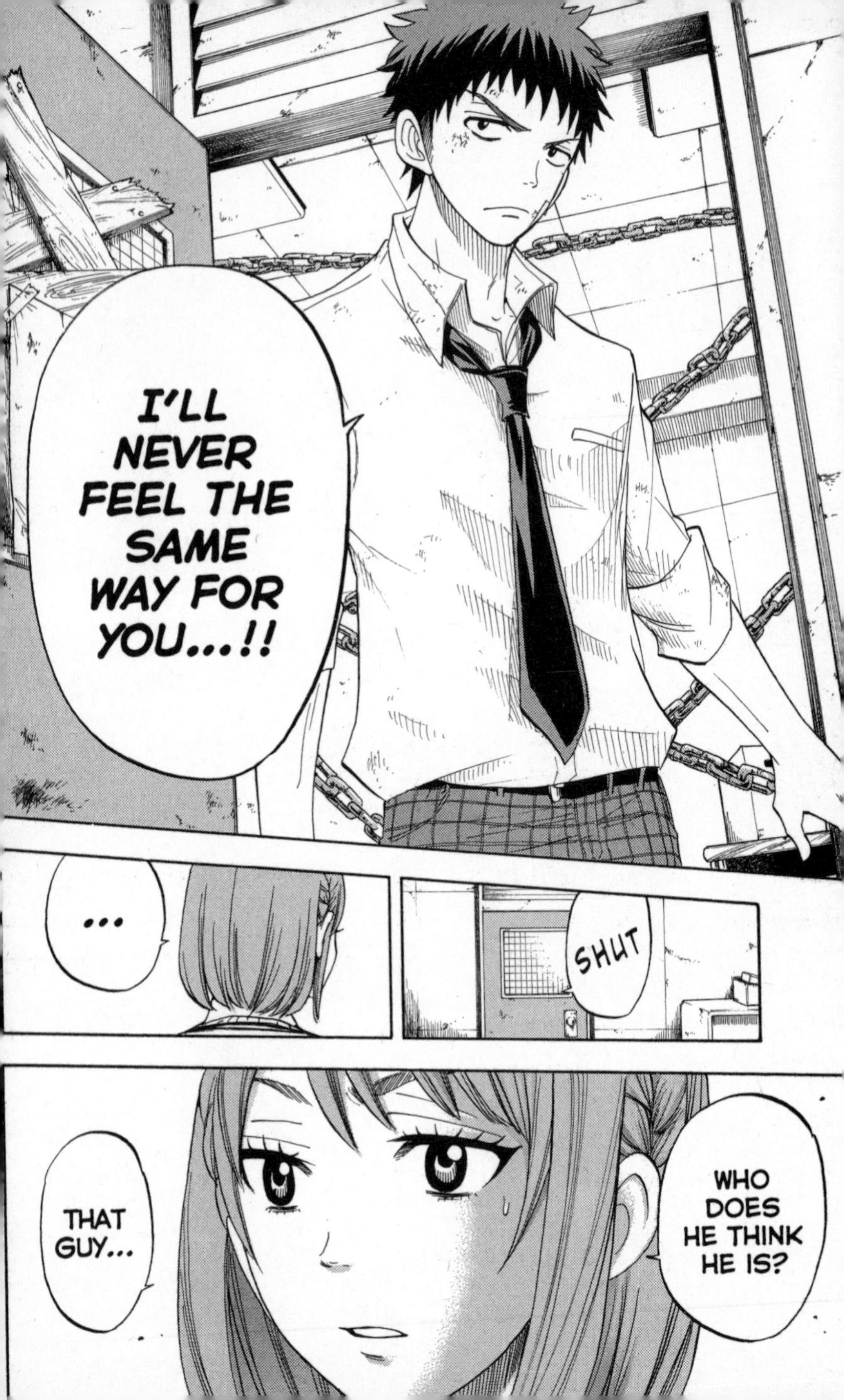
I'LL NEVER FEEL THE SAME WAY FOR YOU...!!
SHUT
...
WHO DOES HE THINK HE IS?
THAT GUY...

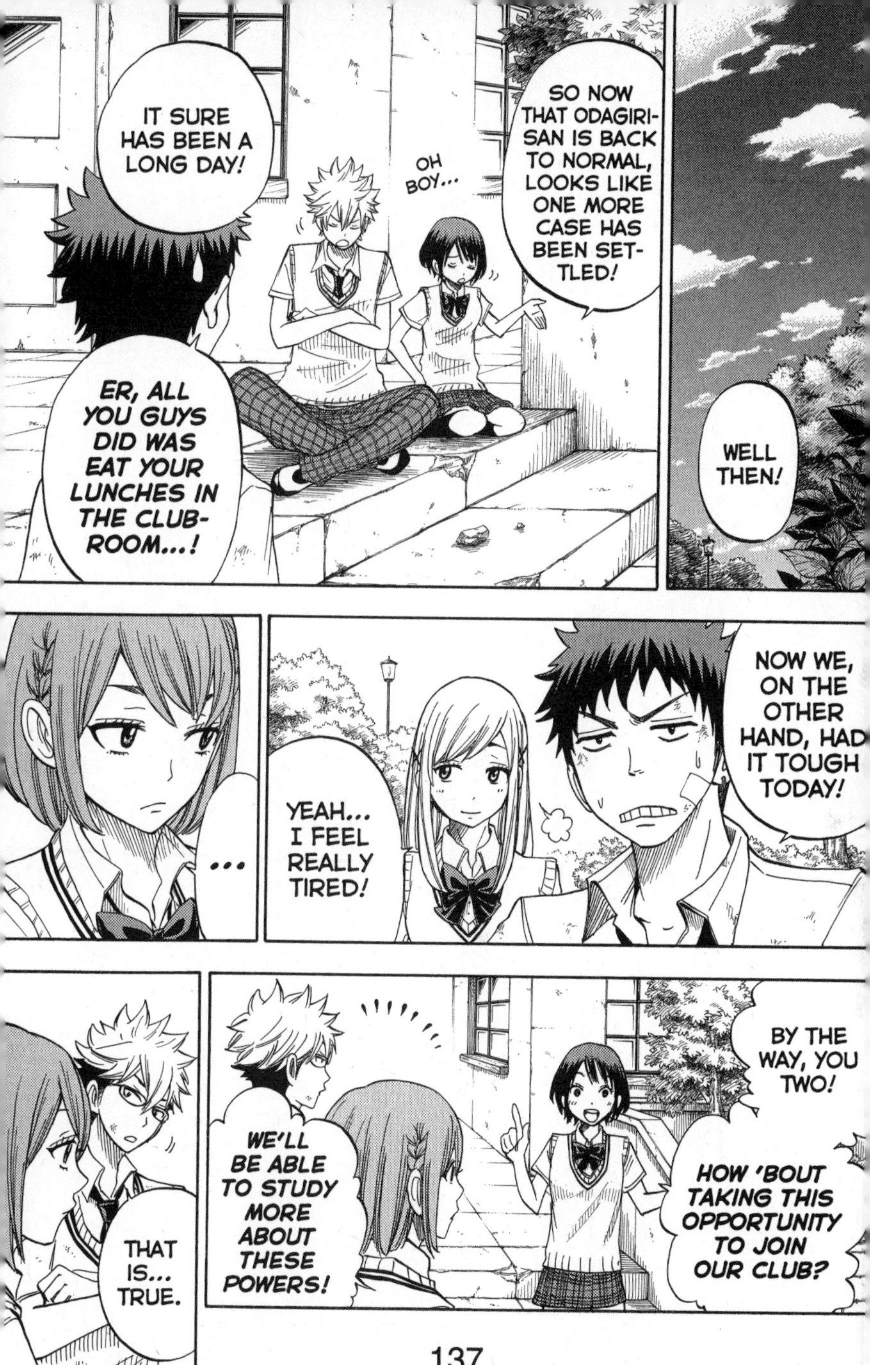
WELL THEN!
SO NOW THAT ODAGIRI-SAN IS BACK TO NORMAL, LOOKS LIKE ONE MORE CASE HAS BEEN SET-TLED!
OH BOY...
IT SURE HAS BEEN A LONG DAY!
ER, ALL YOU GUYS DID WAS EAT YOUR LUNCHES IN THE CLUB-ROOM...!
NOW WE, ON THE OTHER HAND, HAD IT TOUGH TODAY!
YEAH... I FEEL REALLY TIRED!
...
BY THE WAY, YOU TWO!
HOW 'BOUT TAKING THIS OPPORTUNITY TO JOIN OUR CLUB?
WE'LL BE ABLE TO STUDY MORE ABOUT THESE POWERS!
THAT IS... TRUE.

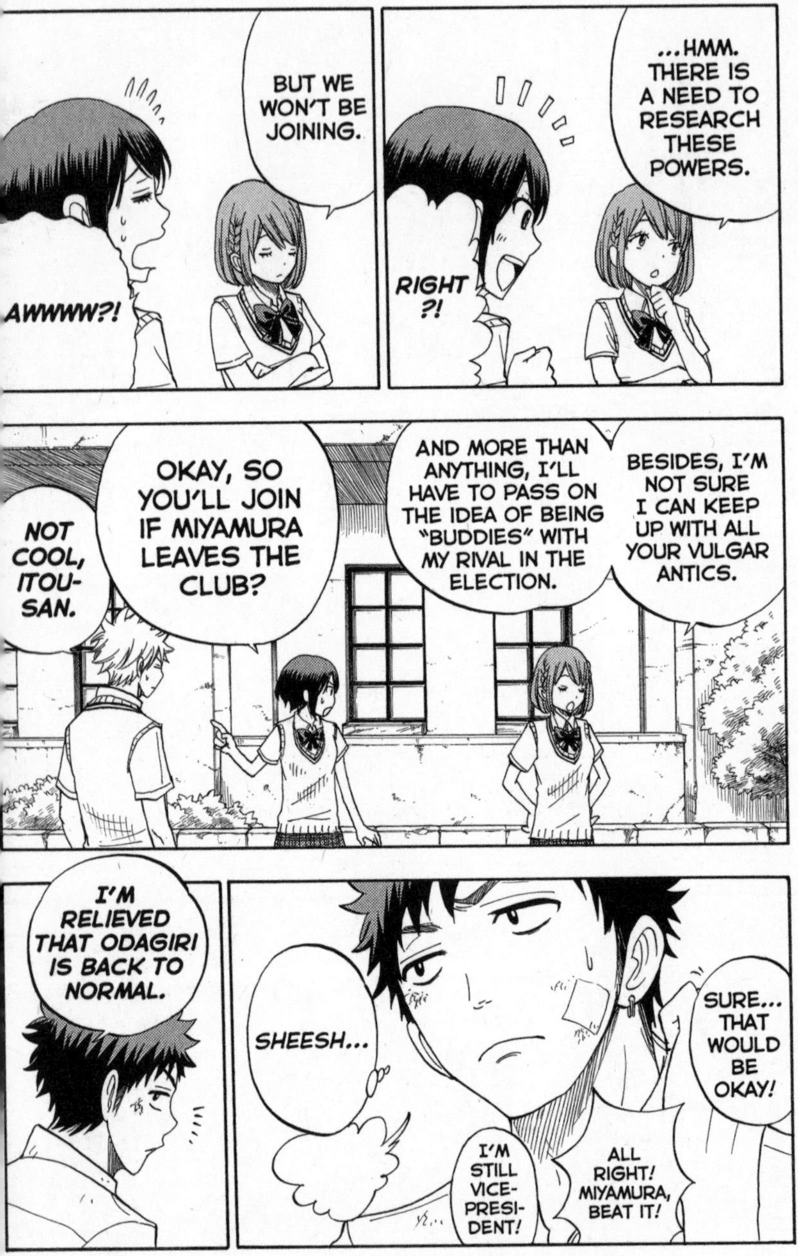
...HMM. THERE IS A NEED TO RESEARCH THESE POWERS.
RIGHT ?!
BUT WE WON'T BE JOINING.
AWWWW?!
BESIDES, I'M NOT SURE I CAN KEEP UP WITH ALL YOUR VULGAR ANTICS.
AND MORE THAN ANYTHING, I'LL HAVE TO PASS ON THE IDEA OF BEING "BUDDIES" WITH MY RIVAL IN THE ELECTION.
OKAY, SO YOU'LL JOIN IF MIYAMURA LEAVES THE CLUB?
NOT COOL, ITOU-SAN.
SURE... THAT WOULD BE OKAY!
ALL RIGHT! MIYAMURA, BEAT IT!
I'M STILL VICE-PRESIDENT!
SHEESH...
I'M RELIEVED THAT ODAGIRI IS BACK TO NORMAL.

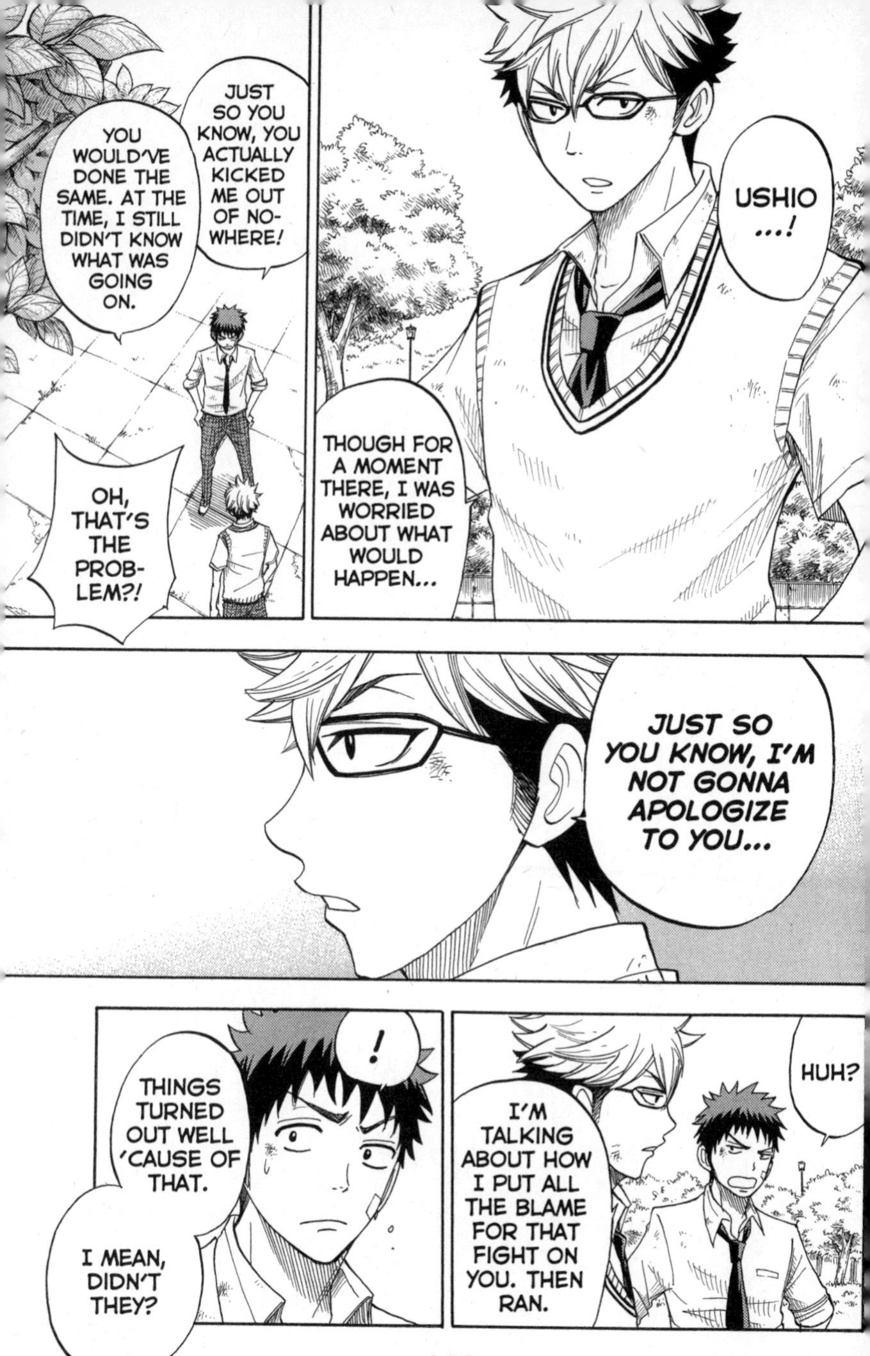
USHIO ...!
THOUGH FOR A MOMENT THERE, I WAS WORRIED ABOUT WHAT WOULD HAPPEN...
JUST SO YOU KNOW, YOU ACTUALLY KICKED ME OUT OF NO-WHERE!
YOU WOULD'VE DONE THE SAME. AT THE TIME, I STILL DIDN'T KNOW WHAT WAS GOING ON.
OH, THAT'S THE PROB-LEM?!
JUST SO YOU KNOW, I'M NOT GONNA APOLOGIZE TO YOU...
HUH?
I'M TALKING ABOUT HOW I PUT ALL THE BLAME FOR THAT FIGHT ON YOU. THEN RAN.
!
THINGS TURNED OUT WELL 'CAUSE OF THAT.
I MEAN, DIDN'T THEY?

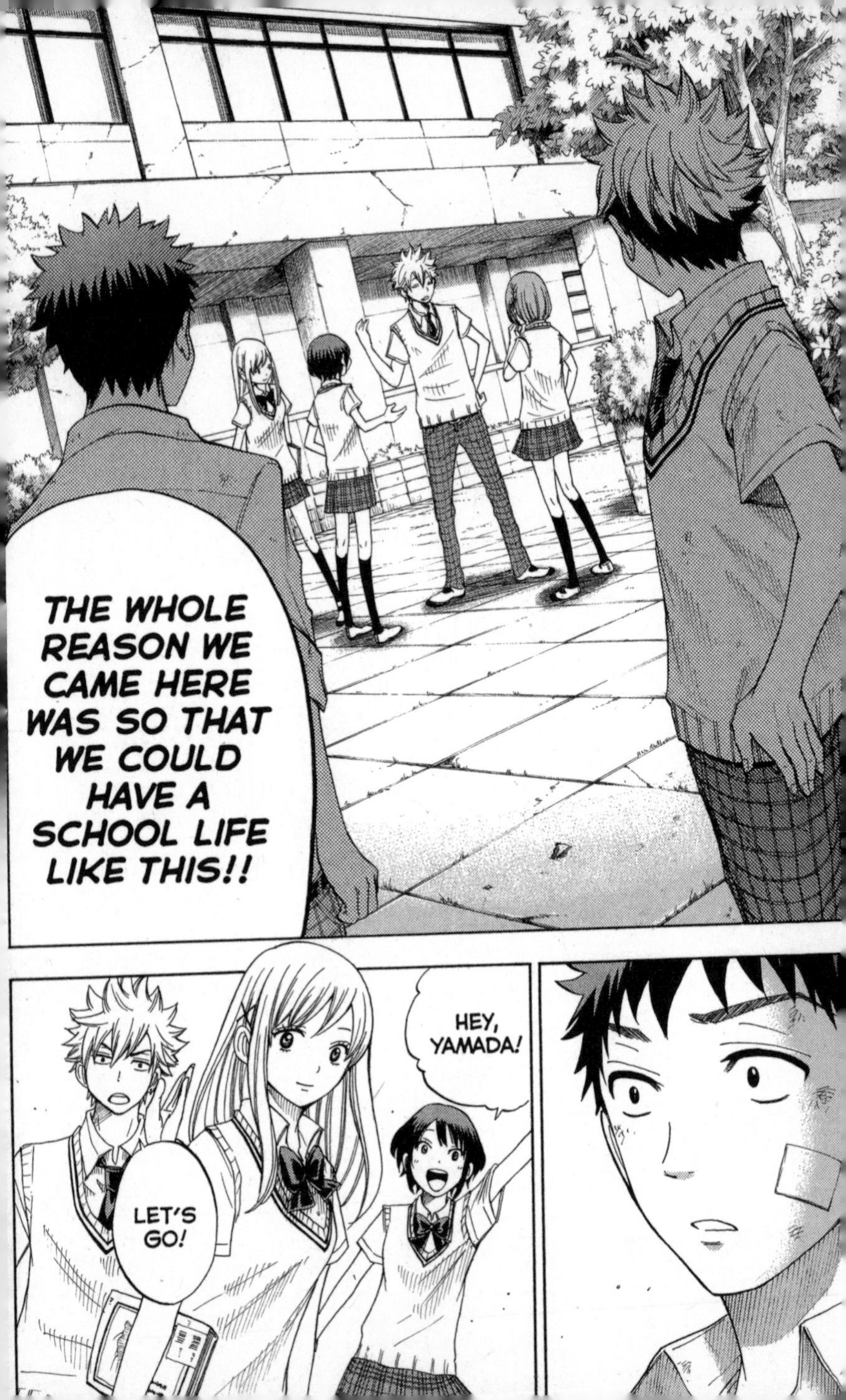
THE WHOLE REASON WE CAME HERE WAS SO THAT WE COULD HAVE A SCHOOL LIFE LIKE THIS!!
HEY, YAMADA!
LET'S GO!

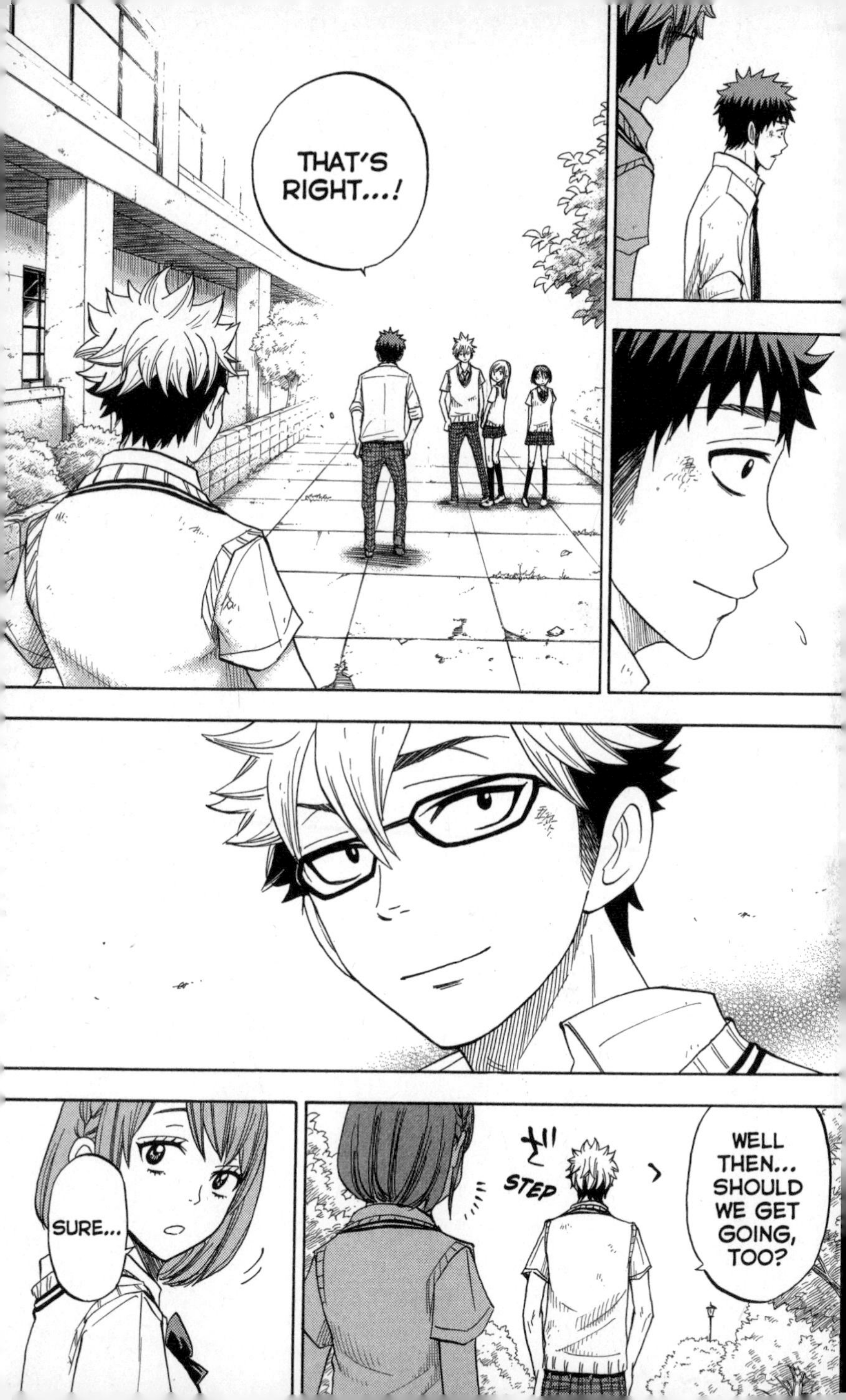
THAT'S RIGHT...!
STEP
WELL THEN... SHOULD WE GET GOING, TOO?
SURE...

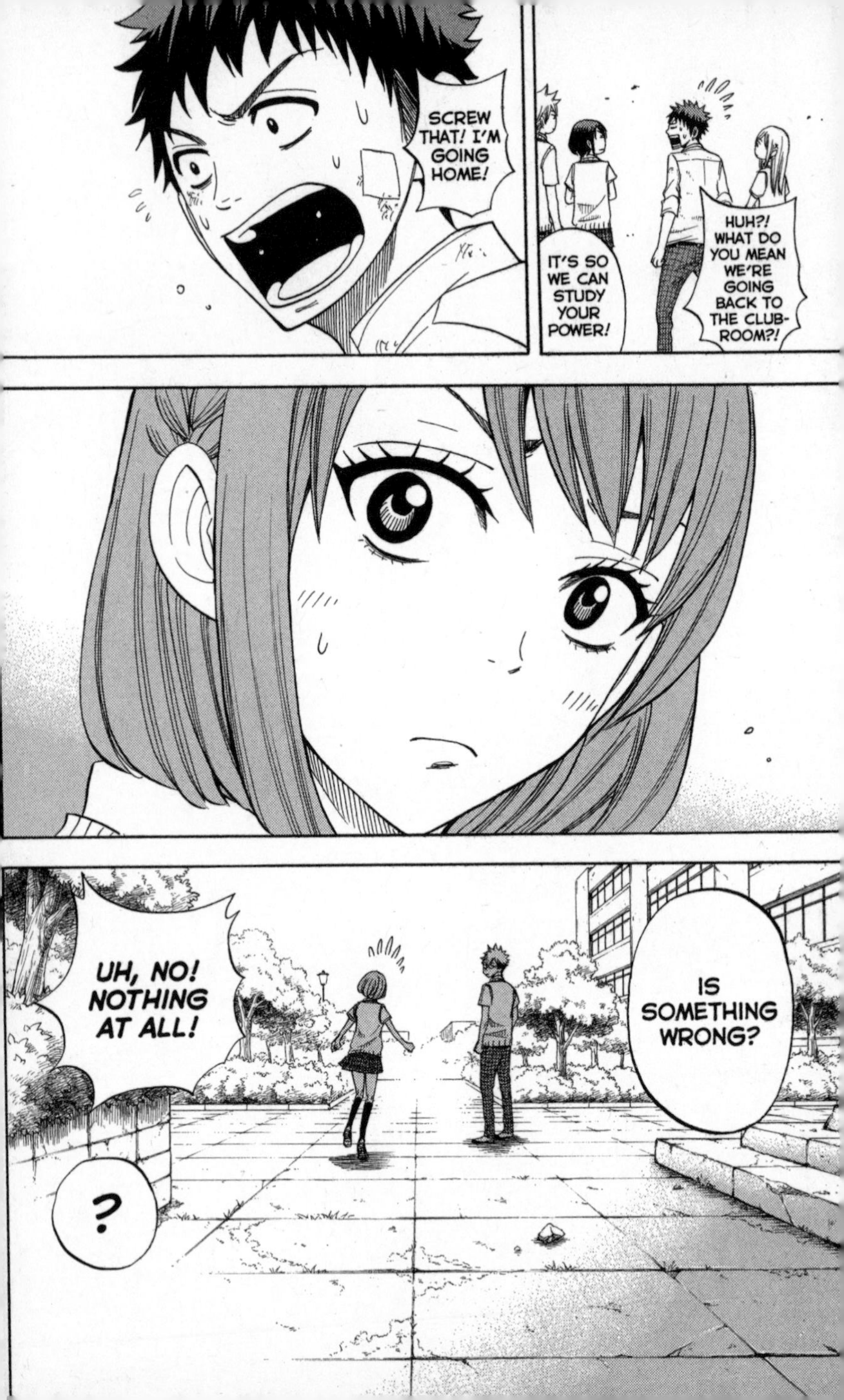
HUH?! WHAT DO YOU MEAN WE'RE GOING BACK TO THE CLUB-ROOM?!
IT'S SO WE CAN STUDY YOUR POWER!
SCREW THAT! I'M GOING HOME!
IS SOMETHING WRONG?
UH, NO! NOTHING AT ALL!
?

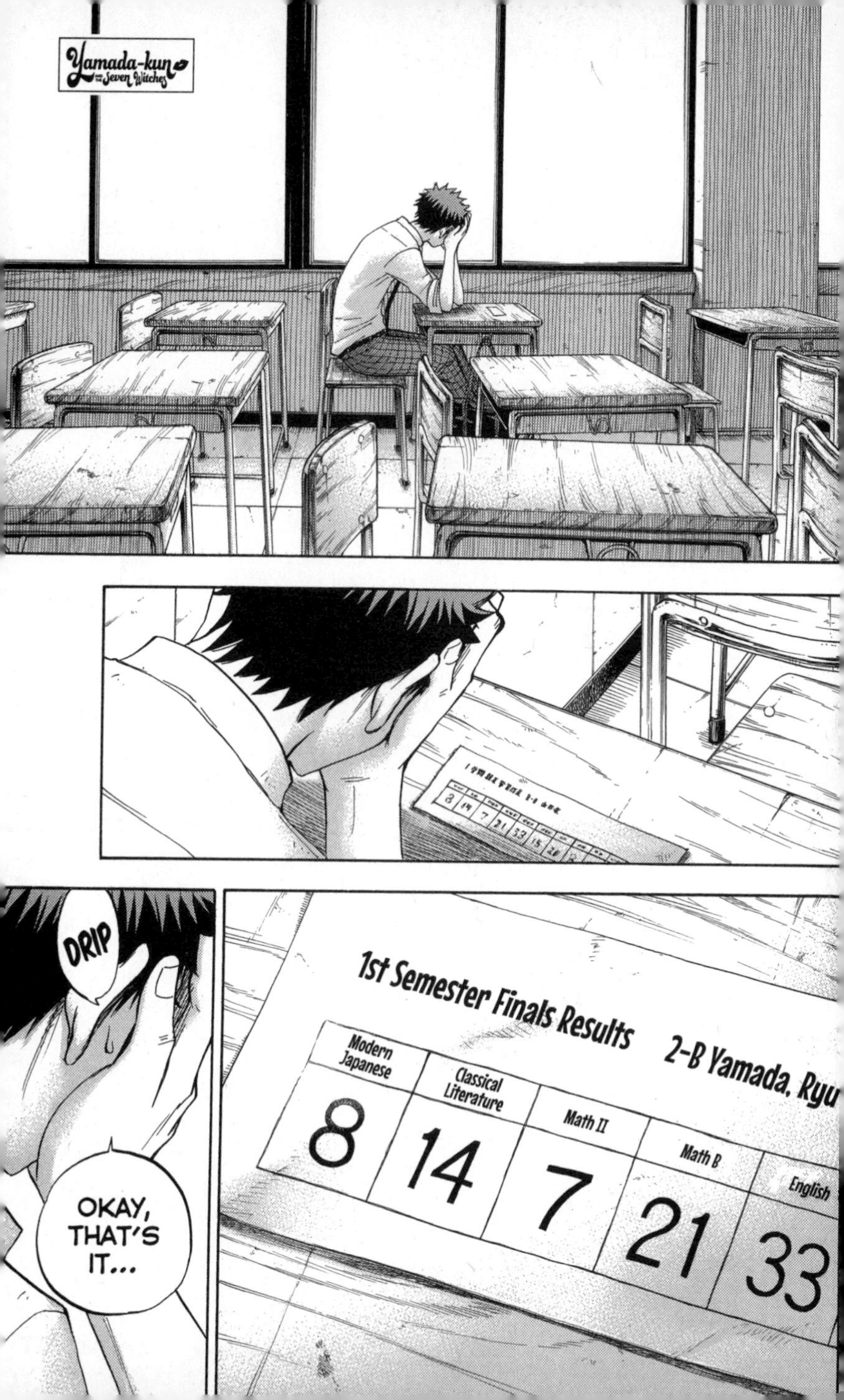
Yamada-kun
Seven Witches
1st Semester Finals Results
2-B Yamada, Ryu
Modern Japanese
8
Classical Literature
14
Math II
7
Math B
21
English
33
DRIP
OKAY, THAT'S IT...

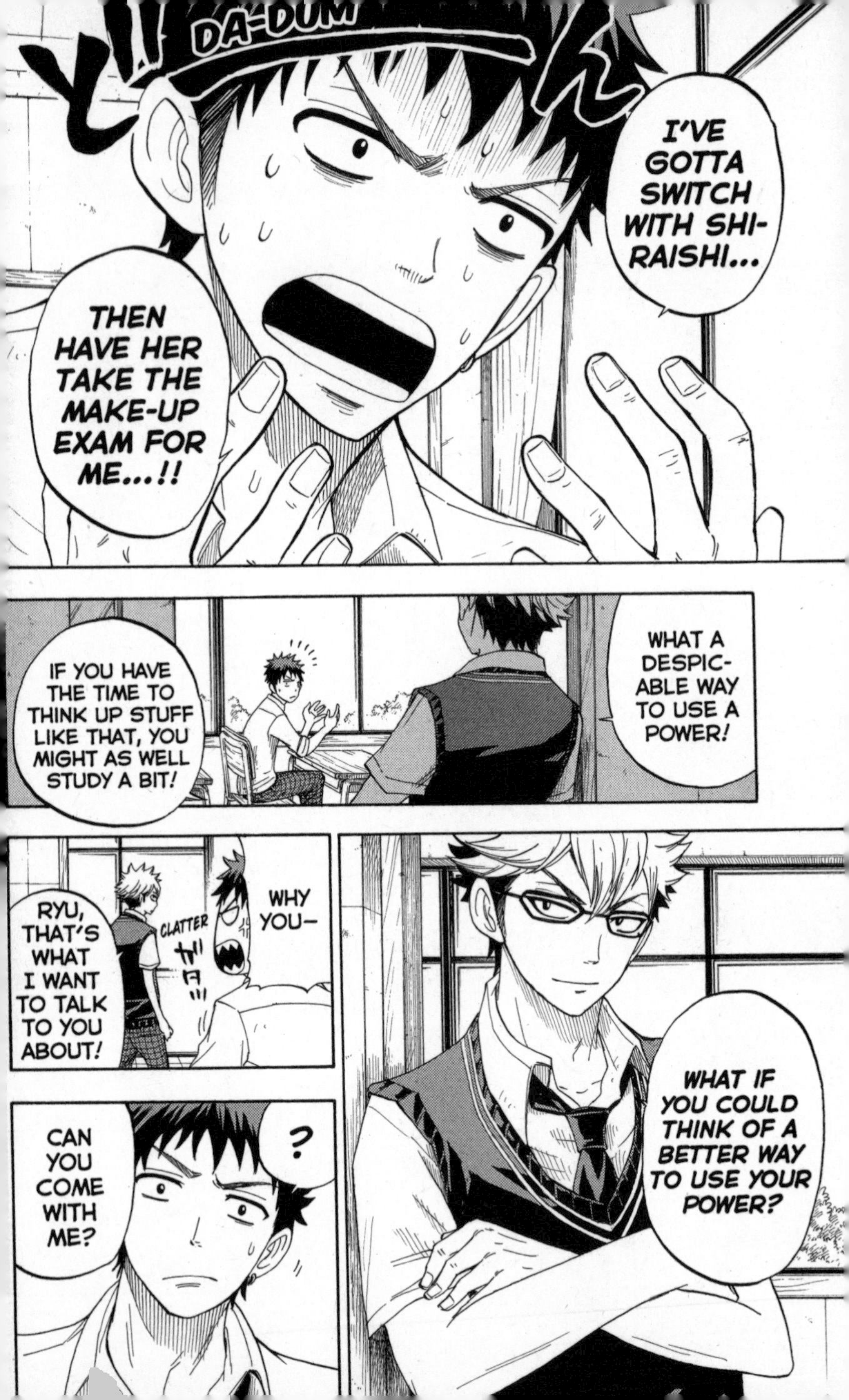
DA-DUM
I'VE GOTTA SWITCH WITH SHI-RAISHI...
THEN HAVE HER TAKE THE MAKE-UP EXAM FOR ME...!!
WHAT A DESPIC-ABLE WAY TO USE A POWER!
IF YOU HAVE THE TIME TO THINK UP STUFF LIKE THAT, YOU MIGHT AS WELL STUDY A BIT!
WHAT IF YOU COULD THINK OF A BETTER WAY TO USE YOUR POWER?
WHY YOU—
CLATTER
RYU, THAT'S WHAT I WANT TO TALK TO YOU ABOUT!
?
CAN YOU COME WITH ME?

CHAPTER 24: We gotta find 'em!

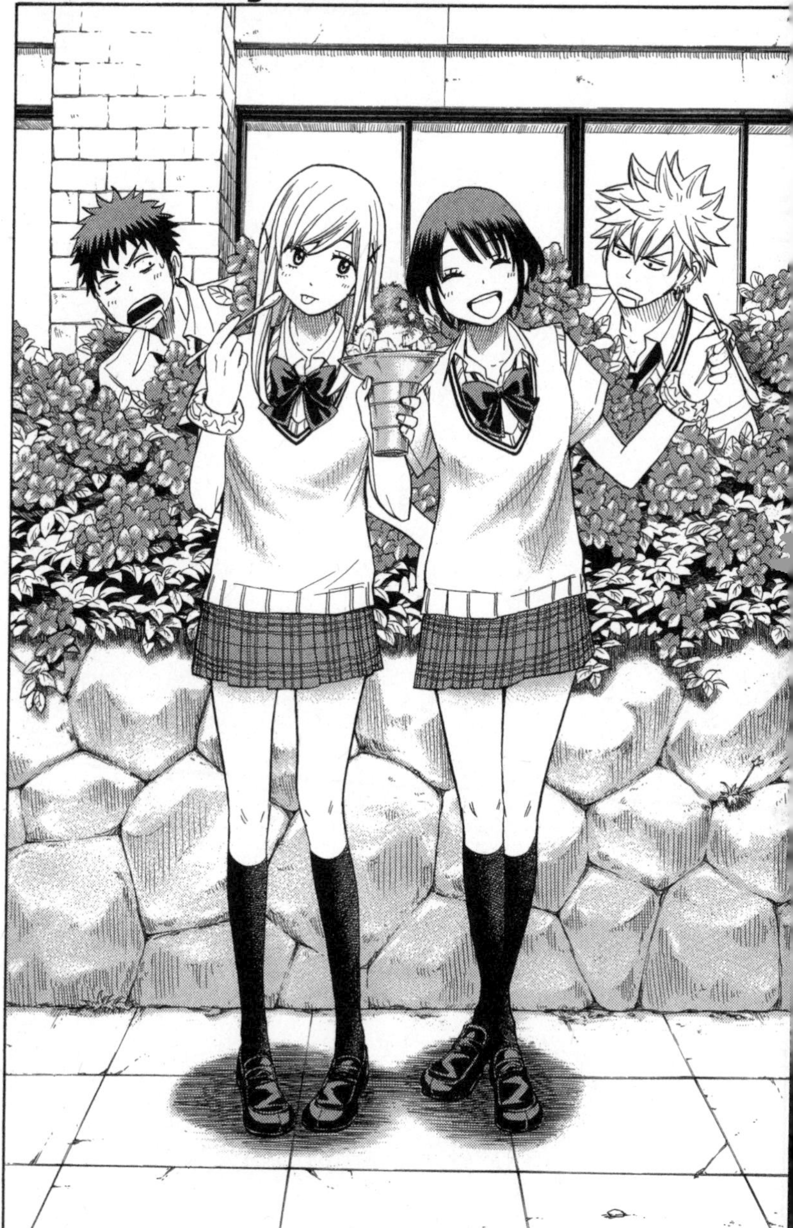

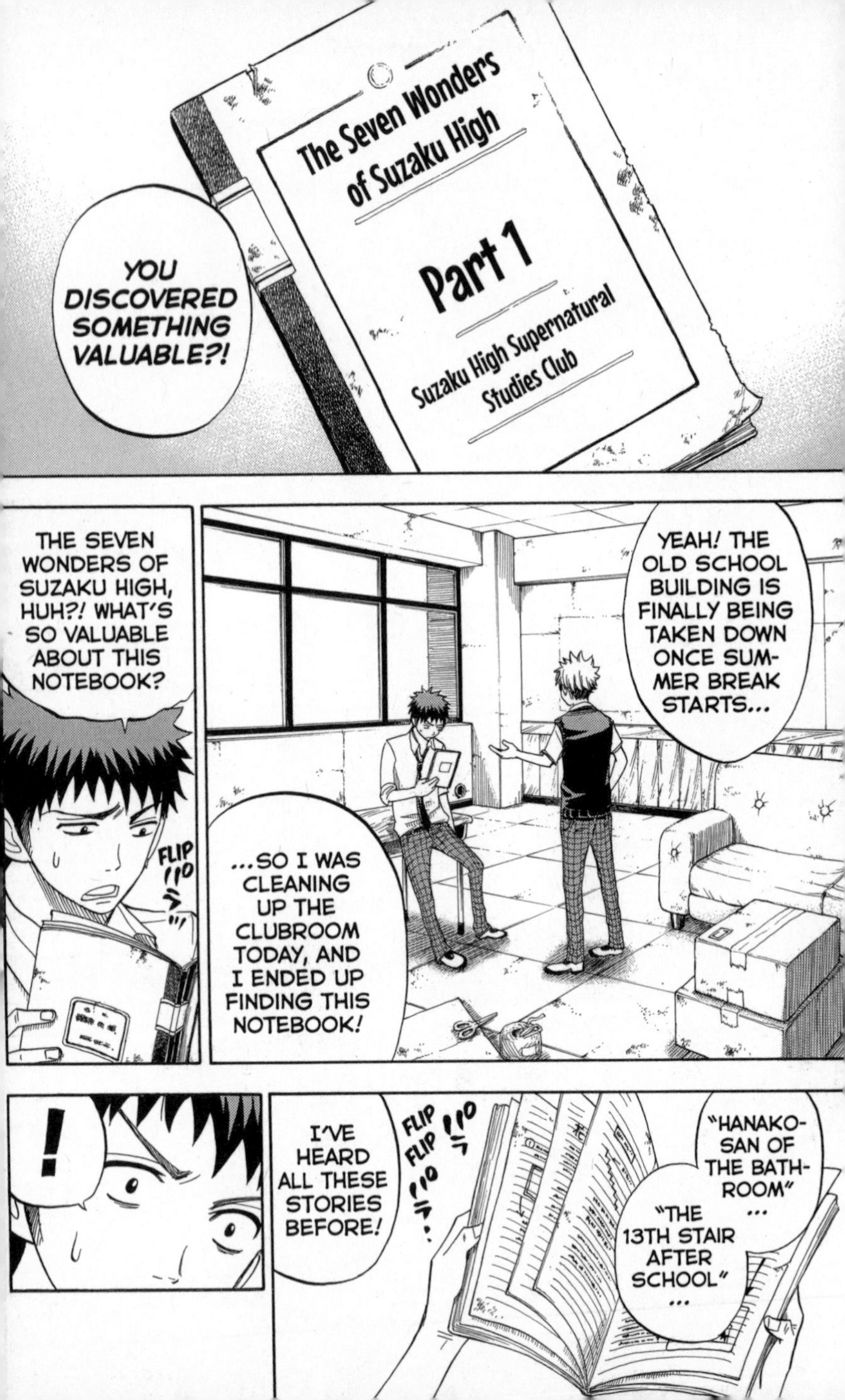
The Seven Wonders of Suzaku High
Part 1
Suzaku High Supernatural Studies Club
YOU DISCOVERED SOMETHING VALUABLE?!
YEAH! THE OLD SCHOOL BUILDING IS FINALLY BEING TAKEN DOWN ONCE SUMMER BREAK STARTS...
...SO I WAS CLEANING UP THE CLUBROOM TODAY, AND I ENDED UP FINDING THIS NOTEBOOK!
THE SEVEN WONDERS OF SUZAKU HIGH, HUH?! WHAT'S SO VALUABLE ABOUT THIS NOTEBOOK?
FLIP
"HANAKO-SAN OF THE BATHROOM"...
"THE 13TH STAIR AFTER SCHOOL"...
FLIP FLIP
I'VE HEARD ALL THESE STORIES BEFORE!
!

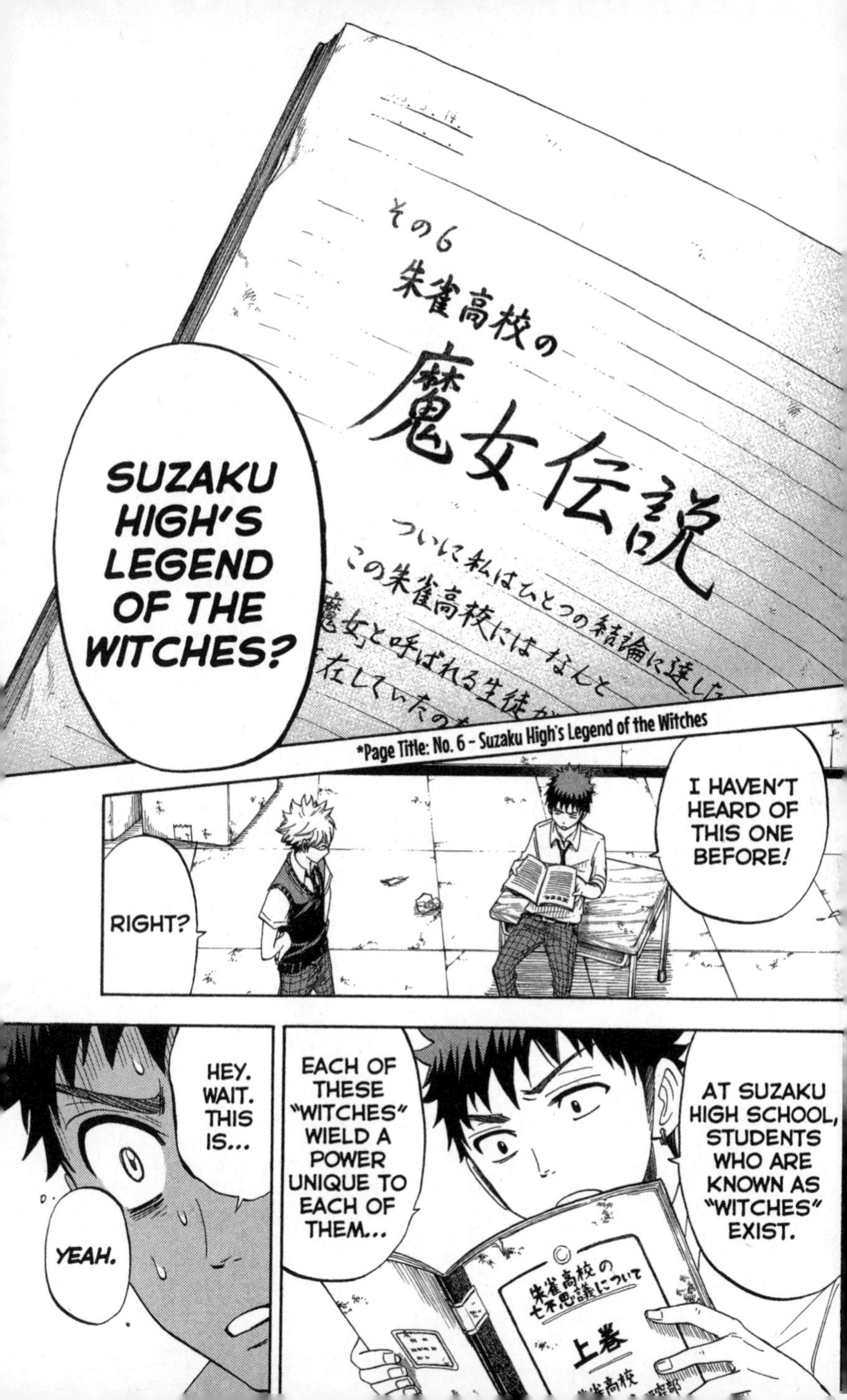
その6
朱雀高校の
魔女伝説
ついに私はひとつの結論に達し
この朱雀高校には なんと
魔女と呼ばれる生徒
在していた
SUZAKU HIGH'S LEGEND OF THE WITCHES?
*Page Title: No. 6 - Suzaku High's Legend of the Witches
I HAVEN'T HEARD OF THIS ONE BEFORE!
RIGHT?
AT SUZAKU HIGH SCHOOL, STUDENTS WHO ARE KNOWN AS "WITCHES" EXIST.
朱雀高校の七不思議について
上巻
EACH OF THESE "WITCHES" WIELD A POWER UNIQUE TO EACH OF THEM...
HEY. WAIT. THIS IS...
YEAH.

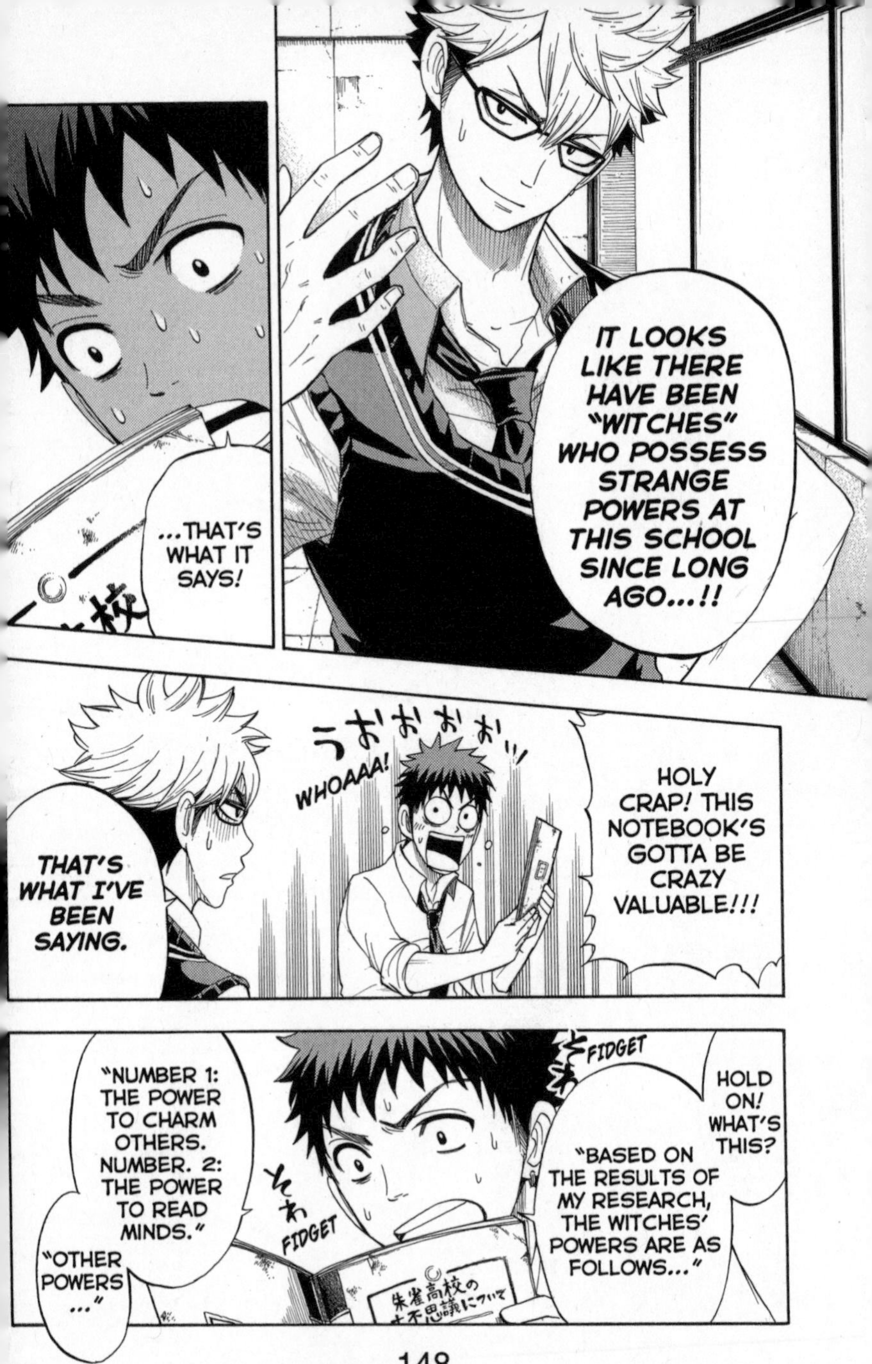
IT LOOKS LIKE THERE HAVE BEEN "WITCHES" WHO POSSESS STRANGE POWERS AT THIS SCHOOL SINCE LONG AGO...!!
...THAT'S WHAT IT SAYS!
HOLY CRAP! THIS NOTEBOOK'S GOTTA BE CRAZY VALUABLE!!!
うおおおお!!
WHOAAA!
THAT'S WHAT I'VE BEEN SAYING.
HOLD ON! WHAT'S THIS?
FIDGET
"BASED ON THE RESULTS OF MY RESEARCH, THE WITCHES' POWERS ARE AS FOLLOWS..."
"NUMBER 1: THE POWER TO CHARM OTHERS. NUMBER. 2: THE POWER TO READ MINDS."
FIDGET
"OTHER POWERS ..."
朱雀高校の

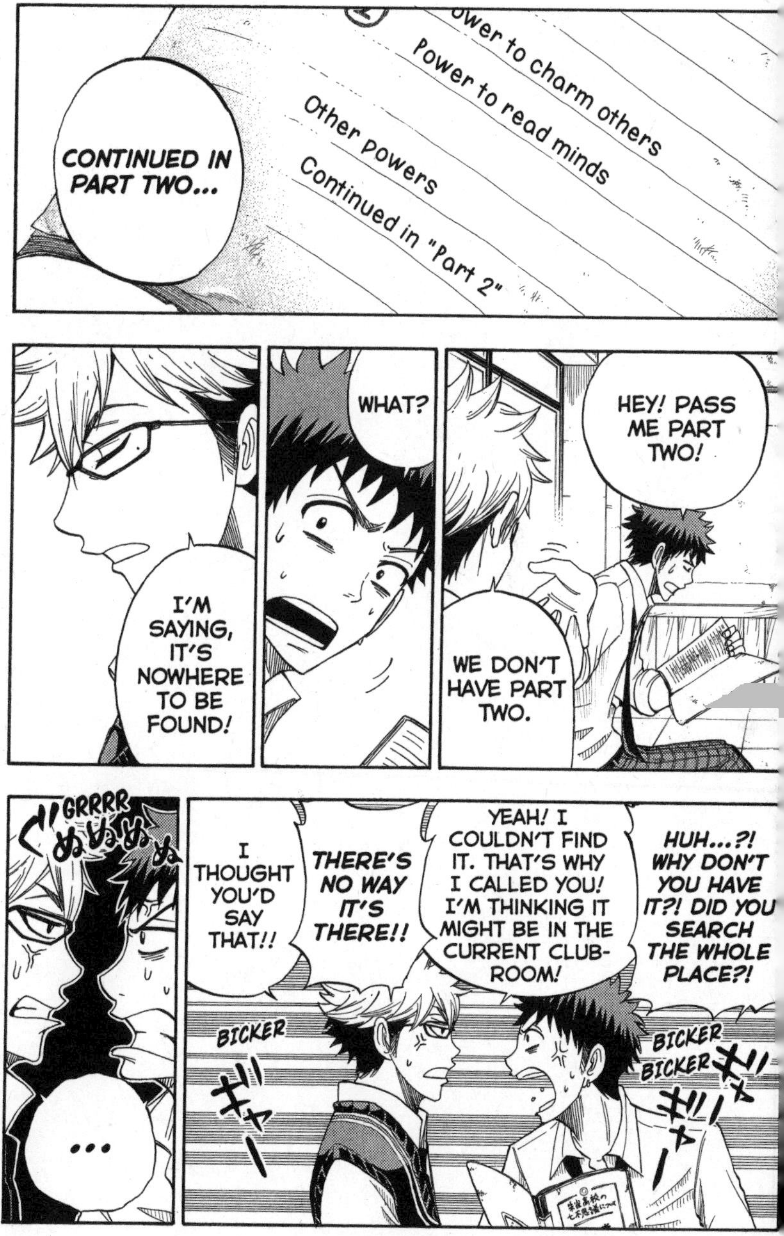
...ower to charm others
Power to read minds
Other powers
Continued in "Part 2"
CONTINUED IN PART TWO...
HEY! PASS ME PART TWO!
WE DON'T HAVE PART TWO.
WHAT?
I'M SAYING, IT'S NOWHERE TO BE FOUND!
HUH...?! WHY DON'T YOU HAVE IT?! DID YOU SEARCH THE WHOLE PLACE?!
YEAH! I COULDN'T FIND IT. THAT'S WHY I CALLED YOU! I'M THINKING IT MIGHT BE IN THE CURRENT CLUB-ROOM!
THERE'S NO WAY IT'S THERE!!
I THOUGHT YOU'D SAY THAT!!
BICKER BICKER
BICKER
GRRRR
ぐぬぬぬぬ
...

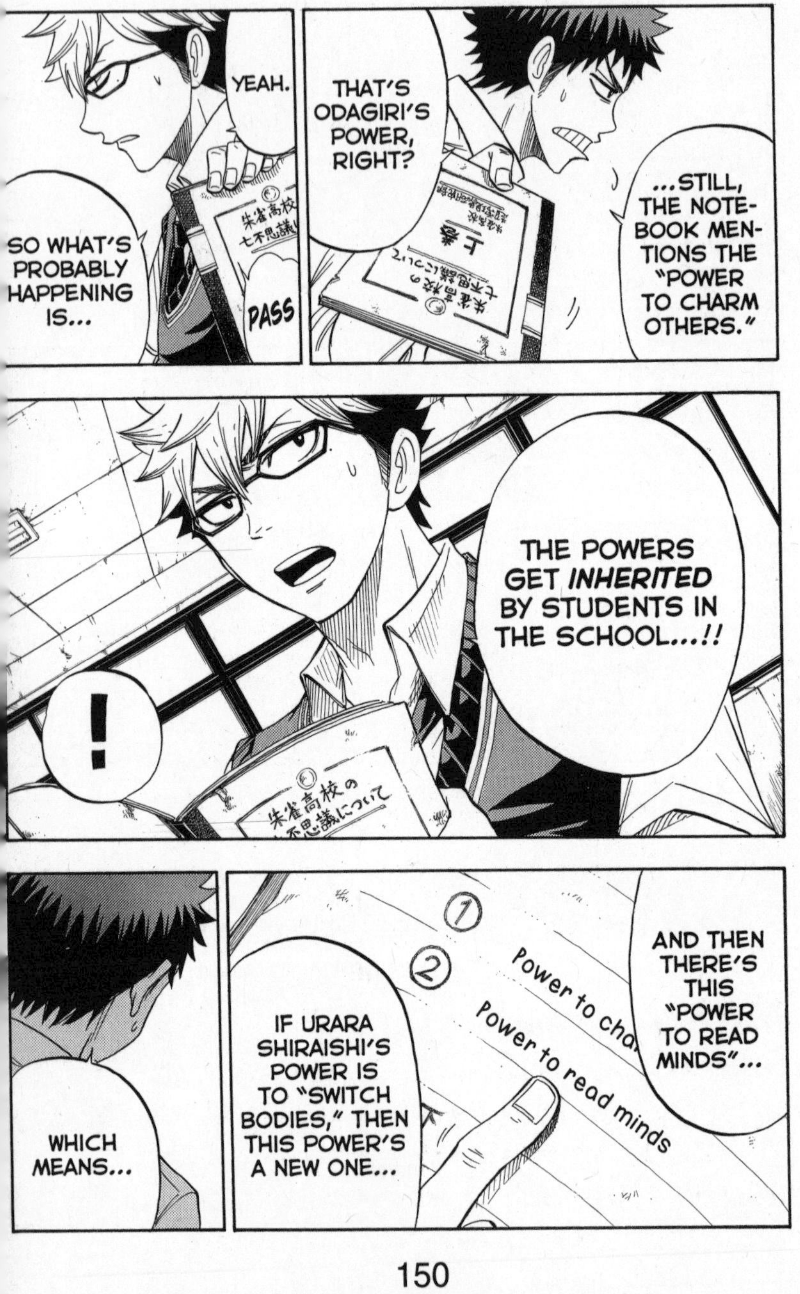
...STILL, THE NOTE-BOOK MEN-TIONS THE "POWER TO CHARM OTHERS."
THAT'S ODAGIRI'S POWER, RIGHT?
YEAH.
PASS
SO WHAT'S PROBABLY HAPPENING IS...
THE POWERS GET *INHERITED* BY STUDENTS IN THE SCHOOL...!!
!
AND THEN THERE'S THIS "POWER TO READ MINDS"...
1
2
Power to cha
Power to read minds
IF URARA SHIRAISHI'S POWER IS TO "SWITCH BODIES," THEN THIS POWER'S A NEW ONE...
WHICH MEANS...

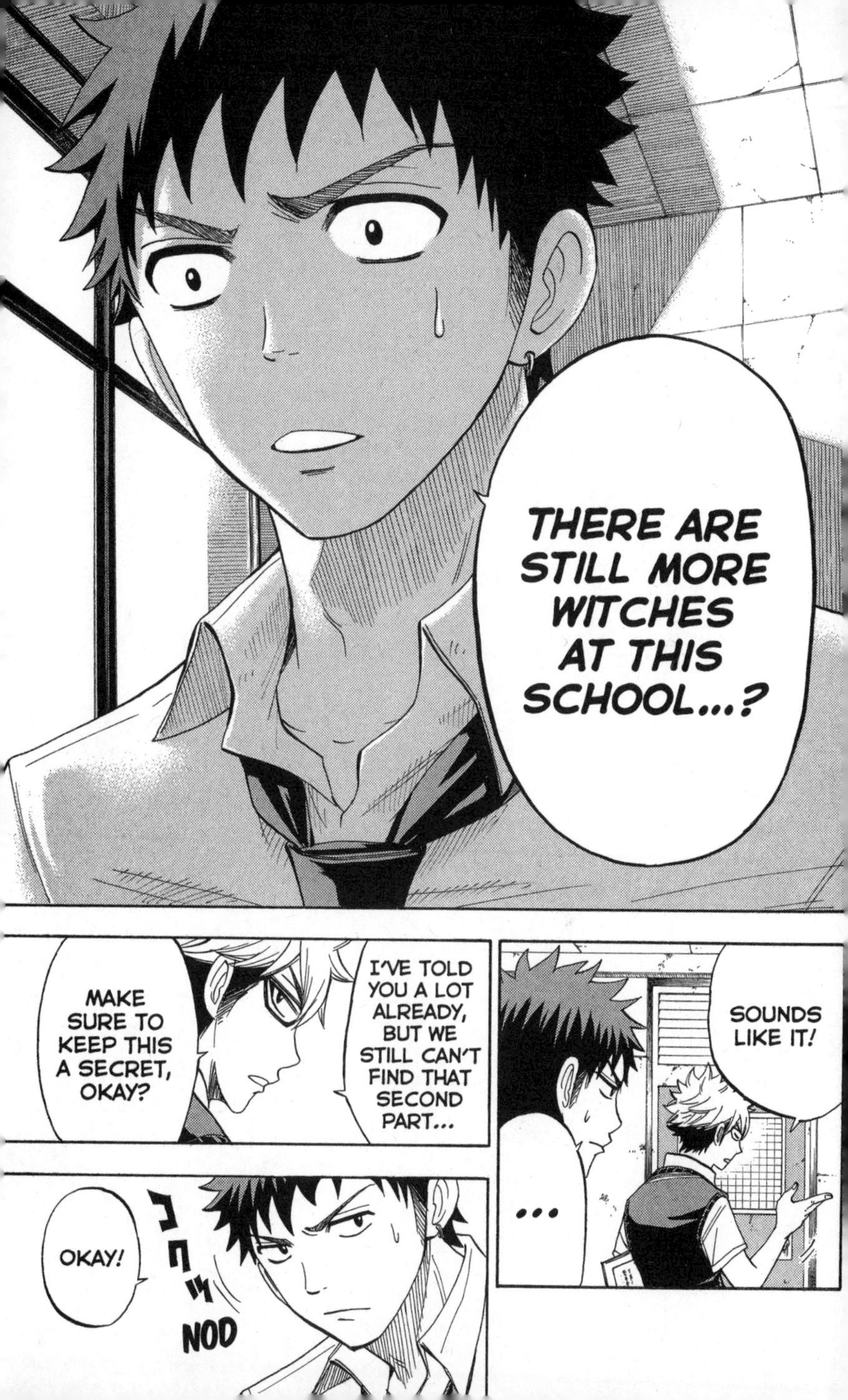
THERE ARE STILL MORE WITCHES AT THIS SCHOOL...?
SOUNDS LIKE IT!
...
I'VE TOLD YOU A LOT ALREADY, BUT WE STILL CAN'T FIND THAT SECOND PART...
MAKE SURE TO KEEP THIS A SECRET, OKAY?
OKAY!
NOD

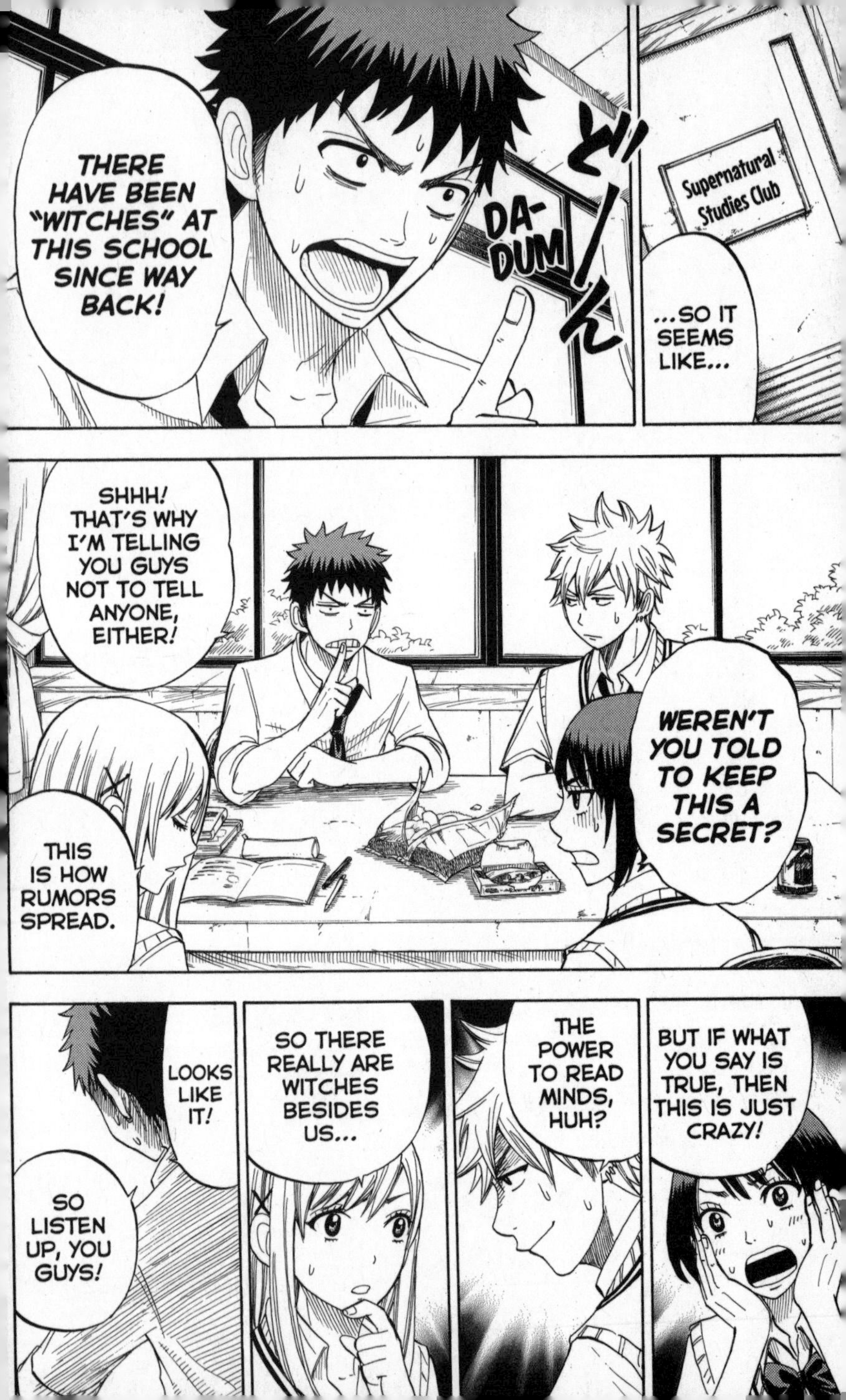
Supernatural Studies Club
...SO IT SEEMS LIKE...
どーん
DA-DUM
THERE HAVE BEEN "WITCHES" AT THIS SCHOOL SINCE WAY BACK!
WEREN'T YOU TOLD TO KEEP THIS A SECRET?
SHHH! THAT'S WHY I'M TELLING YOU GUYS NOT TO TELL ANYONE, EITHER!
THIS IS HOW RUMORS SPREAD.
BUT IF WHAT YOU SAY IS TRUE, THEN THIS IS JUST CRAZY!
THE POWER TO READ MINDS, HUH?
SO THERE REALLY ARE WITCHES BESIDES US...
LOOKS LIKE IT!
SO LISTEN UP, YOU GUYS!

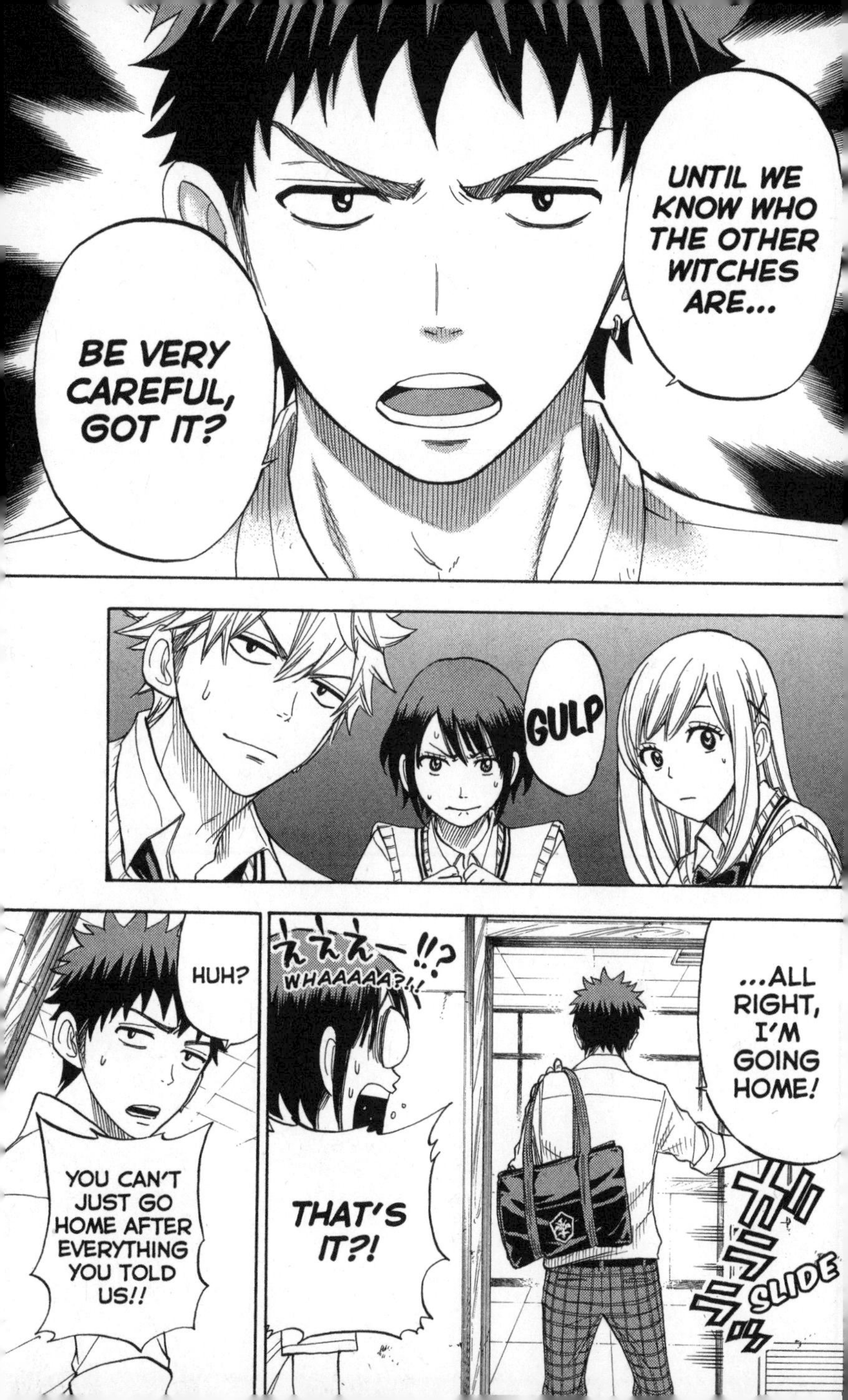
UNTIL WE KNOW WHO THE OTHER WITCHES ARE...
BE VERY CAREFUL, GOT IT?
GULP
...ALL RIGHT, I'M GOING HOME!
SLIDE
えええー!!?
WHAAAAA?!!
THAT'S IT?!
HUH?
YOU CAN'T JUST GO HOME AFTER EVERYTHING YOU TOLD US!!

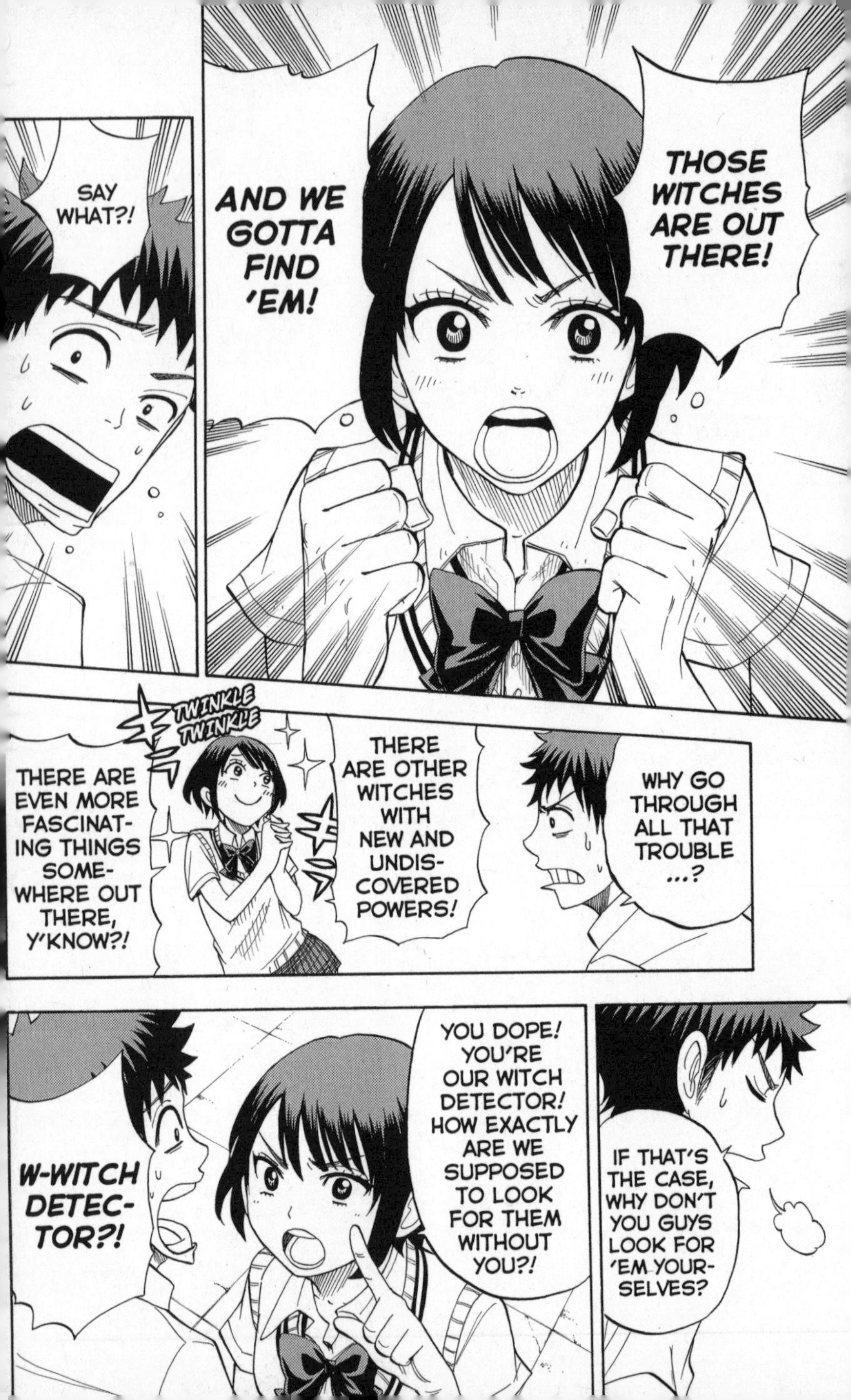
THOSE WITCHES ARE OUT THERE!
AND WE GOTTA FIND 'EM!
SAY WHAT?!
WHY GO THROUGH ALL THAT TROUBLE ...?
THERE ARE OTHER WITCHES WITH NEW AND UNDIS-COVERED POWERS!
TWINKLE TWINKLE
THERE ARE EVEN MORE FASCINAT-ING THINGS SOME-WHERE OUT THERE, Y'KNOW?!
IF THAT'S THE CASE, WHY DON'T YOU GUYS LOOK FOR 'EM YOUR-SELVES?
YOU DOPE! YOU'RE OUR WITCH DETECTOR! HOW EXACTLY ARE WE SUPPOSED TO LOOK FOR THEM WITHOUT YOU?!
W-WITCH DETEC-TOR?!

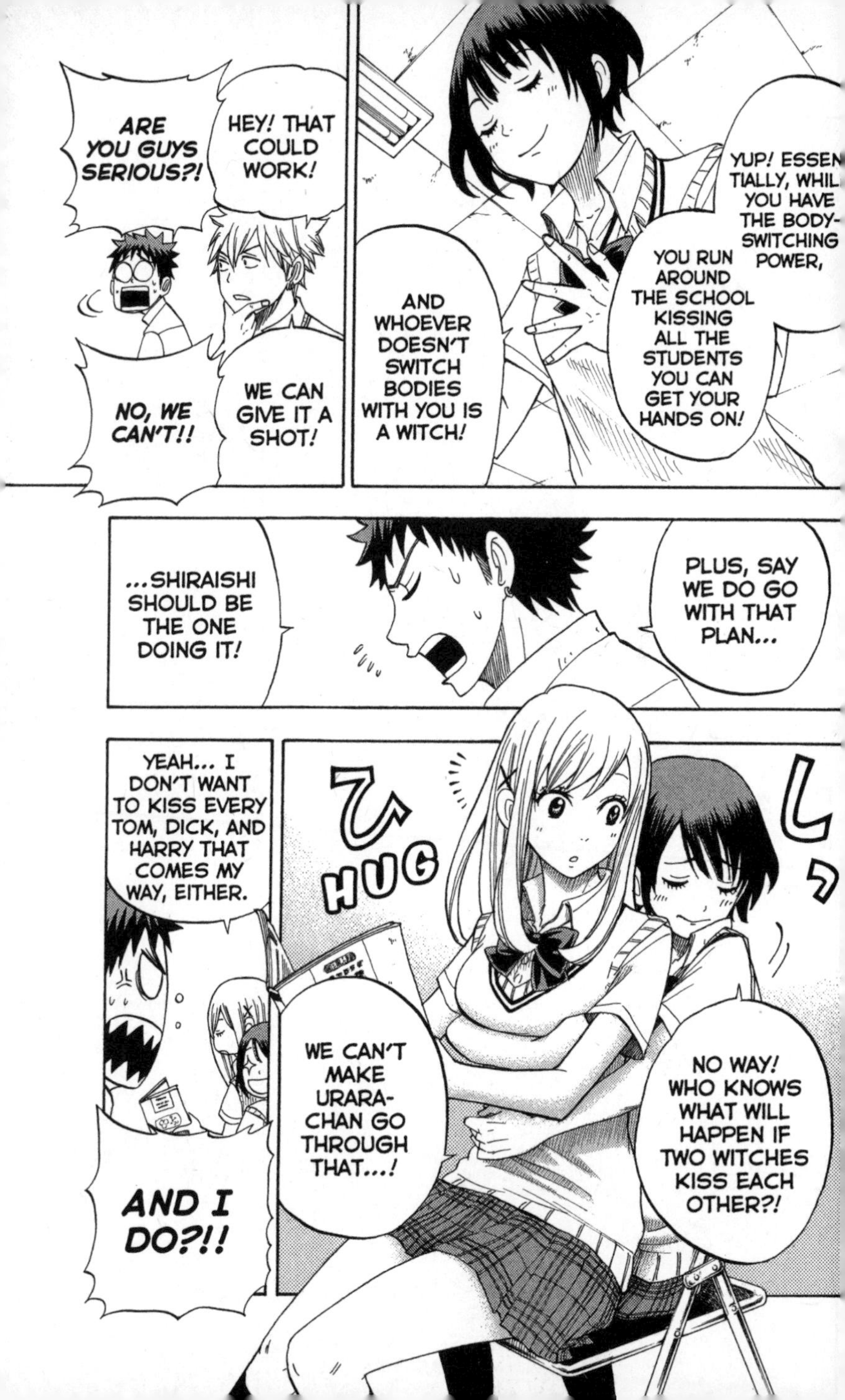
YUP! ESSENTIALLY, WHIL YOU HAVE THE BODY-SWITCHING POWER,
YOU RUN AROUND THE SCHOOL KISSING ALL THE STUDENTS YOU CAN GET YOUR HANDS ON!
AND WHOEVER DOESN'T SWITCH BODIES WITH YOU IS A WITCH!
HEY! THAT COULD WORK!
ARE YOU GUYS SERIOUS?!
WE CAN GIVE IT A SHOT!
NO, WE CAN'T!!
PLUS, SAY WE DO GO WITH THAT PLAN...
...SHIRAISHI SHOULD BE THE ONE DOING IT!
HUG
NO WAY! WHO KNOWS WHAT WILL HAPPEN IF TWO WITCHES KISS EACH OTHER?!
WE CAN'T MAKE URARA-CHAN GO THROUGH THAT...!
YEAH... I DON'T WANT TO KISS EVERY TOM, DICK, AND HARRY THAT COMES MY WAY, EITHER.
AND I DO?!!

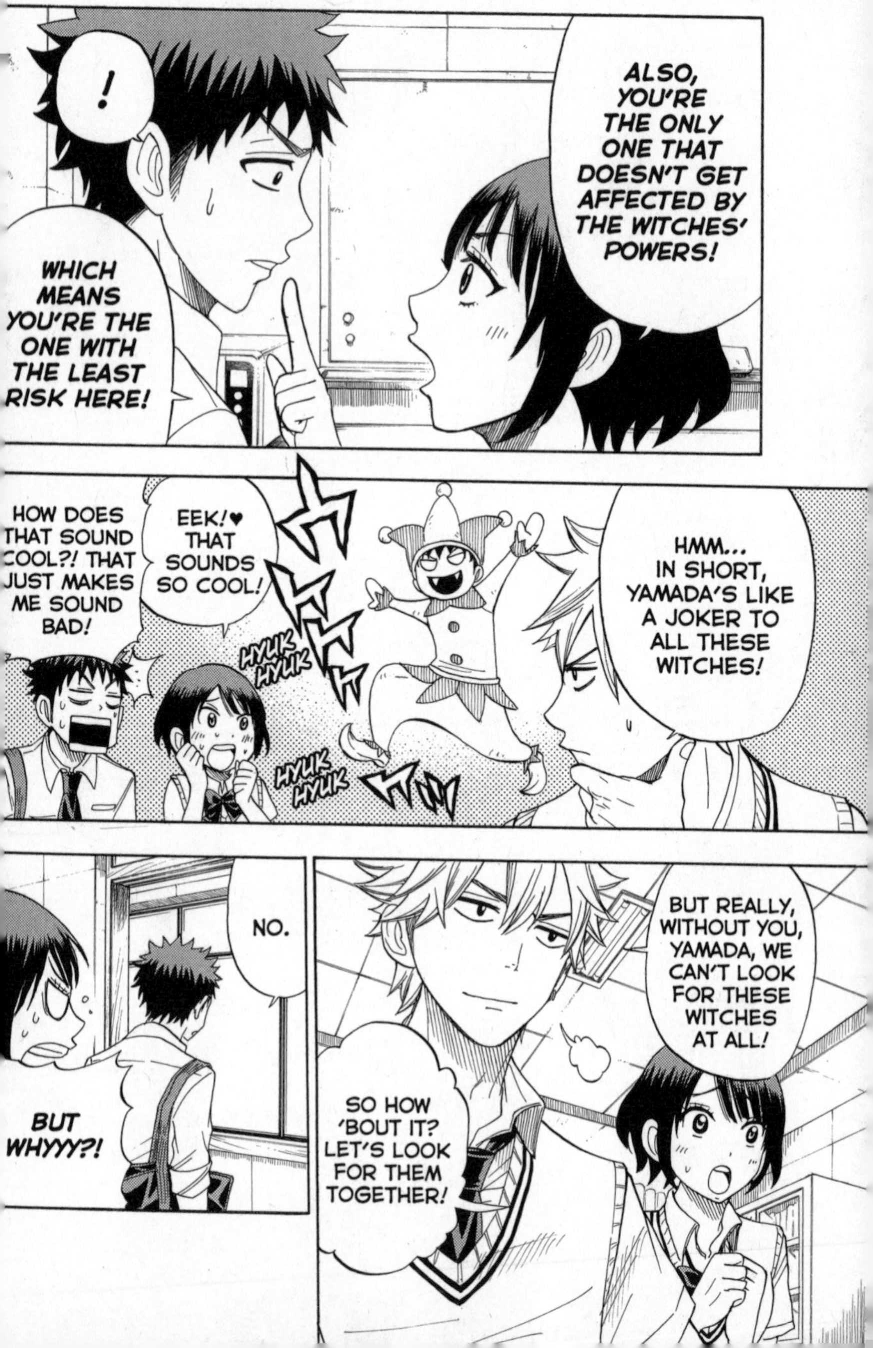
ALSO, YOU'RE THE ONLY ONE THAT DOESN'T GET AFFECTED BY THE WITCHES' POWERS!
!
WHICH MEANS YOU'RE THE ONE WITH THE LEAST RISK HERE!
HMM... IN SHORT, YAMADA'S LIKE A JOKER TO ALL THESE WITCHES!
HYUK HYUK
HYUK HYUK
EEK!♥ THAT SOUNDS SO COOL!
HOW DOES THAT SOUND COOL?! THAT JUST MAKES ME SOUND BAD!
BUT REALLY, WITHOUT YOU, YAMADA, WE CAN'T LOOK FOR THESE WITCHES AT ALL!
SO HOW 'BOUT IT? LET'S LOOK FOR THEM TOGETHER!
NO.
BUT WHYYY?!

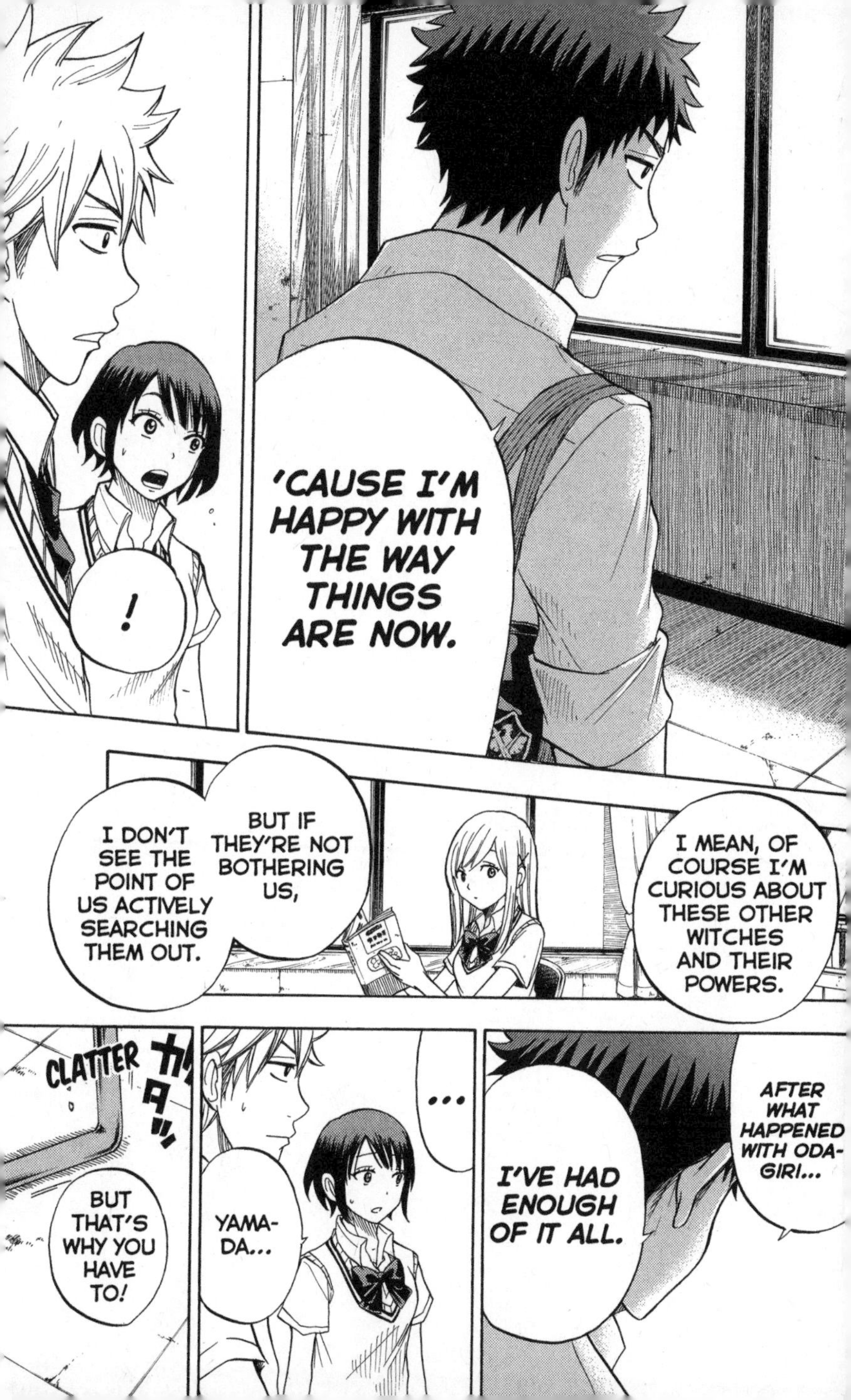
'CAUSE I'M HAPPY WITH THE WAY THINGS ARE NOW.
!
I MEAN, OF COURSE I'M CURIOUS ABOUT THESE OTHER WITCHES AND THEIR POWERS.
BUT IF THEY'RE NOT BOTHERING US,
I DON'T SEE THE POINT OF US ACTIVELY SEARCHING THEM OUT.
AFTER WHAT HAPPENED WITH ODA-GIRI...
I'VE HAD ENOUGH OF IT ALL.
...
YAMA-DA...
CLATTER
カタッ
BUT THAT'S WHY YOU HAVE TO!

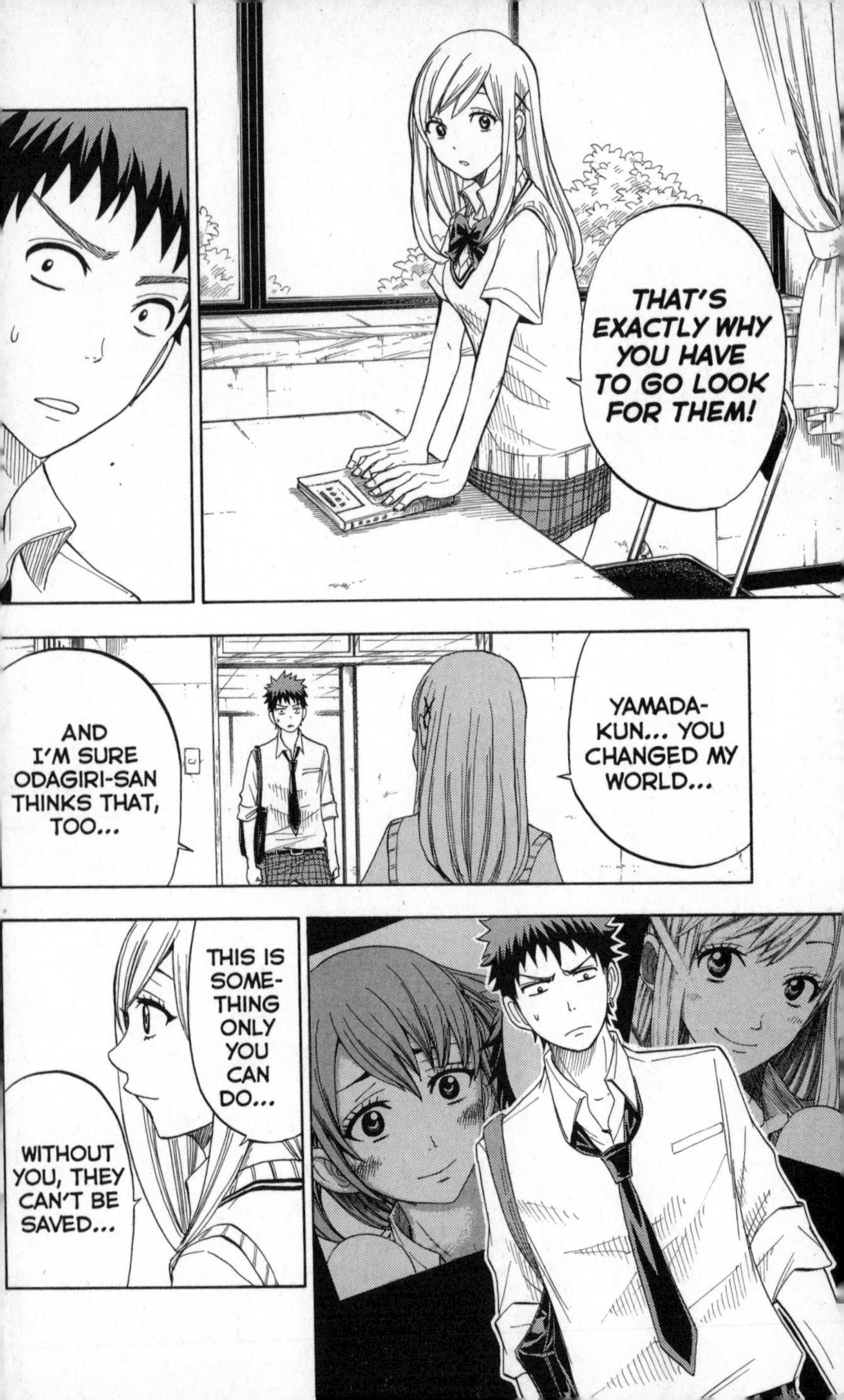
THAT'S EXACTLY WHY YOU HAVE TO GO LOOK FOR THEM!
YAMADA-KUN... YOU CHANGED MY WORLD...
AND I'M SURE ODAGIRI-SAN THINKS THAT, TOO...
THIS IS SOME-THING ONLY YOU CAN DO...
WITHOUT YOU, THEY CAN'T BE SAVED...

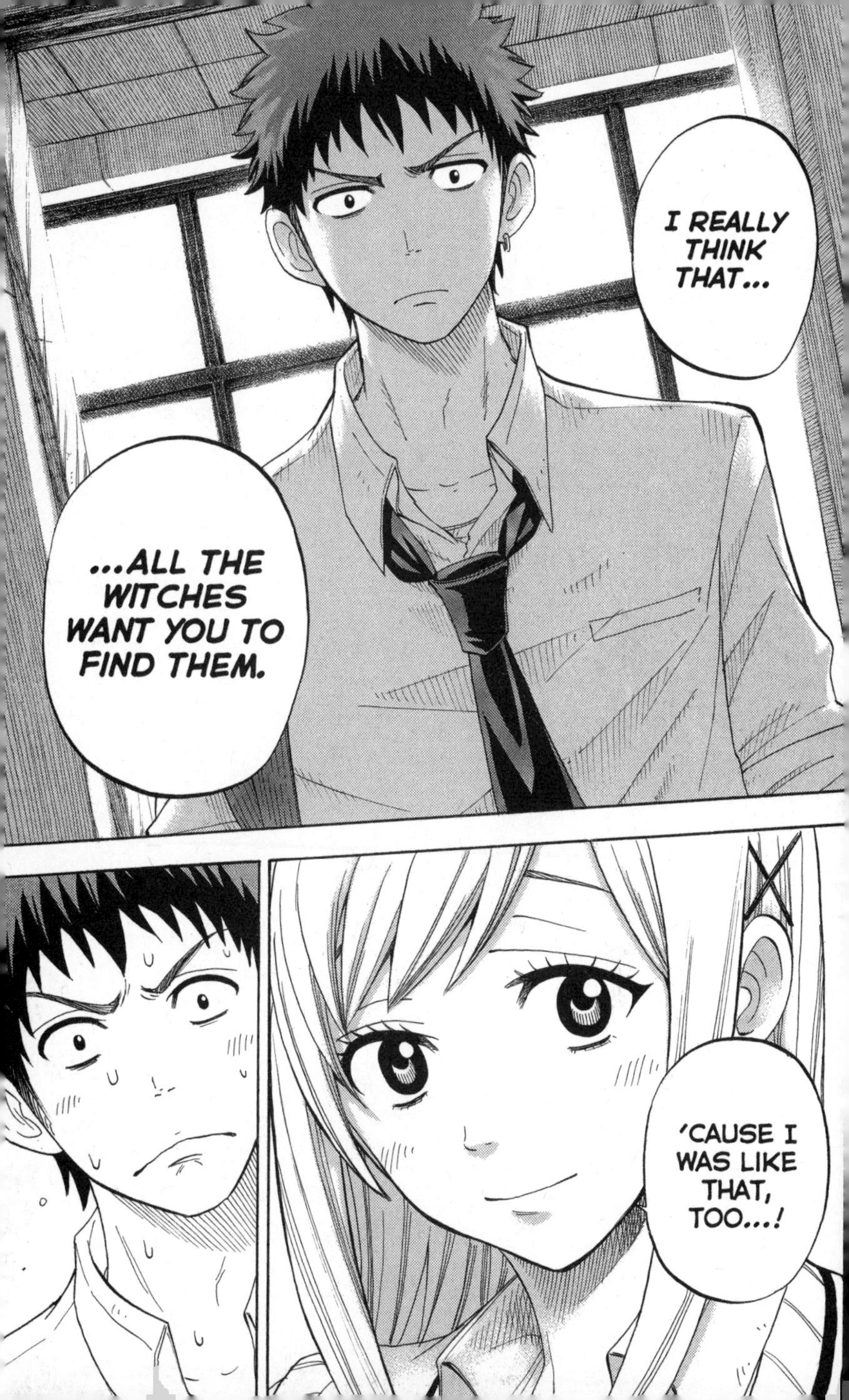
I REALLY THINK THAT...
...ALL THE WITCHES WANT YOU TO FIND THEM.
'CAUSE I WAS LIKE THAT, TOO...!

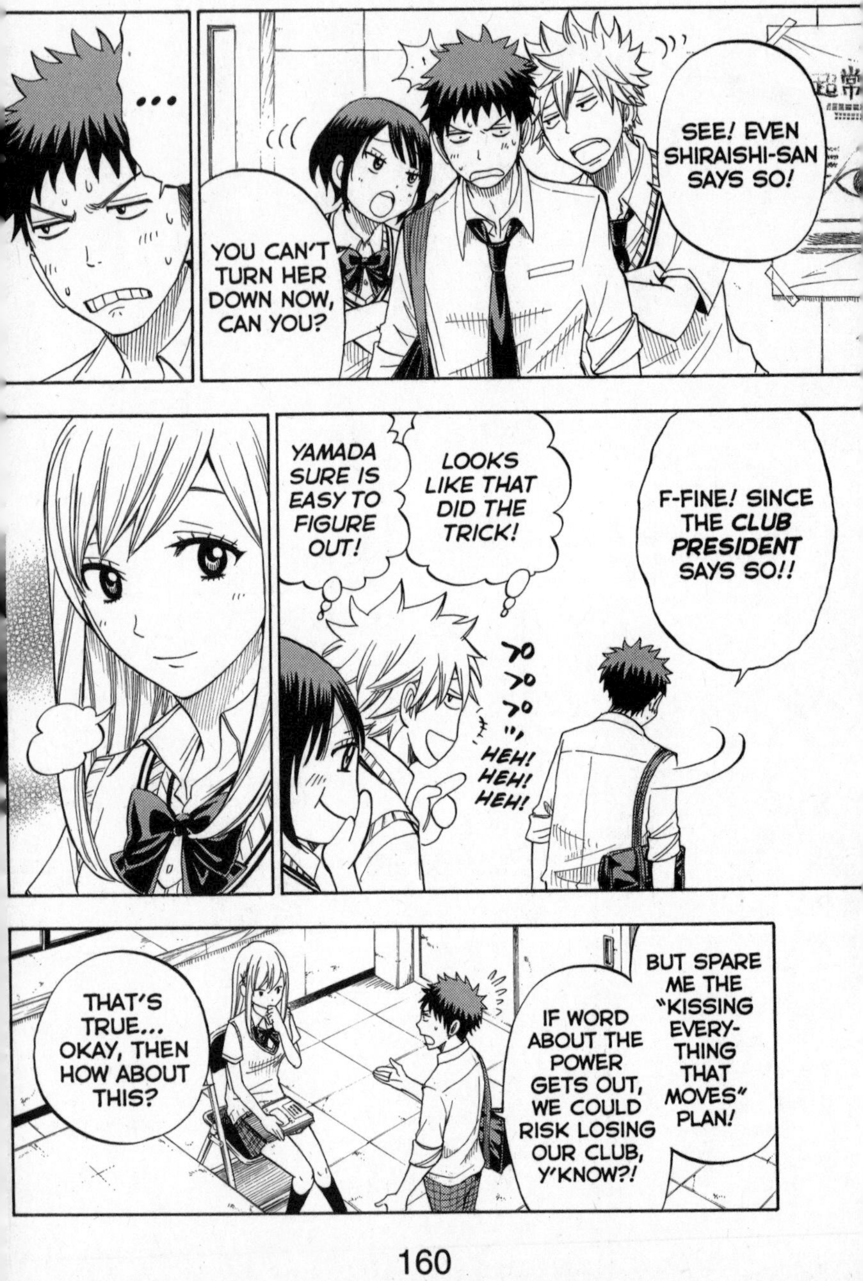
SEE! EVEN SHIRAISHI-SAN SAYS SO!
YOU CAN'T TURN HER DOWN NOW, CAN YOU?
...
F-FINE! SINCE THE CLUB PRESIDENT SAYS SO!!
LOOKS LIKE THAT DID THE TRICK!
YAMADA SURE IS EASY TO FIGURE OUT!
HEH! HEH! HEH!
BUT SPARE ME THE "KISSING EVERYTHING THAT MOVES" PLAN!
IF WORD ABOUT THE POWER GETS OUT, WE COULD RISK LOSING OUR CLUB, Y'KNOW?!
THAT'S TRUE... OKAY, THEN HOW ABOUT THIS?

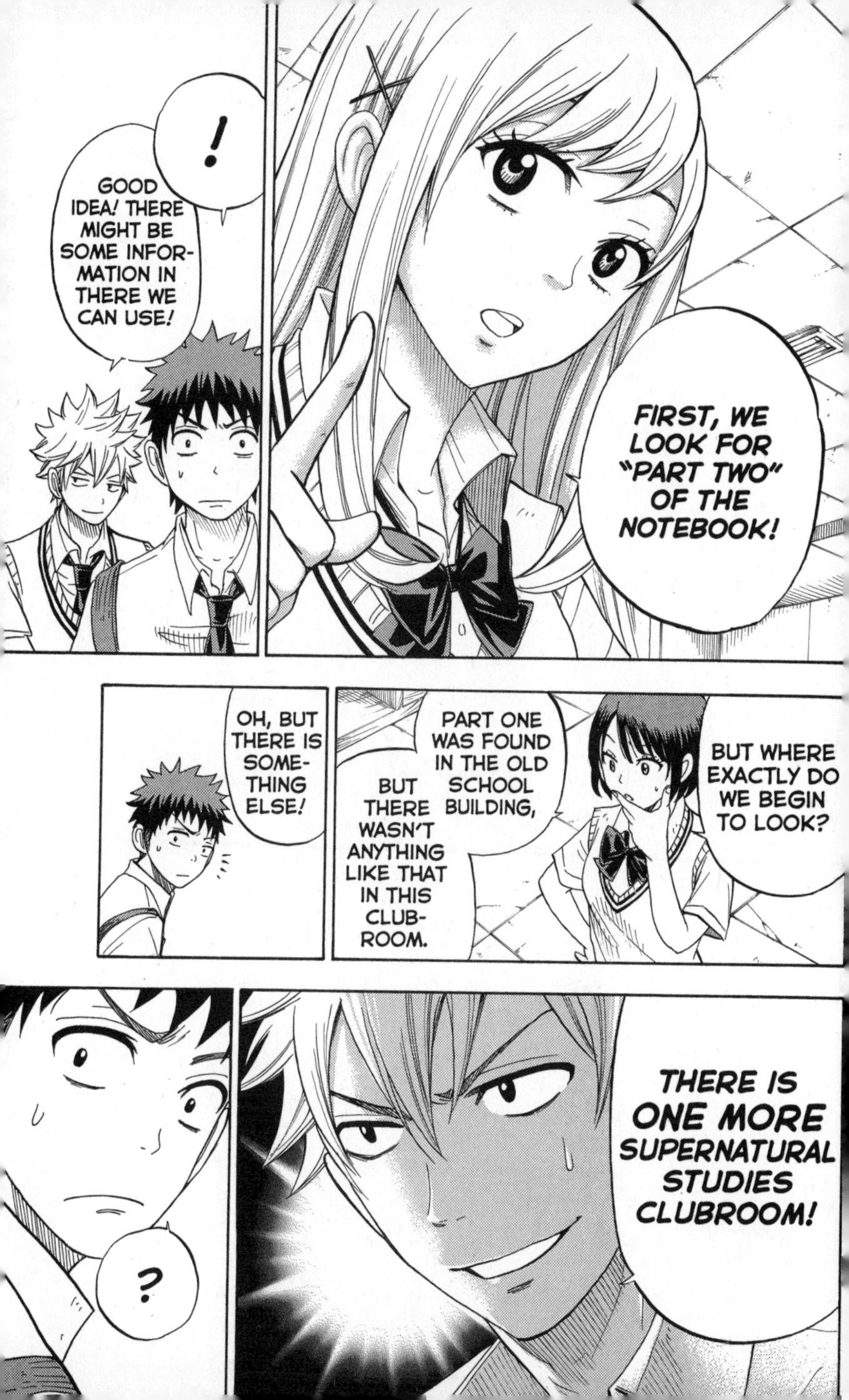
FIRST, WE LOOK FOR "PART TWO" OF THE NOTEBOOK!
!
GOOD IDEA! THERE MIGHT BE SOME INFORMATION IN THERE WE CAN USE!
BUT WHERE EXACTLY DO WE BEGIN TO LOOK?
PART ONE WAS FOUND IN THE OLD SCHOOL BUILDING,
BUT THERE WASN'T ANYTHING LIKE THAT IN THIS CLUBROOM.
OH, BUT THERE IS SOMETHING ELSE!
THERE IS ONE MORE SUPERNATURAL STUDIES CLUBROOM!
?

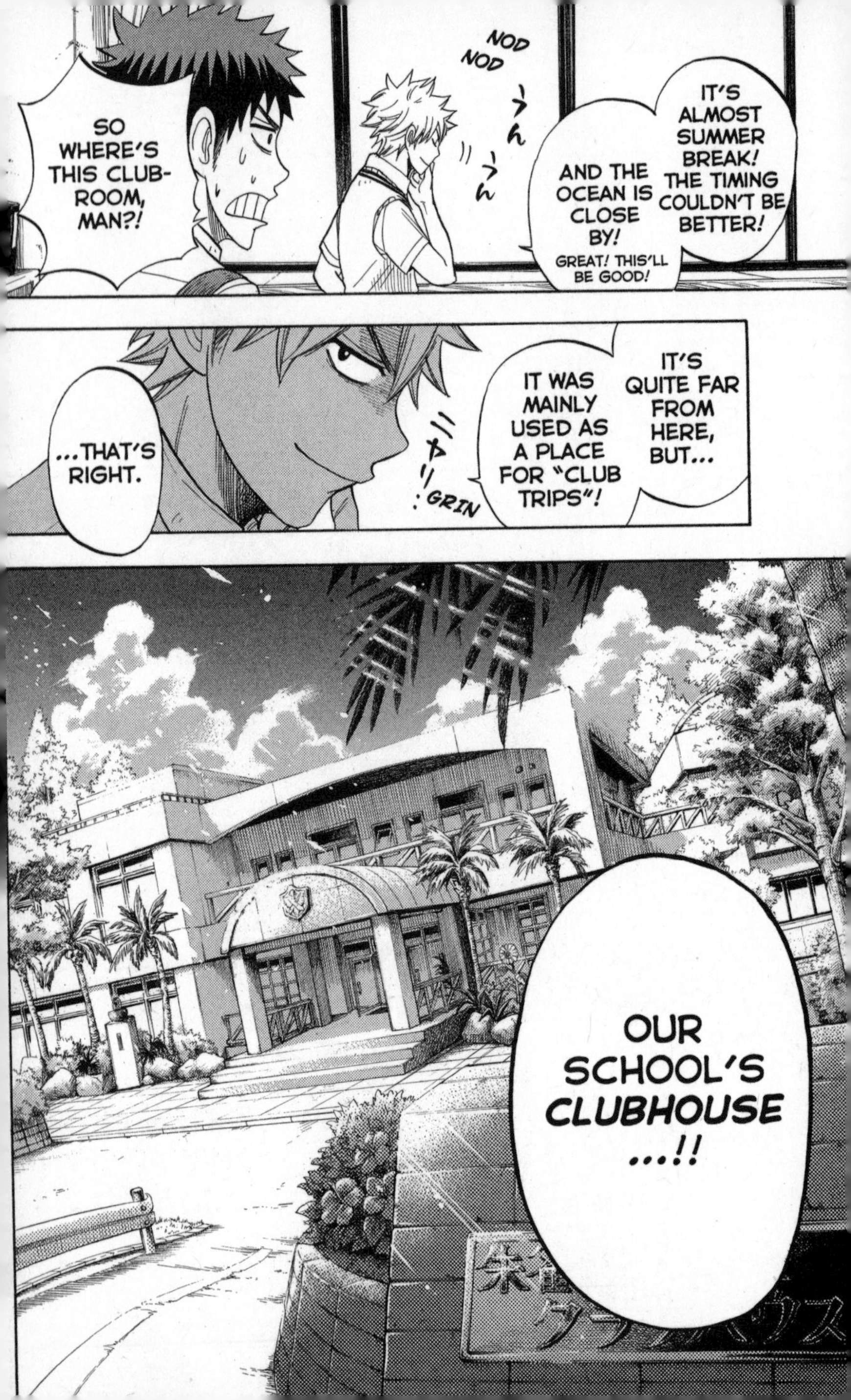
IT'S ALMOST SUMMER BREAK! THE TIMING COULDN'T BE BETTER!
AND THE OCEAN IS CLOSE BY!
GREAT! THIS'LL BE GOOD!
NOD NOD
うん うん
SO WHERE'S THIS CLUB-ROOM, MAN?!
IT'S QUITE FAR FROM HERE, BUT...
IT WAS MAINLY USED AS A PLACE FOR "CLUB TRIPS"!
ニヤリ
GRIN
...THAT'S RIGHT.
OUR SCHOOL'S CLUBHOUSE ...!!

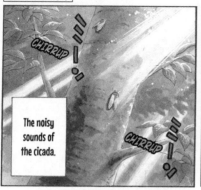

CHIRRUP

CHIRRUP

The noisy sounds of the cicada.

Blue skies.

White clouds.

Today, summer break is here!!

TIME FOR OUR CLUB TRIP!!

CHAPTER 25: Chirrup! Chirrup!

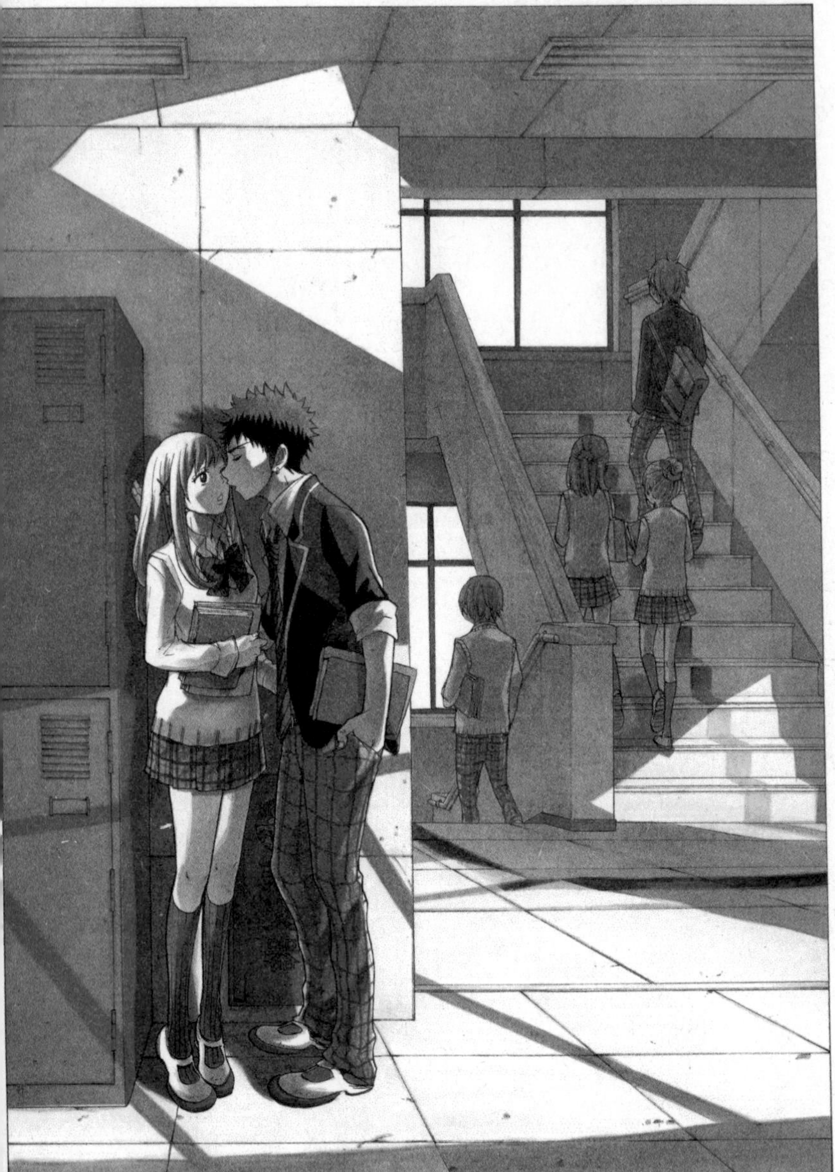

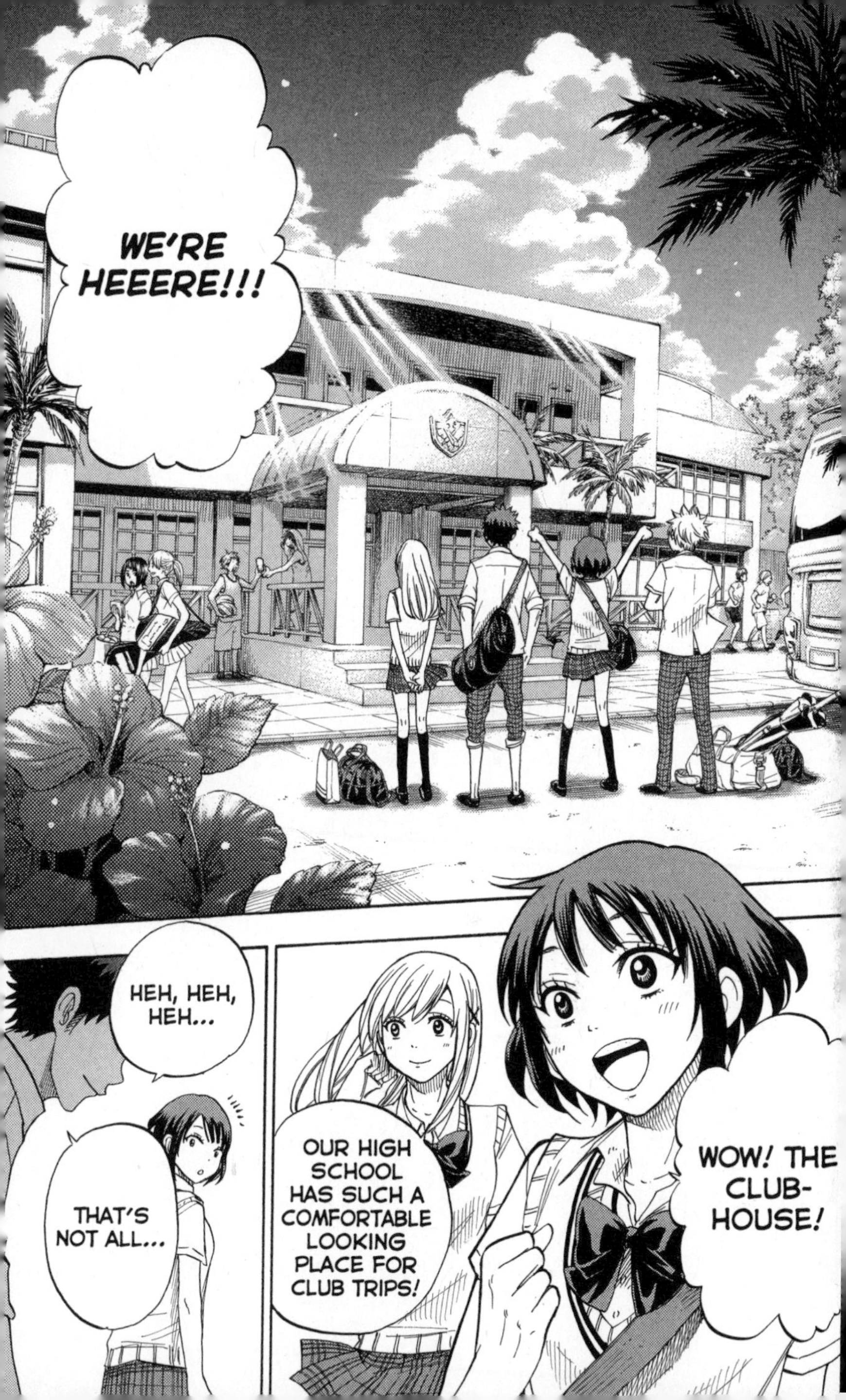
WE'RE HEEERE!!!
WOW! THE CLUB-HOUSE!
OUR HIGH SCHOOL HAS SUCH A COMFORTABLE LOOKING PLACE FOR CLUB TRIPS!
HEH, HEH, HEH...
THAT'S NOT ALL...

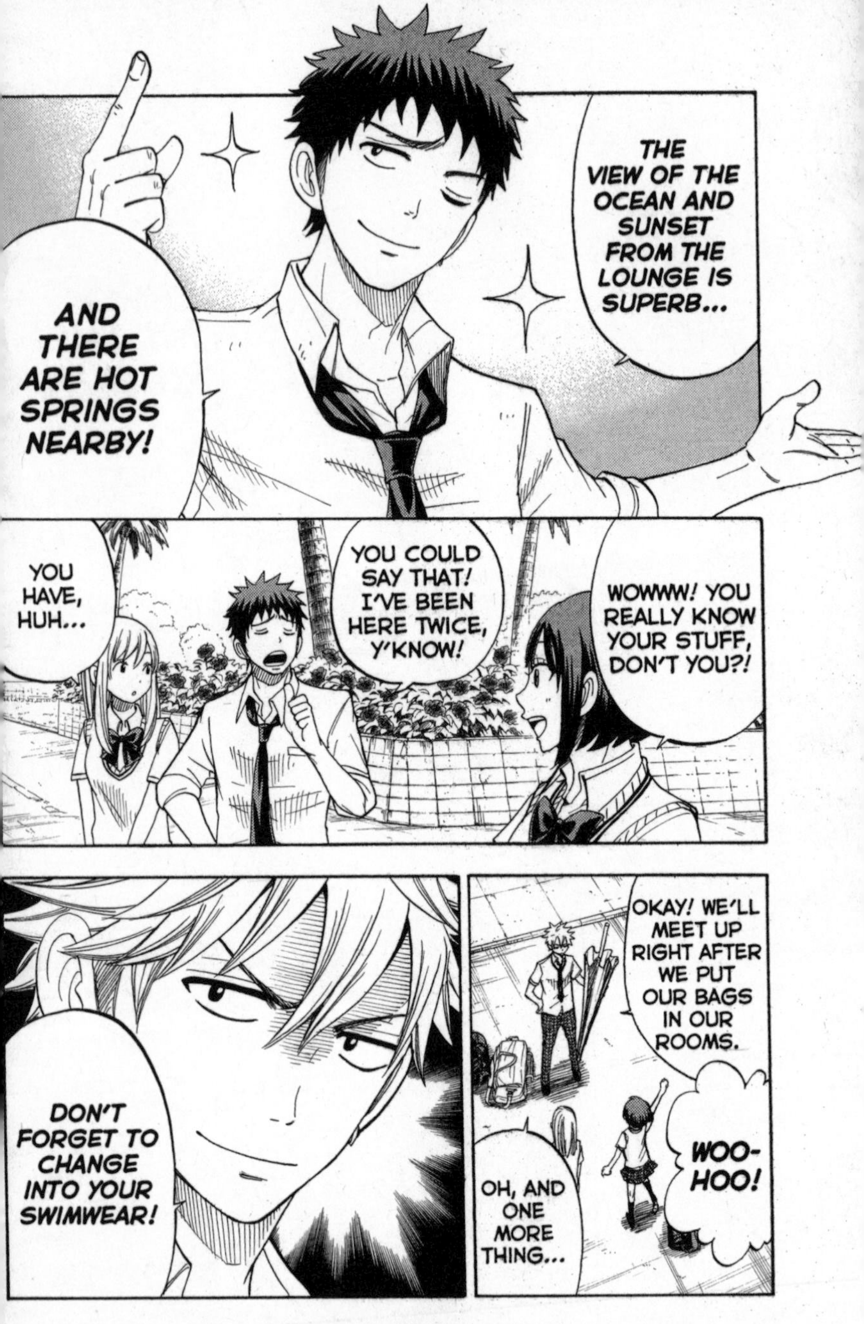
THE VIEW OF THE OCEAN AND SUNSET FROM THE LOUNGE IS SUPERB...
AND THERE ARE HOT SPRINGS NEARBY!
WOWWW! YOU REALLY KNOW YOUR STUFF, DON'T YOU?!
YOU COULD SAY THAT! I'VE BEEN HERE TWICE, Y'KNOW!
YOU HAVE, HUH...
OKAY! WE'LL MEET UP RIGHT AFTER WE PUT OUR BAGS IN OUR ROOMS.
WOO-HOO!
OH, AND ONE MORE THING...
DON'T FORGET TO CHANGE INTO YOUR SWIMWEAR!

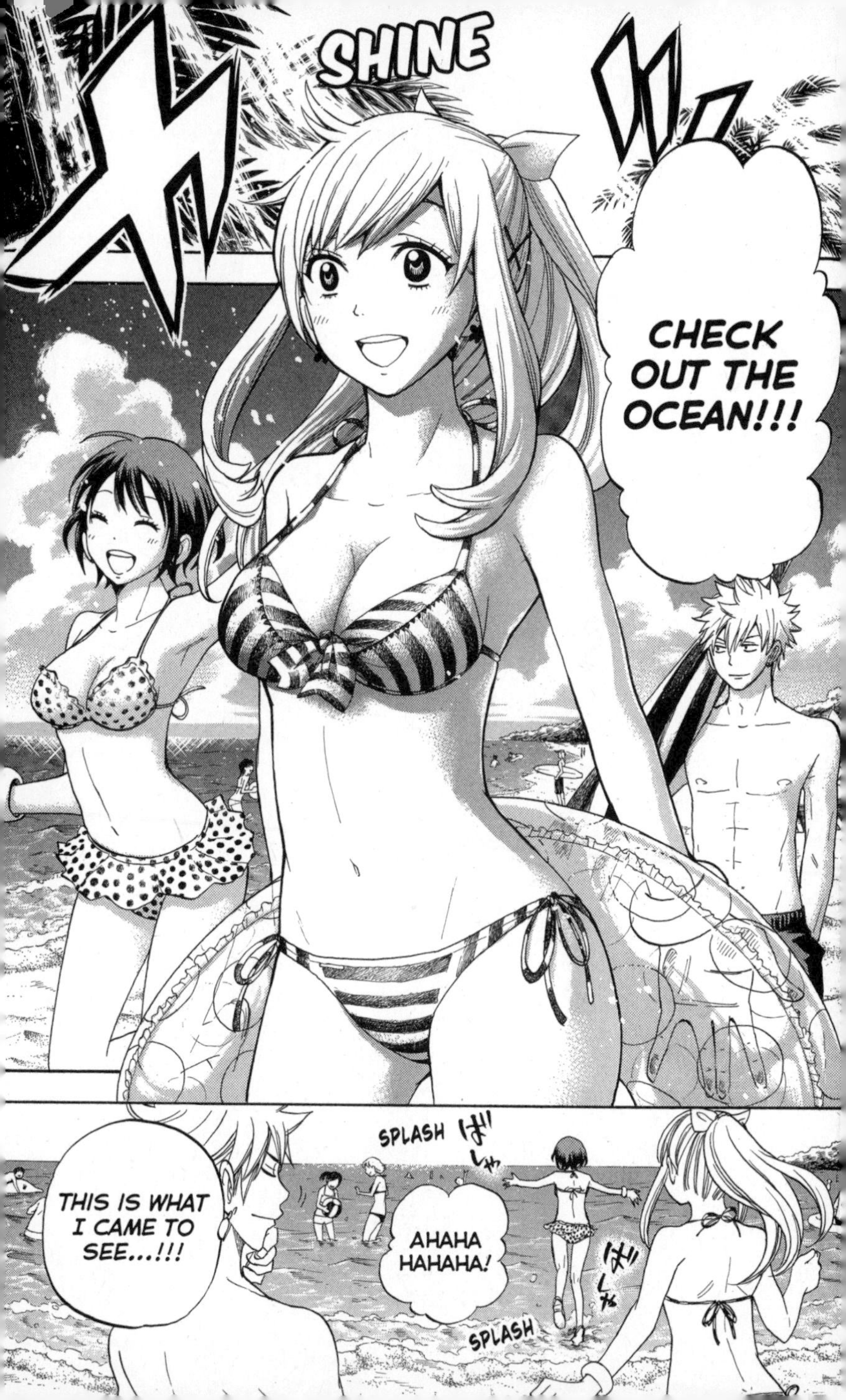
SHINE
CHECK OUT THE OCEAN!!!
SPLASH ぱしゃ
AHAHA HAHAHA!
THIS IS WHAT I CAME TO SEE...!!!
ぱしゃ
SPLASH

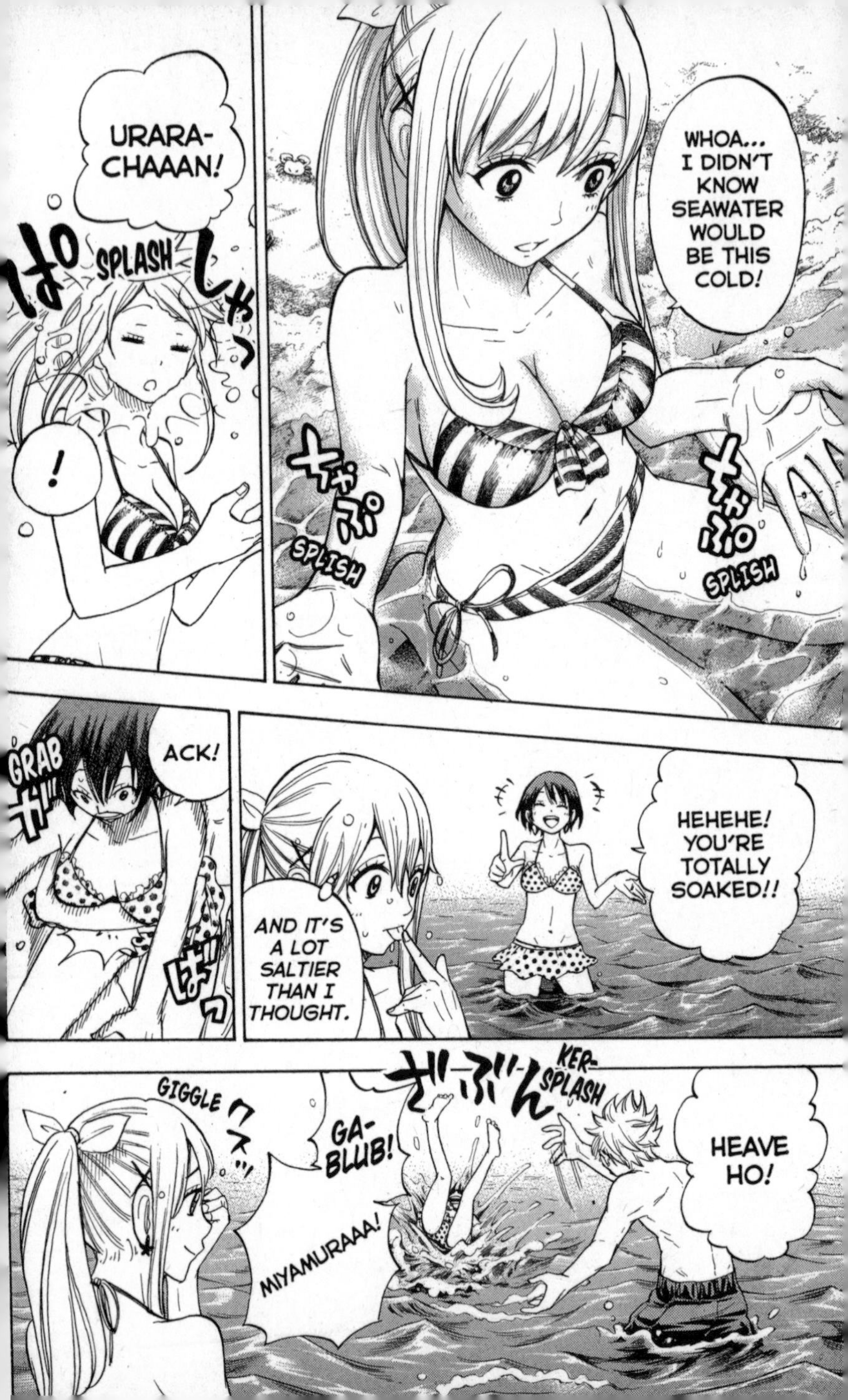
WHOA... I DIDN'T KNOW SEAWATER WOULD BE THIS COLD!
ちゃぷ
SPLISH
ちゃぷ
SPLISH
URARA-CHAAAN!
SPLASH
!
HEHEHE! YOU'RE TOTALLY SOAKED!!
AND IT'S A LOT SALTIER THAN I THOUGHT.
ACK!
GRAB
HEAVE HO!
KER-SPLASH
ざぶーん
GA-BLUB!
MIYAMURAAA!
GIGGLE
クスッ

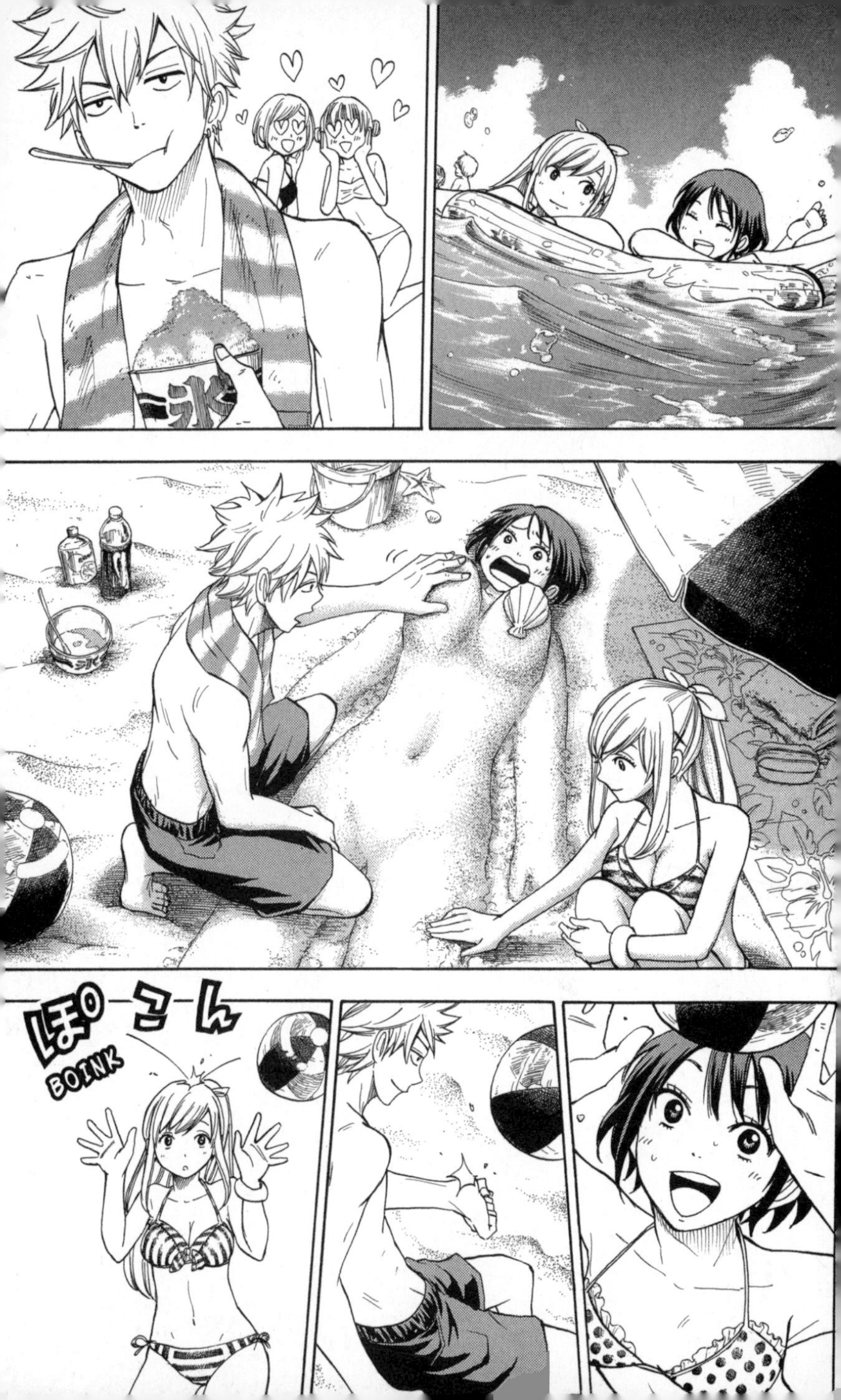
ぽこん
BOINK

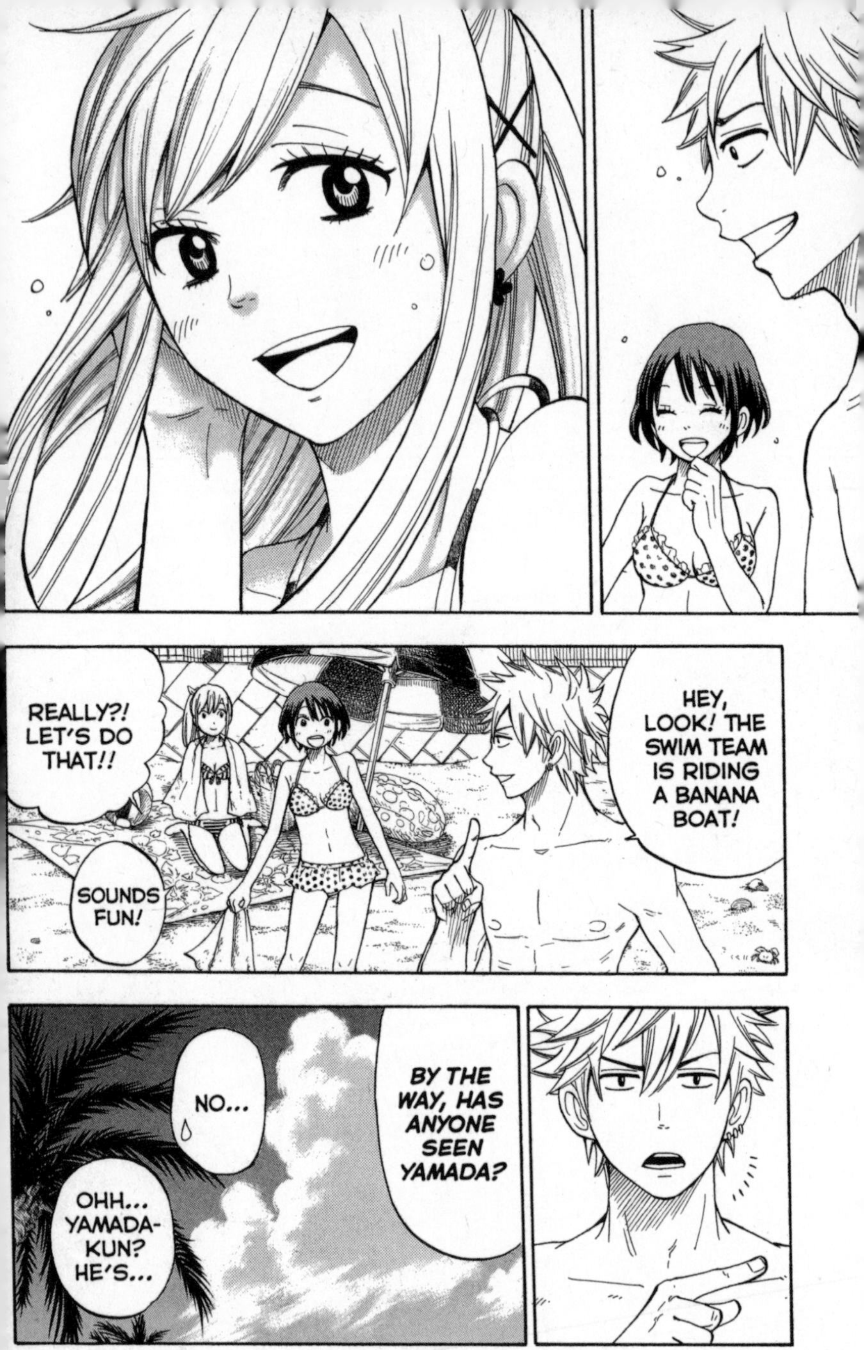
HEY, LOOK! THE SWIM TEAM IS RIDING A BANANA BOAT!
REALLY?! LET'S DO THAT!!
SOUNDS FUN!
BY THE WAY, HAS ANYONE SEEN YAMADA?
NO...
OHH... YAMADA-KUN? HE'S...

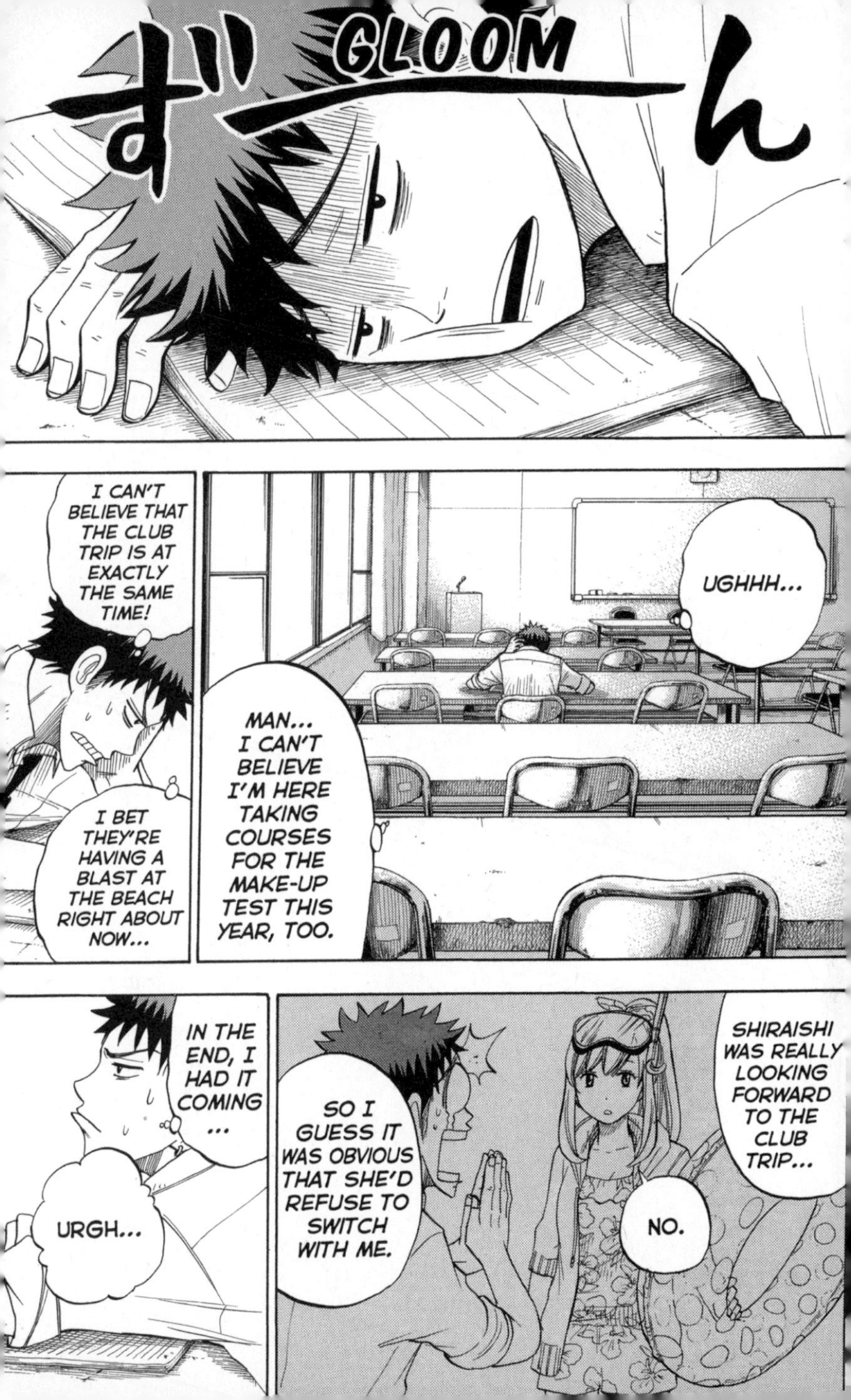
ずーん
GLOOM
UGHHH...
MAN... I CAN'T BELIEVE I'M HERE TAKING COURSES FOR THE MAKE-UP TEST THIS YEAR, TOO.
I CAN'T BELIEVE THAT THE CLUB TRIP IS AT EXACTLY THE SAME TIME!
I BET THEY'RE HAVING A BLAST AT THE BEACH RIGHT ABOUT NOW...
SHIRAISHI WAS REALLY LOOKING FORWARD TO THE CLUB TRIP...
NO.
SO I GUESS IT WAS OBVIOUS THAT SHE'D REFUSE TO SWITCH WITH ME.
IN THE END, I HAD IT COMING...
URGH...

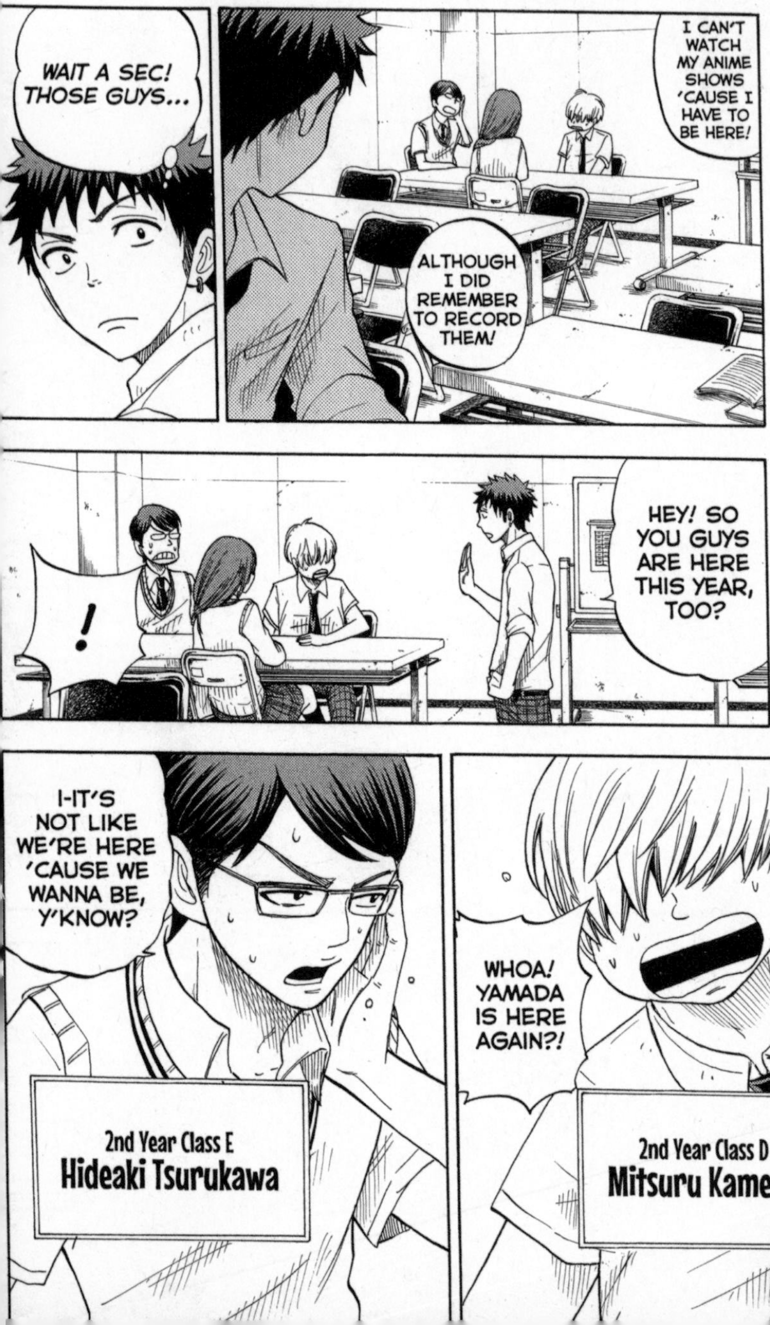
I CAN'T WATCH MY ANIME SHOWS 'CAUSE I HAVE TO BE HERE!
ALTHOUGH I DID REMEMBER TO RECORD THEM!
WAIT A SEC! THOSE GUYS...
HEY! SO YOU GUYS ARE HERE THIS YEAR, TOO?
!
WHOA! YAMADA IS HERE AGAIN?!
2nd Year Class D
Mitsuru Kameda
I-IT'S NOT LIKE WE'RE HERE 'CAUSE WE WANNA BE, Y'KNOW?
2nd Year Class E
Hideaki Tsurukawa

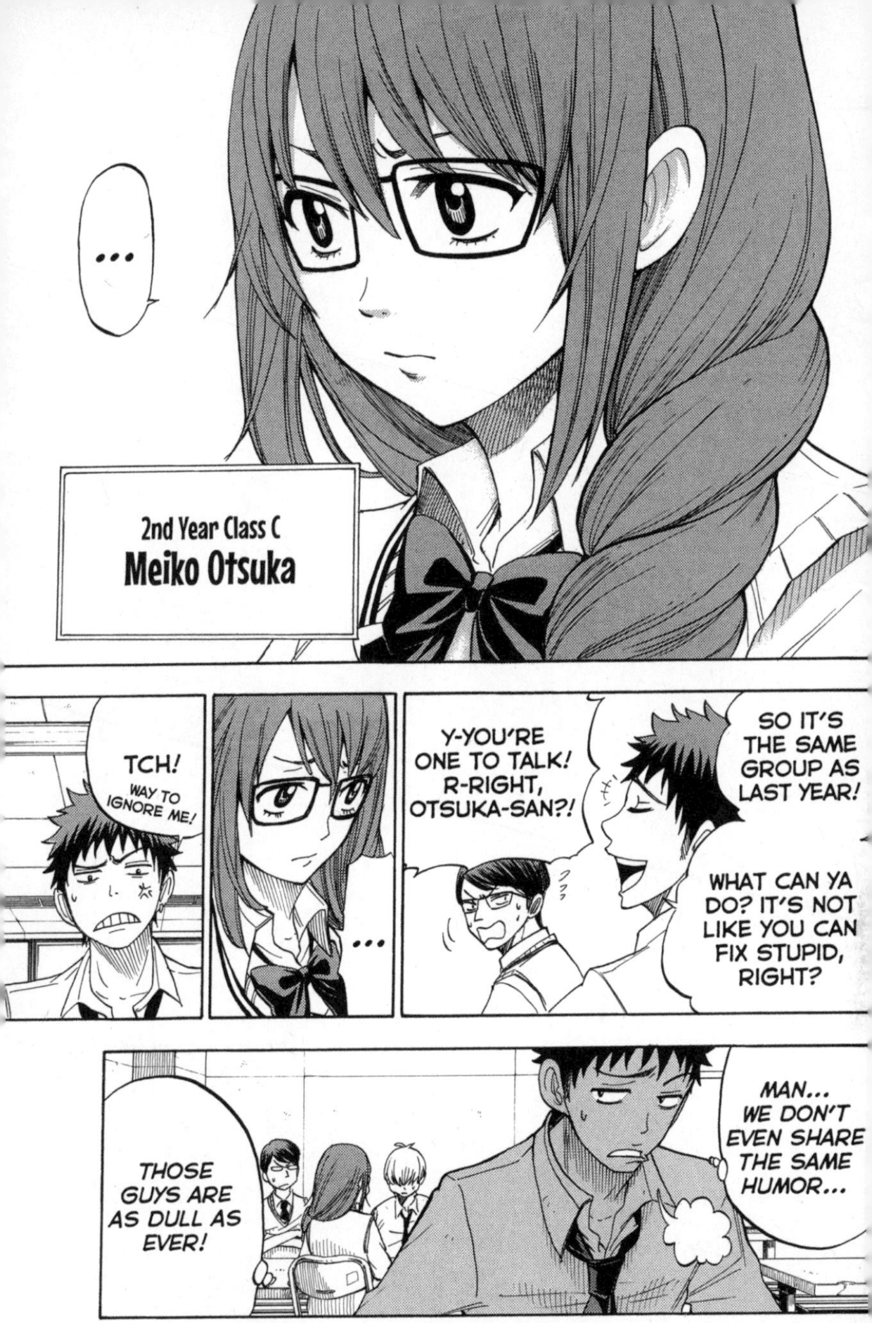
...
2nd Year Class C
Meiko Otsuka
SO IT'S THE SAME GROUP AS LAST YEAR!
WHAT CAN YA DO? IT'S NOT LIKE YOU CAN FIX STUPID, RIGHT?
Y-YOU'RE ONE TO TALK! R-RIGHT, OTSUKA-SAN?!
...
TCH!
WAY TO IGNORE ME!
MAN... WE DON'T EVEN SHARE THE SAME HUMOR...
THOSE GUYS ARE AS DULL AS EVER!

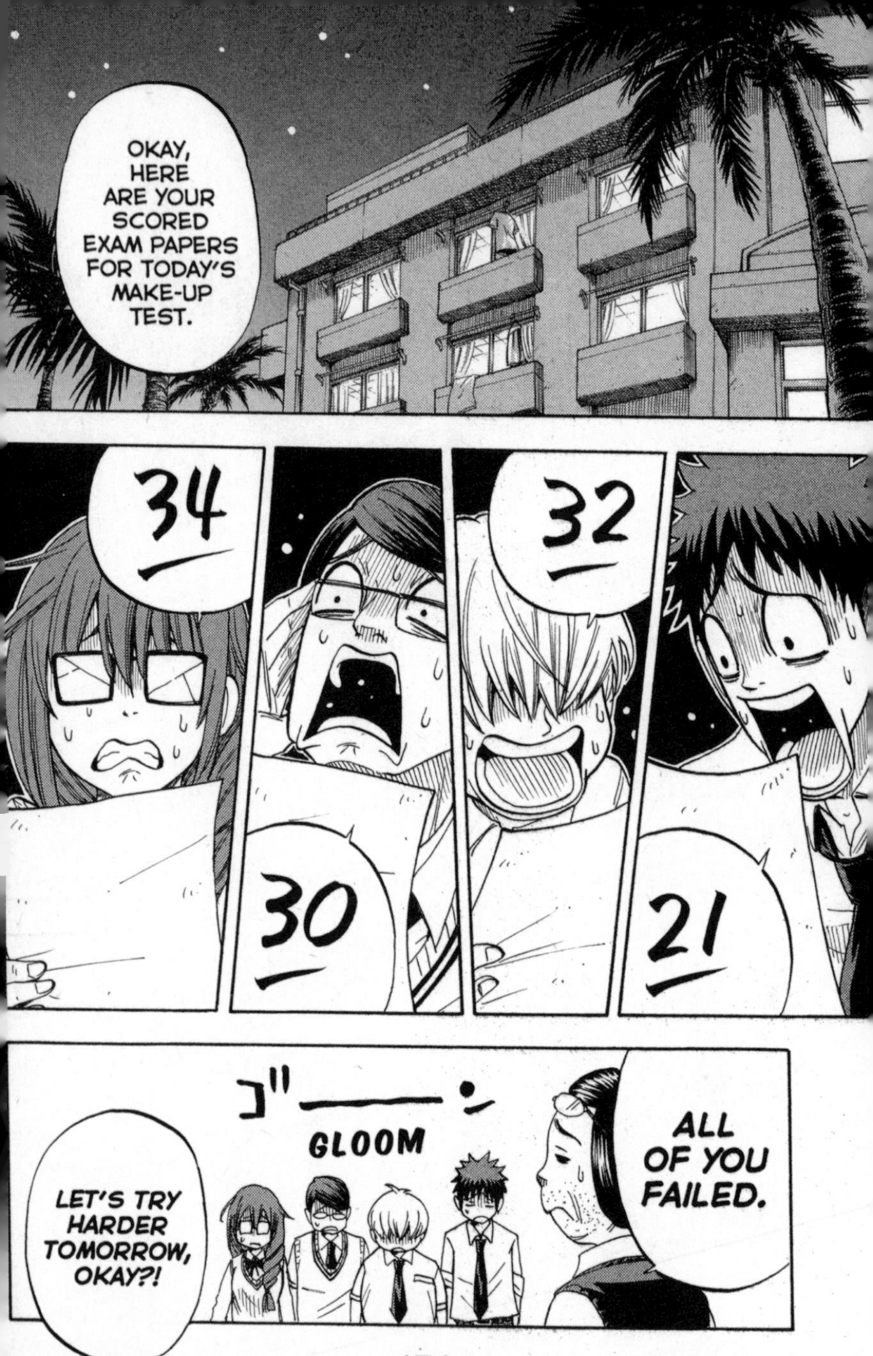
OKAY, HERE ARE YOUR SCORED EXAM PAPERS FOR TODAY'S MAKE-UP TEST.
21
32
30
34
ALL OF YOU FAILED.
ゴーーン
GLOOM
LET'S TRY HARDER TOMORROW, OKAY?!

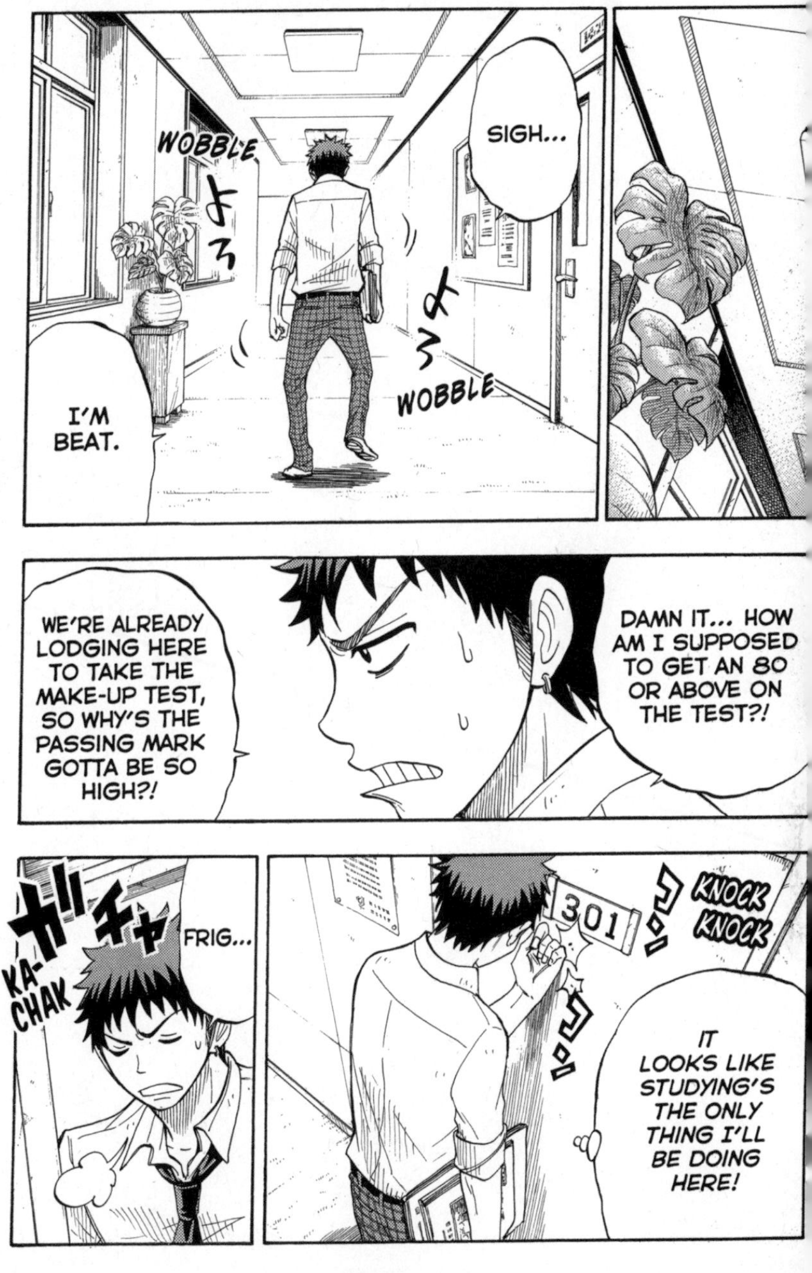

SIGH...
WOBBLE
WOBBLE
I'M BEAT.
DAMN IT... HOW AM I SUPPOSED TO GET AN 80 OR ABOVE ON THE TEST?!
WE'RE ALREADY LODGING HERE TO TAKE THE MAKE-UP TEST, SO WHY'S THE PASSING MARK GOTTA BE SO HIGH?!
301
KNOCK KNOCK
IT LOOKS LIKE STUDYING'S THE ONLY THING I'LL BE DOING HERE!
FRIG...
ガチャ
KA-CHAK

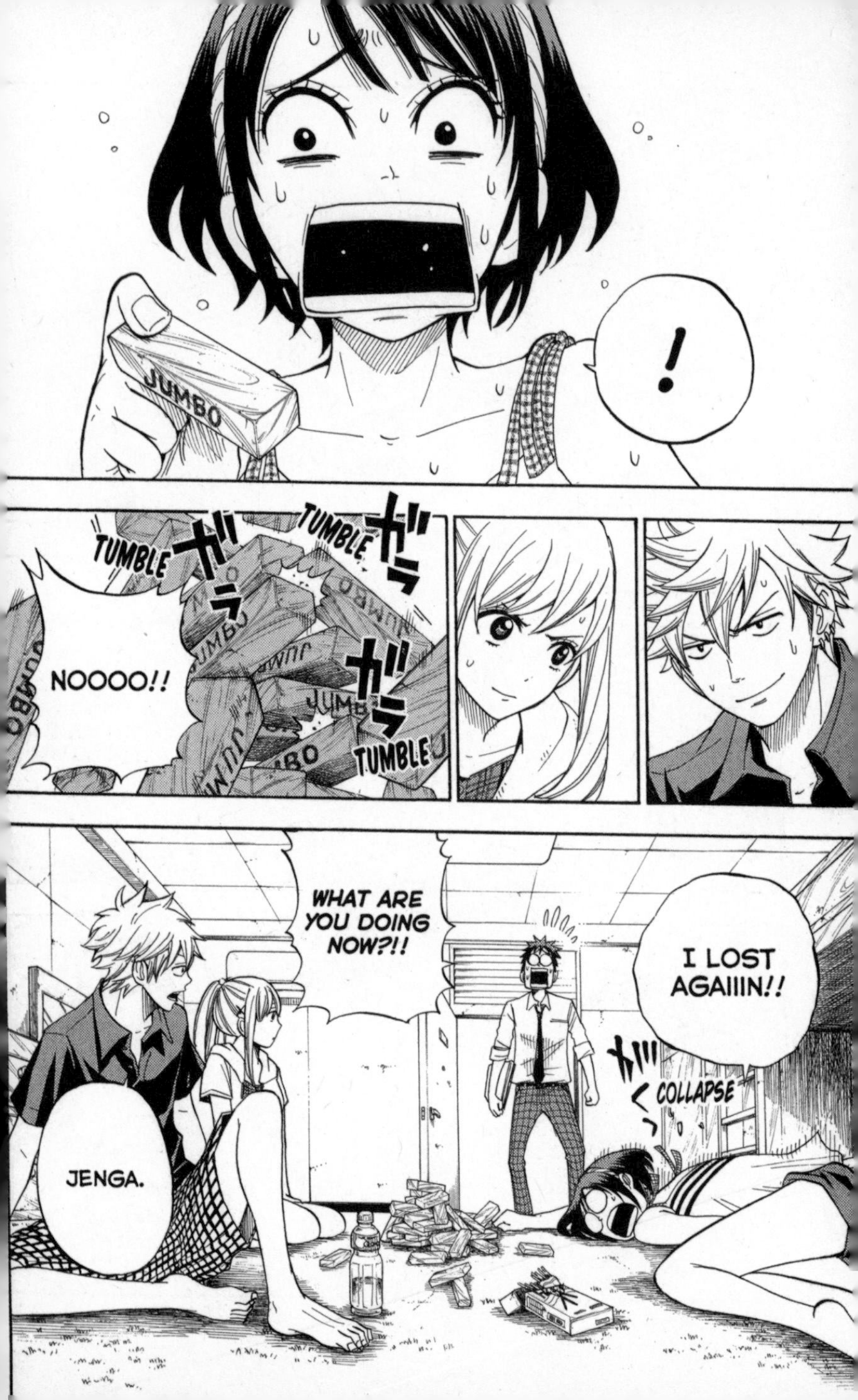
JUMBO
!
TUMBLE
TUMBLE
NOOOO!!
TUMBLE
I LOST AGAIIIN!!
COLLAPSE
WHAT ARE YOU DOING NOW?!!
JENGA.

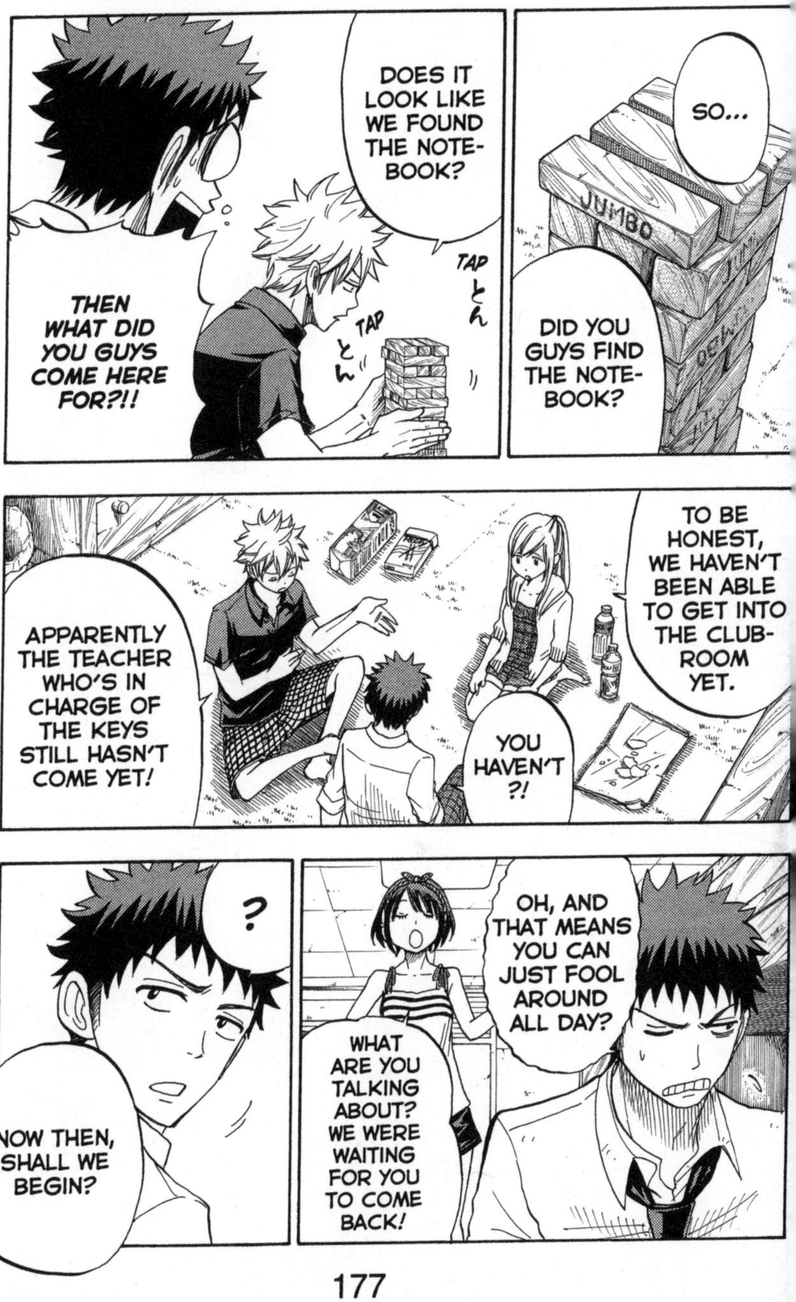
SO...
DID YOU GUYS FIND THE NOTE-BOOK?
DOES IT LOOK LIKE WE FOUND THE NOTE-BOOK?
TAP とん
TAP とん
THEN WHAT DID YOU GUYS COME HERE FOR?!!
TO BE HONEST, WE HAVEN'T BEEN ABLE TO GET INTO THE CLUB-ROOM YET.
YOU HAVEN'T ?!
APPARENTLY THE TEACHER WHO'S IN CHARGE OF THE KEYS STILL HASN'T COME YET!
OH, AND THAT MEANS YOU CAN JUST FOOL AROUND ALL DAY?
WHAT ARE YOU TALKING ABOUT? WE WERE WAITING FOR YOU TO COME BACK!
?
NOW THEN, SHALL WE BEGIN?

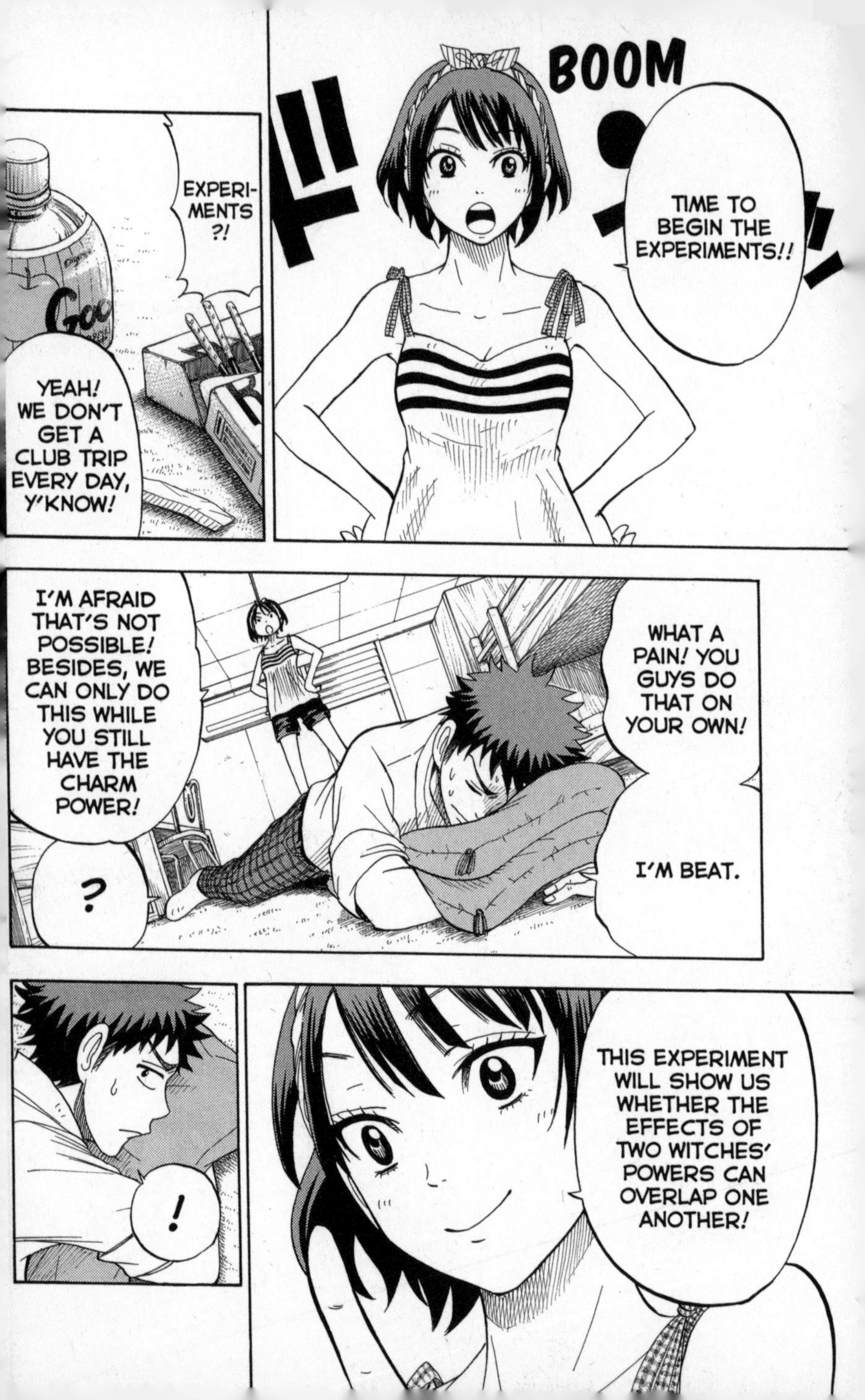
BOOM
TIME TO BEGIN THE EXPERIMENTS!!
EXPERI-MENTS ?!
YEAH! WE DON'T GET A CLUB TRIP EVERY DAY, Y'KNOW!
WHAT A PAIN! YOU GUYS DO THAT ON YOUR OWN!
I'M AFRAID THAT'S NOT POSSIBLE! BESIDES, WE CAN ONLY DO THIS WHILE YOU STILL HAVE THE CHARM POWER!
I'M BEAT.
?
THIS EXPERIMENT WILL SHOW US WHETHER THE EFFECTS OF TWO WITCHES' POWERS CAN OVERLAP ONE ANOTHER!
!

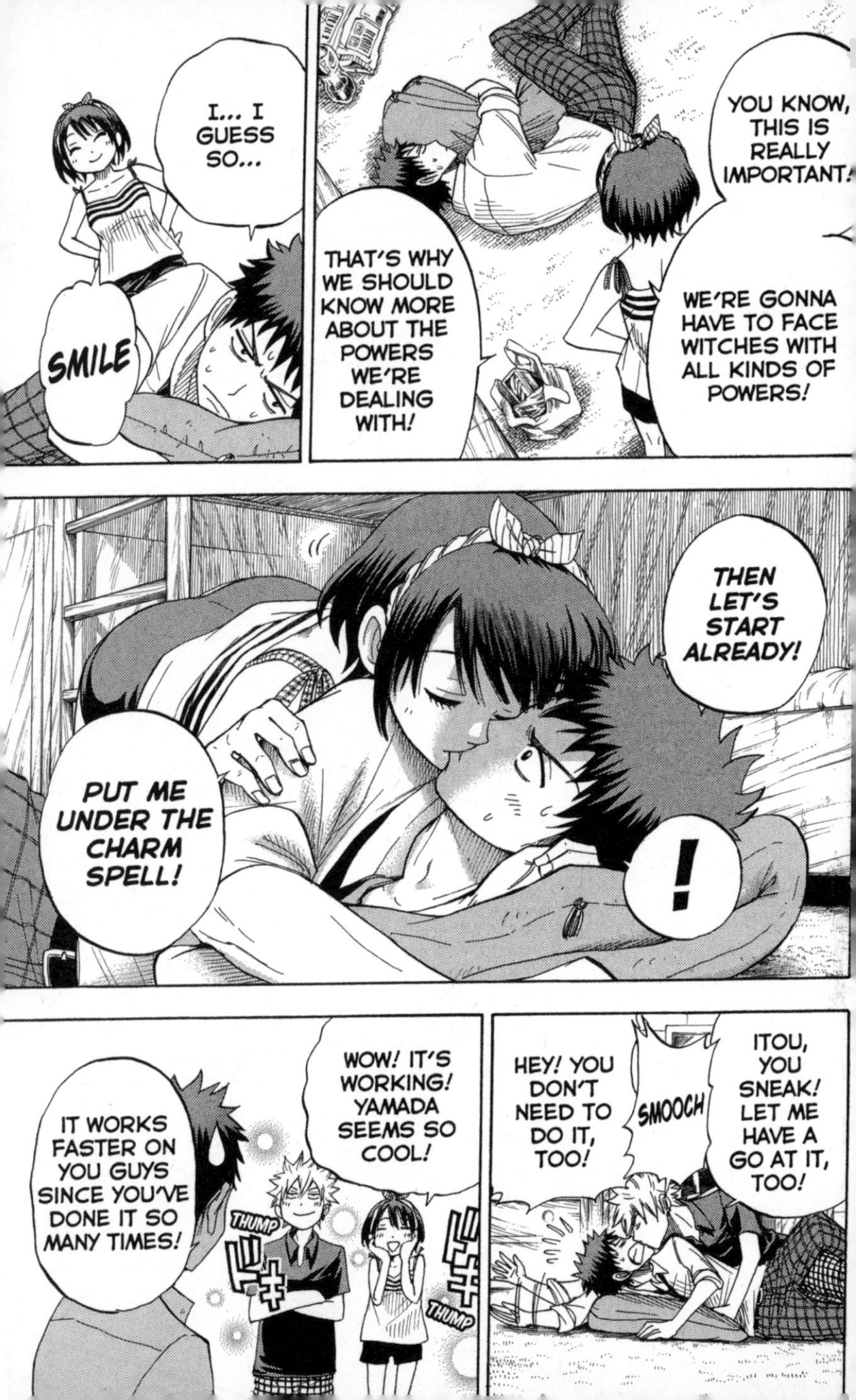
YOU KNOW, THIS IS REALLY IMPORTANT!
WE'RE GONNA HAVE TO FACE WITCHES WITH ALL KINDS OF POWERS!
THAT'S WHY WE SHOULD KNOW MORE ABOUT THE POWERS WE'RE DEALING WITH!
I... I GUESS SO...
SMILE
THEN LET'S START ALREADY!
PUT ME UNDER THE CHARM SPELL!
!
ITOU, YOU SNEAK! LET ME HAVE A GO AT IT, TOO!
SMOOCH
HEY! YOU DON'T NEED TO DO IT, TOO!
WOW! IT'S WORKING! YAMADA SEEMS SO COOL!
THUMP
THUMP
IT WORKS FASTER ON YOU GUYS SINCE YOU'VE DONE IT SO MANY TIMES!

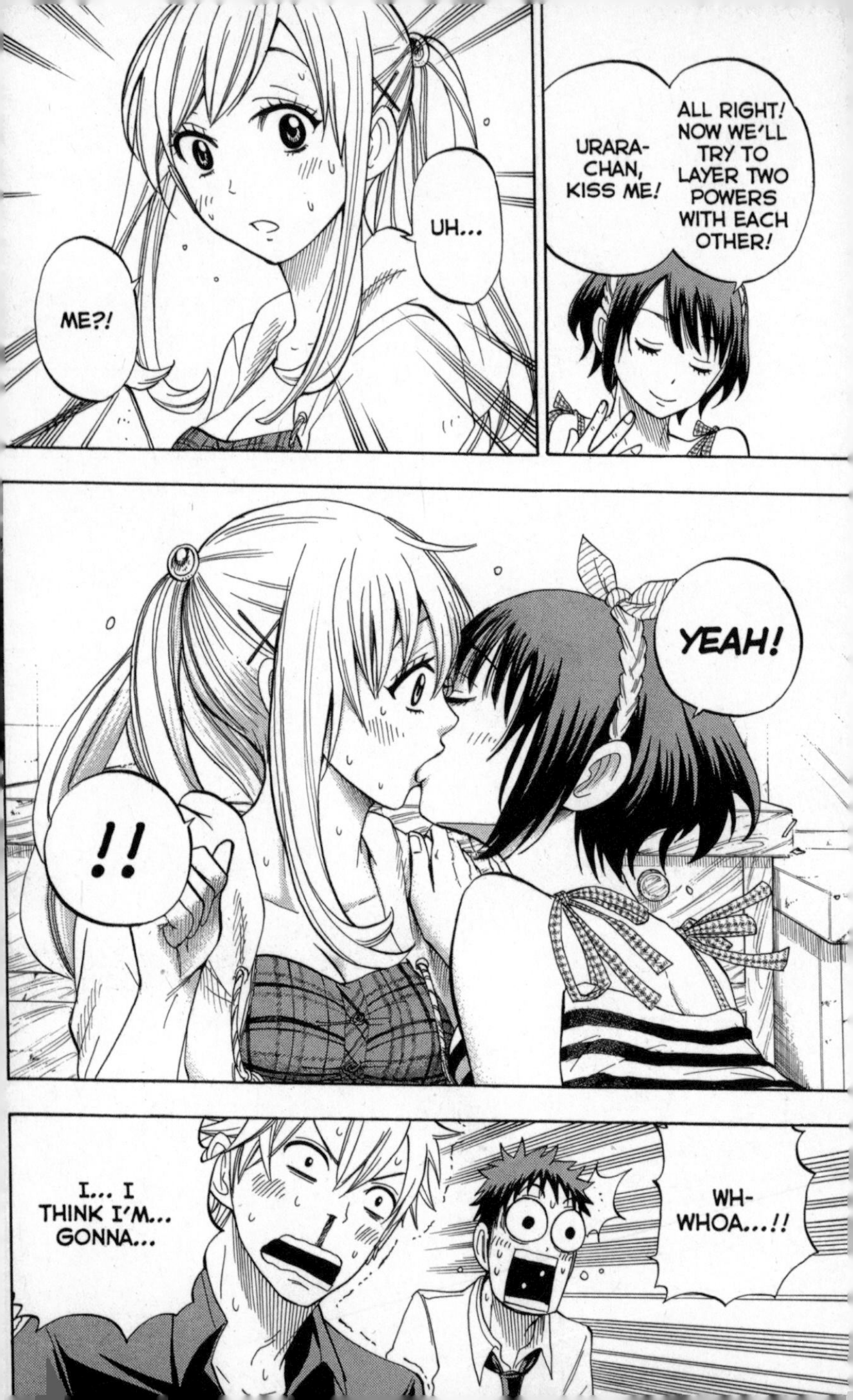
ALL RIGHT! NOW WE'LL TRY TO LAYER TWO POWERS WITH EACH OTHER!
URARA-CHAN, KISS ME!
UH...
ME?!
YEAH!
!!
WH- WHOA...!!
I... I THINK I'M... GONNA...

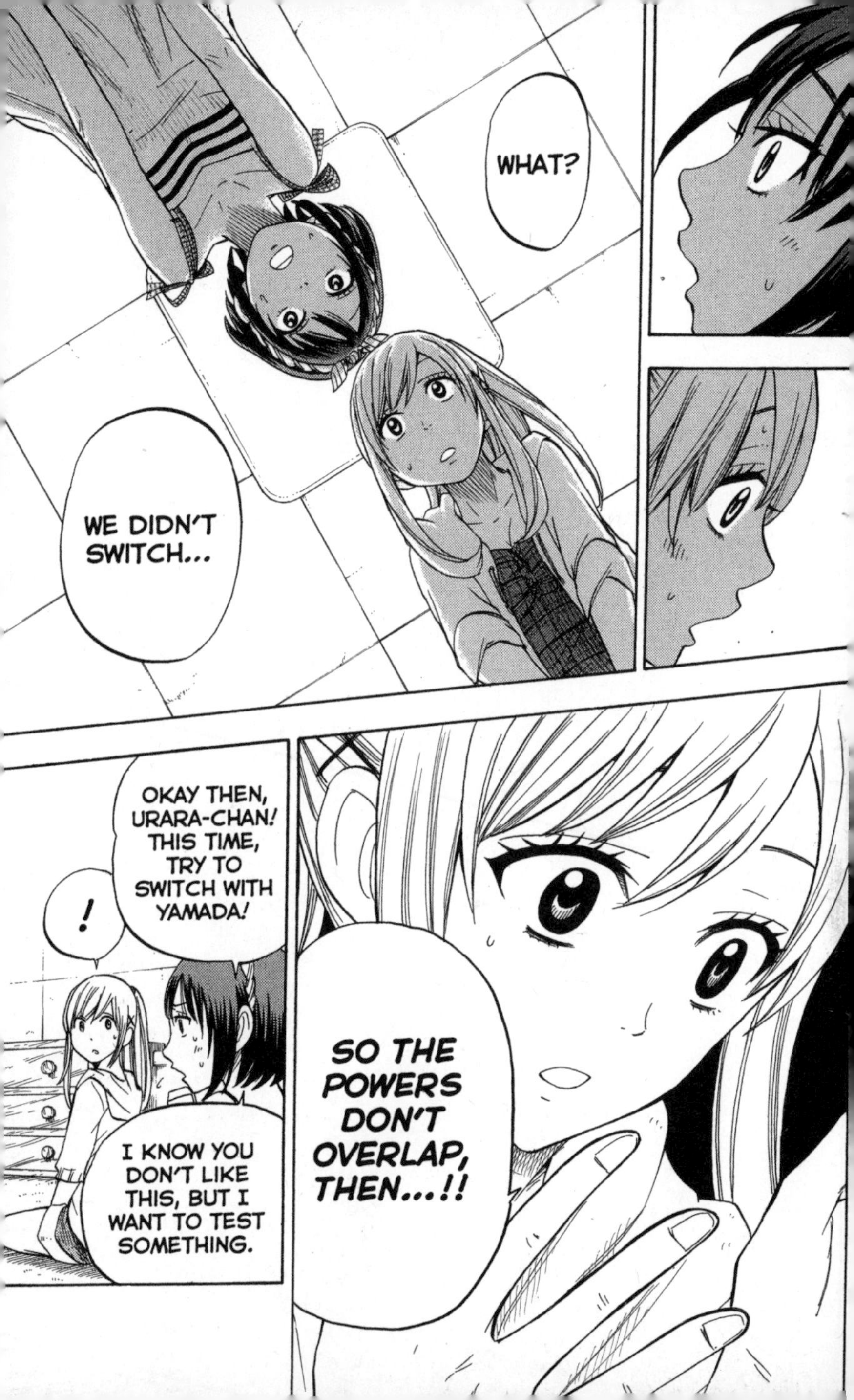
WHAT?
WE DIDN'T SWITCH...
SO THE POWERS DON'T OVERLAP, THEN...!!
OKAY THEN, URARA-CHAN! THIS TIME, TRY TO SWITCH WITH YAMADA!
!
I KNOW YOU DON'T LIKE THIS, BUT I WANT TO TEST SOMETHING.

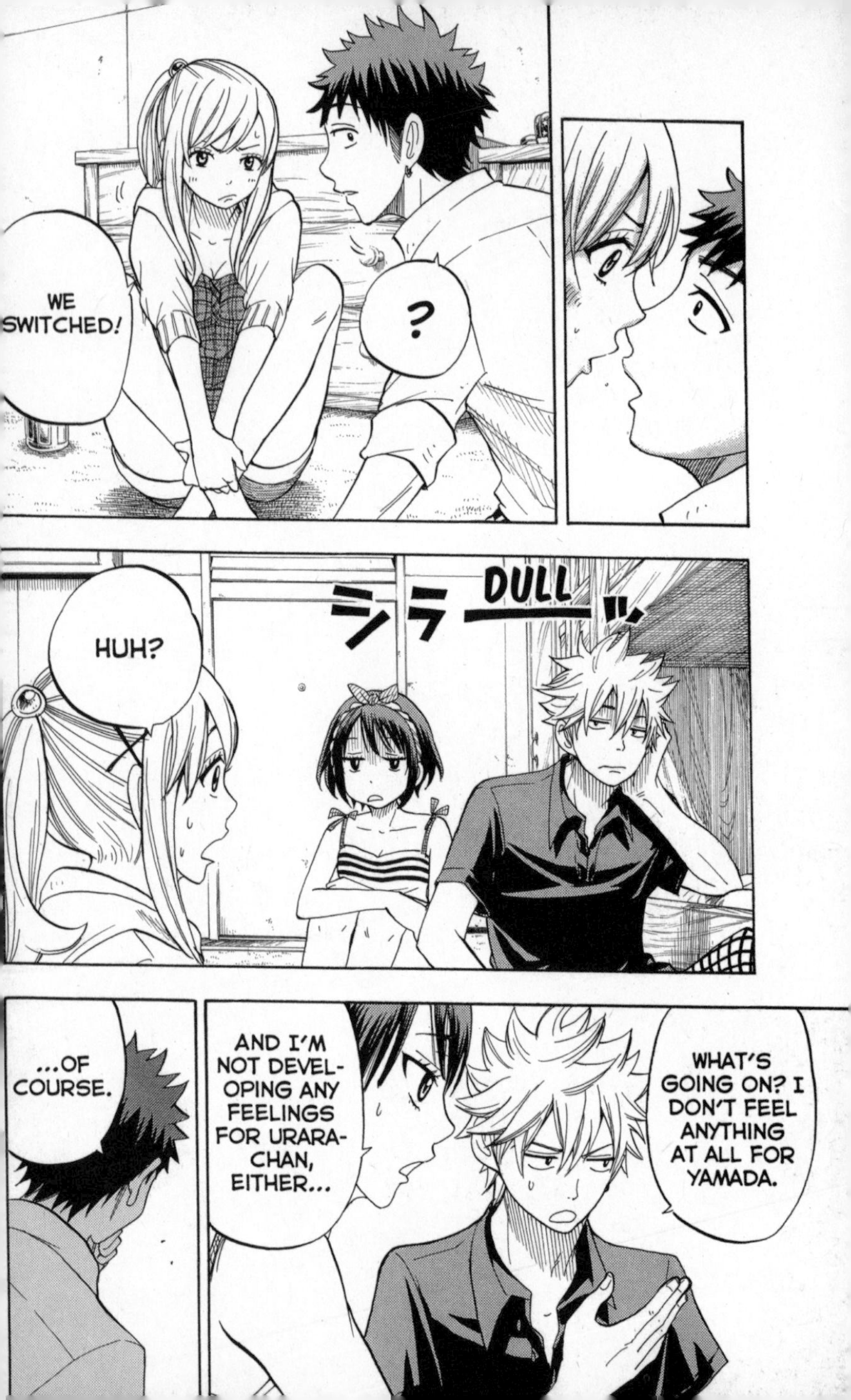
?
WE SWITCHED!
シラー
DULL
HUH?
WHAT'S GOING ON? I DON'T FEEL ANYTHING AT ALL FOR YAMADA.
AND I'M NOT DEVEL-OPING ANY FEELINGS FOR URARA-CHAN, EITHER...
...OF COURSE.

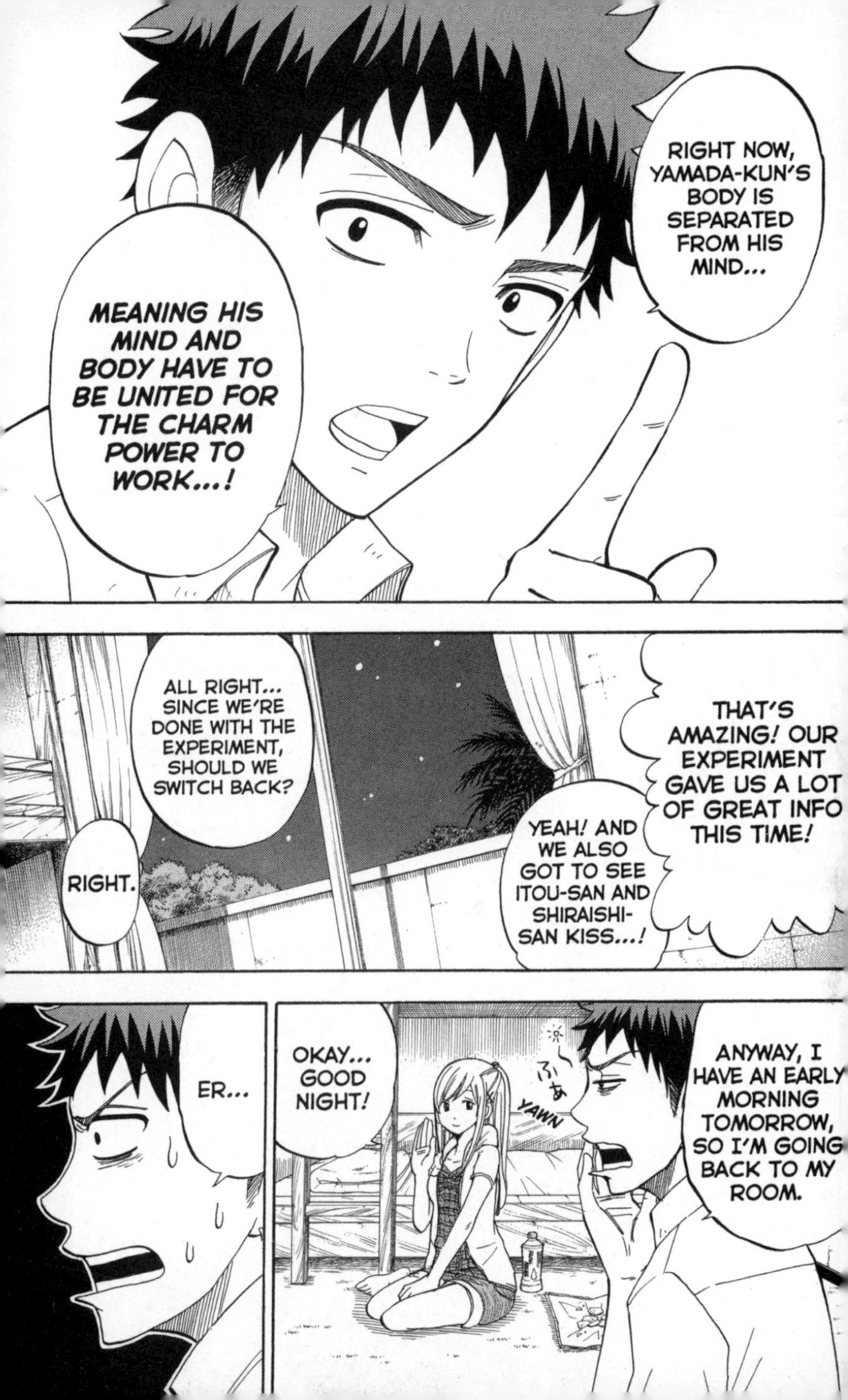
RIGHT NOW, YAMADA-KUN'S BODY IS SEPARATED FROM HIS MIND...
MEANING HIS MIND AND BODY HAVE TO BE UNITED FOR THE CHARM POWER TO WORK...!
THAT'S AMAZING! OUR EXPERIMENT GAVE US A LOT OF GREAT INFO THIS TIME!
YEAH! AND WE ALSO GOT TO SEE ITOU-SAN AND SHIRAISHI-SAN KISS...!
ALL RIGHT... SINCE WE'RE DONE WITH THE EXPERIMENT, SHOULD WE SWITCH BACK?
RIGHT.
ANYWAY, I HAVE AN EARLY MORNING TOMORROW, SO I'M GOING BACK TO MY ROOM.
ふあ
YAWN
OKAY... GOOD NIGHT!
ER...

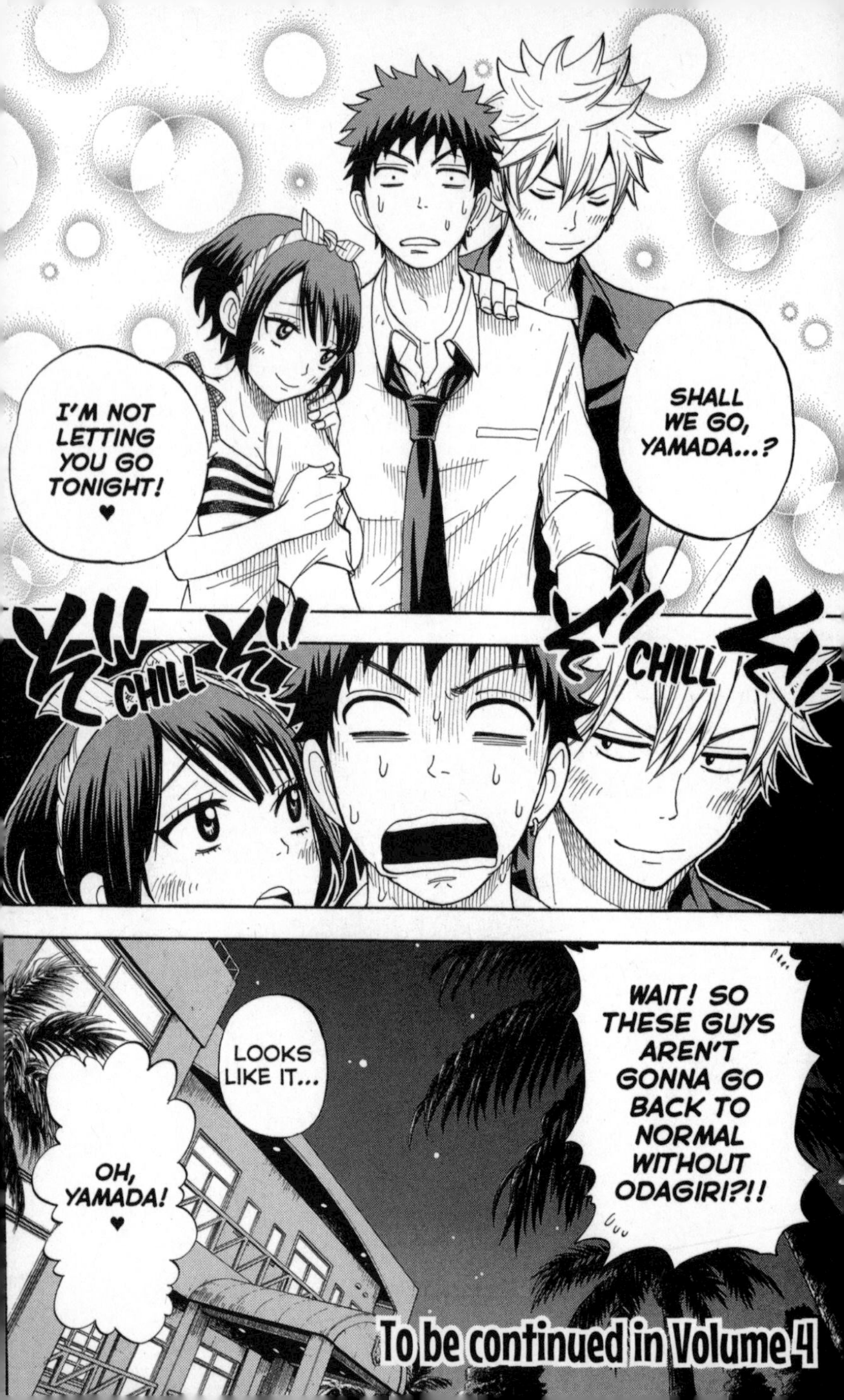
SHALL WE GO, YAMADA...?
I'M NOT LETTING YOU GO TONIGHT! ♥
CHILL
CHILL
WAIT! SO THESE GUYS AREN'T GONNA GO BACK TO NORMAL WITHOUT ODAGIRI?!!
LOOKS LIKE IT...
OH, YAMADA! ♥
To be continued in Volume 4

Miyabi Itou's Witch Research Notes

File. 1 Page 1

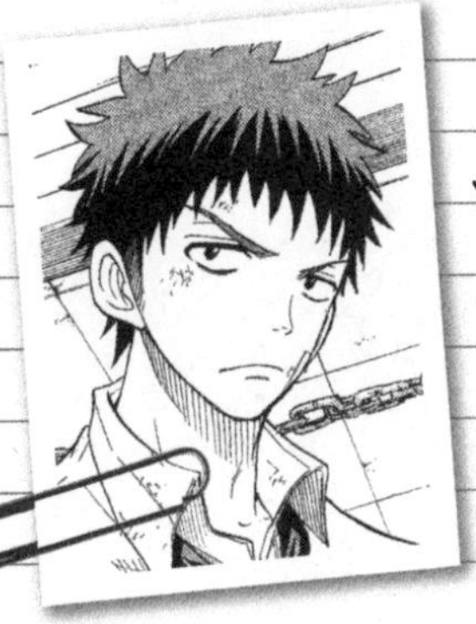

Yamada's power is **Copy!**

★ He copies the powers of whomever he kisses.

- When he kissed Odagiri-san, he copied her powers and then used her charm power on her. (So he reflected her powers back at her?) He's the joker in our deck of cards.

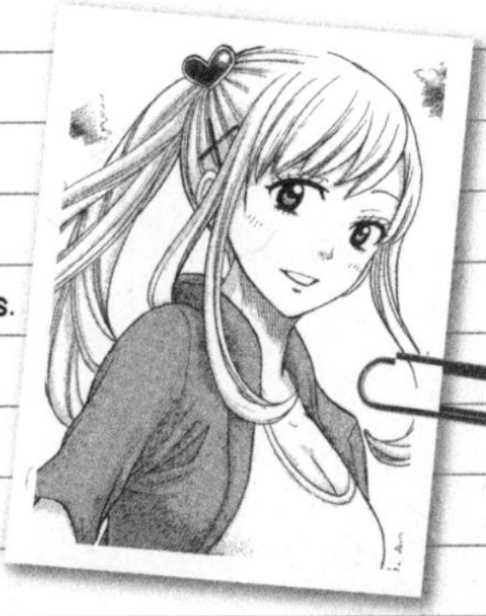

Urara-chan's a witch! **Change!**

★ Has the ability to switch bodies with whomever she kisses.

- The switch happens the moment the kiss is shared.
- Since her power is on the metaphysical level, she can use it even when in a switched body.

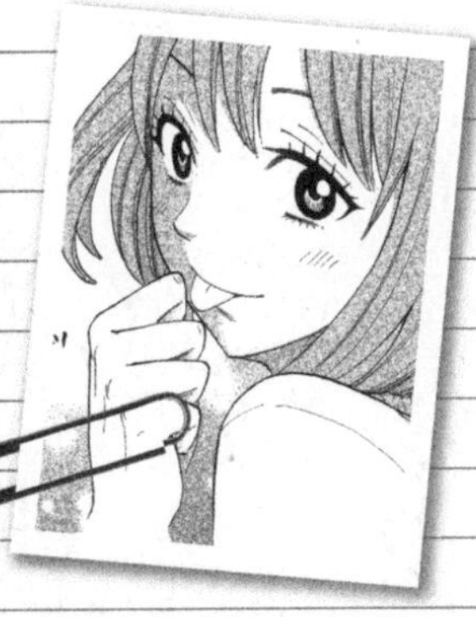

Nene Odagiri's also a witch! **Charm!**

★ Has the ability to charm whomever she kisses.

- It takes some time for the effects to show.
- Kissing that person once more will reset the effects.
- When Yamada uses it, the effects vanish while he's switched into another person's body.

Facts I've Figured Out!

- The old Supernatural Studies Club used to study witches!
- People who possess unique abilities that are only activated when they kiss other people are called witches.
- There have been witches at Suzaku High School for a long time, and their powers have been inherited within the school.

Rules About Witches' Powers that I've Figured Out

- Each person has one power.
- Someone who is under the influence of a witch cannot be placed under the influence of another witch, even if kissed by said other witch.

Problems to Figure Out!

◎ What happens when a witch kisses a witch?

◎ Is Yamada a witch? Or is he something different altogether?

◎ How many other witches are there?

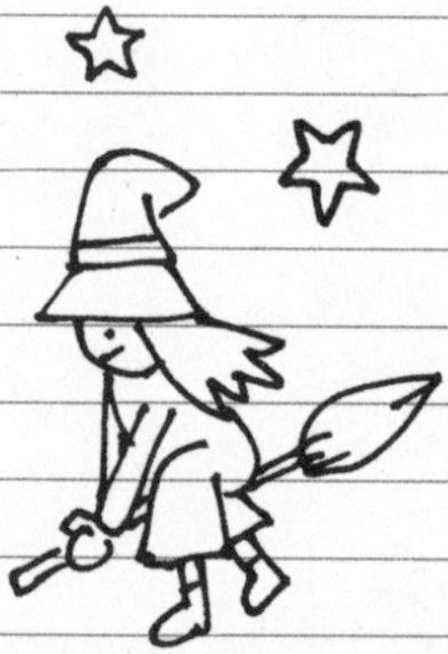

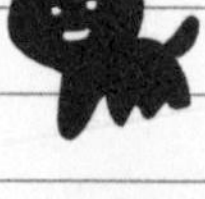

朱雀高等学校
裏ホームページ
SUZAKU HIGH SCHOOL UNDERGROUND WEBSITE

 All right, let's get the column started! Last time, when we made a request for comments and questions, we got a bunch of replies!!

 Hmm, so that means there are people who actually pay attention to this sad little column.

 Hey, don't talk about the column like that!! Now then, let's move on. We'll start with the question we got asked the most!

Q1: On pages 28 and 29 in chapter one of volume one, the teacher featured there looked familiar. Who is he?

H.N. (handle name) Akari-san (as well as many others)

 Ohh, she means **Shinagawa-sensei,** the math teacher.

 I don't know what made him look so familiar, but he came to our school for a temporary stint. When the first semester ended, he went back to the school he came from, **Monshiro High School**.

 He sure brought a lot of his friends into the school... Either way, it seems like the students found him to be interesting so he was pretty popular.

All right, next up!

Q2: Itou-san called the doll that showed up in chapter seven "useless." Did Yamada throw it out?

H.N. Tamutamu-san

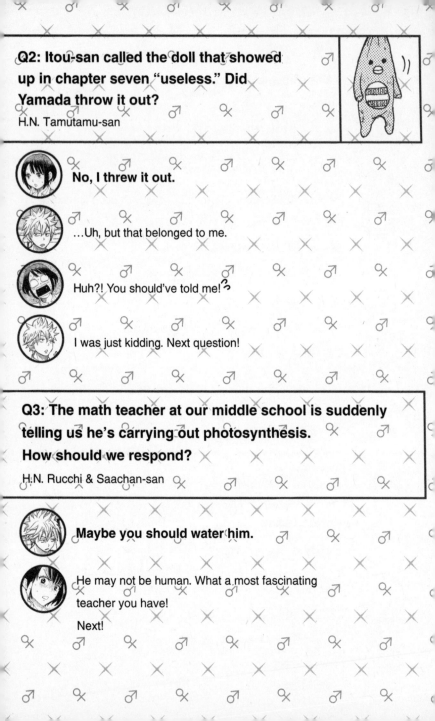

No, I threw it out.

…Uh, but that belonged to me.

Huh?! You should've told me!

I was just kidding. Next question!

Q3: The math teacher at our middle school is suddenly telling us he's carrying out photosynthesis. How should we respond?

H.N. Rucchi & Saachan-san

Maybe you should water him.

He may not be human. What a most fascinating teacher you have!

Next!

Q4: Urara-chan's grades are at the top of her class. So where do the other characters stand?

H.N. Yoshirun-san

Itou-san, you and Yamada are **dunces**, aren't you?

H-how rude! For your information, I get such good grades that I don't even need to take extra lessons! So don't lump me together with Yamada!

Well, as for myself, if I really tried I could probably have the second highest grades in our class.

Anyone can make empty promises! Well, that's all we have for you today!

Please send your correspondence here ↓

Yamada-kun and the Seven Witches: Underground Website
c/o Kodansha Comics
451 Park Ave. South, 7th Floor
New York, NY 10016

Don't forget to include your handle name (pen name) and measurements!

You don't need to know their measurements!

Translation Notes

Yakisoba, page 30

Yakisoba, or fried buckwheat noodles, can often be found at outdoor events in Japan. The dish is usually prepared with pieces of pork, cabbage, onions, carrots, *yakisoba* sauce and buckwheat noodles. The ingredients are stir-fried and topped with Japanese garnishes, including seaweed powder, pickled ginger, fish flakes, and mayonnaise. *Yakisoba* can also be seen between a bun in sandwich form, which is called *Yakisoba Pan* or *Yakisoba Bread.*

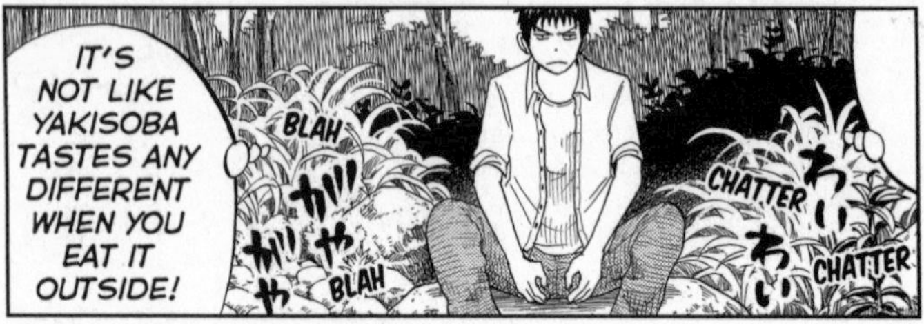
わいわい
CHATTER
CHATTER
ガヤガヤ
BLAH
BLAH
IT'S NOT LIKE YAKISOBA TASTES ANY DIFFERENT WHEN YOU EAT IT OUTSIDE!

Classical Japanese script, page 110

The scribbled text that Yamada is looking at in this scene is a form of Japanese cursive called *sousho.* The literal translation of *sousho* is "grass script" due to its flowing style in which the brush almost never leaves the paper. As a result, it is mostly indecipherable to anyone who is not an expert in Japanese calligraphy. In addition to the style of cursive used, because this is classical Japanese, it's likely that obsolete forms of Japanese syllabary are present in the text, as well as antiquated grammar and speech patterns. Though it's not equivalent in many ways, the book Yamada is looking at is similar to looking at a book written in Middle English cursive.

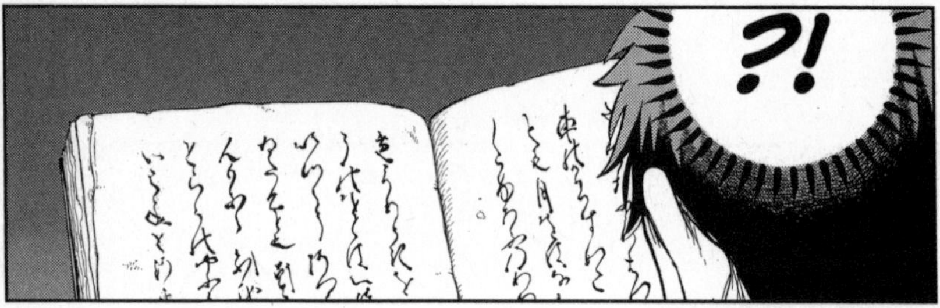
?!

Go, page 111

Go or *igo* is a two-player board game with origins in ancient China that has been played in Japan since the 7th century. The basic concept of *go* is to capture your opponent's pieces by encircling them, and the game involves a high level of strategy. In fact, the number of possible game outcomes far outnumbers chess, making *go* the more complex of the two board games.

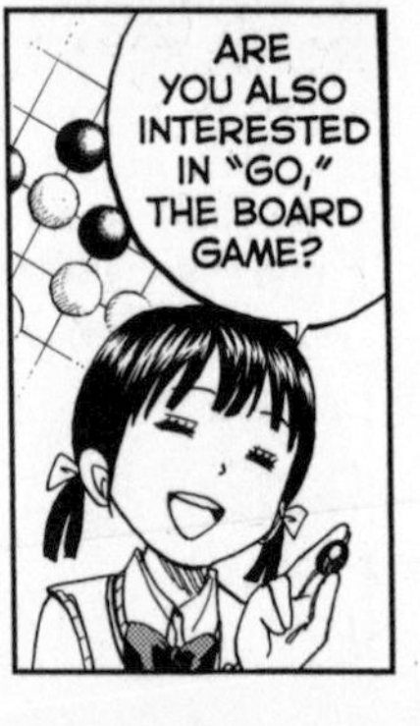
ARE YOU ALSO INTERESTED IN "GO," THE BOARD GAME?

Translation Notes

Mental abacus calculation, page 111

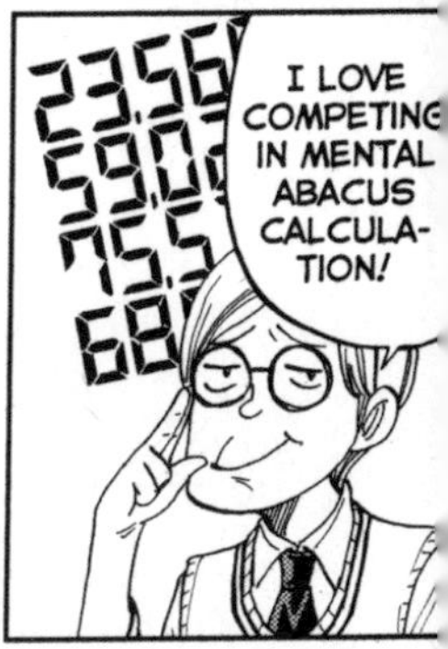
I LOVE COMPETING IN MENTAL ABACUS CALCULATION!

In this panel, what this proud poindexter is actually boasting about is something called "Flash *Anzan*" or "Flash Mental Calculation." In Japan, though the abacus is definitely not in fashion, it is still taught to a large number of children, and for enthusiasts and learners there are several abacus competitions throughout Japan. One of the most prestigious of these competitions is the All Japan Soroban (abacus) Championship, and one of the sections of this competition is the aforementioned "Flash Anzan." This section involves flashing several numbers on a screen, after which contestants are asked to total the numbers as quickly as possible with the abacus in their minds.

Hanako-san of the Bathroom, page 146

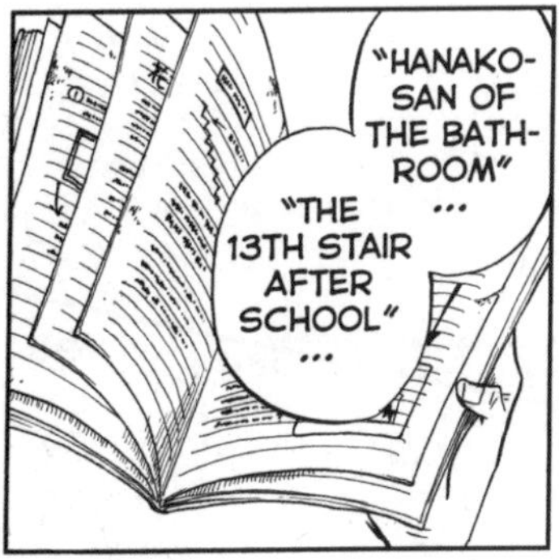
"HANAKO-SAN OF THE BATHROOM" ...
"THE 13TH STAIR AFTER SCHOOL" ...

Along with stories like the "Slit-Mouthed Woman," Hanako-san of the Bathroom is one of the most recognizable urban legends of Japan. Legend has it that one should visit the bathroom on the third floor of your school at night and knock on the door of the third stall while asking, "Is Hanako-san there?" After this, a voice will respond, "Yes." If you open the door, a girl in a red dress sporting a bowl cut will drag you into the toilet.

The 13th Stair After School, page 146

This is another urban legend that often passes around Japanese schools. If you visit school at night, you may find a mysterious flight of stairs with 13 steps. Stepping on the 13th step will cause a noose to drop from the ceiling or send you to the afterlife. It is also said that to get to the main stage of the gallows, you have to ascend 13 steps, so it's possible that the urban legend came from this idea.

Monshiro High School, page 187

Fans of Miki Yoshikawa may recognize this high school as the one from her previous work, "Yankee-kun to Megane-chan." This series had considerable success in Japan and was produced as a 10-episode live-action series. The Singaporean publishing company Chaung Yi also published this series in English under the title "Flunk Punk Rumble."

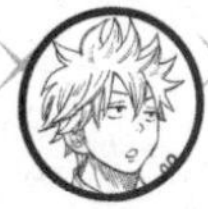

I don't know what made him look so familiar, but he came to our school for a temporary stint. When the first semester ended, he went back to the school he came from, **Monshiro High School**.

Yamada-kun and the Seven Witches volume 3 is a work of fiction. Names, characters, places, and incidents are the products of the author's imagination or are used fictitiously. Any resemblance to actual events, locales, or persons, living or dead, is entirely coincidental.

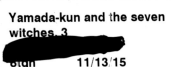

A Kodansha Comics Trade Paperback Original.

Published in the United States by Kodansha Comics,
an imprint of Kodansha USA Publishing, LLC, New York.

Publication rights for this English edition arranged through Kodansha Ltd., Tokyo.

First published in Japan in 2012 by Kodansha Ltd., Tokyo, as *Yamada-kun to Nananin no Majo* volume 3.

ISBN 978-1-63236-070-0

Printed in the United States of America.

www.kodanshacomics.com

9 8 7 6 5 4 3 2 1

Translator: David Rhie
Lettering: Sara Linsely
Editing: Ajani Oloye
Kodansha Comics Edition Cover Design: Phil Balsman